Economics and Its Enemies

Economics and Its Enemies

Two Centuries of Anti-Economics

William Oliver Coleman
University of Tasmania

palgrave
macmillan

First published 2002 by
PALGRAVE MACMILLAN
Houndmills, Basingstoke, Hampshire RG21 6XS and
175 Fifth Avenue, New York, N.Y. 10010
Companies and representatives throughout the world

PALGRAVE MACMILLAN is the global academic imprint of the Palgrave
Macmillan division of St. Martin's Press, LLC and of Palgrave Macmillan Ltd.
Macmillan® is a registered trademark in the United States, United Kingdom
and other countries. Palgrave is a registered trademark in the European
Union and other countries.

ISBN 0–333–79001–4

This book is printed on paper suitable for recycling and made from fully
managed and sustained forest sources.

A catalogue record for this book is available from the British Library.

Library of Congress Cataloging-in-Publication Data
Coleman, William Oliver, 1959–
Economics and its enemies: two centuries of anti-economics / William Oliver
Coleman.
   p. cm.
Includes bibliographical references and index.
ISBN 0–333–79001–4
1. Economics–History. 2. Economics–Moral and ethical
aspects–History. I. Title.
HB75 .C695 2002
330′.09′033—dc21   2002025142

10 9 8 7 6 5 4 3 2
11 10 09 08 07 06 05 04 03

Printed and bound in Great Britain by
Antony Rowe Ltd, Chippenham and Eastbourne

For Anna

Contents

Acknowledgements

My thanks are due to Anna Taitslina for the Russian translations, and constructive criticism of earlier drafts; to Yuri Tupolenko for corrections and comments; to the participants in the History of Economics Seminar of Duke University, and the participants in the Department of Economics seminar of Queen Mary College; and for the never-failing Document Delivery Service of the University of Tasmania.

Part I

1
The Damnation of Economics

1.1 The phenomenon of anti-economics

From almost its beginnings economics has been shadowed by a kind of negative doppelgänger, which has mocked, denigrated and wished ill on its positive counterpart. This clamorously hostile figure we will call 'anti-economics'. This book tells the story of anti-economics, and seeks to take its measure.

Four illustrations of anti-economics

The *École Normale Supérieure* of Paris. In June 2000 students circulate with considerable success a petition calling for an end to the 'hegemony of neoclassical economic theory' that, they say, cuts economics off from reality, and should be replaced by other 'approaches' that consider 'concrete realities'. The petition soon becomes a *cause célèbre*. The Minister of Education quickly announces that he would study closely the appeal from the students. *Le Monde, L'Humanité, L'Express, Les Echos, Marianne, La Tribune, Politis*, and French radio and television rush to take up the students' cause. The media agree that economics is suffering – the 'malaise is general and of longstanding'; it is in crisis; it had become lost in an 'imaginary world' and has an 'obsession to produce a social physics'. 'A debate should be opened on this subject' one paper declares. Another with glee predicts that the coming year 'promises to be agitated'.

Mexico City. In the wake of the ratification of the North American Free Trade Agreement in 1993 a play entitled 'La Muerte Deliberada de Cuatro Neoliberales' [The Deliberate Death of Four Neo-Liberals] is staged to critical approval, and commercial success, in the Mexican capital. The play opens with four Mexican economics post-grads studying in the United States, throwing a party for an old peer group friend, now an anthropologist, and his girlfriend. The banter of their party soon turns to NAFTA, and thence to the merits of economic models. The post-grads take one position, the anthropologist another. Their exchange is lengthy, inconclusive, and unhappy. The girlfriend is silent. Finally, she produces a hand grenade, and tosses it in the midst of the four neo-liberals. Curtain falls.

Bologna, 19 March 2002. Marco Biagi (1950–2002), professor of labour at the University of Modena, and adviser to the Italian Ministry of Labour, is shot dead by two gunmen on a motor scooter, while returning home from teaching. The Partito Comunista Combattente claims responsibility. Pundits are reminded of the murder of Ezio Tarantelli (1941–85), an economist at the University of Rome and author of papers in the *American Economic Review* and the *Review of Economic Studies*, who was killed by the Red Brigades while leaving the economics faculty car park on 27 March 1985.

My post box. Each month a brown envelope arrives. Each contains the latest issue of the newsletter of the 'The Anti-Economists League'. On the front page of each newsletter is printed the League's frank purpose: 'To eliminate the economist from government policy making'.

These are not the maverick idiosyncrasies of solitary authors or obscure sects. Anti-economics is not a reflection of the exceptional or anomalous; it is a conductor of modern history's most powerful ideological charges; socialism, liberalism, nationalism, conservatism, radicalism, humanitarianism, and moralism. It is well represented among the rival wisdoms of our times; environmentalism, managerialism, feminism, and, emphatically, the convulsion against globalisation. (Henderson 1981; Waring 1988; Demming 1993). It is a favourite of journalists (Parker 1993; and see Coleman and Hagger 2001 and Coleman 2001b). Its embrace extends in some surprising directions. It is found amongst wealthy financiers (Soros 1994) and does not exclude economists. 'Against Economics', 'Debunking Economics', 'The Death of Economics', 'The Principles of Economics. Some Lies My Teachers Told Me': all these books and papers have been written by economists (Kanth 1997; Keen 2001; Ormerod 1994; Boland 1992). None other than *The Economist* has joined the charge. The leading article of the 23 August 1997 issue was entitled 'The Puzzling Failure of Economics'.

Neither is anti-economics a passing vogue of the contemporary scene; it can be traced back, in undulations, to the eighteenth century. The hostility of the 1990s was preceded by the 1970s New Left critique of economics. This was the period of *Economics: an Anti-Text*; *l'Anti-economique*; and *The Anti-Samuelson* (Green and Nore 1977; Attali and Guillaume 1974; Linder 1977).

In the quarter-century before 1970 – the 'Age of Keynes' – full employment and buoyant growth did not secure economics from hostile fire. At the close of that Age the economic historian Michael Postan (1968) complained of

'A Plague of Economists'; and at its beginning T.S. Ashton (another economic historian) observed that economists 'have so often been reproved for being unrealistic or dogmatic that the best of them have developed an inferiority-complex' (Ashton 1946, p. 93).

The Great Depression was the obvious occasion of Barbara Wootton's 1938 *Lament for Economics* (reviewed with great praise by the British press), and A.A. Berle's 'The Lost Art of Economics' (Berle 1938). The millenarian gospels of salvation of the 1930s (technocracy, Marxism, social credit, fascism) also provided many examples of phosphorescent anti-economics. Neither did the prosperity of the 1920s preserve economics from disesteem. In that decade, F.A. Fetter (1925) observed, economics was unpopular with both the business and the editorial page.

In the late nineteenth century, a surge of historical and national consciousness provided a thick and luxuriant anti-economics. The German Historical School of Economics dismissed Adam Smith's vision of economic development as 'almost childish', and his successors as 'only several generations of sterile epigones'. Their English 'historical' counterparts felt the same way. In 1888 J.E.T. Rogers, an Oxford economic historian, announced: 'Political Economy is in a bad way: its authority is repudiated, its conclusions are assailed, its arguments are compared to the dissertations held in Milton's Limbo, its practical suggestions are conceived to be not much better than those of the philosophers in Laputa, and one of its authorities, as I myself heard, was contemptuously advised to betake himself to Saturn. And the criticism is just' (Rogers 1888, p. vii).

The mid-Victorian period saw equally crushing condemnations of economics from three vastly influential thinkers. In 1867 Karl Marx published his *Capital*, subtitled *A Critique of Political Economy*, which contained some of the lushest tracts of anti-economics that ever sprouted. In 1860 Ruskin hurled the most terrific invective at economists: 'Nothing in history has ever been so disgraceful to the human intellect as the acceptance among us of the common doctrines of political economy' (Ruskin 1862, p. 61). In 1849 Thomas Carlyle branded it the 'Dismal Science' for fathering some of 'the damnablest notions that ever came into the head of any *two*-legged animal without feathers' (Carlyle [1850] 1898, p. 282).

The 1830s and 1840s saw economics attacked by the visionaries of a society based on an ethic of brotherhood. Auguste Comte, speaking of the social tensions of the industrial revolution, complained that 'instead of recognising in the urgent remonstrances called forth by this chasm in our social order one of the most eminent and pressing occasions for the application of social science, our economists can do nothing better than repeat, with pitiless pedantry, their barren aphorism of absolute industrial liberty' (Comte [1855] 1974, p. 448). Another such visionary, Pierre Leroux, perhaps best known as the originator of the word 'socialism', wrote that economics 'is no more than the doctrine of usury timidly introduced at first by a passing error of Protestant theologians, and elevated since by an immeasurable insolence' (Leroux 1849, p. 207).

The early nineteenth century saw several 'reactionary' critics of liberalism assail economics. In Prussia Adam Müller waged a polemical war against Adam Smith on behalf of a conservative aristocracy. In Napoleonic France Bonald, a theorist of absolute monarchy, wrote that no book could be 'more abstract and more useless' than the *Wealth of Nations*. In England, S.T. Coleridge, the advocate of Christian Monarchy and class order, repudiated the pretended science as a 'solemn humbug' ([1836] 1969d, pp. 205).

One may easily pursue anti-economics back some distance into the eighteenth century. In France and Spain of the 1770s physiocracy received the fierce opprobrium of Denis Diderot, Ferdinando Galiani, and Simon-Nicolas-Henri Linguet, in what was the first outbreak of anti-economics (see, for example, Coleman 1995, pp. 117–24).

The enmity of authors to economics does not eclipse the enmity of the public. Both friends and foes of economics have agreed that the public is a significant bearer of anti-economics. To consider just the nineteenth century, the economic historian William Cunningham in 1878 claimed that 'the mercantile public' is not swayed by economics, 'working-class leaders notoriously disregard it, and foreign statesmen do not pretend to listen to its preachings' (Cunningham 1878, p. 369). In 1876 Walter Bagehot declared political economy 'lies rather dead in the public mind' (Bagehot [1876] 1915, p. 92). At about the same time a sympathiser with Bagehot estimated that 'Political Economy is confined to a few experts, and is held in general aversion as one of the driest and most repulsive of sciences' (Moffat 1878, p. 5). In 1868 J.S. Mill lamented that political economy was 'thoroughly unpopular with a large and not the least philanthropic portion of the people of England' (quoted in Forget 1992, p. 55); in 1845 *The Times* demanded of economists 'Confess the plain fact: political economy won't do ... The science may be bottomed in truth, and it may also admit earthly realisation in AD 2500. But if you wish yourselves or your grandchildren to see the fruit of your labours, you must cut across' (quoted in Edwards 1993, p. 39). In 1836 James Mill suggested that most MPs 'not only disclaim all confidence in the doctrines of political economy, but treat its pretensions to science as imposture' (Mill [1836] 1966, p. 381); in 1830 Thomas Macaulay judged that political economy had become 'an object of disgust to a majority of the community' (Macaulay [1830] 1890, p. 179). In 1823 David Ricardo in Parliament lamented that political economy had become a matter of 'ridicule and reproach' (quoted in Cannan 1894, p. 412).

Embracing both celebrated authors and the anonymous public, anti-economics does not omit the state. Ministries of Culture, Research Councils, and Broadcasting Commissions, even Governors-General, have patronised at some expense exercises in anti-economics.[1] Anti-economics has, on occasion, been pursued with literally deadly force by the state.

Anti-economics is, then, one of the western world's more prominent demonologies of the intellect. It stands today along alongside anti-psychiatry, and the ritual denunciations of 'positivism' amongst critics of science.

But in the face of this barrage economists have been almost silent. There have been some excellent single papers, and even some book-length treatments (Bastable 1884; Viner 1963; Castles 1984; Levy 2001). But there has been just one spirited and extensive retort that meets anti-economist polemic with counter-polemic: Leon Walras's almost completely forgotten *L'Économie Politique et la Justice* (Walras 1860). Overall, there has been a strong tendency to do nothing. The steady refusal of Malthus and Marshall of the invitations of anti-economists to do battle is illustrative of this equanimity (Winch 1996; Maloney 1985),[2] as is Bagehot's observation that a political economist in a rage makes an amusing sight: 'their violence is so meagre'.

This book, however, proposes not to maintain a silence. It undertakes to provide a history, analysis and critique of anti-economics, from its earliest appearance to its efflorescence in the present day.

1.2 The identity of the accuser

What is an anti-economist?

An anti-economist is whoever sees economics as a bane.[3] To the anti-economist the offence of economics is that it is harmful, it is 'pernicious' (Moffat 1878, p. 5). It must, therefore, be done away with. Its teachings must be discredited, its honours (such as the Nobel prize) abolished, its representatives barred from public institutions, its institutional identity effaced, its centres of propagation encumbered or eliminated.

The anti-economist believes, in addition, that no germ of good can be found anywhere within the poisonous canker. To the anti-economist there is no value to be salvaged from economics in its present state. It contains no rudiment of insight; it is 'dead', 'bankrupt', 'collapsed'. And this is necessarily so: economics is a bad seed, a misgrowth which can never progress. The anti-economist, therefore, is not a mender or reformer of learning, but a revolutionary. To the anti-economist the only way to discover economic truth is to throw out all economics and start all over again. This stringent heuristic is a key and identifying attribute of the anti-economist.[4]

The anti-economist's attitude is well captured by the anti-economist Clarence Ayres' summary of Veblen's attitude to economics: Veblen, said Ayres, 'criticised accepted economic theories, not as incomplete or even wrong in specific detail, but as utterly false and deluded from beginning to end. Like Dewey he clearly implied that we should be much better off if we were to dispense with the whole question-begging rubrics "with no other verdict than 'good riddance'"' (Ayres 1935, p. 36).[5]

The not very mild verdict of the anti-economist on the proper fate of economics craves some justification. And it is in the matter of justification that another central feature of anti-economics comes into view: 'The Critique'. The anti-economist is confident that the credence or toleration afforded economics will be drastically reduced by a searching examination of its doctrines and method. Anti-economics has, therefore, proliferated critiques and 'anti-texts': the critical examination of economics that supposedly proves its worthlessness. So if anti-economics *is* a hostility to economics, then what anti-economics *does* is produce critiques, in copious quantities.

This elucidation of what an anti-economist is, allows the elucidation of what it is not.

Anti-economics is not, simply, 'disagreement' with economics. To disagree with a doctrine is not to say that it is nonsense, bankrupt, or pernicious.

Anti-economics is not, simply, 'criticism' of economics. Economics journals are crowded with criticism of economics, and economists may sympathise with some of the criticism of anti-economists: J.S. Mill is a distinguished example. But anti-economists are justified in dismissing this as not 'real' criticism: for that criticism is not advanced with the purpose of demonstrating that economics is a bane. Thus while J.S. Mill was critical of the narrowness of the scope of economics, and was repelled by its 'philistine' emphasis on material progress, and was happy to make a gaping exemption of Ireland from the 'laws' of political economy, he maintained to the end of his life the great value of political economy (Forget 1992).

1.3 The identity of the accused

If 'anti-economics' amounts to a wish to destroy economics, one must ask what counts as 'economics'? Is, for example, Marxist economics 'economics'? Is an intention to fundamentally discredit Marxian economics (for example, Böhm-Bawerk [1896] 1949) a piece of anti-economics? Not by our definition.

By our definition anti-economics is a hostility to only one sort of economics. This economics is that stream of thought which stretches from the eighteenth century to the present day, and which embraces Smith, Ricardo, Mill, Walras, Keynes, Hicks and living persons. This continuity of thought could be called the 'Mainstream'. But, following Walras, we will call it *la Grande Tradition*.

> the science itself...from her birth to the apogee of her glory, grows bit by bit, follows her path, and persists in her tendencies. Political economy is not in the latest work entitled *Course* or *Handbook*, it is in the sum of truths which are laid down in her name, it is in the tradition faithfully followed from its birth until the present moment. It is there that it exists, as proud of its passing defeats as its conclusive triumphs. (Walras 1860, p. xxx)

Three misunderstandings of the Tradition should be avoided.

First, the Tradition is composed, not of persons, but of ideas (such as affirmations, controversies, inquiries). It is an idea which does (or does not) belong, not a person. Thus it is not that Malthus does (or does not) belong. Rather his ideas on population do belong to the Tradition, but his ideas on effective demand do not. The Tradition is better represented as a sequence of classic texts than a sequence of persons (*Wealth of Nations*, *Principles of Political Economy and Taxation*, *Principles of Political Economy With Some of Their Applications to Social Philosophy*, *Principles of Economics* and so on).

Second, the notion of Tradition is not an exercise in 'Whig history'. The Tradition is not composed purely of those who fought on the side of those who are currently victors (that is, neoclassical theorising). The Tradition, for example, excludes the theories of Daniel Bernouilli and Hermann Gossen, for their ideas had no influence. The Tradition also includes some who fought on other sides than the current victors (Keynes, for example).

Third, the Tradition is not a single ideology; or a doctrinal uniformity; or a great idea successively articulated and refined over two centuries (such as 'the invisible hand'). It cannot be, since it is not restricted to a set of affirmations or doctrines; it includes debates without any resolution, and inquiries without conclusion. In any case, the Tradition has proved capable of reversing at a later date its earlier affirmations (its varied stances on 'the invisible hand' are proof of that).

With the notion of the Tradition clarified, some misconceptions about anti-economics can be averted.

Anti-economics does not include all criticisms of the Great Tradition. Not all criticisms of the Tradition constitute anti-economics because it is criticisms of the Tradition that have made the Tradition. The Tradition has developed by repudiations of part of the Tradition in an earlier state, as it was left by predecessors. These repudiations may be substantial, but they do not constitute anti-economics. It would be a mistake, for example, to identify the very substantial criticism of Keynes and Jevons as anti-economics. 'Objectively' these censures were not anti-economics: they were not destructive of the Tradition; they were accepted in some form by the Tradition, and contributed to its further development. 'Subjectively' these censures were not anti-economics; they were not intended to destroy the Tradition.[6]

Therefore, to reject anti-economics is not to reject criticism of the Great Tradition. And it is no part of our thesis that economics is anything other than insufficient, in need of (good) criticism, and has only grown because of (good) criticism. Indeed, one deficiency of a large part of anti-economics is its doctrinal conservatism, its attachment to doctrines that the Great Tradition has discarded. So, for example, 'historical critics' of the nineteenth century preferred Smith to Ricardo; and Marxian economics prefers Ricardo to Jevons.

Anti-economics excludes hostility to 'unorthodox economics'. The conception of the Tradition as a continuity means that excluded from it are any economics that have not contributed to its subsequent development. Thus the Tradition excludes the ideas of Karl Marx, Frédéric Bastiat, Henry George, Gustav von Schmoller and Pierro Sraffa, as these ideas have had no impact on it. Thus any furies directed against these 'unorthodox' economics are not part of our subject matter.

Anti-economics includes more than hostility to neoclassical economics. Anti-economics is much more than disapproval of neoclassical economics, since the Tradition is much more than neoclassical economics. The Tradition stretches from Smith to modern times; it embraces classical, neoclassical, and Keynesian schools, and anti-economics embraces furies against all these. The *General Theory* is an example. It is an anti-neoclassical work, but because it was enormously important for the course of economic thinking (including neoclassical thinking), it is part of the Tradition. Thus the denigration of Keynes by the 'old left' and the nomenclatura of the Soviet Union (Turner 1969) is part of anti-economics.

Anti-economics is not merely opposition to economic liberalism. A large part of anti-economics draws its energy from an anger at economic liberalism. Certainly, the easiest way for an economist to exchange unpopularity for popularity is to advocate some illiberal measure. Thus Nobel Laureate James Tobin proposes a tax on foreign currency transactions, and (without intending it) is rewarded by the bubbly admiration of the 27,000 member Association for the Taxation of Financial Transactions for the Aid of Citizens. Further, economic liberalism constitutes a key premise in a popular case against the Tradition, that goes as follows: 'The Tradition favours economic liberalism. Economic liberalism is unsatisfactory. Therefore, the Tradition is unsatisfactory.'[7]

Yet for several reasons it would be an error to conclude that anti-economics 'reduces to' a hostility to economic liberalism.

Firstly, several significant economic liberals are hostile to the Tradition. These include Richard Cobden (who dismissed the 'dry bones of political economy'), George Poulett Scrope, J.E.T. Rogers, P.W.S. Andrews, the neoconservative 'supply side economists' associated with Irving Kristol, and several twentieth-century Austrians.[8] Murray Rothbard (1995), for example, subjects almost every figure in the Great Tradition to abuse, especially Adam Smith.[9] The conclusion is plain: even if antipathy to economic liberalism is sufficient for an antipathy to the Tradition, it is not necessary for such an antipathy. There are varieties of opposition to the Tradition which are not sourced in opposition to the market.

Second, the Tradition does not, in truth, always favour economic liberalism.

1. The Keynesian Revolution upholds the usefulness of state intervention, and yet is part of the Great Tradition.
2. Neoclassical economics should not be identified with economic liberalism. The economically literate person is aware of the swarm of neoclassical

economics arguments against laissez-faire, especially issues involving natural monopolies, externalities and public goods. The 'left neoclassical' is a fairly frequent figure in the history of economic thought: Leon Walras, Knut Wicksell, Maurice Allais, Oskar Lange, Hirofumi Uzawa.

3. Even the classical economists cannot be adequately represented as advocates of laissez-faire, an expression they rarely used. Ricardo opposed the abolition of the Corn Laws (Grampp 1960, p. 18); Smith supported the Navigation Acts.[10]

There is, in summary, a distance between the Tradition and economic liberalism. That distance means that in *logical* terms a dissatisfaction with the Tradition cannot be reduced to a dissatisfaction with economic liberalism. And a vindication of the Tradition does not reduce to a vindication of a rigorous economic liberalism. Our topic is a distinct one.

1.4 'A fine bill of indictment': an inventory of the charges against economics

If the anti-economist is confident that the toleration afforded economics will be drastically reduced by a critique of economics, what does that critique maintain? This question cannot be answered. Anti-economics does not comprise a single critique of economics. Anti-economics is a heterogeneous aggregate of positions united only by finding economics objectionable. Many of these positions are actually contrary to one another. So, for example, economics has been criticised for seeking to resemble the natural sciences (Werner Sombart), and it is criticised for not seeking to resemble natural science (Auguste Comte); it has been criticised for facilitating industrialisation (J.K. Ingram), and it is criticised for not facilitating industrialisation (development advocates); it has often been criticised for being 'scholastic' by empiricists (Comte, William Beveridge), but on occasion it has been criticised for *not* being scholastic (de Quincey; see Coats, 1964); it is criticised for being unchristian, and for being Christian;[11] it is criticised for overemphasising competition, and for neglecting competition (Engels manages to take both positions [1844] 1973, p. 205); it is criticised for acting as a palliative for social dissension (Marx), and for acting as a breeder of class hatred (Cunningham 1894, p. 2); it has been criticised for being anti-socialist (Marx) and pro-socialist (H.S. Foxwell).[12] It has been criticised for being a rigid system of belief, and it has been criticised for being a squabble of inconsistent opinions. Economics has been faulted for a cynical and low estimate of humankind (by assuming everyone a knave), and faulted for a guilelessly generous opinion of mankind (by assuming away human aggression in the manner of an eighteenth-century philanthropist). It has been criticised for being materialistic, and even for being *in*sufficiently materialistic (William Thompson quoted in Eagleton 1999).

It will prove helpful to organise these highly various objections to economics under three headings: objections to doctrine; objections to practice; and objections to subject. These headings might be equivalently expressed as objections to economics, objection to economists, and objections to the economic.

Objections to doctrine

Economic theories, anti-economists hold, are valueless either to seekers of knowledge, or improvers of society. There are a number of variants of this general claim.

Economics is false.   This sentiment embraces a number of complaints; the vernacular dissatisfaction with the poor forecasting capacity of economic models; the historian's objection to 'unrealistic assumptions' of economic theory; the renegade economist's parade of the 'anomalies' literature, and the collectivist's ire at the free market tendency of economics.

This sentiment extends to the normative principles. So it is held that *the normative doctrines of economics are false*. The normative principles, it is asserted, are not sufficiently alive to distributional questions; they are overly material in their values, they neglect the intrinsic value of the aesthetic, spiritual, and environmental dimensions of our existence.

Economics is useless.   Sometimes it is urged that the theses of economics are not so much false as useless. Economics lacks fruit, rather than light. The social ameliorationist will complain that *economic theories are useless to government* (Wootton 1938). The management pundit will scoff that *economic theories are useless to business*. Others have protested that *economic theories are useless to the consumer* (Shubik 1970). The charge of lack of utility extends to the research of economics. *Economic research is useless*. Economists are not researching important questions; they are playing mind games. A particular target here is the apparent triviality of the 'normal science' of economics, its lack of 'relevance' to the day's pressing issues. This was a favourite theme of the New Left of the 1970s (Heilbronner 1970), and one shared by right-wing commentators two decades later (Anderson 1992).

Economics may be useless because it is wrong. Alternatively, economics may be useless, not because it is wrong, but because its content, although true, is trivial: *economic theories are truistical* (Rogers 1888). Its content may be so trivial that it is no more than definition of certain terms: *economic theories are tautological* (Rogers 1888). Finally, economics may be useless not because its claims are false, or because its claims are trivial, but because they are unfalsifiable and without predictive content: *economic theories provide no guide to the consequences of actions* (Hutchison 1938).

Economics is harmful.   In this objection economics is worse than useless. Its remedies make you ill. Economists themselves have been fairly free in faulting each other in this respect. But such 'internal' criticism typically directs itself to only one tendency within economics.[13] Anti-economists do not so restrict their criticism, and have pictured the injury of economics going far deeper and wider than economists have entertained. Economics has nurtured egoism and greed, it has plunged the labouring class (or the Third World) into misery (Frank 1976), it has been responsible for the 'catastrophic dimensions' of famine (Beloff 1968), it has incited class war and revolution, it has despoiled the natural environment and artistic heritage, it has frustrated the rightful aspirations of the nation-states.

Objections to practice

Objections to the practice of economics have been prominent in anti-economics.

Economists are methodologically inadequate.   The way economists reach and justify their theses is commonly subject to objection.

Many of these criticisms of methodology centre on the 'ancient feud' between fact and theory. A common criticism is that 'economists have been too theoretical' in their method. (This has been voiced by Richard Jones, Gustav Schmoller, William Beveridge, T.W. Hutchison, Leontief, Comte.) However, it is also sometimes that 'economics is too empirical' in its method (Hollis and Nell 1975; Mises 1962).

Another axis of criticism concerns the role of scientific and humanistic method in economics. In the late twentieth century it was common to object that 'economics is too scientific', or tries too hard to be scientific (McCloskey 1983). In this complaint 'scientistic' economics, by seeking to resemble physics, is absorbed in mathematics, diverted into a spurious precision, oblivious to the unmeasurable, and neglectful of the power of language. However, in the mid and late nineteenth century it was more frequently complained that 'economics is too unscientific'; economics was lost in verbal disputes, and it should instead embrace the measurable and quantifiable, and become more like physics. This was the complaint of the Comtean positivists, such as J.K. Ingram ([1888] 1910).

The strictures over language have been parallelled by strictures over the use of mathematics. It has been frequently held that economics is too mathematical (Rothbard 1995), while others have held that economics is insufficiently mathematical (John von Neumann; see Dore et al. 1988, and Rashid 1994, p. 286).

A related axis of criticism has concerned the role of laws in economics. It has been widely objected 'that economics is too law-like'. This objection holds that there are no economic laws, be they empirical or theoretical; there are no economic truths unrestricted in time or place; every case is unique, and the method of generalities is wrong. The 'historical' critics of economics are prominent on this critical front, although it also embraces some theorists.[14] At the same time, hastening from quite the opposite direction, there is another (disparate) collection of critics who have complained that 'economics is too lawless' (Hollis and Nell 1975; Mises 1962).

Economists are conceited.   To some anti-economists the unacknowledged deficiency in economists' methods has led economists to exaggerate their capability to know, control and predict the world. Indeed, say anti-economists, *economists suffer from hubris* (Ravenstone 1821, p. 415). The truth is, they say, *economists can never know more than non-economists.* Any attainable economic truths are obvious to any sensible and experienced person. A specialism in economics is at best redundant, certainly wasteful, and probably misleading. An economist could never have more authority than non-economists to speak on an economic question. Regrettably *economists claim a spurious authority*, expect others to defer to their judgements without challenge, and 'bandy' what authority the public does (mistakenly) award them to discourage alternative positions being entertained (Manne 1993).

Economists are biased.   Even if their methods are potentially effective, the practice of economics is marred by an ideological bias. Economists select (knowingly or not) the premises in theoretical arguments, and the evidence in empirical arguments, to suit their prior beliefs. The prior beliefs of bias are most commonly supposed to be political. At the close of the twentieth century the common accusation was that 'economists are right wing'. However, up to the last part of the twentieth century the commoner accusation within English speaking countries was 'economists are left wing' (Lonigan 1944; Bastable 1884).

Economists are bidden.   In this complaint it is not that economists are irrationally attached to some private vision but that their judgements are for sale. In its most extreme form the thesis is that economists have a cynical or corrupt unconcern about truth, and consciously observe at the behest of wealth and power. So rather than being doctrinaires imposing their ideas on hapless neighbours, they are bland accomplices of the establishment. This was the claim of Marx regarding economics after 1830. The stricture may be put in a more moderate (and plausible) form. Truth is a cold and austere dish. The material and non-material rewards (acclaim, influence) promised by wealth and power have, claim critics, subverted the economist's judgement of truth in a manner of which the economist is hardly conscious.

Objections to subject

Charges against economics as a subject may be brought under two headings: the scope of the subject, and the value of the subject.

The scope of economics. The delimitation of the scope of any subject is judicious only if one can understand the matter contained within those limits, without an understanding of the matter outside those limits. Anti-economists maintain that markets and market systems cannot be understood as long as non-market phenomena are not understood. Put briefly, the economy cannot be understood by reference only to the economy, and thus the customary scope of economics is injudicious. Two grounds for this contention are advanced:

1. *The Holistic Objection: 'The Market Cannot Be Understood in Isolation From Society'.* This position claims there is a mutual interdependence between the market and the non-market (Comte [1855] 1974).[15] An illustration may be helpful. It is obvious that the tax regime affects the distribution of wealth; that effect, economists believe, is part of their province of knowledge. However, it is also true that the distribution of wealth can affect the tax regime. Thus there are links running from the socio-political to the economic, as well as from the economic to the socio-political. The critical point is that understanding economic movements requires an understanding of both links. So, for example, while technological invention will have direct impact on the distribution of wealth (and economists have theories of that) that change in wealth will, by forces economists do not understand, change the tax laws, and that will in turn (by forces economists do understand) change the distribution of wealth. Therefore, to gauge rightly the impact of invention on the distribution of wealth we must know the feedbacks from the socio-political to the economic.

    The market, then, is only a component part of a single, integrated social mechanism; it is a unity made out of the interaction of many different parts.[16] Economics has ignored this and is therefore (in the language of economists) too 'partial'. More popularly expressed, the holistic objection states that the political, the social and the economic all work as a system, and that economics is, therefore, 'too narrow'.

2. *The Reductionist Objection: 'The Market is Reducible to Other Phenomena'.* In the Holistic Objection, the market was just one moving part of the social machine. In the Reductionist Objection the market is not even a moving part of the social mechanism. It is just a passive and incidental, if conspicuous, feature. It is the exterior of the machine, and those exterior movements are just the expression of deeper interior movements beneath.

    There have been a variety of candidates for the deeper forces which market phenomena may be reduced to, and that would be the object of knowledge of the putative social super science. There are sociological candidates. In this category sit Marxists, who believe that the 'superficial buying and selling' of the market is only a camouflage of certain fundamental social relations; a veil for social structure (that is itself insecurely balanced upon the juggernaut of 'history'). Alternatively, it may be held that psychology is the deeper force to which economics may be reduced (for example, Schmoller, see Mayer 1988, p. 571; Eysenck 1990). Finally, it is widely held that politics is the deeper force to which economics may be reduced. This belief may be found in journalists, demi-savants and political rulers who see everything as a part of a struggle for power; or (at least) that everything is significant only in so far as it is part of the struggle for power.

The deep forces to which market forces may be reduced have not always been held to be specifically human. In this vein some environmentalists have aspired to a 'human ecology' that would give a fundamental explanation of the phenomena that market forces reflect. Others have sought to reduce economic phenomena to an expression of the laws of thermodynamics (Soddy 1922; Scott 1933).

The value of the economic

Both the holistic and reductionist objections to economics claim that economic matters cannot be well understood while non-economic issues are ill understood. This robs economics of its intellectual significance. But neither objection implies that economic phenomena are without significance.

By contrast, a different position of anti-economics states that knowledge of markets and market systems *is* unimportant. This stream of criticism, therefore, impugns the value of the success of any inquiry into the economic. This stream has several variants.

Economic considerations are not important.   In this objection money does not make the world go around. Human affairs have not been driven by 'economic' considerations; that is, the materialist interpretation of history is wrong. Economists, in their avid search for economic motives behind every action, are wrong headed.[17]

Economic considerations should not be important.   In this objection money should not make the world go around. This sentiment has wide appeal: it appeals to the romantic who finds material comfort insipid; to the aesthetic who finds material progress uglifying;[18] to the environmentalist who finds the manufactured world alienating; and to the various visionaries of the ideal society, who have rarely rated the standard of living as of much moment. To these, wealth does not equal happiness, or fulfilment, or anything worth seeking. To these, what economics knows about is not worth knowing. Thomas Carlyle: 'Political philosophy ... should tell us what is meant by "country", by what causes men are happy, moral, religious and the contrary. Instead, it tells us how flannel jackets are exchanged for pork hams' (quoted in Halliday 1950, p. 198).[19]

A more extreme formulation of this position finds material comfort vicious in itself. A scorn of material comfort is as old as philosophy, and seems to arise in any society of a certain mental sophistication. The Cynics of Hellenic society elevated 'inner wealth' over outer wealth; Christianity encouraged asceticism and devalued bodily ease; Rousseau and others in the eighteenth century castigated 'luxury', and championed physical endurance. Certain social critics in Imperial Germany exhibited a dismay about 'luxury' (see Breckman 1991); rigorists like the anti-economist Werner Sombart objected to 'comfortism' and glorified martial virtues. Today the displeasure with 'consumerism' stands in for the displeasure with comfortism. In this stance the very concern of economists to raise living standards is derisible.

How the economic system works is unimportant; how it should work is important. The final objection to the value of economics is that of the moralist. The moralist is no more concerned to read an account of how the economic system does work, than an abolitionist would be concerned to consult a manual of slave management. The utopian in this respect is the same as the moralist: they find no significance in the 'how' of the present system. The present system is irrational, and certainly not utopian. It is not to be understood, it is to be abolished. [20]

1.5 An overview of the analysis

Having identified the weapons, tactics and protagonists of this struggle, we are ready to embark on the undertaking of this book; a history, analysis and appraisal of anti-economics.

Our general historical thesis will be that a cluster of anti-economics germinated in the wake of the dissolution of the Enlightenment. It was the Enlightenment – tranquil in politics, universalist in outlook, collected in its emotional sensibility – that had provided the environment for the birth of economics. It was its end that produced an environment noxious to its survival.

In analytical terms the book is divided into three parts.

Part II, composed of Chapters 2, 3, 4, and 5, examines a suite of anti-economics that have in common a fundamentally political attitude: they see the world in political terms. To their mind the political is more basic than the economic.

Chapter 2 takes up the dissatisfaction that the Right felt with economics in the wake of the Enlightenment's success in destroying the old order. The free market (with which economists were identified) was seen as subversive of the social order.

Chapter 3 turns to the offence the Left took at economics in the wake of the failure of the French Revolution to permanently destroy all order. The Left saw the free market (with which economists were identified) as constructive of a resurgent social order in the post-Revolutionary world based on wealth, rather than rank.

Chapter 4 concerns a rejection of economics born of a resentment of the notion that there was a single, global centre of political and cultural pre-eminence, to which all other polities and cultures must orientate themselves, and that they must imitate. This resentment was articulated in nationalism, which emerged in the mid-nineteenth century somewhat later than Right and Left doctrines, and managed to combine both 'right' and 'left' postures. In economics this resentment manifested itself in a rejection of the universalism of classical economics; and an advocacy of historical and cultural relativism.

Chapter 5 concerns the resolve of certain constructivist totalitarian regimes of the mid-twentieth century to eliminate economics as part of their merciless commitment to contrive an entirely new human existence.

Part III, composed of chapters 6, 7, 8, 9, and 10 is concerned with anti-economics which have in common that they are not primarily political in consciousness. Although they may be exploited by political forces they are politically inert by themselves; they are on their own account either anti-political, apolitical, or only quixotically political. These types of anti-economics, have their focus on the individual, rather than the state.

This part begins with two chapters concerned with the contest between science and morality. Chapter 6 takes up critics who find offence in economics on account of its supposed cultivation of, and foundation in, scientific quantitative methods, instead of intuitive thought and emotion. Chapter 7 deals with moralists' denial of an economics existing usefully and independently of any moral notions. In the minds of these moralists the project of 'positive economics' is a manifestation of the error of supposing that knowledge is the solution to the world's problems, when, in truth, morality is the solution.

The next two chapters turn to specific, supposed, moral failures of economics. Chapter 8 focuses on the doctrine that egoism is the fundamental problem of the world, and that correspondingly the fundamental remedy of the world's problems is altruism. Economics is seen by the partisans of this doctrine as aiding and abetting egoism, and thereby clearing a straight path for inhumanity. Chapter 9 deals with those who object to economics on the grounds that it implicitly takes human satisfaction to be the measure of all things. Economics finds several enemies in those who insist that certain things have value regardless of the service they provide human satisfaction. Prominent among these is the environmental movement.

Chapter 10 turns to a genus of anti-economics which is rooted in an exaggeration, rather than a repudiation of the eighteenth century, and which faults economics, not for serving wealth, but for not serving wealth. We deal there with certain 'gospels of wealth' that dispute the market is the path to prosperity. These include the gospel of energy, the gospel of technology and engineering, and the gospel of work, which flourished from the late nineteenth to the mid-twentieth century.

Part IV turns from 'the case' to 'the campaign'; it deals with the means and resources of anti-economics, and why they have been deployed with so little return.

In Chapter 11 we take up one of the potent fuels of anti-economics: the offence taken by vested interests at economics on account of its pursuit of the public interest.

Chapter 12 takes up one of the favoured rhetorical strategies of anti-economics; the faulting of the presumption of authority of the economic expert at the cost of a disregard for the independent judgement of the economic layperson.

Chapter 13 compares anti-economics with another enmity, anti-Semitism, and argues that for the first 150 of its 200 years anti-economics was homologous with anti-Semitism.

Chapter 14 seeks to identify the location of the morbidity of anti-economics. It identifies some proximate causes of the failure of anti-economics to effectively criticise economics, and goes on to argue that anti-economics must fail. Although anti-economics must fail, it contends that a critical culture within economics is useful, and outlines the activities of that culture.

Part II

2
The 'Wretched Procurers of Sedition'

The oldest and most enduring species of anti-economics is 'Right' anti-economics. This species of anti-economics sees the market as destructive of a desirable social order, identifies economists as the market's advocate, and consequently judges them to accommodate, wittingly or unwittingly, the destruction of this desirable social order. To Right anti-economists, economists are the apostles of disorder; the ideologists of anarchy, 'the wretched procurers of sedition'.[1]

It was the Enlightenment's benign posture towards the market that provoked in reaction the original Right anti-economics. And it was the calamitous conclusion of the Enlightenment in the events of 1792 and 1793 that inflamed that reaction. The trauma of the French Revolution led conservatives to seek the causes of this disaster, and in their search for the guilty some found the economic liberals were culpable.

But we will contend that Right anti-economics was not restricted merely to the 'reactionary' champions of the *Ancien Régime*. We argue that within a generation of 1789 this Right species of anti-economics was assimilated by new 'visionary' Right ideologies that were concerned to herald and construct a new order on the ruins of the old. We maintain, in fact, that Right anti-economics has retained vigorous life throughout the twentieth century, even if in the guise of anti-Right self-consciousness.

2.1 Enlightenment dissenters

The Enlightenment makes peace with the market

The Enlightenment saw the market as benign, and this was a novelty. Before the Enlightenment essentially only two types of social realm were recognised: order (based on authority), and anarchy (based on force). The market, therefore, was either a piece of the socio-political order, or it was a species of anarchy. If the market was not to be treated as anarchy, it had to be made part of the socio-political order; by regulating the economic activity of the social classes (see Lévy-Bruhl 1933), by policing the consumption of social classes, and by dictating the prices of the commodities the different classes exchanged.

It was during the eighteenth century that this older watchfulness of authority to the market relaxed. This was encouraged by the new perception that the market was a realm of social action distinct from order and anarchy: independence. To be 'not-order' was no longer equivalent to anarchy. The older policy of assimilating the market into the social order decayed, and was subject to attack.[2]

The theorisers of this perceived new market realm were economists, and they were confident it was not seditious of the social order. A political conservative, such as David Hume, could, with only one or two slight hesitations, embrace the free market. And this was the presumption of society at large.

But even in the eighteenth century there were Right gadflies, including Simon-Nicolas-Henri Linguet and Ferdinand Galiani who challenged this complacent state of mind. These dissident authors conjured with three theses concerning the incongruity of the economics of the day with the social order.

Thesis 1. The market is antagonistic to order on account of its economic ramifications. This was argued on two grounds:

i.   The social order in significant measure consisted of violations of the free market by feudal privileges and encumbrances. The Right freely identified order with privilege. In the words of Robert Southey, 'Vested interests are the keystone of the social edifice' (quoted in Roberts 1979, p. 86).[3]
ii. The social order required (and was even constituted by) a certain distribution of income that a free market would threaten. The economic equilibrium, went this complaint, will jar with the political equilibrium.

Thesis 2. The market is destructive of the social order on account of its political ramifications. This was argued on two grounds:

i.   Free-market emphasis on consent and choice weakens the cement of the social order; the attachments and ties of life.
ii. Economic liberalism is antagonistic to the social order on account of its fraternity with political liberalism. This fraternity required little ingenuity to argue for. Both political and economic liberalism amounted to an elevation of consent and choice over authority or force. If the market could be based on consent, why not political life? If economists preach liberty in one sphere, would it not be heard in the other? If privilege and monopoly are scorned in economic matters, why not scorn them in political matters? Certainly, some members of the party of Enlightenment identified economic liberalism with political liberalism: 'For many

philosophes . . . there was no difference between the police which terrorised merchants and monitored or requisitioned grain on the one hand and the police which burned books and deprived men of their freedom on the other' (Kaplan 1976, p. 14).[4]

Thesis 3. A pre-eminence of the economic is antagonistic to the social order. This was argued on two grounds:

i. The economic criterion neglects the sentiments and virtues that solidify a social order; piety, patriotism, allegiance, devotion to family.
ii. The economic criterion undermines traditional authority since authority had no material function. What was more materially useless than the instruments and ornaments of traditional power?

Well before the French Revolution several of these claims had already been pressed by Linguet, Galiani and Jacques Necker.

Linguet

Life

Simon-Nicolas-Henri Linguet (1736–94) may be described as the first anti-economist. He was also a poet, playwright, engineer, renegade lawyer, social theorist and rogue journalist who pursued a fierce feud with the French *Économistes* in the 1770s in his *Du Pain et du Bled* (1774), *Réponse aux Docteurs Modernes* (1771), and *Théorie du Libelle* (1775).

Linguet was born, appropriately or inappropriately, on 14 July 1736. His early adult years were consumed in unsuccessful false starts, and troubled by accusations by former employers of theft. He found his true talent as a popular writer, and issued a stream of combative pamphlets. The court room may have seemed a more gainful forum for his dialectical talents, but this ambition ended with quarrels with his legal peers, and his expulsion from the order of advocates in 1775. He left for England where he published a newspaper to voice his views, *Annales Politiques, Civiles et Littéraires*. On his return in 1780 he was imprisoned by means of a *lettre de cachet* in the Bastille for 22 months. He wrote a celebrated exposé of that institution, and won the favour of the populace of pre-Revolutionary Paris. By 1788 his statuette sold in the streets; his waxwork stood in the Madame Tusssaud's of the day, situated between Voltaire and Frederick the Great.

With the advent of the Revolution, Linguet became an ardent advocate of Royal absolutism, and favoured 'complete support for the crown and for its unimpaired authority' (Paskoff 1983, p. 31) Consequently, he opposed calling the Estates General. He urged the public: 'Rally round the king, form a wall around him; support his authority and the independence of his crown' (quoted in Paskoff 1983, p. 32). During the Terror he was arrested on account of correspondence between himself and the King. He was 'tried and condemned by the Revolutionary Tribunal on June 27 [1794], and guillotined the same day' (Vyverberg 1970, p. 476).

Ideology

Linguet's theory of society was pessimistic and brutal. The social order was a matter of inequality. The perfection of this order lay in the perfection of inequality: the division of the population into the powerful and the powerless, masters in command and masses in servitude. Economic inequality was the necessary complement to political inequality. Thus the coexistence of wealth and poverty is 'both the base and the bond of society' (quoted in Vyverberg 1970, p. 477). The poverty of the mass in serfdom was certainly more endurable than their fate under freedom. Domesticated animals never die of starvation, neither do enslaved humans. It is only wild animals and free humans which perish. Thus Linguet urges, 'Believe me, and nothing more: for three quarters of men it is enough to know how to obey' (Linguet 1774, p. 305).

On these premises any spirit of liberty is anathema. Any notion of social contract is a formula for anarchy. 'Who does not see that such a contract would hold the germ of the most terrible and continual revolutions?' Linguet believed that eighteenth-century society was fostering the spirit of liberty and was thereby doomed. Linguet did not, however, envisage a red revolution. Rather, he foresaw a kind of black revolution, in which a new master class would arise and reinstitute servitude for a gratefully acquiescent populace (Linguet 1780, p. 103).

Anti-economics

The emergence of physiocracy in the 1760s, the appointment of the economic liberal Turgot to comptroller-general of finances in 1774, and attempts to deregulate the market in grain, provoked Linguet to several literary rampages against economics.

The catalyst of this frenzy was the publication in 1767 of Linguet's ambitious treatise on politics *Théorie des Lois Civiles*. This offended the *Économistes* by its disregard of Natural Law and its championship of Asiatic Despotism over modern freedom, and was negatively reviewed by Du Pont (Paskoff 1983). It was in 1774, with the appointment of Turgot to comptroller-general, that Linguet saw the occasion to counterattack. In *Pain et Bled* (Bread and Wheat) the *Économistes* are damned as 'despicable, ridiculous, impertinent, fanatics, liars, dangerous, of bad faith, charlatanry and indecency'; a 'monstrous mixture of French frivolity and the pedantic inhuman pettiness of the English' (quoted in Paskoff 1983, p. 68), and the authors of 'famine, misery, despair, migrations'. But they are worse than all these.

'They propose to kill the human race in order to make it happy. They say the best way to secure their needs is for them to die of hunger. This is a brief summary of their gospel' (Linguet 1774, p. xiv). He adds 'millions of families have been murdered'. In *Pain et Bled*, evidently, ordinary calumny gives way to phantasmagoria.

One manifestation of the fantastic dimension of Linguet are his tirades against bread. 'Bread is a murderous drug, of which corruption is the first element; that we are obliged to alter by a poison (leaven) in order to make the rest less unhealthy' (Linguet 1771, p. 168). Bread is a foodstuff 'against nature', which destroys the body, and than which there is nothing more dangerous. Bakers, as drug peddlers, are blamed for the degeneration of the human race.

Pain et Bled was met with a disdainful rebuttal in the *Théorie du Paradoxe* (1775) of André Morellet (1727–1819), an active supporter of the *Économistes*. Linguet growled, 'I have sworn never to allow myself to be attacked without striking back' (quoted in Paskoff 1983, p. 8). He struck back with a production which is singular even by the standards of the literature of anti-economics: the *Théorie du Libelle* (1775). This purports to be a dialogue between Morellet and a youth, 'P'. In his chambers Morellet threatens the youth with ruin unless he pens a denunciation of Linguet, from whom the youth has earlier received a kindness. Morellet offers the distracted P a positive incentive: he will receive 2000 *écus* for this piece of literary assassination. But, adds Morellet, it will not be sufficient to merely chastise Linguet; Linguet must be silenced. Morellet then plucks from his pocket a manuscript that Linguet had planned to publish, but which Morellet had seized by the censors. 'He attacks our principles by the root. Goodbye to science and net product if this had appeared'. But it does not end well for Morellet. On the last page the valiant youth rebels against his corruptor and storms out defiant, leaving Morellet bewildered in the face of this unyielding purity. The *Théorie du Libelle* sold 4000 copies within a week (Paskoff 1983, p. 9).

The primal source of Linguet's revulsion against the *Économistes* was their attraction to freedom: 'Here is the favourite divinity of the economists' (Linguet 1771, 2, p. 120). In Linguet's judgement, liberty is a 'poisoned plant that makes furious all those who breathe its fragrance'. It did so by allowing the subordinated to think and discuss their situation. Certain *Économistes* had suggested that a free discussion of the polity would only strengthen authority. 'Ah! Do you not see that you are venturing perhaps the most dreadful of all principles; that you place in the light of day an axiom that can overthrow crowns and overturn empires?' (Linguet 1774, pp. 291–3). 'Be sure that as soon as each citizen has the prerogative to weigh, in his own little private sanctuary, the conduct of his governors ... all is lost' (Linguet 1774, p. 296).

Other *Économistes* had contended that the freedom they sought was economic freedom, not political freedom. But political liberty and economic liberty are equated by Linguet. 'Whatever limits you wish to place on this freedom, it is impossible to prevent it from spreading to the great ends of politics. From wheat, the thinkers of this type will not wait to raise themselves up to the throne' (Linguet 1774, p. 296). The *Économistes*, therefore, are saying: '*authority does not impose anything on us*'. They are the 'panegyrists of English anarchy' (Linguet 1771, 1, p. 192). This thesis is illustrated with a favourite historical metaphor of Linguet's: the identification of the Enlightenment with the Reformation, the previous great rebellion against authority. Economists are to the Enlightenment as Protestants are to the Reformation. They are comparable to Luther and Calvin 'They [too] broke holy bonds that tradition and habit had filled the people. They raised themselves up against ancient fetters strengthened by the awe of centuries. They demanded, as you, reason and evidence, and the natural and essential order... They proclaimed, as you, the most complete freedom of thought, and in that they were at least logical' (Linguet 1774, p. 372). The *Économistes* were, indeed, comparable to the most shocking rebels of Protestantism. 'In the sixteenth century, in the flood of sects which disgraced and tore apart religion, there arose the Anabaptists, who flattered themselves that they yielded a service to small babies by taking their life after baptism, because by this they obtained them an indestructible happiness. The economists are the Anabaptists of philosophy' (Linguet 1774, p. xiv).

Galiani

Ferdinando Galiani (1728–87) was an active member of Parisian salon life of the 1760s who advanced an anti-economics that was in large measure similar to Linguet's.

Galiani had been an early sympathiser with the *Économistes*, but by 1770 he had acquired a loathing for physiocracy. Physiocracy was 'a veritable occult sect, with all the faults of sects, jargon, system, a taste for persecution, a hatred of outsiders, back-biting, spite, and small mindedness' (1881, 1, p. 114). 'If you want me to be frank, I think Quesnay is the Antichrist and his rural physiognomy is the Apocalypse' (1881, 1, p. 129).

Galiani launched a public censure of physiocracy and grain liberalisation in his *Dialogues sur le Commerce des Bleds* (1770). Lacking the choler of his private expressions, the *Dialogues* is intended as an ingenious battle of wits over the program of liberalisation of the grain trade. It achieved great popular success: Voltaire compared it to Plato.

The *Dialogues*' case against physiocracy was largely methodological: general theories are generally wrong. Every case is a special case, and so while liberalisation is in some circumstances advantageous, often times it is not. But the nervous core of Galiani's opposition to economic liberalisation lay not in methodological considerations, but in political ones. Like Linguet, his fundamental objection to economists was that they were a threat to political order. They were 'Jansenists' (the 'puritan' dissidents of seventeenth-century Catholicism who represented the courts of justice against royal absolutism). They were 'la Fronde' (the series of anti-royal civil disturbances in mid-seventeenth-century France).

Like Linguet, Galiani took economic order and political order to be entwined. 'If you succeed in modifying the corn administration too much in France you alter the form and constitution of government' (quoted in Faccarello 1998, p. 132). Like Linguet he took inequality to be the base of the political order; the brute fact was that the social order required the exploitation of the peasant mass.

But, unlike Linguet, his grievance against economists was not that their doctrines corroded subservience, but that economic freedom would redistribute income from the nobility to the peasantry. 'The monarchy essentially hinges on an inequality of estates; the inequality of estates on a low price of food; and a low price of food on constraints' (Faccarello 1998, p. 133). Therefore,

> When the economists say that it is good that the price of wheat be very high, they do not utter nonsense, nor stupidity; but they choose a very seditious language... The whole system of all countries in the world is founded on an ancient violence that was committed and sustained against the possessors of the only true goods. We sit straddled on the peasantry. Kings, Popes, courts, the Sorbonne, the Order of Saint-Esprit right up to the Order of Saint-Michel have all climbed on top of them, and have lowered the price of bread.
>
> (Galiani 1881, 1, p. 329)

Necker

There is a final, third figure who may be bracketed with Linguet and Galiani – one very different in style, but similar in doctrine – Jacques Necker (1732–1804), a successful banker and less successful administrator of royal finances. Amidst the public reaction against Turgot's deregulation of the grain trade Necker published in 1775 a defence of grain regulation, *De la Législation et du Commerce des Grains*, which expressed sentiments in concurrence with Linguet and Galiani. The 'social architecture', said Necker, refuses free trade (Faccarello 1998, p. 135). The economists' love of liberty is merely an infantile rejection of authority. 'The unlimited love of liberty in political economy and the exaggerated hate of prohibition go back to man's childhood' (quoted in Faccarello 1998, p. 141).

Linguet the scoundrel journalist, Galiani the salon sophist, and Necker the politic banker; all three manifested an anti-economics that was to recur in later centuries; all three are types which recur centuries later in the history of anti-economics.

2.2   Counter-revolutionary convictions

'You have greatly hastened this useful revolution'

With the advent of the Revolution the dissolution of order was no longer a disquieting prospect, but a shocking reality, and the Right's search for the sources of subversion quickened. The older distrust of economists was now inflamed by a perception that they had been forward in participating in the terrible events of 1789 onwards. This perception was held even by those concerned to defend economics, such as Dmitrii Golitsyn (1734–1803, Russian ambassador to France, 1762–68). Golitsyn was an admirer of Turgot, yet in 1796 he wrote that certain former pupils of the first economists 'who kept the jargon but not their teachers' conduct... had themselves elected to the National Assembly and the National Convention, had embraced their spirit and their atrocities' (Golitsyn 1796, p. 7). He adds with regret, 'The horrors in which they participated during the course of this monstrous revolution, sufficed to make light minds and unreflective people believe that they acted thus by systematic principle, and to conclude that these principles were the basis of the system of the *Économistes*' (Golitsyn 1796, p. 8).

Who were these former pupils of the first economists who had supposedly embraced the atrocities of the Assembly and Convention?

Golitsyn is undoubtedly referring to Marie-Jean-Antoine-Nicolas de Caritat, Marquis de Condorcet (1743–94), a disciple and eulogist of Turgot. He was the author of the liberal *Lettres sur le Commerce des Grains* (1774), a well-received and widely-read *Vie de Turgot* (1786), and a 1791 French paraphrase of the *Wealth of Nations* (Diatkine 1993). Elected to the Legislative Assembly, in 1791, Condorcet was the first to declare for a republic, and was later a member of the National Convention. In the trial of the King he voted in favour of the strongest punishment short of death.

Another 'former pupil' was Pierre-Samuel Du Pont de Nemours (1739–1817). Du Pont was an assistant of Turgot, an editor of various physiocratic journals, and compiler of the 'collected papers' of his friend and physiocratic mentor François Quesnay. In 1789 he was elected a member of the Estates General, representing the Third Estate of Nemours. He was prominent in the Tennis Court Oath of 20 June, and later posed for David's *Serment de Jeu de Paume* (Tennis Court Oath), where he appears in the first rank of figures. He twice presided over the new National Assembly and often served as its secretary. Raised in a devout Huguenot household, Du Pont successfully campaigned in the last months of 1789 for the state expropriation of the property of the Catholic Church (Jolly 1956, p. 87).

Du Pont believed that both the *Économistes* and Adam Smith could claim a share of the inspiration of the constitutional changes of 1789. In the ferment preceding the calling of the Estates General he wrote to Smith in May 1788: 'you have greatly hastened this useful revolution' (Smith 1977, p. 277). Dugald Stewart, Smith's biographer, literary executor and successor as Professor of Moral and Political Philosophy in Edinburgh, might have agreed. Stewart had spent the summers of 1788 and 1789 in Paris, where he was admitted to observe the proceedings of the Estates General. 'He sympathised strongly with the early revolutionary movement, and did not give up his hopes of a satisfactory issue even at the outbreak of the war and the beginning of the Terror' (*Dictionary of National Biography – DNB*).

Another economist of the Revolution was Jean-Baptiste Say (1767–1832), who was employed by Mirabeau in the production of the influential radical journal *Courier de Provençe*. The youthful Say was presumably indiscernible in the midst of the Revolutionary panorama, but his biographers have stressed how he 'was an active revolutionary throughout the 1790s and an ardent republican from 1794' (Whatmore 1998, p. 441; Steiner 1990, p. 176).

Thus the *Économistes* were vulnerable to the search by anti-revolutionary forces for the origins of this disaster.[5]

An early example of the search for the guilty – and the discovery of economists – is provided by Jacques Mallet du Pan's *Considérations sur la Nature de la Révolution de France* (1793). Mallet du Pan (1749–1800) had been a journalist for Linguet's journalistic mouthpiece, *Annales Politiques, Civiles et Littéraires*. In *Annales* du Pan had specialised in economic subjects in which he was 'severely critical towards the sect of the economists' (Mallet 1902, p. 17). He eulogised Necker and was unsympathetic to Turgot. In *Considérations* in 1793 Turgot was again a target. Mallet du Pan complained that opinion in pre-Revolutionary France had 'confused, without pause, freedom with the most anarchic democracy. This delirium reached a point such that there was a minister of state, Mr Turgot, who . . . poured derision and contempt on the foundations of English government, on the limits to popular power, and on the institutions restraining a legislative anarchy' (Mallet du Pan 1793, p. 6).

A more extravagant use of anti-economics in the counter-revolutionary inquisition is provided by Augustin Barruel (1741–1820). Barruel was a Jesuit of noble birth who won celebrity through anti-*philosophe* journalism. The lynching of 220 priests in the September massacres of 1792 put Barruel into flight to England, where he befriended Edmund Burke. In 1797 he published what was to become 'one of the founding documents of the right wing interpretation of the French Revolution' (Hofman 1993, p. 28), *Mémoires Pour Servir a l'Histoire du Jacobinisme* ([1797] 1800). Its thesis was simple: the French Revolution was a plot conceived by various enemies of Christianity, ranging from *philosophes* to Masons. In Barruel's massive four-volume dragnet of virtually every imperfectly orthodox thinker, economists were not to escape. They were found guilty of deism, Rousseauianism and *lèse-majesté*.

A Doctor, known in France by the name of Quesnay, so well insinuated himself in the good graces and esteem of Louis 16 [sic] that this prince called him his *Thinker*. Quesnay indeed appeared to have pondered deeply all that makes for happiness of the people, he desired it frankly;

but he was with all this only a man of vain systems and the founder of this species of sophists called *economists*, since they greatly busied themselves with, or at least spoke much on, the economy...If some of these Economists did not stray far from their speculations, it is at least certain that these authors ill concealed their hatred of Christianity.

(Barruel [1797] 1800, p. 378)[6]

The *Économistes'* offensive deism was accompanied by an attachment to right and reason, which Barruel held was subversive of respect to things established. Barruel quotes Du Pont to illustrate, 'It is necessary to admit, we are told by the honeyed mouth of Du Pont "that most nations are the victims of a infinity of crimes and misdeeds, that could not take place, if they studied natural right, reasoned social justice, and the true and sound policies that have enlightened the largest number of minds"' (Barruel [1797] 1800, p. 183). But what, perhaps, most affronted Barruel was the physiocrats' fondness for the notion that an aware and thinking public opinion could prove a useful resource in policy making. To Barruel the very fact of the public having an opinion, any opinion, was subversive. Sovereign authority would be destroyed by any presumption of the public to judge a question for themselves (Vyvyerberg 1970).

Overall, the *Économistes* were deemed by Barruel to be equivalent to Rousseau, for, 'the more moderate of these sophists, at least those under the standard of Quesnay who wished to appear moderate, did not give the people an account more flattering [than Jacques Rousseau] on the origin and actual state of their government' (Barruel [1797] 1800, p. 183). In equating the *Économistes* with Rousseau, Barruel was inaugurating a comparison that was to be put to work by Right anti-economists time and again in the subsequent century.

But however much he may have gratified the prejudgements of the Right, Barruel's indiscriminate conspiracy hunting was not always taken seriously by his natural audience. A Right anti-economist of considerably more intellectual distinction was Louis-Gabriel-Ambroise Vicomte de Bonald (1754–1840), an advocate of absolute monarchy and ecclesiastical authority. His anti-economics includes 'Sur l'Économie Politique' and 'De la Richesse des Nations', both written in 1810.

The starting point of Bonald's anti-economics was the thesis that market society could not conserve itself. It was a state of disequilibrium. At the social level the disequilibrium was manifested in the social problems of market society (exemplified by the towns), which had higher unemployment, crime, crowding, inequality of wealth and suicide than non-market society (indicated by rural society). At the more political level market society was prone to war on account of the struggle for markets. 'Europe is found in a moral and political disorder such that nothing like it has been seen since the beginning of the world in civilised states, a disorder against which the political economy of Adam Smith and others is certainly powerless' (Bonald [1810] 1864b, p. 300).

Political economy's powerlessness was due to it being given over to the 'two divinities of the modern age' freedom and equality (Bonald [1810] 1864b, p. 303). This grievance had already been aired by Linguet and Barreul, but Bonald stressed, in addition, that political economy was also useless on account of its materialism. Governments, complained Bonald, are

> always preoccupied with *political economy* ... have thought there were not enough cultivators, although all was cultivated ... that there was not enough commerce, although perhaps there was too much ... not enough money, as if they could ever have enough for cupidity. But at the same time they allowed themselves to be persuaded that they had too much religion, too much morals, too much severity in laws ... too much dependence within the family, too much respect of the inferior classes to the superior classes, not enough liberty, and finally, not enough equality.
> (Bonald [1810] 1864b, p. 299)

'Morals and laws' Bonald contended 'are thus the true and even the only wealth of societies, families or nations; that is to say the true and only means of their existence and conservation' (Bonald [1810] 1864c, p. 308). Therefore, although 'governments are accustomed to regard ... material wealth as the sole source of the strength of nations' (Bonald [1810] 1864b, p. 310), Adam Smith had not treated the true Wealth of Nations.[7] Smith's political economy was, consequently, a 'great uselessness': it 'makes those who study it neither more economic or politic; and which, when one has read all the writings that it has given birth, one does not know how to govern men any more than one knows how to write poems when one has read all the poets' (Bonald [1810] 1864b, p. 299).[8]

In the Restoration, Bonald became the favoured philosopher of the 'ultras', was made a peer in 1823, and placed in charge of censorship by Charles X in 1827. He gloated that this last office permitted him to pursue a 'thought inquisition' (Klinck 1994, p. 712). The official attitude to political economy was, therefore, at best cool. The French political economists saw themselves as liberals, and 'in the eyes of Bourbons, a liberal was a revolutionary' (Bernstein 1971, p. 26).[9]

An indication of the *froideur* that political economy faced in Restoration France is given by the difficulties experienced by its leading figure, Jean-Baptiste Say. He had sought in the early years of the Restoration to create a chair of economics. This proposal, however, was not sympathetically received by the Chamber of Deputies.

To create chairs in political economy would have passed for treachery. Was it a science? No. Only a machine of war under a specious name. The name alone constitutes a revolt against the established powers and prevailing practices, a critique of existing and projected laws, an attack on the respect which must enfold the law. Thus they speak on the majority benches.

(Reybaud 1864, p. 952)

To increase a planned chair's chances of success the word '*politique*' (that sounded too charged) was dropped from its title, and a chair in 'industrial economy' was subsequently established at a private college, the Conservatoire des Arts et Métiers. But Say was soon in conflict with the 'ultra' forces again, over an attempt to resurrect the corporations of the *Ancien Régime* (see Sibalis 1988). It was, perhaps, Say's public intervention in this controversy which prompted police to place secret auditors in his lectures, and in the lectures of some colleagues.[10] The police agent reported the 'pernicious doctrines that the professors of these lectures inculcate little by little in the mind of the people who frequent them' (Liesse 1901, p. 172). In 1826 the police also compiled a dossier on Adolphe Blanqui (1798–1854), Say's protégé who was to assume the chair at the Conservatoire on Say's death. The dossier accused Blanqui of 'outrageous liberalism' and of being 'full of sarcasm against non-constitutional governments' (Staum 1998, p. 105).[11]

Comte and Toussenel

The deposition of Charles X and the advent of the July Monarchy in 1830 ended official hostility towards political economy. It also marked an end to a purely 'reactionary' anti-economics that was concerned to defend, restore and justify the *Ancien Régime*. But the Right ideas did not fade away. Instead they were assimilated into certain 'visionary' Right ideologies, that turned away from the elite and towards the mass, from the past and towards the future, and from repairing an old order to constructing a new one. Principal among these visionary ideologies were Fourierism and Saint-Simonianism, and each fathered an anti-economist, Auguste Comte and Alphonse Toussenel.[12]

While often seen to be part of the pre-history of socialism, the Saint-Simonians shared a wholly Right concern about the ungovernability of modern society: 'True men of ability no longer are or can be appreciated' they complained. 'The legitimacy of the power of those who exercise it is questioned. Governors and governed are at war' (Enfantin [1828] 1972, p. 54). The source of this disorder was traced by Saint-Simonians to liberalism: 'Apostles of liberty, will you yet long repeat that revolt is the holiest duty?' (Enfantin [1828] 1972, p. 260). The subversive character of liberalism is evinced in its role in the French Revolution: 'if we wished to designate who contributed to the destruction of the old French monarchy, we would be well obliged to name Malesherbes and Marat, Turgot and Hébert, la Gironde et la Montagne, save to establish the nuances between them'

(Enfantin 1832, p. 54). Thus to the Saint-Simonians Turgot was just as responsible as Jacques-René Hébert (the leader of the ultra left *enragées*), and Malesherbes (the royal official who supported Turgot) was just as a culpable as Jean-Paul Marat.

Auguste Comte (1798–1857) began as a Saint-Simonian, and fortified the Saint-Simonian judgements of the negative consequences of liberalism with Bonald's similar opinion (quoted in Mauduit 1929, p. 30). Thus with Saint-Simonians he imputed to economists some degree of responsibility for the end of the *Ancien Régime*: 'the political school of the negative doctrine is usually supposed to be represented by Rousseau; but we must not overlook the participation in it of the political sect of the economists who bore a large share in the disorganisation of the ancient social system' (Comte [1855] 1974, p. 681). And, with Bonald, Comte believed that economics contributed to social disorder through its advocacy of the free market. 'All economic relations between nations, cultivators, factory hands, traders left to themselves, without social discipline lead to the most grave conflicts' (quoted in Mauduit 1929, p. 24). Faced with this 'chasm in the social order' caused by, for example, machinery, 'our economists can do nothing better than repeat with pitiless pedantry, their barren aphorism of absolute industrial liberty' (Comte [1855] 1974, p. 449). This 'offspring of Protestantism', complains Comte, is now fathering a new rebellion, socialism (Comte [1855] 1974, p. 681).

A still more vivid example of Right anti-economics in a visionary author, is provided by the wild raging of Alphonse Toussenel (1803–85), a partisan of Charles Fourier, the 'utopian socialist' who advocated communal association.[13] Toussenel edited the Fourierist journal *Démocratie Pacifique*, and during the Second Republic was a member of the Commission of Luxembourg, a sort of socialist department of labour.

Despite these Left credentials, Toussenel absorbed most of the characteristic theses of Right anti-economics in France: the equivalence of economics to rebellion, its equivalence to Protestantism, its odious English origins, its deleterious impact on social conditions. All this is repeatedly pressed in the work for which he is best known: *Les Juifs, Rois de l'Époque* (1847). In these two volumes of frantic wrath he quickly identifies economists as an enemy of order.

Regicide is only, after all, the deadly and logical conclusion of the belief in the inborn antagonism of governments and peoples, of the dogma of the economists which the French government finances with students and a chair to propagate their science. The other symptoms of the revolutionary virus that the doctors of economism have inoculated the French nation, reveal themselves in the growing crime statistics, the success of newspaper crime sheets, and the state of our prisons.

(Toussenel 1847, 1, p. 94)

Toussenel resumes Linguet's thesis that economics is an importation of English anarchy. 'From the English economists, who first produced it under the venal patronage of their false science, it passed straight to the French encyclopaedists. The philosophers of the late century, belonging to this sect, gave it polish and shine, and by epigram put it into the currency of ideas of the period' (Toussenel 1847, 1, p. 48). He traces the passage of the virus in the approach of the French Revolution 'After Diderot came the economists, who wrote that *government is the born enemy of the people* . . . The people adopted, from before '89, this fatal doctrine . . . they logically concluded that the *people are all the more happy the weaker the acts of government, the more disarmed its power*' (Toussenel 1847, 1, p. 47). This theory of 'languishing government' says Toussenel, went 'straight to the abolition of the monarchy, and nobility of the blood'. This theory, he adds mordantly, 'said its last word in its deed of January 21 [1793]'.[14]

Germany

Right anti-economics was not restricted to France. Germany also had its Right critics of physiocracy before the revolutionary outburst. Justus Möser (1720–94) was a conservative critic of capitalism, who wrote against physiocracy, and its 'Iroquois philosopher' Quesnay. And in Germany, as in France, the advent of the revolution brought an encyclopedic inquisitor of subversion, Johann August Starck (1741–1816). In his *Der Triumph der Philosophie im Achtzehnten Jahrhundert* (1804) Starck faults (among Masons, Protestants, British empiricists) physiocracy's 'critique of the prevailing social and economic system [that] threatened established customs and property rights' (Epstein 1966, p. 510).[15]

But the greatest outburst came with the controversy over reforms, reminiscent of Turgot's, which were introduced by chief minister Karl von Stein (1757–1831) and were designed to reinvigorate a humbled and ailing Prussian state. His October Edict of 1807 ended serfdom, curtailed guild privilege, and legalised the alienability of noble land to non-nobles. Stein had read and annotated the *Wealth of Nations* and his reforms 'were recognised by friend and foe alike, to be applications of the laissez-faire theory of Adam Smith as popularised' (Epstein 1966, p. 181). Stein's attempts to end serfdom provoked the fury of the Junker class. General F.A.L. von der Marwitz complained of the reformers, 'They had studied Adam Smith without realising that he speaks only of money, because in such a country as England . . . the study of money can be carried to the extreme without overthrowing the constitution; but in a country without a constitution and without living legislation . . . a state organisation based on this money theory . . . must destroy the state' (quoted in Hasek 1925, p. 146). In this remonstration the nobility had a literary ally in Adam Müller (1779–1829), a romantic defender of the feudal order and a critic of the 'simplistic principles' of Adam Smith.[16]

2.3 The 'consuming pestilence to the empire'[17]

'The peace of the cottage and the happiness of the palace'

Before 1789 an English Right anti-economics barely existed.[18] The pre-eminent English conservative of the period, Samuel Johnson, was conscious of the possibility that the market was corrosive of the established social structure, but was no anti-economist.[19] The leading British economic authors of the period, Hume and Smith, were censured more on account of their religious tenets than any economic doctrines they maintained.[20]

It is in the wake of the French Revolution that a Right anti-economics emerged in Great Britain. In its immediate aftermath there was the same tendency as in France for the Right to identify economists as being among the phalanxes of subversives. As Dugald Stewart observed in 1794: 'It was not unusual, even among men of some talents and information, to confound, studiously, the speculative doctrines of political economy, with those discussions concerning the first principles of Government which happened unfortunately at that time to agitate the public mind. The doctrine of a Free Trade was itself represented as of a revolutionary tendency' (quoted in Rashid 1986, p. 60).[21] Stewart, who had delivered the only lectures on political economy given at any university in the British Isles during the 1790s, had in the *Elements of the Philosophy of the Human Mind* of 1792 praised the physiocrats for conjuring with a vision of the ideal state and goading governments to reach towards it, and had quoted Condorcet with approval. Two Lords of Session (that is, two judges of the supreme Scottish court) demanded Stewart retract these words. 'For some years', says the *DNB*, Stewart 'was not cordially received' in Edinburgh.

The one conservative to pursue in print the supposed link between political economy and subversion was John Robison (1739–1805), the Professor of Natural Philosophy at Edinburgh, and author in 1798 of *Proofs of a Conspiracy against All the Religions and Governments of Europe*. In this he approvingly refers to Barreul's identification of a 'Gang of public corruptors',

> The most eminent members were d'Alembert, Diderot, Condorcet, La Harpe, Turgot, Lamoignon. They took the name of Oeconomists, and affected to be continually occupied with plans for improving Commerce, manufactures, Agriculture, Finance, and published from time to time respectable performances on those subjects. But their darling project was to destroy Christianity and all Religion, and to bring about a total change of Government.
>
> (Robison 1798, p. 536)

But Robison's concern of 1798 about a 'total change of government' was soon to be overshadowed by the national struggle with France. This struggle closed in 1815 with the conclusive triumph of the conservative power. But in its triumph the United Kingdom found itself confounded by the release of accumulated tensions over privileged treatment of interests and institutions. These tensions encompassed the political (electoral reform), the religious (Catholic Emancipation), and the economic (the Corn Laws). In the Britain of the 1820s and 1830s political economists took the 'radical' view on all these, and the economic liberalism of political economy was associated with criticism of the existing socio-political order. This made for a rich field for Right anti-economics.[22] Nevertheless, there was never an official anti-economics in Great Britain, for the Right did not flourish in the ruling circles. 'By the 1820s an authentically Tory party had disappeared' (Eastwood 1989, p. 331), and a succession of semi-liberal Tories and Whigs fitfully accommodated the pressure to change. Britain's ruling circles were, then, not hostile to political economy,[23] and the Right anti-economists of Great Britain were little more than hostile spectators, usually disregarded, and always in retreat. They were composed of journalists, maverick politicians, and visionaries.

Tory journalists

John Wilson Croker, John Wilson, David Robinson and Archibald Alison articulated anti-economics in the two leading Tory organs of the age: the *Quarterly Review* and *Blackwood's Edinburgh Magazine*. Their anti-economics was prolific, 'comprehensive', and extreme.

John Wilson Croker (1780–1857) was a man of letters, and a Tory ideologist who was reputedly the first to designate the Tories as 'Conservatives'. He was sufficiently opposed to the Reform Bill of 1832 to resign from Parliament when it was passed. His judgement of political economy may serve as an exemplar of the attitude of all anti-economists: political economy was a 'pseudo-science' that 'might be esteemed the great folly of the age, if it were not in its consequences to be one of the great evils, and if there were not reason to apprehend that eventually it may prove the greatest curse' (quoted in Coleridge 1969d, p. 490).

John Wilson (1785–1854) was the editor of *Blackwood's Magazine*, a tireless ragger of Thomas McCulloch, and inventor of an absurd slur against David Ricardo. Ricardo had, said Wilson, secured a commission of £64,000 on a £2 million loan raised for the Greek rebellion against the Turks. Unfortunately for the truth of this assertion, Ricardo was dead at the time the loan was raised (Grampp 1976, p. 557).

It was David Robinson (1787–1849), a *Blackwood's* journalist, who was perhaps the archetypical Tory anti-economist journalist. The centrepiece of his anti-economic oeuvre is a multi-part critique of political economy, headed 'To the Heads of the University of Oxford', who had recently appointed a Professor of Political Economy.[24]

That which bears the name of Political Economy, is now taught at your University... If it be not a science, but a mass of fictions, you are by teaching it deeply disgracing your university, and destroying your own reputation as men of science. You are converting that noble and hallowed seat of learning, which has so long ranked amidst the first of England's boasts and treasures, into the parent of ignorance and error, and the enemy of truth and philosophy.

(Robinson 1829, p. 510)

Shrill and extreme, Robinson nevertheless managed to strike analytical land by raising issues slighted by classical economics; effective demand, uncertainty, the distinction between long-run and short-run equilibrium. So by the generally weak standards of anti-economics 'To the Heads of the University of Oxford' is a relatively robust performance (see Rashid 1978). Nevertheless, this analytical performance was beside the point: 'They might not always say it in so many words, but the tacit assumption was that economic analysis was really irrelevant, and that England should not permit the sort of change that would follow from dropping the old controls of custom and government associated with the dominance of a landed aristocracy' (Fetter 1965, p. 430; see also Fetter 1958 and 1960).

What was really at stake is seen better in Robinson's, 'The Faction' (Robinson 1827). This is a bitter tirade over 'catholic treason', the recognition of the newly independent states of South America, and the new Jury Law. The Faction (that is, the Whigs) intend to 'abolish the Usury Laws, the Test Acts, the Laws of Primogeniture and Entail, the Poor Laws, the laws that impose disabilities on the Catholics... In all this it is to be guided, not by expediency and the state of the empire, but by its fallacious inventions, which it dignifies with the names – Political Economy, and Abstract Right' (Robinson 1827, p. 424).[25]

Archibald Alison (1792–1867), also of *Blackwood's*, was a well-liked lawyer and historian of prodigious energy and vehement views. He was an adversary of the Great Reform Bill, an ardent protectionist (Alison 1850), defender of slavery and 'a strong opponent of the North in the American civil war' (*DNB*). Political economy, complains Alison, 'imported from France', has been 'progressively applied to every part of the social body', so that the press now enjoys the 'utmost licentiousness', crime has increased 'TEN TIMES', 'the worst Chartist or Socialist doctrines' are tolerated, and 'combinations among workmen to raise their wages [are] declared legal and carried into practice' (Alison 1845, p. 530). He was also the author of a two-volume effort to refute Malthus on account of the Deity's providential oversight of man's happiness, *The Principles of Population and their Connection with Human Happiness* (1840).

We may conclude the treatment of Tory journalists by making mention of William Lilly (1840–1919), Catholic convert, lawyer, historian, *écrivain* and anti-economist of a fervour to match Ruskin, but without his bizarre genius (see Lilly and Devas 1904). Like Croker and his company Lilly was a furious opponent of democracy, for the 'the majority is not merely irrational but senseless'. As late as 1907 (!) he was praising the unreformed House of Commons prior to 1832. The origins of the False Democracy of 1907 lay in the French Revolution, and Political Economy had the same terrible genesis. 'The truth is, that the old "orthodox" Political Economy is really a growth of the *philosophe* school which so largely influenced Adam Smith. Consciously or unconsciously, its exponents are dominated by the extreme individualism of which Rousseau became the most popular exponent' (Lilly and Devas 1904, p. xv).[26] After Smith came Ricardo, whose 'seeming impartial and scientific theory on hypothetical landlords was, in fact, meant as a weapon against the real living country gentlemen and the existing corn laws' (Lilly and Devas in Byles 1904, p. 226). But from that dark time 'the yoke of this now shattered science – pseudo-science is a more correctly descriptive term – was riveted, for the better part of a century, upon the neck of a people specially proud of its freedom' (Lilly and Devas 1904, p. xxiii).

Poets

Three poets deserve mention among Right anti-economists: S.T. Coleridge, Robert Southey and William Wordsworth.[27] All three were enthusiasts for the French Revolution in their youth, who had by the 1820s adopted reactionary postures: angrily opposing, for example, the Roman Catholic Relief Act (1829) of the Tory government of the Duke of Wellington.

S.T. Coleridge (1772–1834) left no extended anti-economics, just fragments of derision of the 'solemn humbug' of political economy, and the 'democratical oligarchy of glib economists'. William Wordsworth's (1770–1850) opposition to political economy was also parenthetical, however pungent: bitterly disapproving references to *Wealth of Nations* in his poetry,[28] footnote scorn of Smith's literary taste, and sporadic struggles to frustrate the political ambitions of political economists.[29] In 1818, for example, he threw himself into a campaign to defeat Henry Brougham's attempt to win a seat in the House of Commons. 'One of the most importunate of that class of Economists which Parliament contained', he warned the electors 'now, Gentleman, solicits the honour of representing you' (Wordsworth 1974b, p. 169).[30]

Robert Southey (1774–1843) was a shallower mind, but of sufficiently greater application to articulate his anti-economics in a number of pieces of journalism (Southey 1803, 1831). Southey seems to have seen society as an intricate contrivance, the complexities of which composed an integral part. His youthful perception that it was a bad contrivance made him a radical. His later perception that it was a good contrivance made him an ultra conservative, with a faith in the *Ancien Régime* in all its Gothic convolutions. Reform was just a wrecking interference and reformers were equated with revolutionaries. Thus MPs such as Joseph Hume, campaigning for retrenchment in the name of political economy, were described as surrogate Jacobins (Southey [1832] 1971, pp. 128, 129, 141).

Maverick politicians

Politicians composed another group of Right anti-economists. Their leading theme is that the economic equilibrium jars with the political equilibrium. The market gave so little income to the labouring class that economic destitution could led to political convulsion.[31] This thesis is well put by the Rev. Dr Folliot in Peacock's *Crotchet Castle* who blamed insurrection on maldistribution, maldistribution on the free market, and a free market on political economy.

Chief among these politician anti-economists were Michael Sadler, Richard Oastler and George Poulett Scrope.

Michael Sadler (1780–1835; Tory MP from 1829–32) campaigned actively against Catholic emancipation (two of his speeches ran to half a million copies), actively against electoral reform, and actively in favour of the restriction of factory hours. Economists were 'pests of society and the persecutors of the poor' (*DNB*). He was also author of an anti-Malthusian tract, the *Law of Population*, that declared that political economy was 'made up of "shreds and patches", partly of truisms, partly of palpable blunders, but principally of a string of unconnected paradoxes' (Sadler [1830] 1971, p. 9).

In the campaign for shorter working hours Sadler was joined by Richard Oastler (1789–1861), who opposed Catholic emancipation, electoral reform and disestablishment of the Church of England, despised dissenters, and achieved fame in the battle for the 10-hour bill. His favoured maxim was 'a place for everything and everything in its place'. Everything which threatened this placing was identified as one. 'The Demon called *Liberalism* who is now stalking through the land ... assuming first one name and then another: March of Intellect, Political Economy, Free Trade, Liberal Principals, etc., but always destroying the peace of the cottage and the happiness of the palace' (quoted in Driver 1946, p. 295).

George Poulett Scrope (1797–1876; MP from 1833–68) was the *parvenue* lord of the Manor House of Castle Combe who published in the *Quarterly Review* a 51-page critique of the doctrines of Malthus and McCulloch. There he protested the political economists' 'opposition to the most obvious facts and reasonings', and claimed they had 'propagated so many dangerous fallacies, and established so few useful truths' (Scrope 1831, p. 2). Scrope's performance is one of the best in the anti-economics corpus. He was an important geologist, and his scientific, analytic mind fell upon several frailties in classical economics. But at the bottom of his anti-economics, as he forthrightly owns, was a dissatisfaction with political economy on account of the 'mischievous' 'notions likely to prevail among the masses' if its tenets were accepted (Scrope 1873, p. i).

Thomas Charles Banfield (1800?–82) was a Secretary to the Privy Council thanks to the patronage of Peel. In *Six Letters to the Right Hon. Sir Robert Peel, Bart., Being an Attempt to Expose the Dangerous Tendency of the Theory of Rent Advocated by Mr Ricardo, and the Writers of his School*, he declared that Ricardo's theory 'has done more mischief to this country in misdirecting the course of the industrious classes and shaking its political institutions to their foundation, than the efforts of the most powerful declared enemies could have accomplished' (Banfield, 1843, p. 5).[32]

Three visionaries of the enslaved society

The Right anti-economics of nineteenth-century Britain that we have examined thus far was defensive, even reactionary; it was concerned to preserve, repair and buttress an old order. But, as in France, anti-economics with a backward gaze did not secure the greatest influence in the mid-nineteenth century. Instead, a greater influence was won by Right doctrinaires who threw away a concrete past, in the hope of building a marvellous future based on the supremacy of command and obedience.

George Fitzhugh (1806–81) was an anti-economist, and one of the most enthusiastic ideologists of slavery who emerged in the ante-bellum American South. He was not content to have slavery merely defended as the South's 'peculiar institution'; to Fitzhugh slavery was an institution of universal desirability, in all times and places. He was sufficiently convinced of this that he looked forward to converting the North to the slave system.

The principal threat to the slave society, says Fitzhugh, is what he calls the 'Free Society', and the 'Free Society', therefore, was his target. If his *Sociology for the South: or, the Failure of Free Society*, should contain, he said, 'suggestions that will enlist abler pens to show that free society is a failure and its philosophy false, our highest ambitions will be gratified'. To Fitzhugh the ideology of free society is political economy. The first sentence of the first chapter of *Sociology for the South* opens fire at political economy for its responsibility for the free society. 'Political economy is the science of free society. Its theory and its history alike establish this position. Its fundamental maxims, *Laissez-faire* and *pas trop gouverner* are at war with all kinds of slavery, for they in fact assert that individuals and peoples prosper most when governed least' (Fitzhugh [1854] 1960, p. 47). However, it is not the case, says Fitzhugh, that peoples prosper most when governed least, since part of the human population needed 'support and protection', and another part 'much and rigorous government'. All civilisations of ages past had recognised this, and had consequently instituted slavery in some form or another. Regrettably feudalism left in its retreat a free society that had been raised on the hazardous tonic of political economy: 'The ink was hardly dry with which Adam Smith wrote his *Wealth of Nations*, lauding the benign influences of free society, ere the hunger and want and naked-ness of that society engendered a revolutionary explosion that shook the world to its centre' (Fitzhugh [1854] 1960, p. 66). 'It is time, high time', concludes Fitzhugh 'that political economy was banished from our schools' (Fitzhugh [1854] 1960, p. 120).

Thomas Carlyle (1795–1881) is, perhaps, the pre-eminent representative of Right anti-economics. Yet he was unconcerned with defending the remainders of the *Ancien Régime*; he applauded the repeal of Corn Laws; and saw the Chartists' demands as legitimate, at least insofar as they were a demand for justice rather than power. Nevertheless, his conviction of the centrality of the command relationship produced a Right anti-economics that rivalled Linguet in its disgust at modern freedom.

Economics, Carlyle complained, 'reduces the duty of human governors to that of letting men alone' (Carlyle [1849], 1899a, p. 354). 'By multifarious devices we have been endeavouring to dispense with governing; and by very superficial speculations, of laissez-faire, supply-and-demand, etc. etc. to persuade ourselves that it is best so' (Carlyle [1850] 1898, p. 23). Thus in the British middle-class household we see the 'over-fed White Flunkey' being 'bribed by high feeding to do the shews of obedience'. However, 'Cash payment never was, or could except for a few years be, the union-bond of man to man' (Carlyle [1843], 1897, p. 188) It is not possible 'to buy obedience with money...from a huge and ever-increasing insupportably foolish class of human creatures' (quoted in Castles 1997, p. 3). Consequently the English working man had chiefly 'gluttony and mutiny' in his heart, not 'obedience' (Carlyle [1849] 1899, p. 364). This extinction of obedience was not in the true interest of the foolish populace: it produced the spectacle of 'mutinous serving maids' having failed 'to work and obey' posing as 'distressed needle-women' in order to impress credulous philanthropists. Carlyle therefore declares to the populace: 'Your want of wants, I say, is that you be *commanded* in this world, not being able to command yourselves' (Carlyle [1850] 1898, p. 42).

The consequences of this lack of command were more terrible than idleness; it would be revolution. 'Cut every human relation which has anywhere grown uneasy sheer asunder; reduce whatever was compulsory to voluntary, whatever was permanent among us to nomadic: – in other words, loosen by assiduous wedges in every joint, the whole fabric of social existence, stone from stone; till at last, all now being loose enough, be overset by a sudden outburst of revolutionary rage' (Carlyle [1850] 1898, p. 25).

Carlyle has his own preventive remedies. He put in a public declaration of a imaginary British prime minister to the British proletariat.

Nomadism I give you notice has ended; needful permanency, soldier-like obedience, and the opportunity and the necessity of hard steady labour for your living have begun...

[Here numerous persons with big wigs many of them, and austere aspect, whom I take to be professors of the Dismal Science start up in an agitated vehement manner: but the Premier resolutely beckons them down again.]

Industrial Colonels, Workmasters, Taskmasters, Life-commanders... I perceive you do need...

[Here arises indescribable uproar, no longer repressible, from all manner of Economists, Emancipationists, Constitutionalists and miscellaneous Professors of the Dismal Science, pretty numerously scattered about.]

To each of you I will then say: Here is work for you: strike into it with manlike, soldierlike obedience... Refuse to strike into it, shirk the heavy labour, disobey the rules, I will admonish and endeavour to incite you; if in vain I will flog you; if still in vain I will at last shoot you.

(Carlyle [1850] 1898, pp. 42–6)

John Ruskin (1819–1900) vies with Carlyle as the pre-eminent anti-economist of the Right, and (like Carlyle) is remembered almost as well for his crazed anti-economics as he is for anything else. Adam Smith, in Ruskin's mind, was a 'half-bred and half witted Scotchman' (quoted in Fain 1956, p. 108) with 'an entirely damned state of soul' (quoted in Anthony 1983, p. 75).

Ruskin's mind was too personal in its contents to conjure with the sociological generalities of Right anti-economics, but he shared Carlyle's preoccupation with hierarchy and command, and expressed them pungently in his anti-economics. Ruskin described himself as a 'violent Tory of the old school' with a 'most sincere love of kings, and a dislike of everybody who attempted to disobey them'. Ruskin once sought to identify the divide between J.S. Mill and himself thus: Mill and company 'are for Liberty, and I am for Lordship; they are Mob's men, and I am a King's man' (quoted in Ford 1947/48, p. 229). He once told a House of Commons committee of his 'dread' that 'workmen [would be] tempted to think of rising above their own rank... they wish to become something better than workmen, and I want to keep them in that class' (quoted in Castles 1997, p. 5). In sympathy with this hierarchical outlook, Ruskin approved of slavery as a universal institution. In *Munera Pulveris. Six Essays on the Elements of Political Economy* he declared 'Slavery is not a political institution at all, *but an inherent, natural, and eternal inheritance* of a large portion of the human race' (Ruskin [1872] 1891, p. 166, emphasis in original).

The English historicists

The quickening of academic life in the late nineteenth century was the scene for another version of Right anti-economics: 'historical schools of economics'. Here the enemy of social order shifted from liberalism to socialism; economics was now decried as a father of socialism rather than a child of liberalism. The causal link was that political economy fostered an individualism and social disunion, that made property vulnerable to socialism. We will mention Herbert Somerton Foxwell (1849–1936) and William Cunningham (1849–1919).

Foxwell was a Cambridge specialist in the history of economic thought who believed that political economy stimulated socialism; Ricardo's *Principles of Political Economy* was a 'disastrous book, which gave us Marxian socialism and the Class War'. Socialism, in Foxwell's account, was the offspring of liberal radicalism, in that it was based on the notion of individual right; a producer has a right to what he produces. This sense of the producer's right to production was only underlined by Ricardo's labour theory of value. 'It was Ricardo's crude generalisations which gave modern socialism its fancied scientific basis, and provoked, if they did not justify, its revolutionary form' (Foxwell [1899] 1962, p. xl).[33] Thus, 'Ricardo, by this imperfect presentation of economic doctrine, did more than any intentionally socialist writer to sap the foundations of that form of society which he was trying to explain' (Foxwell [1899] 1962, p. xli).

Cunningham was a Cambridge economic history don, who pursued a long feud with Alfred Marshall, and economics in general. Cunningham was an imperialist, a collectivist and a paternalist. By Cunningham's reckoning, England's employers were a good hearted and fatherly lot, who would have had amiable and close relations with their employees in the nineteenth century, but for the spoiling intervention of economists, who imposed laissez-faire over the best impulses of employers.[34] 'Economists have', he concluded, 'in the mere analysis of economic conceptions, been mischief-makers, who have tended to set class against class' (Cunningham 1894, p. 3).

2.4 Twentieth-century revivals

Purely 'reactionary' forms of anti-economics were extinct long before the twentieth century opened. But right anti-economics is not a museum piece. It has flourished in the twentieth century.

Corporatism

In the first half of the twentieth century some conservative instincts for order fell upon the project of synthesising a new, modernised social structure. This project is associated with the term 'Corporatism'.

Perhaps the thinker most distinctively associated with corporatism is Mihaïl Manoïlesco (1891–1950?). Manoïlesco was a Romanian central banker and industry minister, an anti-Semitic nationalist, a close associate of the Iron Guard, an advocate of the one-party system, and a prominent evangelist of the corporatist state. In *Le Siècle du Corporatisme* (The Century of Corporatism, 1934) he envisaged a non-neutral state engaged with 'organised collectivities'. Not surprisingly he was a 'keen observer of Italian Theory and practice', and was an honoured guest (with Werner Sombart) at a conference on corporatism held at Ferrara in May 1932 (Adler 1995). And not suprisingly, he was an anti-economist. Economics was a 'half-science', that ignored organised collectivities. His *The Theory of Protection and International Trade* (1931) purported to refute the 'individualist' theory of trade, and justify protection in the face of that theory. Manoïlesco gratefully quoted Marx on the disruptive impact of free trade: 'A free-trade system works for destruction. It causes great antagonism between the proletariat and the bourgeoisie. I favour free-trade only in the revolutionary sense' (quoted in Manoïlesco 1931).

Werner Sombart (1863–1941) was another leading corporatist anti-economist of the 1930s. *Deutscher Sozialismus* (1934) heralded the end of the 'economic age', and the advent of a new 'total ordering of life' in which the population would be partitioned into distinct 'estates', so that all public relationships would be defined through estate membership. This vision was complementary to his anti-economics. In his *Die Drei Nationalokonomien* of 1930, he had identified the methodology of economics with 'secularisation, urbanisation, the growth of technological conception of knowledge, the phenomenon of individualism, and the disappearance of the traditional community' (Ringer 1969, p. 388). Sombart hailed Ruskin and Carlyle as his inspiration.

Othmar Spann (1878–1950), the philosopher of 'spiritual Germandom' in inter-war Austria, was another Right anti-economist (see his anti-text, Spann [1912] 1930, pp. 150–3) who manifested corporatist themes in his aspiration to realise a hierarchical society based on 'estates' (Riha 1985). Of the corporatist anti-economists, Spann is the most closely linked to the Right anti-economists of the early nineteenth century: Adam Müller receives Spann's luxurious tribute (Spann [1912] 1930, p. 167).

Societarianism

There was a second strand of revival of Right anti-economics, which one could refer to as 'communitarianism', but we will call 'societarianism'; as the word 'society' glows even brighter in the minds in question than 'community'. Societarianism amounts to an intuition as to the overriding importance and value of 'society'. Societarianism, unlike corporatism, typically has no connection with fascism. Indeed, it usually sees itself as Left. But in its stress on ties and attachments, in its sometimes frank hankering after the past, it is by our account Right.[35]

The seminal theoretician of societarianism is Karl Polanyi (1886–1964), who pursued with tenacity the long-standing Right notion of the market as solvent of bonds and ties. In Polanyi's telling of history, markets were 'embedded' in society, until the advent of the Great Transformation of the early nineteenth century, in which markets were removed from social control, with deleterious social consequences. What makes Polanyi an anti-economist is the stress he puts on the political economy for securing this removal. 'The creation of a labour market was an act of vivisection performed on the body of society by such as were steeled to their task by an assurance which only science can provide' (Polanyi [1944] 1957, p. 127). Those 'steeled to their task' were Ricardo and Malthus, who had 'relinquished Adam Smith's humanistic foundations' (Polanyi [1944] 1957, p. 115) in favour of an 'animalistic approach'.[36]

2.5 Right and Left: an analysis

The chapter has presented an account of an energetic and vehement Right anti-economics. Yet the use of 'Right' here is an oversimplification that now requires correction to secure a better understanding of our subject. This correction consists of abandoning a single axis scheme of ideological organisation for one that uses two axes.

The first axis of the schema runs from 'Right' at one pole to 'Left' at the other. Right is defined as an attraction to 'order'. Order amounts, in the first place, to calm and stability, that then shades off into structure and pattern, which shades off finally into inequality and hierarchy. Left is defined as an aversion to order; and amounts at bottom to attraction to motion, change, and turbulence, that shades into fluidity and formlessness, which shades finally into indistinctness and therefore equality.

The second axis in the schema runs from 'liberalism' at one pole to 'anti-liberalism' at the other. Liberalism is defined as an attraction to the prerogative of the individual, freedom and 'plurality'. The anti-liberal, by contrast, is attracted to the prerogative of the collective, 'unity'.

The two axes provides four basic ideological positions: liberal Right, anti-liberal Right, liberal Left, anti-liberal Left. The liberal Right is attracted to order and plurality. The illiberal Right is attracted to order and unity. The liberal Left is attracted to turbulence and plurality. Finally, the anti-liberal Left is attracted to turbulence and unity. To make these ideas more concrete, F.A. Hayek may be considered a representative of the liberal Right, John Stuart Mill of the liberal Left, Karl Marx of the anti-liberal Left, and August Comte of the anti-liberal Right.

The anti-economics of the Right that we have dealt with in this chapter is, therefore, properly described as the anti-economics of the anti-liberal Right.[37] The liberal Right, by contrast will refuse anti-economics. The liberal Right comprehends the principal eighteenth-century British economists (Hume, Smith), who believed in a society that was hierarchical but free. They were all at peace with the prevailing 'system of subordination' of that century (see Clark 1985); they admitted the 'natural and respectable distinctions of birth and fortune' (Smith [1776] 1937, p. 897). And they had little interest in programmes to efface the significance of those natural and respectable distinctions. They were, apparently, indifferent to electoral reform: Smith never censured the Scottish 'rotten boroughs' (see Viner 1965, p. 85), but merely noted that the representation of the people in the House of Commons is not always 'very equal' (Smith [1776] 1937, p. 551). Adam Smith was doubtful of the theory of a social contract, Hume denied it, and Josiah Tucker abhorred it. Finally, Smith was, it seems, cool towards the French Revolution.[38]

Further, the principal eighteenth-century British economists did *not* believe the market destroyed authority; they thought it was part of a system of subordination (see Shelton 1981 on Tucker). The free market accommodates the useful calm/stability/structure/inequality/hierarchy that they were drawn to. In summary, attracted to both freedom and order, the liberal Right of the eighteenth century believed in their complementarity.

The French-speaking economists of the eighteenth century were more Left than their British counterparts, and that is reflected in their itch for constitutional change. Turgot wished for annual elections and a more equal right of representation, and in 1775, assisted by Du Pont, formulated a scheme for elected parish, district, and provincial councils, culminating in a General Assembly (Stephens 1895, p. 113). Yet Du Pont was a firm advocate of constitutional monarchy. Louis XVI: 'Ah! Mr Du Pont; we find you wherever we have need of you!' (Jolly 1956, p. 124). The end of the monarchy threatened his own end, Danton called for his arrest, and Du Pont went into hiding in August 1792.

To the mind of the anti-liberal Right the outcome of the French Revolution constituted a rebuttal of the presumption of the liberal Right about the complementarity of liberalism and order. Thus 'Right anti-economics' can be seen as a riposte of anti-liberal Right to liberal Right: it asserts that the freedom favoured by the liberal Right is inconsistent with the order they also favour.

In the specific historical context in which the thesis emerged it seems the riposte of illiberal Right to liberal Right was justified: economics was obviously hostile to the *Ancien Régime*.[39] Firstly, economists' approval of the competitive market made it antagonistic to feudal survivals and the mercantilist creations of royal absolutism. Thus the *Wealth of Nations*, opposed established churches, slighted the universities, scorned primogeniture and entails, disparaged tithes, campaigned against the East India Company that 'oppresses and domineers' (a legislative creation), and derided the prevailing (mercantilist) rationale of Empire. Secondly, their economic liberalism was facilitating of political liberalism. The eighteenth-century economists were economic liberals, not political liberals in the nineteenth-century mould. But political liberalism was to some degree explored and even condoned by conservatives such as Hume. Halévy: 'Had not Hume, in his *Treatise*, already rejected the theory of certain philosophers that "men are utterly incapable of society without government"? It remained for Thomas Paine to push this idea to its revolutionary conclusions' (Halévy [1928] 1949a, pp. 128, 190).[40] Thirdly, the materialism of political economy appeared to make the political caste, and the rentier, parasitical.

> In a Civilised Society the poor provide both for themselves and the enormous luxury of their Superiors. The rent, which goes to support the vanity of the slothful landlord, is all earned by the industry of the peasant... All the indolent and frivolous retainers upon a Court, are, in the same manner, fed clothed and lodged by the labour of those who pay the taxes which support them.
>
> (Adam Smith, quoted in Scott 1937, p. 326)

Robert Southey, reading Smith in his radical phase, in 1794, drew his conclusion: 'According to the computation of Adam Smith – one man in twenty is employed in providing the necessaries and comforts of life... and this cursed state of society degrades thy creatures to brutes by obliging them to hard labour so to acquire a poor pitiful livelihood – while the kings, nobles and priests fatten on their toil and cry out "all is well"' (quoted in Eastwood 1989, p. 326).[41]

Yet liberal Right was not without a reply to the riposte of illiberal Right: their reply would be that it is the refusal of liberalism which threatens to tear apart any order at all. Thus it was the thesis of Whigs that the French Revolution was provoked by resistance to liberal reform. In the same vein Malthus, another member of the liberal Right, held that the anti liberalism of Poor Laws threatened order.

Thus defended, political economy and economic liberalism, could be retained and esteemed by certain members of the liberal Right throughout the nineteenth century (T.B. Macaulay; editors of *The Economist* such as James Wilson, and Robert Lowe). Indeed, political economy was *not* unpopular with some not so liberal Right ideologists such as Edmund Burke.[42]

At the same time almost all of the significant political economists of the nineteenth century, with the exception of Malthus, would be better classified as 'liberal Left' rather than 'liberal Right'. It was as if the tumult of 1789 made a liberal Right position untenable for political economists; and feeling pressed to drop either Right or liberalism, they dropped the Right; and liberal Left sentiment swelled. This period that extended perhaps up to the 1830s was when political economy was at its most radical.

This was the period when certain working-class figures of militant background were attracted to political economy. Francis Place (1771–1854) was a leather breeches maker, a member of the London Corresponding Society and a youthful strike organiser who became a publiciser of political economy.

For this purpose Place made full use of *The Republican* edited by Richard Carlile (1790–1843), a tinsmith, who had been sentenced to six years imprisonment for publishing works by Tom Paine (Wiener 1980).[43] This was the period when class resentment of the patrician is easily discovered in political economy. It is conspicuous in James Mill.[44] It was the period when an attachment to the ideals of the French Revolution (though not the deeds) was characteristic of English political economy. To Mill the Girondins were 'the purest and most disinterested body of men, considered as a party, who ever figured in history' (quoted in Dinwiddy 1989, p. 450).[45] Mill named his own ideological circle 'Utilitarians' after a dissident group so named in John Galt's novel about the 1790s, that were 'seceding from Christianity' (Galt [1821] 1936, p. 208).

It was, indeed, a time when the prospect of revolution seemed to hold allure to some political economists. One addict of insurrection, Auguste Blanqui (a brother of Adolphe), described the temper of Jean-Baptiste Say in the 1820s: 'Jean-Baptiste Say had ideas very revolutionary for his time. He detested at the same time the Bourbons and Bonaparte... One Sunday he told us, the preceding night, on hearing a disturbance in a neighbouring barracks, his heart pounded with joy and hope. He thought it was a popular uprising' (Blanqui 1885, p. 138). Alas! it was only a garrison departing for new quarters.[46]

But the political economists were not revolutionaries; no one ever made a revolutionary slogan out of political economy;[47] the liberal Left remained liberal. And in that they were open to riposte from the anti-liberal Left. If the riposte of the anti-liberal Right to liberal Right was that pluralism was subversive of order, then anti-liberal Left had a riposte to make to liberal Left: that pluralism *was* constructive of order, and on account of aversion to order, the Left should repudiate it.

3
The 'Apostles of the Rich'

The preceding chapter argued that the French Revolution stimulated among the illiberal Right a hostility to economics, as the search for the original authors of subversion led to, among many others, economic liberals

In this chapter we turn from a Right anti-economics to Left anti-economics. In other words, we turn from a form of anti-economics arising from an attraction to social order, to an anti-economics arising from a repulsion from the social order. Whereas Right anti-economics assumed that the market was destructive of social order (and therefore bad), Left anti-economics supposed it was constructive of the social order and therefore (also) bad. This Left interpretation of the relation of the market to the social order readily suggests a verdict on economics. Whereas to Right anti-economists, economics by its advocacy of the market is disruptive of social order, to the Left, economics, through its advocacy of the market, is merely buttressing the social order. Whereas to Right anti-economists, economists are the 'wretched procurers of sedition', to radical anti-economists they were the 'apostles of the rich'.[1] So here we arrive at the classic interpretation of economics by the Left. Economics is supportive and reinforcing of the norms and structures of existing society. It is an ideological effusion of those structures. It is there to justify, legitimate, rationalise and apologise for the rule of wealth, capitalism and plutocracy.[2]

We will contend that this Left form of anti-economics was stimulated by the French Revolution, along with a Right economics. However, it had its origin, not in the advent of the Revolution, but in the Revolution's arrest and demise well short of the dissolution of the social order. In their frustration at this, the anti-liberal Left placed the blame upon the emergence of 'capitalism'. In this illiberal Left account of the Revolution, an old social order based on rank had been abolished only for a new social order based on wealth to replace it.

The anti-liberal Right also sometimes shared the Left identification of the market with a new order. Thus the anti-liberal Right had its own version of 'Left' anti-economics: rightful authority had been usurped; financiers and capitalists had seized power and office from its rightful possessors. Thus in the aftermath of the Age of Revolution both Left and anti-liberal Right joined in censuring wealth as a power structure, and economists as its advocate, although they had diametrically opposed views as to the direction in which society should shift.

In this chapter we argue that, contrary to Left anti-economics, the *Grande Tradition* has not justified, legitimated and apologised for ruling order; and that, instead, these censures may be justifiably made of anti-economics, both Left and Right.

3.1   The Judas of the Revolution

Revolution and Restoration

The French Revolution was resolutely liberal Left in its first two years: political and economic freedom were to be pursued together. But out of the frustration of the Left at the failure of a new world to materialise was born the notion that the old feudal order had been destroyed only to be replaced by a new order based on wealth. Historians have sought to identify the germination of such notions in the most frustrated of the Left, the ultra-revolutionary *enragés*, and have sometimes settled upon Jean Theophile Victor Leclerc (1770–?), a fanatic agitator, who expressed such thoughts in 1793 (Rose 1998, p. 143). But the howl of this *enragé* was not heard. It was only in the Restoration that the equivalence between the new commercial society and old feudalism was clearly articulated. And then it was articulated, not by any insurrectionists, but by the tender-hearted Saint-Simonians. In *Exposition of the Doctrine of Saint-Simon* (1828–29), Barthélemy-Prosper Enfantin (1796–1864) (a 'supreme father' of the Saint-Simonian moment after Saint-Simon's death in 1825) asserted that the most repressive aspect of feudalism, vassalage, existed in contemporary France as much as it had in medieval France:

> At last the exploitation of man by man, which we have shown in its most direct and uncouth form in the past, namely slavery, continues to a very large extent in the relations between owners and workers, masters and wage earners ... At first sight it seems as if no comparison could be made. However, it must be realised that the more recent situation is only a pro-longation of the earlier. The relation of master and wage earner is the last transformation which slavery has undergone. If the exploitation of man by man no longer has the same brutal character of antiquity and assumes more gentler forms today, it is, nevertheless, no less real.
>
> (Enfantin [1828] 1972, p. 82)[3]

At almost the same time, William Cobbett (1763–1835) expressed a similar sentiment of equivalence:

> Hume and other historians rail against the feudal-system; and we 'enlightened' and 'free' creatures as we are, look back with scorn, or at least with surprise and pity, to the 'vassalage', of our forefathers. But, if the matter were . . . well and truly examined, we should find, that the people of these villages were as free in the days of William Rufus as are the people of the present day; and that vassalage, only under other names, exists now as completely as it existed then.
>
> (Cobbett [1830] 1967, p. 125)

In 1847 Alphonse Toussenel put the same thought in the context of Revolutionary experience: 'The French people, supposedly emancipated by the revolution of '89 from the yoke of feudal nobility, has only changed masters' (quoted in Glasberg 1974, p. 64). To Toussenel money-power betrayed the Revolution in order to establish itself:

> Judas of the revolution . . . in the morning of your establishment in power in 1830 you had already separated the nation into two camps, in virtue of theory imprudently borrowed from England [political economy] . . . Judas of the revolution . . . it was you again, the children of 89, who on the dawn of the fall of the old regime, and more than 50 years after the night of 4 August, recreated the dukes and the counts . . . And how the time was well chosen, you see, in order to establish a new edifice of gentlemen . . . as the dukes of the old edifice sold their old coats of arms to the Jews in order to serve as lieutenants in the stock market of the railways.
>
> (Toussenel 1847, p. 256)

In 1849 the frenzied anti-economist Pierre Leroux (1797–1871)[4] expressed the equivalence in terms of spirit: 'we do not think that Europe is liberated from the spirit of feudalism, that the feudal period is over, that a new era began in 1789 . . . The feudal spirit is essentially a spirit of conquest. Marvellous! The spirit of the contemporary world, the industrial spirit, the capitalist spirit, the Jewish spirit, is it anything else?' (Leroux 1849, p. 39).

Marx adopted the equivalence between the new commercial society and the old feudalism, and expressed it in his own sweeping and metaphysical style. 'Economic categories are only the theoretical expressions, the abstractions of the social relations in production' (Marx [1847] 1963, p. 92).[5] The social relation in contemporary society was that between capitalist and proletarian. And what is the character of that social relation? It is the relation of exploiter to exploited. To Marx this is the pre-eminent social relation in all societies in all times. To Marx the same binary social order of producer and parasite endures and pervades all ages: 'Etruscan theocrat, civis

Romanus, Norman baron, American slave-owner, Wallachian Boyard, modern landlord or capitalist' (Marx [1887] 1954, p. 226), it's all the same. Thus to Marx the end of the *Ancien Régime* was just a change of parasite. 'The bourgeoisie took possession of the old productive forces it had developed under feudalism' (Marx [1847] 1963, p. 103). Feudal property became bourgeois property, without any substantive difference. What is the difference between owning the rights to mill in the locality (feudal monopoly), and owning all the mills in the locality (bourgeois monopoly)?

Marx provided the classic and enduring presentation of the equivalence of the market to a social order, but the thesis has received some development since. At the beginning of the twentieth century the notion was extended to the realm of international relations. With the Anglo-Boer War in mind, *Imperialism*, by J.A. Hobson (1858–1940) contended that imperialism, the rule of one country by another, was a matter of the rule of wealth. As is well known, Lenin made this notion part of the Marxist canon. In the post-war period a similar notion was articulated by 'dependency theorists', who have provided some of the most fanatical anti-economists (see for example Frank, 1976), who extended the notion of an exploitative order to an international context; so that there is a hierarchy (the United States, say, at the top, and Guatemala, say, at the bottom) of which the market is the instrument.

But it was in the last third of the twentieth century that the identification of the market with the social order was developed in a thoroughly un-Marxian manner. Ordering of society by ethnicity, race and gender became the object of animus, and in this animus the market was not infrequently identified with this objectionable structure. More radical still was the assault of environmentalists on the basis of order: the elevation of human over the non-human. Again the market was convicted as the vehicle and instrument of this flawed hierarchy.

3.2   The market and the social order

The critics of the market had three arguments for their thesis that capitalism amounted to a social order equivalent to, say, feudalism: the argument from plutocracy, the argument from practical equivalence, and the argument from property.

The argument from plutocracy

In the early 1830s the spirit of the times revived from obscurity a disused term, 'plutocracy'; the society where wealth makes laws.[6] To the anti-economists this term was a fitting description of contemporary society.

Toussenel: 'there is no government other than the bank...the King, the Chambers, exist only on the condition of serving its exigencies and caprices' (quoted in Glasberg 1974, p. 64).

The American anti-economist John Pickering: 'We have no titled nobility it is true; but we have institutions composed exclusively of capitalists, whose influence has often controlled even our legislators, from whom they have obtained special privileges which in their operation produce the same evils in society that titles of nobility do in other countries' (Pickering 1847, p. 5).

Saint-Simonians: 'And in this state of legal emancipation he can exist only under the conditions imposed on him by a class small in numbers, namely that class of men who have been invested through legislation, the daughter of conquest, with the monopoly of riches' (Enfantin [1828] 1972, p. 83).

The argument from practical equivalence

This popular argument contends that A is a slave of B if A's refusal of B's direction would reduce A to a state of extremity. Thus the destitute freeman is a true slave, and since the great mass of the population is dependent on the employer to avoid destitution they are, in practice, in servile status. The Saint-Simonians explain:

> The worker is not like the slave, the direct property of his master. His condition, which is never permanent, is fixed by a transaction with a master. But is this transaction free on the part of the worker? It is not, since he is obliged to accept it under penalty of death, for he is reduced to expecting his nourishment each day only from his work of the previous day.
> (Enfantin [1828] 1972, p. 82)

John Pickering, in *The Working Man's Political Economy* (1847), presents the helplessness of the worker more emphatically. 'Therefore is he turned on the street *to starve, to beg, or to steal*; he must do one or the other, there is no alternative; or to *die*. (*These are the privileges of the Free Labourer)'* (Pickering 1847, p. 4).

The argument from property

There is a third argument for the market constituting a social order. It has been expressed since the time of Rousseau, and has loudly resonated throughout the Left since: *the essence of the market is not freedom but property*. Property is a system of control and exclusion, it is a set of walls or stakes between and around people. By the position of the walls property will rank people; putting some higher than others. Property, therefore, amounts to a social order An aversion to order will manifest itself in an aversion to property.

It was Jean-Jacques Rousseau (1712–78) who, in his *Discours sur l'Origine et les Fondements de l'Inégalité parmi les Hommes* (Discourse on the Origins and Foundation of Inequality among Men) (1754), had traced all social order to the abstract notion of property. 'The first man, having enclosed a piece of ground, to whom it occurred to say this is mine, and found people sufficiently simple to believe him, was the true founder of civil society'. Further, in keeping with a radical hostility to order, Rousseau held the civil society that resulted was not good, but bad. 'How many crimes, wars, murders, how many miseries and horrors Mankind would have been spared by him who, pulling up the stakes or filling in the ditch, had cried out to his kind: Beware of listening to this imposter' ([1754] 1997a, p. 164).[7]

The upshot was that, whereas the anti-liberal Right dislikes the market because it is not a social tie, the Rousseauian radical dislikes the market because it is a social tie (a matter of 'social control'). Man is born free but everywhere he is in chains, and one of these chains is property.[8]

3.3 Hired prize-fighters

The function of political economy

If the market is a new form of social order, and if economists are advocates of the market, then economists are the champions and apologists of this new social order. As soon as the notion of the market as a social order quickened, this inference was made, and from the 1820s it finds articulation among anti-economists. Thus Thomas Hodgskin, 'It is the ... demands of capital sanctioned by the laws of society ... enforced by the legislature, and warmly defended by the political economists, which keep ... the labourer in poverty and misery ... capitalists may well be pleased with a science which both justifies their claims, and holds them up to our admiration, as the great means of civilising and improving the world' (quoted in Thompson 1984b, p. 21).[9] In 1828 the Saint-Simonians announced, 'The economists of the eighteenth century based their political system on the interests of the owners ... Malthus and Ricardo ... justify as best they can the political organisation in which one part of the population lives at the expense of the other part' (Enfantin [1828] 1972, pp. 119–21).

This clear identification of political economy with the capitalist enemy found its practical culmination in the abolition during the Revolution of 1848 of J.B Say's old chair in political economy.[10]

The identification of political economy with the capitalist enemy found its rhetorical and intellectual culmination in Marx. Marx believed that social order amounted to a superior and a subordinate group held in antagonistic relation. The development of reality ('history') was, at critical points, favourable in a material sense to the subordinate group, sending them 'up' and 'in', and unfavourable to the superior group. At this critical point the subordinate group have an interest in the recognition of reality, and the superior group have an interest in hiding it. The construction of camouflage, distortions, illusions and idols is ordained by the superior group. These will be torn down by agents of the subordinate group to reveal reality. In applying this theory to economics Marx believed that from 1830 the newly established superior group (capital) was threatened by the insurgent subordinate group (labour), and political economists served as the priests of the idols of capitalism. Of political economy Marx said that from 1830,

> it was thenceforth no longer a question, whether this theorem or that was true, but whether it was useful to capital or harmful, expedient or inexpedient, politically dangerous or not. In place of disinterested inquirers, there were hired prize-fighters; in place of genuine scientific research, the bad conscience and the evil of apologetic.
>
> (Marx [1887] 1954, p. 25)

As 'mere sophists and sycophants of the ruling classes' (Marx), the 'function' of political economy was to hide the producer/parasite relation. This is the standard, defamatory Marxist categorisation of economists.

The function of Marxism, by contrast, was to expose this producer/ parasite relation. Whereas the binary producer/parasite relation was manifest under feudalism ('every serf knows what he expends in the service of the lord' (Marx [1887] 1954, p. 82)), under capitalism that transparency disappears. Whereas political economy concerned itself with a new space in the social world composed of consent rather than force and authority, Marx conceived his critique of political economy as demonstrating the endurance of the producer/parasite relation.

Marxist theory of the function of political economy and its critique is open to several criticisms: the social order is not a matter of an unambiguous ranking of superior and subordinate (and thus there may be conflict among the 'rulers' and among the 'ruled'); that 'history' (that is, the trends in material reality) may favour all groups, or none; that recognition of reality *best* serves no group's interest, since every group will always be better served by some illusion, and thus no group is 'on the side of truth'; that the better perception of reality may *better* serve *all* groups' interests than prevailing perceptions (and so all groups may be on the side of truth against the alternative); that the recognition of reality is not merely a matter of tearing away man-made camouflage (the problem of knowledge is far deeper than that); that distortions (illusions) and so on may contain some truth despite being distortions.

In any case, Left anti-economics no longer takes the trouble to adhere to a materialist theory of history. The thesis that economics is an effusion of social structure is instead supported by several more specific claims.

1. Economists, it is alleged, are simply hired prize-fighters: the mercenaries of the ruling elements of the social order.
2. Economists are of elite social background. This thesis, however ridiculous, has been advanced by some *marxisante* anti-economists (for example Pusey 1991).
3. Economic doctrines favour wealth. Economics is an ideology of wealth, and economists are its ideologues.

Not hired prize-fighters

In rebuttal, it may be simply observed that no blatant 'prize' for hire has ever been found. The advocates of the Marxist thesis may persist by embarking upon a search for the less blatant prizes by which mankind may be rewarded. But no such assiduous inquiry is needed to discover the anti-economists themselves have sometimes enjoyed some very palpable prizes for their services. Thus Linguet was pensioned and ennobled by the Hapsburg Emperor Joseph II, and in 1826 Müller was ennobled by Emperor Francis II on the recommendation of Metternich. Years earlier Friedrich Gentz, Metternich's propagandist and personal adviser, had suggested to Müller that he write a book in defence of nobility, and 'pointed out that he would thereby make his fortune' (quoted in Aris 1936, p. 304). Müller's eventual elevation to the peerage was advocated by Metternich on the grounds that 'in the past twenty years he has employed his talents as an author on behalf of good and right, of the monarchical principle and of religion' (quoted in Bowen 1971, p. 33). One historian of ideas has said of Müller, 'With the extraordinary versatility of a badly paid intellectual, this type was at one and the same time a philosopher of history and a propagandist, a "typical concocter of justifications", who quickly found an ideological superstructure for any political cause that employed him' (Bramsted 1967, p. 39).[11]

One English anti-economist also enjoyed a (modest) connection between his doctrinal position and his worldly recompense. In 1812 Wordsworth sought financial assistance from Lord Lowther, and was consequently made Distributor of Stamps for the county of Westmorland, bringing £400 a year. 'It was perhaps inevitable that, in thus placing himself under an obligation to the great Tory peer, he should at least modify the future expression of his political sympathies; it is hardly likely for example, that he would have taken such an active and public part in the 1818 election' (Todd 1957, p. 158), in which he campaigned against Henry Brougham.[12]

Not of the ruling order

If the obvious ever needed stating, the political economists tended to come from middling backgrounds, a considerable distance from the strata above and below.[13] One indicator of this distance from the ruling order is the comparison of the attributes of an institution of that ruling order with the attributes of a sample of economists. The ruling order institution we will use is the House of Commons. The sample of 'economists' we will use is the membership of the Political Economy Club in the year of Ricardo's death in 1823. It will be found that 35 per cent of the unreformed House of Commons consisted of baronets, Irish peers or sons of Scottish and English peers. No such gracious distinctions were ever borne by members of the Political Economy Club. It is also found that 55 per cent of the unreformed

House of Commons had university degrees as against only 31 per cent of Political Economy Club members.[14]

Later in the nineteenth century, the social background of the economist was still a remove from the establishment, and still considerably apart from the populace. If we use Cambridge University as the elite institution (instead of the House of Commons), and use the Royal Economic Society (instead of the Political Economy Club) we find that 41.5 per cent of Society members in 1891 had fathers in the Church or the law, or were landowners, compared to 59 per cent of Cambridge graduates (Coats and Coats 1970). In the same vein, between 1850 and 1899, 39 per cent of Society members attended the top 23 public schools, compared to 52 per cent of Cambridge graduates. The Royal Economic Society was plainly not representative of the ruling order.[15]

The proximity of the social background of economists and elite groups cannot be easily measured in the United States or other large countries, partly owing to lack of data,[16] and partly owing to more straggling social structures.[17] But with respect to the United States, the author of one 1970s anti-text allowed 'economists are members of the American meritocracy. Traditionally, advanced degrees have opened doors to professional status, financial reward and upward class mobility to hordes of lower middle-class Jews, Irish, Italians, and in the last decade, blacks, women and Hispanics' (Lekachman 1976, p. 184).[18] On another simple, if imperfect, indicator of social positioning – the native born/immigrant dichotomy – economics also appears non-elite in the US. Economics graduate schools in the US today have a higher proportion of foreigners than any other faculty, except engineering. 'Today's entering classes are probably less than one-half US citizens' (Krueger 1991, p. 1040).

Not ideologues of wealth

The third alleged sign that economics is an effusion of the social structure lies in the favour with which its doctrines (supposedly) treat wealth. Economics, it is construed, is not a disinterested inquiry, but one biased in favour of wealth.

In truth, the conclusions of modern economics are a meagre tool for interests vested in property (see Chapter 11). In truth, economics has recoiled from proposals beloved of the party of wealth; such as the reduction of capital gains tax.[19] Nevertheless, the Malthusianism of classical economists may with some justice be taken to be a 'defence of wealth', on account of Malthus' tireless insistence that poverty would not be eliminated by transfers from the rich to the poor, such as the tax-financed supplementation of wages. Yet Ricardo's call for the elimination of such supplementation 'by the most gradual steps' does not seem a very energetic defence of wealth. Further, Ricardo's objections to these transfers seem distinctly contingent upon the particularities of the Old Poor Law, for Ricardo did *not* believe the 'systems of equality' in their generality would be threatened by a subsistence crisis. Ricardo expressly denied the claim that *'under a system of equality population would press with more force against the means of subsistence than it does now'* (Ricardo 1952b, p. 49), and on account of his denial indulged Owen's plan to cover England in quadrilateral communes. In the same vein, Mill's Malthusianism never deterred him from seeking remedies for the 'prodigious inequality' of wealth.[20]

Further, it must be allowed that some who expressly sought economic doctrines favourable to property found classical economics singularly disappointing for this purpose, and adopted an anti-economist posture in consequence. Consider the anti-economist George Poulett Scrope. He became interested in political economy on the eve of the Great Reform Bill by which 'the power of directing the Legislation of Britain was about to pass ... from the hands of the few into those of the many'.

> What lessons were they ['the many'] likely to imbibe from the current doctrines of Political Economy? Were these lessons fitted to reconcile them to the hardships of a condition of almost ceaseless toil for, in many cases, but a meagre subsistence; and this in a country overflowing with wealth enjoyed in idleness by some at the expense (as it might at first sight appear to them) of the labour of others?
>
> (Scrope 1873, p. vii)

Scrope answers his question with regret. 'On the examination of the works of the most noted economists of the day, Messrs Ricardo, Jas. Mill, Maculloch [sic], Malthus, Chalmers and Whateley, I could not discover in them any answer likely to satisfy the mind of a half-educated man of plain common sense and honesty who should seek there some justification for the great disparity of fortunes and circumstances that strike the eye on every side.' All he found was whimsical, inconsistent definitions, fanciful hypothetical illustrations, 'confused arguments' and strange theorems. To rebut this 'mischievous' political economy, Scrope published in 1833 his *Political Economy for Plain People.* 'I maintained in it that under a system of law combining freedom of industry and exchange with security to property so acquired ... any miseries that men may endure through the lack of the material comforts of life, can only be occasioned by their own wilful default' (Scrope 1873, p. ix).

Further, some observers who would have been repelled by an economics in the service of property found classical political economy unobjectionable. It is not difficult to find working-class writers who praised political economy. John Wade was the editor of a 'radical working class paper' in 1818–19 (see Thompson 1984, p. 25) who extolled Ricardo ('a tower of strength') and Smith ('the enlightened and benevolent author') over their attitude to wages; E.P. Thompson claims that the *Wealth of Nations* and the *Rights of Man* were two 'handbooks' of radicals in the first decades of the nineteenth century (see Biagini 1987, p. 831); Noel Thompson has proposed a category of 'Smithian socialists'; Baigini has recorded the approving interest of the Trade Union press in Adam Smith in mid-Victorian England: 'Adam Smith and Jeremy Bentham were looked upon with gratitude' (Biagini 1987, pp. 826, 831, 817).

Neither could political economy be said to be apologetic for the ill that great wealth might seem to be concomitant with: poverty. Any such apology would presumably make light of the state of poverty, speciously diminish its prevalence, and unreasonably find a utility in whatever poverty remains. Yet the doctrine of political economy most vulnerable to an accusation of such an apology, Malthusianism, does none of these. Malthusianism never attempts to make light of a state of poverty, and it thereby contrasts with William Paley's (1743–1805) *Reasons for Contentment, Addressed to the Labouring Part of the British Public* of 1793. Malthusianism never attempts to diminish the frequency of poverty; the urgency of its doctrines rested upon its prevalence. And Malthusianism ignores the classic exonerations of poverty.[21] Malthusianism, at least in its mature formulation of the 'second edition' of *Principle of Population*, did *not* say poverty was inevitable. And it did not say it possessed economic utility.[22]

Neither did political economy apologise for certain other blights of the Industrial Revolution, such as child labour. They did not consider child labour a 'potent' means of transforming society, nor did they believe its prohibition was 'inconsistent with large scale industry' or 'reactionary'. These views were those of Karl Marx.

> A *general prohibition* of child labour is incompatible with the existence of large-scale industry and hence an empty, pious wish. Its realisation – if it were possible – would be reactionary, since... an early combination of productive labour with education is one of the most potent means of transforming present-day society.
>
> (Marx [1875] 1969, p. 172)[23]

Neither, contrary to myth (for example, Mills 1963), did political economy ever press a 'harmony of interests' that would, in some measure, reconcile those at the bottom to being at the bottom. Political economy has never said that the operation of the market process would benefit all. In Ricardian economics the process of growth would benefit landlords, but harm the interest of the remainder of society. The same economics suggested, much to the affront of Tory critics, that wages and profits were in 'eternal conflict' (Robinson 1829, p. 513).

In summary, political economists were not priests of power. In truth the two societies where economists have been priests of power were societies where economists made the *Grande Tradition* an object of derision or vituperation: Imperial Germany and the Soviet Union.

The function of the German Historical School

From 1870 the German academy appointed itself the priests of a kind of national 'cultural church', on guard against any falling away from the German 'mission'. One of the tasks of this mission was the elimination of 'Smithianismus'. Whereas previous to the 1870s, economists played a minor role in German academic and public life, from 1870 (as one later recalled) 'our national history called economics to this forefront' (Barkin 1970, p. 11). At the fore of this forefront was Gustav von Schmoller (1838–1917) and the German Historical School (GHS) that he led into battle against 'Smithians'.

The GHS was approved by the political establishment; in 1874 Kaiser Wilhelm I caused a 'sensation' by attending a lecture by Schmoller on social policy, and Bismarck said he would have joined Schmoller's academic association, if only he had the time. The GHS was heeded by the political establishment; Schmoller's opinions were 'carefully studied' by ministers (Barkin 1970, p. 9). The GHS was patronised by the political establishment; Schmoller was 'well acquainted' with Bismarck, and counted six other ministers as personal friends.[24] Schmoller was sufficiently close to the Kaiser for the former chancellor Bernhard von Bülow to use him as intermediary (Barkin 1970, p. 9).

And the GHS was utilised by the political establishment; they energetically defended and advocated government policy. Grand Admiral Tirpitz in his memoirs recalled that the GHS responded 'almost to a man' to his requests for scholarly pieces supporting the naval building programme (Ascher 1963, p. 284). In particular, Schmoller 'hastened to do the admiral's bidding' in support of the programme (Barkin 1970, p. 10). It has been reasonably written that 'The glorification of the Prussian state and its rulers was probably the most characteristic feature of Schmoller's work' (Schefold 1987, p. 257).

The function of 'Marxist-Leninist political economy'

'Marxist-Leninist political economy' was the pre-eminent device of ideological legitimation of the Soviet Union and its satellites in Eastern Europe. It is appropriate that economists in the Soviet Union were dubbed 'priests' (Katsenelinboigen 1980, p. 18).

A pungent illustration is provided by the life of the 'priest' and economic historian Jürgen Kuczynski (1904–97). He is especially interesting given that he was one of the most coarsely enthusiastic propagators of the Marxian thesis that orthodox economists were 'mere sophists and sycophants of the ruling classes' (see *New Fashions in Wage Theory: Keynes–Robinson–Hicks–Rueff* of 1937 and *Die Politökonomische Apologetik des Monopolkapitals in der Periode der Allgemeine Krise des Kapitalismus*, 1952).

Arriving in the UK in 1937 as a Communist Party refugee from Germany, Kuczynski quickly wrote an attack on economics, *New Fashions in Wage Theory*. Keynes was the leading western economist and Keynes is his leading target. Keynes is described as an 'opportunist theoretician supplying with a semblance of a theory the anarchic attempts of the ruling class to hold together a decaying economic society'. What, according to Marxist doctrine, did such attempts of the ruling class constitute in the 1930s? They constituted, of course, fascism, and Kuczynski does not pause to pass the atrocious judgement: 'Ten years before, Mr Keynes had finally parted ways with Liberalism: now he embraces Fascism' (Kuczynski 1937, p. 14).

The second part of Kuczynski's *New Fashions* consists of a number of statistical essays which in Abba Lerner's judgement 'are almost unbelievably bad', and display a 'Philistine contempt for arguments used, as long as the conclusions are correct' (Lerner 1938, p. 116). This concocter of justifications displays a similar condescension of the truth in *The Condition of the Workers in Great Britain, Germany and the Soviet Union* (1939), recording with joy the 'breath-taking improvement' in the Soviet Union, that 'has no parallel in the history of labour', leaving conditions in food, clothing and housing better in the Soviet Union than in Great Britain and Germany (Kuczynski 1939, p. 90).[25]

In 1950 Walter Ulbricht lured Kuczynski to East Germany 'with a house in Weissensee large enough to accommodate his extensive personal library and the promise of an economic portfolio in government'.[26] He was installed in the Volkskammer in 1950, made President of the Society for German–Soviet Friendship, and continued publishing. In 1952 there appeared *The Economic Apologetic of Monopoly Capitalism in the Period of the General Crisis of Capitalism*, in which the most quoted authority is Joseph Stalin, receiving 19 citations. In 1956 he proved to his satisfaction that (at a time when food was still rationed in East Germany) general food consumption in West Germany had fallen beneath 1914 levels. The increased consumption of some products in the West (sugar, tea, coffee, alcohol and tobacco) 'is explained by the fact that, by using drugs, workers could more easily stand the increased tempo of work for the profit of capitalists'.[27]

During the 1970s Kuczynski cultivated Erich Honecker 'to the point of sycophancy' (*The Australian* 18 August 1997). He was decorated with the Karl Marx Order, and the Friedrich Engels Prize, and was the beneficiary of colloquia in his honour organised by the East German Academy of Sciences on the occasions of his seventieth, seventy-fifth and eightieth birthdays. He died in 1997, the steadfast subaltern of a police-state.

Marxist-Leninist 'political economy' cannot be said to have been misused by the likes of Kuczynski; almost the only function of this entity was to provide rationales for the twists and turns in the policies favoured by political power. In this vein it has been observed that 'A feature characteristic of the GDR's official economics was also that, when the textbook *Politische Ökonomie* was scrapped in the course of attacks launched against Ulbricht's economic conception in 1971, many authors rapidly mutated into critics. The same people had no difficulty in furnishing political arguments for Honecker's DSS only a short time later' (Krause 1998, p. 306). In the same vein, in 1987, in the face of 'out of control debt', declining competitiveness in manufacturing, and faltering exports, a press campaign in praise of the Honecker era economy was staged. 'All the standard East German "mouthpiece" economists were dragged out for this' (Kopstein, 1997, p. 102). It is the official DDR economist who may truly be described as an 'opportunist theoretician supplying with a semblance of a theory the anarchic attempts of the ruling class to hold together a decaying economic society'.

The tendency for the doctrinaires of the GHS and 'Marxist-Leninist political economy' to become the mouthpieces of the state is easily explained. It is a matter of a vulnerability lying in their ideological tenets. The German Historical School exalted the state. And Marxism took no real offence at the state; the state was *not* the cause of exploitation. If one believes the great state is the author of great good, or potentially so, then whatever its current defects and difficulties, its potentialities are to be preserved by defending it. It is the contrary mindset that will provide a guard against making oneself an agent of state authority. It is the state of mind that sees the great state as a great ill that provides some safeguard. Insofar as the *Grande Tradition* is correlate with economic liberalism, then the *Grande Tradition* has this guard.

The guard which economic liberalism puts against utilisation by the state apparatus is illustrated by the contrast between Sismondi, on one side, and Say and Du Pont on the other. Sismondi had cordial relations with Napoleon; Say and Du Pont had hostile relations. After the first edition of *Traité d'Économie Politique* Say was invited by Napoleon to dine at Malmaison, the Emperor's private residence. Napoleon expounded vividly on how he planned to restore finance, and urged Say to make a new edition of the *Traité* that would justify in the eyes of the public the necessary measures. Say declined.[28] Napoleon dismissed Say from the Tribunate, the debating chamber of the Consulate, and had the publication of a second edition forbidden. Du Pont was equally resistant to the regime's policies: in 1809 Du Pont led the Chamber of Commerce of Paris in protesting to Napoleon against the prohibition of the export of grain. Napoleon responded: 'I have received a hodgepodge of ideas...on the grain trade that is altogether ridiculous...It is the twaddle of an economist...As far as I am concerned, I ask you not to send me any more such nonsense. I have no need of the drivel or the lessons of M. Du Pont de Nemours and some merchants' (quoted in Betts 1987, p. 196).[29]

4
The Dream of Nationhood

Earlier chapters dealt with a Left and a Right anti-economics. We now turn to a species of anti-economics that challenges a thesis that is shared by Left anti-economics, Right anti-economics, and economics itself: that human economic experience, in so far as it can be understood at all, is a unity; in so far as markets can be rationalised, the laws and regularities that do so encompass all markets; in so far as human drives behind those markets can be accounted for, the laws and regularities that do so encompass all human beings. Heterogeneity in manners and markets are not denied, but they are lawless and cannot be explained by reference to less than universal categories.

In this chapter we turn to a species of anti-economics which denies this fundamental homogeneity of human experience: relativism. Relativism holds that economic reality is not one. There are no significant economic claims that always hold true, across all time and space. There are no institutions or policies that will always be the best fitted ('natural') to humankind's economic life. There may be truths, but no absolute truths. All economic truths will be relative to some sub-universal category; to historical epoch; or to culture; to race; to the state of technology... To relativist anti-economics the *Grande Tradition* has violated relativity by purporting to create an economics for all economies, centring on 'economic man', and the market. It has in fact, under the guise of universalism, sought to advance policies which are to the advantage of the powerful, and to the disadvantage of the less powerful. Economic inquiry should see through this false universalism; it should abandon any vision of the world as a set of homogeneous free markets, and allow for institutions, customs, and politics, anchored to 'nation', 'culture' and 'history'.

Relativism is a man-of-war that has been borne by several contrary currents; conservatism, radicalism, Left and Right. But we will argue that another political principle has been the great emotional motor of relativistic anti-economics: nationalism. Here lies the nervous core of relativism; a resentful identification of an aspiration to universalism with a reality of imperialism. We therefore trace the appearance of relativist economics to the nationalist reflux of opinion against the universalism of the eighteenth century, and its condensation in varieties of 'national economics' in the nineteenth.

We further argue that in the twentieth century national economics retreated from the developed world to reappear as 'development economics' in the Third World. And in the developed world 'culture' took the place of 'nation' as the catchword of relativism.

4.1   The 'fraction of the human race'

The contentions of relativism

Relativism comprises a suite of linked cosmological contentions: unicity, hysteresis and historicism.

Unicity contends that everything is unique. Each thing is the sole member of its kind, or class. Thus the properties of any one thing are different from every other thing. This contention implies a universe without generalisations or laws. It does not, however, posit a world of mystery: each event may be explicable; but the explanation of one event will give no assistance to the explanation of any other. Therefore, the method of research must consist of the examination and allowance for all detail. This method of detail includes the 'historical' method. This method holds, in the words of the anti-economist Ferdinand Galiani, 'General reasonings and nothing are pretty much the same thing' (Galiani 1881, 2, p. 274).[1]

Hysteresis gives unicity historical form. In this cosmology the critical detail of a thing is the detail of its past. The whole profile of its past state is relevant to its current properties. This has an epistemological significance: knowledge becomes 'genetic'; things are to be understood in terms of their past, or in terms of their 'origins'. Hysteresis also has a cosmological significance; all change is now qualitative change. For if a thing moves from A to B and back to B, it is not left unchanged. It is changed by the very movement from A to B and back again. All change is irreversible.

Historicism posits a pattern to the qualitative and irreversible change of hysteresis. Historicism supposes that qualitative states succeed one another so as to approach nearer to some end. Such a succession of qualitative states might be called 'development' and the clear metaphor of this change is the biological change from infant to adult. Historicism, therefore, says that all history is development.[2] If you like, historicism puts the story back into history. More formally, historicism holds that there are laws of succession: so pastoralism succeeds hunter-gatherers; and capitalism succeeds feudalism that succeeds primitive communism.

The implications of nationalism

Economics was born in a period when these contentions of relativism were refused. It was born in the Enlightenment in which the unity of man's behaviour was assumed. As Hume put it: 'It is universally acknowledged that there is a great uniformity among the actions of men, in all nations and ages' (Hume [1777] 1975, p. 83). Differences in national characters were allowed to exist, but they were held to be haphazard and external. The only laws of 'sentiments, inclinations, and the course of life' were uniform across the human race.[3] This 'uniformitarianism' has been described as 'the first and fundamental principle' of the Enlightenment (Lovejoy, 1948, p. 79), and was fully assimilated by classical economics.[4] To the classical economists there were no natural divisions in human experience by human nature, or society's material context. There were, undeniably, differences between persons and societies in terms of knowledge. Thus societies could develop or progress, and so make the eighteenth century better than the thirteenth. But the eighteenth century was better not because it had better motivations, or because it was less stupid, but because it knew more. And, since reality is one, this growth of knowledge amounted to the development of one single, universally assimilating thing, 'civilisation'. 'Civilisation' was the expression that Smith and the other political economists conjured with, not 'culture'.[5]

It was in the aftermath of the Age of Revolution that the Enlightenment's vision of a universal civilisation lost prestige and presence. Both the enthusiasm and the hostility towards the Napoleonic Empire stimulated a counter-ideology: nationalism. The enthusiasts saw in the Empire a thrilling example of national reinvigoration and self-assertion. The critics saw a supposedly universal culture now exposed as having a specifically national affiliation – French – and used to domineer other cultures. The universal, it was concluded, was a sham, and an exploitation of the weak by the strong.

This nationalism lent itself easily to the cosmological contentions of relativism.

Nationalism as unicity.   Nationalism says the world is, must be and should be divided into unique nations (that is, distinct collective entities composed of persons sharing a set of attributes such that they constitute a complete and integral social system). Nationalism is against the universal, the syncretic or the plural.

Nationalism as hysteresis.   The critical national sense of identity is moored to history, experiences and memories. Nations are made by history. They lend themselves to historical explanation. They are not recreated every morning; they owe their creation to circumstances in the past that have since disappeared. Their borders are the bequest of the vanished past; their distinctive institutions and customs would be impossible to invent if they did already not exist.

Nationalism as historicism.   Nineteenth-century nationalism put the nation state in a historicist sequence. The claim was that there was a historical tendency for the nation-state to succeed particularist non-national states, as baroque dynastic structures were replaced by efficient nation-states. 'The small separate States of earlier times were no longer equal to the comprehensive economic tasks of the present. They had either to disappear in one large national State, as in Italy, or surrender considerable portions of their independence ... to a federal State, as did the individual States in the German Empire' (Bücher 1912, p. 140). The nation-state was both a result of development, and an agent of development; it was the product of the present and producer of the future.

Thus in the nineteenth century nationalism gave life to relativist contentions, provided them with a clear articulation, and bore them into the fray of intellectual combat.

In this fray nationalism was plainly set in opposition to the *Grande Tradition*.

Firstly, nationalism is antagonistic to the Tradition's methodology.[6] Nationalist unicity is flatly inconsistent with the uniformitarianism of the Tradition, and dooms any attempt at generalisation. Nationalist hysteresis compels a genetic epistemology, where all explanation is to be found in origins. And nationalist historicism makes doubtful any inquiry that is not historically self-conscious. In nationalist historicism there is no possibility that some reality may shrug off its historical circumstances, and be a reality in all ages. Nationalism, thus, makes an easy ally with 'history' against 'theory'. Finally, the nationalist thesis of the nation as an integral whole makes irrelevant any specialist study of the economic, and instead requires all consideration of the economic to be done within a multi-disciplinary context.

Secondly, nationalism has a significant anti-liberal potentiality. As the rifts that divide mankind are deepened, the significance of the collective that is enclosed must be correspondingly increased. With deep enough divisions there follows the nationalist conviction that it is only by participating in their national entity that the individual is fulfilled; and it is only by the maximisation of that participation that fulfilment is maximised. From that it is a short step to the key nationalist position: the political recognition of these clefts, and the erection of a national state, will be the answer to all problems; it will be the act that restores life; the kiss of the prince to the slumbering princess.

Nationalism, in summary, required the creation of a new economics, and the elimination of the old.

4.2   The national economists

National economics first appeared in the aftermath of the Napoleonic era. The Napoleonic wars had sharpened national feeling on the two sides of the English Channel, and the 'cosmopolitan' posture of political economy excited the resentment of patriot anti-economists in both France and England.

Thus Coleridge complained that political economy had denationalised England. The French anti-economists and passionate anglophobes Leroux and Alban de Villeneuve-Bargemont bitterly alleged the English origins of political economy. Leroux declares this imported English political economy is 'the negation of our principles of unity and equality' (Leroux 1850, p. 382).

But a nationalist inspired relativistic anti-economics did not appear in France or Britain; it appeared instead in the margins of the metropolitan culture.[7] It was on the circumference that a resentment of the centre's putative universal culture gave the prospect of a national economics a particular appeal.

Anti-imperial national economics

The first national anti-economics was the precipitation of a compound of sentiments in Ireland, the United States, and Germany; three countries exhibiting, respectively, a defeated nationalism, a victorious nationalism, and a restless but confined nationalism.

In 1779 a youthful Irishman, Mathew Carey (1760–1839), published a protest against mistreatment of Catholics in Ireland. In the face of a reward for the apprehension of this subversive author, Carey removed to Paris, where he discussed the revolutionary potential of Ireland with Lafayette. Returning to Ireland Carey became editor of *Volunteer's Journal*, 'the object of which was to defend Ireland, economically and politically, against the encroachments of England' (Mitchell 1958, p. 490). Jailed for one year for nationalist agitation, he fled upon his release to the United States.

In the new American nation the germ of economic nationalism had already been cultivated by Alexander Hamilton (1755–1804), an unwavering nationalist, who as Washington's Secretary for the Treasury from 1789 sought the establishment of a national debt, a National Bank, and (in the *Report on Manufactures* of 1791) a tariff. These aspirations matured in the aftermath of the War of 1812 when nascent US industry was exposed to British imports, and the Philadelphia Society for the Promotion of National Industry was formed. From 1820 Mathew Carey became a keen advocate of the Society's doctrines, and as a result thought he should furnish his mind with some political economy.

As the Wealth of Nations was universally regarded as a sort of text book, I began with it, and to my astonishment found, *in ipso limine*, some of the most pernicious maxims that ever led to sacrifice the prosperity and happiness of nations ... To a person wholly unbiased by prejudice, it must be a matter of astonishment, how a work, resting on such a sandy and miserable foundation, could have obtained, and still more, have so long preserved its celebrity. The monstrous absurdity of these doctrines, and the facility with which they might be refuted, induced me to enter the lists against this Goliath, with the sling and stone of truth.

(Carey [1829] 1970, p. 48)

There followed *Essays on Political Economy* and the *Addresses of the Philadelphia Society for the Promotion of National Industry* in which the stone is hurled at Smith and on behalf of protectionist nationalism. 'It is the mighty question', Carey wrote of the book's concern on its opening page, 'whether we shall be really or nominally independent' (Carey 1822, p. 2).

In 1825 Mathew Carey was joined in Philadelphia by Friedrich List (1789–1846), the pre-eminent figure of national economics. In the years just prior to his emigration he had helped organise the German Association for Trade and Commerce, and pressed its goal of a German customs union. 'The objective of abolishing internal duties is . . . clearly stated to be the fostering of German national unity' (Tribe, 1988, p. 21). A 10-month prison sentence for liberal political activities in Württemburg prompted him to enlist in the entourage of Lafayette, then touring the United States. He found there that the protectionist issue had been kindled by Mathew Carey, and in 1825 Hamilton's report had been reissued.[8] List became an American citizen, and, in Schumpeter's opinion 'fully Americanized' (Schumpeter 1954, p. 505).

The result was *American Political Economy*, of 1827. It calls for the United States to 'declare war' against the system of 'Adam Smith and Co'. If they did not the future would record that the United States became weak and died, trusting in the infallibility of two books imported into the country, one from Scotland, the other from France – 'books, the general failure of which was shortly afterwards acknowledged by every individual' (List [1827] 1909, p. 152).

In List's view the source of Smith's error lies in not adding to his 'general principles the modifications caused by the fraction of the human race into national bodies'. Nations, says List 'are different in their conditions as individuals are. There are giants and dwarfs, youths and old men, cripples and well-made persons; some are superstitious, dull, indolent, uninstructed, barbarous; others are enlightened, active, enterprising, and civilised' (List [1827] 1909, p. 165). Economics has not heeded this: 'what goes by its name is merely an astrology – but it is possible and desirable to produce an astronomy out of it' (quoted in Henderson 1982, p. 273).

Returned to Germany, List sought to devise the 'astronomy' of economics, and in 1841 his *Das Nationale System der Politischen Oekonomie* was published.

Nationale System presents some themes that were to be fundamental for national economists throughout the nineteenth and twentieth centuries.

1. The esteem of the nation state: 'The highest union of individuals realized up to the present under the rule of law is in the state and the nation' (List [1841] 1909, p. 301).
2. The existences of stages of mental development, and the consequent relativity of all policy.
3. A commendation of 'realpolitik' on account of its supposed recognition of political imperatives (in contrast to the philanthropic illusions of economists).

4. A denigration of theory, and an elevation of practice. List's rhetorical presentation on this issue was in terms of the need to face up to some unbeautiful realities that theory hides. 'Theory did not wish to learn anything from history or experience, from politics or nationality' (List [1841] 1909, p. 293). He also gave new charge to a favourite rhetorical technique of anti-economists – to dismiss any general claim as a 'theory', as opposed, of course, to his own 'facts'.

Listianism became the charter of new and aspirant nation states, of unsettled status in the international diplomatic order and on the fringes of the metropolitan economies.

The 'Old German Historical School'

Listianism found an almost immediate resonance in the so-called Old German Historical School, associated with Wilhelm Roscher and Bruno Hildebrand.

Wilhelm Roscher (1817–94) cannot be well described as an anti-economist; he admired Ricardo and Malthus, and has been with some justice portrayed as a reformulator of J.S. Mill. But he clearly articulated several precepts of relativistic anti-economics.

1. Economic phenomena are best appreciated in the light of their origins. 'He can only rightly judge when, where and why . . . forced-labour, guild rights, [and] monopolistic companies should be abolished, who has fully understood why in their day they had to be introduced' (quoted in Oncken 1926, p. 325).
2. Economic development is characterised by a series of stages (genesis, growth, maturity, and decline) that preclude any universal judgements. The crutch of the old man, says Roscher, would be unsuitable for a man in maturity. As a consequence, 'the historic method will not simply praise or blame any economic institution; for certainly but few institutions have existed which to all people, or in all stages of civilisation have been absolutely beneficent or absolutely detrimental' (quoted in Oncken 1926, p. 325).
3. The nation was a unity. 'Just like life itself, national life forms a whole, the different expressions of which are deeply interwoven. Whoever aims to understands any one aspect of the science must understand them all' (quoted in Priddat 1995, p. 19).

Bruno Hildebrand (1812–78) exemplifies a more combative nationalism, and anti-economics. Hildebrand was an editor, statistician, professor, protectionist and active participant in the Frankfurt National Assembly (May 1848–June 1849) that sought to create a political union of the German speaking states. He held the typical nationalist doctrine that 'the economy of nations is, like their language, literature, law and art a branch of their civilisation' (Ashley 1926, p. 311). He also brandished a programmatic attachment to the historical method. These attitudes are displayed in *Die Nationalökonomie der Gegenwart und Zukunft* (The Economics of the Present and the Future) of 1848. In Hildebrand's view classical economics, in attempting to create a universal truth, had falsely generalised from 'the facts of single peoples or stages of development', and had forgotten man is 'always a child of civilisation and a product of history' (Hildebrand quoted in Koot 1987). Hildebrand's book was, in the judgement of one anti-text, 'perhaps the most trenchant criticism of the Smithian doctrine and method ever written' (Lilly and Devas 1904, p. xxii).

Hungary

Perhaps List's most immediate success outside Germany was in Hungary. The *National System* was translated into Hungarian in 1843. 'Eagerly awaited' by his Hungarian readers, List toured Hungary in 1844 and was elected to the Hungarian Academy. Lajos Kossuth, the nationalist revolutionary, welcomed List, and founded a society for the promotion of national industry, the ultimate purpose of which was to nurture Hungarian independence.

Asia

List's claims resonated around Asia.

Mahadev Govind Ranade (1842–1901), 'the Indian disciple of List'[9] graduated at the top of Bombay University's first bachelor of arts class in 1862. He became a judge, an important figure within the young Indian National Congress (founded in 1885), and wrote *The Rise of the Maratha Power*, a history of the Hindu zealots who established an independent state in the eighteenth century.

In 1892 Ranade published 'Indian Political Economy' (Ranade [1892] 1899) in which he urges students of Indian economic problems to reject the 'preposterous assumptions of the Ricardian School', to recognise the relativity of economic truth, and develop a political economy appropriate for India. This Indian political economy would recognise that free trade, factory laws, free capital markets, and direct taxation might well suit the United Kingdom but not India. It would also reject economic man in favour of anti-economical man: 'With us the average Individual man is, to a large extent, the very antipodes of the Economical man' (Ranade [1892] 1899, p. 9). Any appeal to 'tendencies' to justify economic abstractions was unacceptable: 'You might as well talk of the tendencies of mountains to be washed away into the sea, or of the valleys to fill up, or of the Sun to get cold' ([1892] 1899, p. 10). This relativism draws on more thinkers than List; Leslie (who is quoted by Ranade) is one additional source. But his collectivism – 'the centre round which the Theory should revolve . . . is the Body Politic of which the Individual is a Member' ([1892] 1899, p. 21) – is perfectly Listian.[10]

In the late 1880s List's *Nationale System* was translated into Japanese by Oshima Sadamasu. 'If apples fall towards the ground in England', declared Sadamasu 'we can presume that all apples will fall towards the ground in every country of the world. But in the case of politics, law or economics, what is suitable for England may not be applicable to France, for nations may be old or new, large or small, strong or weak' (quoted in Morris-Suzuki 1989, p. 60). Sadamasu founded the National Economics Association which adopted an 'assertive nationalist tone' (Morris-Suzuki 1989, p. 62).[11]

Ireland

List was also flourished by Irish nationalists. The founder of Sinn Féin, Arthur Griffith (1872–1922) advocated a Listian programme of national development of Ireland through the 'exclusion' of foreign products. In words which recall List, but with a distinguishing bitterness, Griffith branded the *Wealth of Nations* as 'the best example of a subtle scheme for English world-conquest put forward under the guise of an essay on political economy flavoured with that love of man that hooks in the sentimentalists of all countries' (quoted in Daly 1994, p. 84).

Griffith's own anti-economics (of 1918) had been preceded by 'unsparing' attacks on political economy by Irish nationalists over the preceding sixty years (see Boylan and Foley 1991, p. 7). The 'Limerick Declaration' of 1868, that marked the renewal of the campaign for Repeal of the Union, affirmed 'Ireland has had enough of political economy' (*The Times* 2 January 1868). In 1848 the *Irish Tribune* declared that, although political economy would be relatively harmless if confined to 'turnip headed' politicians 'there are others whose poison is more insidious, and who have taken the best means of diffusing it through our veins – such as one [Archbishop] Whately, a goodly specimen of the foreign vermin we have allowed to crawl over us – of such we must be aware' (quoted in Boylan and Foley 1984, p. 137). Somewhat more constructively John Mitchel (1815–75), the leader of the Young Ireland movement of the mid-nineteenth century, appealed for the cultivation of an 'Irish political economy'.

The most extensive articulation of Irish national anti-economics is found in William Dillon (1850–1935), a biographer of John Mitchel, and author of *The Dismal Science. A Criticism of Modern English Political Economy* (1882).

William Dillon was the elder son of a veteran of the abortive rising of Irish nationalists of 1848, Treasurer of the newly-founded Society for the Preservation of the Irish Language, and a committee member of the Irish Land League, which was devoted to destroying the power of landlords.[12]

The Dismal Science censures political economy on the grounds of its 'persistent practice of looking at the phenomena of wealth from a strictly cosmopolitan stand-point, and the consequent neglect to recognise and estimate the existence and effect of national divisions . . . English Economists not only admit that in their method of inquiry national distinctions are ignored, but further...they actually boast of this as a feature in their method which they have reason to be proud of' (Dillon 1882, p. 208).

Renouncing such 'cosmopolitical' economics, Dillon announces he will consider the free trade/protection issue from a 'strictly national view point'. He reworks the Listian theme that England's patronage of free trade was just a means to promote her national interest at the expense of Ireland.

> While England was building up her great manufacturing industry, the growth of manufactures in Ireland was prevented by laws passed expressly and avowedly with that object. Then, when England had got a decisive start, when her manufactures were firmly established, and she had complete control of the market, Ireland was 'put on a footing of perfect equality'. The result was such as might have been, and probably was foreseen.
>
> (Dillon 1882, p. 156)

The Dismal Science's national economics is complemented by an advocacy of an historical and inductive method against political economy's abstractions. It rejects 'the method which proceeds by abstracting one leading passion or motive from human nature and viewing man as a voluntary machine, acted on solely by the desire of wealth, and the aversion to labour' (Dillon 1882, p. 220).[13]

In his methodological passages, Dillon has an evident and acknowledged debt to another Irish born anti-economist, T.E. Cliffe Leslie (1827?–82) whose 'often bitter attacks upon orthodox political economy during the 1870s were rooted especially in the distinctive needs of Ireland, for which economic orthodoxy did not appear to have a solution' (Koot 1975, p. 320).[14]

In a variety of journal publications (see Leslie 1888) Leslie censured political economy for its vicious abstractions: the assumption of perfect knowledge, the disutility of labour, competition, and above all 'interest' (that is, egoism). No rival generalisations could satisfactorily supplant them. The fault was in seeking generalisations. One must eschew conjuring with simplicities, and instead engage in historical inquiry into communities 'one in blood ... and manner of life'.

> A priori political economy has sought to deduce...the nature, amount, and distribution of wealth, from...individual interest; but the conclusion which the study of society makes every day more irresistible, is that the germ from which the existing economy of every nation has been evolved is not the individual... but the primitive community – a community one in blood, property, thought, moral responsibility, and manner of life.
>
> (Leslie 1888, p. 177)

America and Australia

Listian themes echoed in the former colonies of Great Britain.

In the United States Henry Charles Carey (1793–1879), the son of Mathew Carey, pursued the project of a national economics with a greater range of resources than his father. Carey's *Principles of Social Science* ([1859] 1963) is a melange of history and geography in three volumes, directed towards destroying the 'Ricardo-Malthus' theory. Apart from rejecting the Ricardian theory of rent on historical grounds, Carey is best remembered for his opposition to free trade, and one of the roots of this is not hard to uncover. 'In all his writings he was, for a number of reasons, intensely anti-British' (Hebard 1958). By 1863 his *Manual of Social Science* (a condensation of the *Principles*) had been translated into German, and greeted there 'with extraordinary warmth and rash recognition' (Lambi 1963, p. 92).

In Australia a representative of national economics is provided by the almost perfectly forgotten figure of David Syme (1827–1908), whose writings were once distinctly known to many 'who would have been unable to name the capital of Victoria' (La Nauze 1949, p. 98). Syme was a Scottish journalist who emigrated to Melbourne where he championed a tariff to protect local producers against British imports. He wrote an anti-text, *Outlines of an Industrial Science*, that drew heavily on the methodologising of his friend Leslie. But List is there too; as one critic said 'there is a central influence on the formation of Syme's views ... nationalist feeling. A belief in the perversity of a system of political economy which regards political societies as no more than units in the international division of labour is certainly sincere and powerful in Syme' (La Nauze 1949, p. 134). Syme's anti-text was reprinted in Boston, praised by Henry Carey, prescribed as a text, translated into German, and commended by Schmoller.

Two other Australian anti-texts appeared in the late nineteenth century, both presenting socialist sympathy with national colours. *Cinderella: a Manual of Political Economy for Free Men*, by an anonymous and 'obscure Australian workman' (who used 'Cinderella' as a nom de plume), is a Carlylian denunciation of economics that undertakes to curse the Mill-Fawcett school 'with such volcanic blasphemy that the printer's devil should shake in his shoes!'. *Cinderella's* principal grievance is political economy's treatment of capital as a factor of production, commensurate with labour. But *Cinderella* also objects to political economy's neglect of the national aspect of immigration: 'Under the magnificent Law of England ... the whole soil of England might be depopulated and the descendants of the conquerors at Agincourt, Crecy and Naseby be replaced by Central African dwarfs with poisoned arrows, degraded Patagonians and bestial Hottentots and the change would be unknown to those who "govern" by the Mill-Fawcett manuals!' (*Cinderella* 1890, p. 66).

George Lacy is a still more forgotten and obscure figure than Syme or 'Cinderella', but perhaps even more worthy of memory. He is the author of the massive and sprawling anti-text, *Liberty and Law: Being an Attempt at the Refutation of the Individualism of Mr Herbert Spencer and the Political Economists; [...] and a Demonstration of the Worthlessness of the Supposed Dogmas of Orthodox Political Economy*. Lacy's rambling cogitations defy any brief summary. But he has some kinship with historical economics in the style of Leslie: he maintains that political economy must be 'purely inductive' if it is to have 'the least value' (Lacy 1888, p. 195); he stresses mental development of the human race, and he rejects the unity of mankind. Indeed, the very notion of unity moves Lacy to indignant expostulation; 'I must here enter my protest against the commonly accepted theories that the human race is of one species ... I have had much to do with many races of mankind, from the lowest Bushman and Australian Blackfellows to the higher Hottentots, Basutos, Bechuans, Papuans, Kanaks, Negroes, Ethiopians, Pampa Indians, and the yet higher Maoris, Zulus, Cingalese, Hindostanis, Arabs, Swahilis, Moors, Malays, Malagasys, and Chinese, and I cannot, for one instant, believe they are all of one species, or even descended from a single stock' (Lacy 1888, p. 105).

Imperial national economics

In the late nineteenth century national economics broadened its sources of appeal. The socialism that burgeoned after 1848 found the collectivism of nationalism complementary. At the same time, nationalism now appeared to the Right to be a resource for conserving the old order, for preserving society from class war, and securing the integrity of state borders from insurgent minorities. The upshot was that nationalism became 'social' (in the way it had never been in the hands of the firmly anti-socialist List and Hildebrand); a potential ally of dynasty, rather than a necessary foe; and an assertion of the centre against the margin (rather than the margin against the centre).

With this broadened appeal national economics was no longer confined to societies that identified themselves as peripheral. It could now take root in even a great industrial and imperial power such as Great Britain. Thus the very plea for national-historical economics that was designed to rebut British hegemony in the guise of classical political economy was, in the late nineteenth century, adopted by champions of Britain imperialism.

William Cunningham (1849–1919) was one such 'imperial national economist' and the principal academic anti-economist in Great Britain in the thirty years before 1914. His chief targets were Alfred Marshall, Marshall's revived economic science, and the new syllabus that Marshall was developing in Cambridge to teach this.[15] He made war upon Marshall's *Principles of Economics* and his allies in several publications: 'The Perversion of Economic History', 'Economists as Mischief Makers', 'The Relativity of Economic

Doctrine', 'The Comtist Criticism of Economic Science', *The Case against Free Trade*. He sought at the Senate of Cambridge to block the new specialised degree (the Tripos) in economics that Marshall was seeking. He initiated the historicist *Economic Review* as a counter-weight to the Marshallian *Economic Journal*.

Cunningham's ideas are dominated by two themes: relativism and nationalism.

1. Relativism

'If political economy were like Physics and gave us information about unchanging uniformities it would afford very valuable guidance...Fire burns, and always burns, and the burnt child fears it' (Cunningham 1892a, p. 14). Regrettably, says Cunningham 'political economy cannot lay down laws which hold good at all times and all places'. There are two reasons why this is so:

i. The degree of competition is historically contingent (Cunningham 1878, p. 371). The gains of medieval merchants were, for example, obtained largely by gaining temporary monopoly: competition in 'exchange was an occasional incident' (Cunningham 1892a, p. 5).
ii. Motives are historically contingent. Orthodoxy assumed 'the same motives have been at work in all ages, and...therefore, it is possible to formulate economic laws which describe the action of economic causes at all times and in all places' (quoted in Maloney 1976, p. 442). But motives are many more than the egotistic, and have fluctuated.

Setting their face against relativism, economists made general claims that were revealed as a false. They claimed the factory acts would harm employment, but they did not. In their laissez-faire stance they had set class upon class, and divided the nation.

2. Nationalism

Cunningham 'believed in' nationality. It was a vessel of history: 'In the present day, and among the progressive peoples of the world, nationality is the heritage of human experience' (1911, p. 16). It was an expression of varying potentials: 'Humanity can attain to its fullest life...not by toning down national characteristics to a common level, but by affording opportunities for the development of the characteristic features of each separate race' (1911, p. 15). It was no less than the hope of the future: 'the nation is the organ by which the welfare of mankind may be effectively promoted' (1914, p. 98). Regrettably, liberal economics was possessed of 'a-moral and a-national prejudices', and this was why (by his own account) Cunningham hastened to do battle with it (Maloney 1985, p. 92).

One field of battle where Cunningham's sword was drawn was in the fight for Joseph Chamberlain's 'Tariff Reform' scheme of 1902 which would impose a common tariff over the entire British Empire. Thus in Cunningham's protectionism the nationalism of List had transmuted into imperialism. Listian resentment of free trade as the imperialism of the hegemon had become a resentment of free trade as the subverter of empire.

The imperial tariff struggle of 1902 was also the occasion of the publication of one of the classics in anti-economics: William Samuel Lilly and Charles Stanton Devas's reissue of an edited version of *Sophisms of Free-Trade and Popular Political Economy Examined* by Sir John Barnard Byles (1801–1884) (Byles 1904, originally published in 1849). Its frantic 38-page Introduction and numerous editorial interpolations pursue the 'fictions, fallacies, and futilities' of political economy (that 'begins in atheism and ends in abortion') with a grandiloquent absurdity that barely has a parallel even in the literature of anti-economics.

The German Historical School

It was Germany that nurtured the deepest aspirations to articulate the consequences of a relativistic critique of economics. It was the German Historical School (GHS), that from 1870 began a 40-year domination of economic thought in Germany, and that is supremely identified with the 'historical' and 'national' rejection of economic orthodoxy.

Gustav Schmoller (1838–1917) was the undisputed leader of the GHS. To Schmoller the value and vitality of orthodox political economy had perished with the close of the eighteenth century; classical economics 'after 1780 produced only several generations of sterile epigones'; there had seldom been 'a science so damaged by one man as Ricardo' (quoted in Dopper 1993, p. 165); and no 'Smithians' were fit for appointment in a German university.

There were four leading themes in his critique of classical economics.

1. *The disunity of mankind.* Here we have the starting point; Schmoller's basic opposition was to the 'natural' unity of mankind. It is the disunity of man that Schmoller stressed. 'In the eighteenth century the science of State, of society and political economy shared . . . the belief in the natural equality of men', and as a consequence sought to establish a 'human nature in general' (Schmoller 1906, 1, p. 338). But 'there is no general character of man', and on this point he refers with qualified approval to the work of Joseph Arthur Gobineau (1816–82), author of *Essai sur l'Inégalité des Races Humaines* (Schmoller 1906, 1, p. 339). He concludes that 'we must find the laws of the character of man because they are the most important in sociology': he presents sketch appreciations of the character of Negroes, Mongols, Semites, Indo-Europeans (in turn divided into Russians, Italian, French, English and Germans).

2. *The integral nation necessitated an integral social science, not a specialised economics*. Just as one cannot understand physiology without knowledge of anatomy; so one cannot understand economic activity without understanding the social anatomy. As the social anatomy changes, so would economic activity. 'The chemist may dare to abstract from physical properties of a chemical entity but if he investigated atmospheric air and then applied Menger's principle of isolation and argued: "I will consider nitrogen because that is predominant", he would very likely be thrown out of the laboratory immediately' (quoted in Dopfer 1993, p. 153)
3. *The dominance of progressive development*. History possesses a direction, and this should be recognised. Economic doctrine 'should be subordinated to the idea of evolution, which dominates contemporary science' (Schmoller quoted in Pearson 1999, p. 552). This development included institutional development, and the great new form of society would be the nation-state. Development also comprehended the mental, the psychological, and the ethical. Such development creates differences between different ages. 'Demand and supply, as they confront each other in different systems of custom and law, are quite different in their result' (Schmoller 1894, p. 27).
4. *The need for an (inductive) 'historical' method in economics*. Here classical economics was blameworthy. Not even Smith was exempt. He 'fell back again and again on natural law. In spite of historical matters with a common thread, he was still not a real historian but a dogmatic fellow'. Smith's presentation of mercantilism is 'false': he did not use the historical resources available for 1400–1700. His vision that princely politics, established churches and feudalism had tilted economic development away from agriculture 'was an almost childish notion'. 'He, in spite of the knowledge of human and national differences, wanted for all that as a political analyst to apply for all times, climates, races and peoples ... the single formula of economic freedom' (Schmoller 1991, p. 138).

Schmoller, in what he thought was a contrast with Smith, saw his science as serving, not some imaginary human race, but the national community to which he belonged, and to which he was devoted. It was on account of his Prussophile views that he was forced out of the Württemburg civil service. In 1872 he became professor at the Emperor William University of Strasbourg in the newly annexed province of Alsace. As professor he argued for 'vital, but at the time hard-pressed, national industry against foreign supremacy' (quoted in Lambi 1963, p. 91); the peopling of German colonies, and even the establishment of a new German colony in southern Brazil; and a naval expansion to defeat the 'encirclement' of Germany and to re-establish German national politics in 'a grand style'.

American institutionalism

The relativism of the German Historical School and others had some parallel in the American 'institutionalism' that is associated with Thorstein Veblen (1857–1929), a renowned critic of orthodox economics, Richard Theodore Ely (1854–1943), who had studied at Heidelberg, and Ely's institutional colleague, John R. Commons (1862–1945). Commons's starting point was Veblen's suggestion that an 'evolutionary theory of value must be constructed out of the habits and customs of social life'. In *Legal Foundations of Capitalism* Commons was concerned to trace property and transaction in Anglo-American law from 'our Teutonic ancestors' in 'German forests' through three stages: agriculture, commerce and industry. This historical and cultural treatment was complemented by Commons's belief that human kind was deeply divided by race (see Ramstad and Starkey 1995).[16] 'Race differences are established in the very blood and physical constitution... they are most difficult to eradicate'. The tropical races were 'indolent', Negroes 'lacking in "mechanical idea"', and only the 'ambitious races of northern Europe could be industrialised' (Gosset 1963, p. 173).[17] The differences between industrial northern Italy and agrarian southern Italy is due to the greater presence of 'Teuton' blood in the North. All this is reminiscent of the spirit of Schmoller and List.

4.3   Twentieth-century reformulations

The years before the First World War saw nationalism within economics – and without – at the height of its influence, utilised by the anti-liberal Left and by the Right. But the outbreak of the First World War marks the end of national economics in developed countries. In considerable measure this was due to the fall in international esteem of the country which represented excellence in national economics: Germany. National economists outside Germany had greatly admired her. Cunningham 'had long been a friend of Germany' (quoted in Cunningham 1950, p. 119), and in 1870 had written in his diary that 'We can only trust for the rise of a united Germany to dictate to the world' (quoted in Cunningham 1950, p. 119). He had even identified himself with 'the more extreme members of the German Historical School'. But with the outbreak of World War I, Cunningham became militantly anti-German. And he was not alone: a 'tidal wave of anti-Germanic feeling swept across the United States'.

The association of national economics with a disgraced Germany promoted the dissolution of the former collaboration between nationalism and the anti-liberal Left; a collaboration that was manifested, for example, in the institutionalism of Commons and Ely.[18] In the late nineteenth century a part of the Left had assimilated nationalism as favourable to collectivism, and as a useful relativiser. But nationalism now caused offence to the Left on the ground of its reactionary aspect; it seemed to represent an old and barbaric order. Thus Veblen who had 'hailed the publication of Schmoller's *Grundriss* [in 1901] as an outstanding event in economic theory' (Dopfer 1993, p. 146) now anatomised the German pathology (Veblen [1915] 1939). Nationalism now seemed to belong to the Right rather than the Left.

With the defection of the Left, national economics in the wake of World War I retreated to where it began; in those economies marginal to the centre.

Development economics

For about a generation after the liquidation of fascism, development economics was the principal vessel of national economics and relativism. As 1815 marked the beginning of national economics, so 1945 marked the genesis of development economics. In the 30 years that followed, the hegemony of the Atlantic was challenged as poor countries containing a billion people obtained independence. The nationalist excitement over this, and the frustration at their economic marginality, laid the emotional charge for perhaps the biggest flare in economic relativism: development economics. Development economics was raised upon the notion that there should be two economics; one for developed countries and one for underdeveloped countries. What is right for the developed world may be wrong for the underdeveloped. This relativism found a ready application in trade policy. Reflecting its character as a form of national economics, development economics exhibited a painful sensitivity to international trade, and relativism provided the remedy. Free international trade may be beneficial for the developed world, but it is harmful for the developing world.

Three European economists, with a nationalist identification before World War II, were early articulators of national economics as development economics: Mihaïl Manoïlesco (a functionary of Romanian fascism), Thomas Balogh (1905–85) (a one-time supporter of Admiral Horthy in the 1930s), and Gunnar Myrdal (1898–1987), who, with his wife Alva, had in the 1930s 'cast their lot with ethnocentric nationalism. For Gunnar...an almost tribal devotion to the Swedish "folk" drove him in a new direction...a true passion for "Sweden's children"' (Carlson 1990, p. 85).

Manoïlesco had already promoted a national economics for less-developed economies before World War II. His *The Theory of Protection and International Trade* (1931) was an ambitious, if unsuccessful, attempt at a theoretical refutation of comparative advantage (see Irwin 1996), and the 'League of Nations policy' of free trade. His contention was that 'international trade represents in the most categorical form, although the most disguised, the exploitation of one people by another'. 'Economic science', he added 'is in contradiction with history' (Manoïlesco, 1934, p. 28).

Myrdal's *Rich Lands and Poor* of 1957 articulated what he described as 'sane and sound nationalism' and 'rational nationalism' for developing countries

(1957, p. 68). International trade will benefit strong countries, but would impoverish the culture of underdeveloped countries, and strengthen the forces of stagnation (pp. 52, 53).[19] Regrettably, there is a 'cosmopolitan flavour' in 'the most abstract concepts and pronouncements in economics'. Myrdal hopes for a new economics that would go beyond 'outmoded Western liberal economics and Marxism', and that would realise that 'stable equilibrium' is an 'unrealistic assumption' and 'a false analogy'. This new economics would appreciate that 'change does not call forth counter-vailing changes, but supporting changes' (pp. 9, 13) and that society is more a matter of 'dramatic breaks' than uniformities. In service of this notion Myrdal pours scorn upon 'natural law' as frequently as does Schmoller or Veblen.

Thomas Balogh's *Unequal Partners* (1963) is a tract on international economic relations that urges developing countries to spurn free trade. The basis of this counsel is the inadequacy of standard economics on account of the lawlessness of the economic world. This theme was repeatedly pressed in *Unequal Partners*, and brought to the centre of Balogh's anti-text of 1982, *The Irrelevance of Conventional Economics*, whose pre-eminent thesis is that the world is indeterminate. There is no equilibrium; no point of tendency, no effacement of disturbances over time, no resemblance of future to past; no resemblance of the near and far; no stability, reversibility, or indepen-dence and structure. Anything goes. Thus a change in price in response to a shock to demand will not restore equilibrium since the experience of the change in price will change demand *at a given price*, and change supply at a given price. The very movement in price, in other words, will shift the demand and supply schedules.

Balogh flung bile at all who disagreed, that is to say, almost all economists, if not exactly all. Balogh makes a respectful nod to Manoïlesco, and salutes the GHS; it is 'astonishing' that on the basis of the 'twaddle' of orthodox economics 'the historical school was eliminated as a serious effort at elucidating concrete problems' (Balogh 1982, p. 38).

In the post-war period, Manoïlesco's protectionism, the historicism of List and the German Historical School, and the 'permanent disequilibrium' of Balogh and Myrdal, found expression in the 'structuralism' of Raúl Prebisch (1901–86), and the ideas of the UN's Economic Commission for Latin America (ECLA). The ideas of List had already been popularised in Argentina by Vincente Fidel Lopez (1815–1903), a historian of Argentina's struggles for independence, and a professor of political economy. Prebisch was the 'admirer and translator' of Wagner, who is also sometimes included in the GHS.[20] More immediately, ECLA also drew on Manoïlesco who had main-tained (as ECLA did) that less-developed countries will grow only through a policy of planned industrialisation, hastened by import substitution and financed by internal (rather than foreign) capital.[21] The aspiration to a national economics was explicitly stated.[22] The doctrine of ECLA was in essence the doctrine of Balogh and Myrdal; the denial of the existence of equilibrium, at least with respect to the whole 'structure'. 'Lawfulness', in other words, was at a massive discount. The unique, special and distinctive was at a premium.

The cult of culture

But however potent nationalism was in the Third World, its ideological expression in the developed world had been discredited by the world wars and was no longer an effective vehicle of relativism. Yet relativists would still benefit from a relativiser that would challenge the market system's pretensions to naturalness and normality. One alternative relativiser was Marxism, which would turn on 'history' rather than nationality. But this was a rather feeble relativiser.[23] Vast, disparate chunks of the world were reduced to a single category: 'capitalist'. And Marxist relativism was strictly 'materialist'.

Repelled from such a material relativiser, anti-liberals, both Left and Right, were drawn to a new relativiser: 'culture', which had obtained its modern anthropological sense only at the opening of the twentieth century.[24] Culture, not nation, became the great shibboleth of relativists.

The first strand in the case for culture lay in a hypothesis of the GHS: that there was a rupture between the modern and pre-modern world on account of a rupture between pre-modern and modern mentality. Drawing on Max Weber (1864–1920), Sombart and Schmoller held that innovations in the modern mentality included a 'puritan' or 'bourgeois' spirit (calculation and prudence), and a 'capitalist' spirit (acquisitive, inquisitive, audacious).[25] A second strand was the emergence in the 1920s of economic anthropology that 'emphasised the vast gulf between the ancient and modern worlds' (Morley 1998).

The child of GHS and economic anthropolgy was the thought of Karl Polanyi,[26] that was engrossed in a vision of a 'Great Transformation' of the world. Polanyi rejected universals in human conduct. 'The alleged propensity of man to barter, truck, and exchange is almost entirely apocryphal' (Polanyi [1944] 1957, p. 44). Consequently the market structure is not universal: 'market economy is an institutional structure which, as we all too easily forget, has been present at no time except our own, and even then it was only partially present' (Polanyi [1944] 1957, p. 37). And it is certainly not natural; he writes of 'the extreme artificiality of the market economy'. Drawing on GHS authors such as Karl Bücher (1847–1930) and Werner Sombart, Polanyi advances the paradox that the market was the creation of the modern state.[27] Polanyi could only agree with the characterisation of Sombart that the 'capitalist spirit' and the institutions embodying it are purely transitory episodes in the evolution of society. In consequence, the laws of capitalism, indeed all economic laws, are neither final nor universal. There is, then, 'no science of "economy", or Wirtschaft, in the general or universal meaning of theoretical economics' (Harris 1942, p. 832).

An attack on the endurance of the market sphere, complementary to Polanyi's, came at the outbreak of the Second World War with the *The End of Economic Man* (1940) by a life-long friend of Polanyi, Peter Drucker (b. 1909). To Drucker there is one fundamental motivation in humankind: a wish for equality. In the age of faith it was religion that promised equality. In the eighteenth century wealth-making in a market context promised equality. Economic man was, in other words, just an experimental strategy of egalitarian man. The economic man strategy, however, did not succeed. Mankind therefore abandoned playing economic man. The proof of this says Drucker, writing at the close of the 1930s, is that the world no longer obeys economic laws.

In the post-war period culture survived as a relativiser, but it was with the end of the Cold War that it received its greatest exploitation by anti-economists. In 1989 the Soviet bloc was overthrown, Marxism suffered a huge blow to its morale and prestige, and the Left was no longer dominated by its one determinedly internationalist form. Further, for the first time in about a century, the prospect of a single globally dominant form of society suddenly loomed, and the United States was its exemplar. This prospect provoked a deep resentment that was almost immediately condensed in the term 'globalisation', and a jealous pan-Europeanism that aspired to defend the 'distinctiveness' of 'Europe' (see, for example, Bordieu 1998, p. 41). This resentment revived the national economics which in the western world had been quiescent. It revived the same accusation of universalism being the instrument of a particular culture; the same denial of the existence of universal laws; the same insistence on the partition of humankind by culture and age.[28]

A prominent exponent of this resurgent national economics was John Gray (b.1948), in *False Dawn: the Delusions of Global Capitalism* (1998). Its emotional underlay is a boiling antipathy to the United States; its focus of hatred is the 'Washington consensus' of 'market fundamentalism' that presumes to inculcate 'a single worldwide civilization, in which the varied traditions and cultures of the past were superseded by a new, universal community founded on reason'. This consensus, says Gray, amounts to 'a marginalisation of cultural differences in human life that grossly underestimates its political importance'. It treats 'nationalism and ethnic allegiance as ephemeral', and consigns them to 'poverty or extinction'. It revives Herbert Spencer in supposing that 'allegiance' can be formed in the absence of a 'particular cultural tradition'. Finally, it assumes that the market is not derivative on the existence of a cohesive society (and here Gray makes extensive re-use of Polanyi).

In truth, says Gray, the importance and validity of different economic cultures cannot be effaced. In truth there persist 'indigenous types of capitalism that owe little to any western model', especially the 'radically different' Asian institutions that are 'overtaking' western ones.[29] Europe and the USA are themselves distinct, especially since (according to Gray) the USA can hardly be considered European culture given the prospect that Blacks and Hispanics will by 2050 almost constitute a majority (Gray 1998, p. 129).

Gray's stance amounts to a resurrection of the GHS, with which Gray can be paired on several significant counts. Both the GHS and Gray see Marxism and economic liberalism as Enlightenment survivals. Schmoller described Marxism and Manchesterism as 'twin offspring of an unhistorical rationalism, the last musty remnant of the Enlightenment'. To Gray, the kinship of Marxism and 'market fundamentalism' is 'evident'. 'It is like Marxism, a variant of the enlightenment project' (Gray 1995, p. 101). Both see the market as not natural, but as somehow 'artificial'.[30] Both have at their nervous core a defensiveness regarding cultural identity; with Gray the United States has simply been substituted for Great Britain as the loathsome, menacing agent of universalisation.

List, too, is now revived. Thus one densely academic anti-text from Australia, *Beyond Economics: Postmodernity, Globalization and National Sustainability* (Sauer-Thompson and Smith 1996), disparages the 'cosmopolitanism' of Marxism, and is garlanded with quotations from Friedich List (and J.G. Fichte's *Addresses to the German Nation!*). This is done in the perfectly Listian cause of championing the 'semi-peripheral nation state' of Australia in the face of the 'hegemonic core states of America and Japan'. There is, however, one significant innovation in this neo-Listianism: 'nationalism' is now carefully wed to 'culture' rather than anything crudely 'tribal' (naturally).[31]

4.4 Pseudo-science and pseudo-history

The economics that wasn't there

National economics proclaimed itself as the future of economics. But in the wake of this proclamation few tangible outcomes were forthcoming. The little national economics that was done was of low quality, or ephemeral.

Hildebrand announced, with fanfare, a multi-volume work that would revise economics on an historical basis. But the 'first volume' 'was not really historical, as its author admitted' (Lindenfeld 1993 p. 408), and the promised subsequent volumes never appeared. Leslie's prospective treatise on economics on historical principles also never appeared. One historian of the English Historical School has judged that what they 'actually achieved was a disappointment even to themselves. As a contribution to economics proper, little empirical work materialised' (Maloney 1976, p. 449). Certainly, much of the historical research that was carried out was done, not by the Historical School, but by practitioners in the new field of economic history, who were not the progeny of the Historical School, and whose world view was often antagonistic to the School's nationalism and collectivism.[32] Similarly national economics outside Europe had no greater success. In 1942, fifty years after Ranade's call to formulate an Indian economics, one retrospect had to record: 'Again we are disappointed. No new theory appears' (Kellock 1942, p. 253).

What national economics was produced was of poor quality. There is an undeniable superficiality about many of the national economists (Dillon, Symes, Leslie), which is not concealed by their undeniable fluency.[33] 'List's writings are devoid of great interest . . . hence the disappointment with which the modern reader will scan the pages of the *National System* . . . List is a third rate economist and, consequently, a non-runner in the history of economic theory and analysis' (Tribe 1988, p. 19). J.S. Mill, who was not unsympathetic to relativism, declared Carey's *Principles of Social Science* the 'worst book on political economy I ever toiled through' (quoted in Schumpeter 1954, p. 516).

The effectiveness of national and historical economists was hindered by their small appreciation of the neoclassical theory that was the centre of the mainstream they belittled. Cunningham was oblivious to marginalism: so was the entire English Historical School. 'No historicist tried to master the neoclassical "paradigm" and it must be doubted whether most of them would have been able to handle it even if they had tried' (Maloney 1987, p. 148).[34]

Weak in their opponents' strength, the Historical Schools were also weak in their own speciality, history. Their history was not outstanding. Their historicism encouraged them to adopt a false history, that was preoccupied by a vision of progress through stages, and neglectful of constancies. Thus a popular historicist doctrine of money had barter succeeded by commodity money, and that in turn by credit money, even though historical experience refutes the necessity of such progression. At the same time their doctrine of money managed to discount historical experience that rapid monetary expansion was inflationary: a truth revealed in 1776–83, 1789–96 and 1861–65 (not to mention 1170–1240; see Lui 1975).

The Historical Schools' own opponents sometimes seemed stronger in history. Thus McCulloch got the better of the 'historical' anti-Ricardian Richard Jones regarding the presence of rent 'as it exists in England' in ancient Greece and Rome (McCulloch 1831). For, contrary to myth, several of the most important classical economists were not ahistorical, in the sense of being uninterested or ignorant of history; they used it. One historian has averred:

> on examining the works of the political economists it becomes clear that the deafness was entirely on the historians' side. The pioneers of political economy were steeped in the classics, and the writings of Adam Smith, James Steuart and Thomas Malthus are full of references to classical

authors and episodes in ancient history – not merely as illustrations or displays of evidence but as an integral part of their arguments.

(Morley 1998, p. 97)

Further, the efforts of the Historical School to discredit the use of history by the orthodox were unsuccessful. 'Cunningham cited excerpts from the *Principles*, some of which were fair, whereas others involved wilful – and because so transparent, curiously pointless – intellectual dishonesty' (Maloney 1976, p. 442).[35]

It is true that the classical economists *were* 'unhistorical' in that the past was not considered 'a foreign country'. But it was their very willingness to see the past as in an overarching union with the present that encouraged classical economists to use history. Further, it preserved them from two vices of the historical school: 'historicism' and anachronism.

The classical economists were immune to the historicist fallacy that inside every past there was the present struggling to get out:

> Even when political economists became more aware of the differences between antiquity and the nineteenth-century experience, they placed the emphasis on the unique and unprecedented nature of the latter: there is certainly no hint that such development is natural and inevitable. This is a world away from the anachronism of a writer like Weber, who treats the 'failure' of the ancient world to 'develop' as a problem that must be investigated.
>
> (Morley 1998, p. 114)

Further, the classical economists, in extracting and discarding the distinctive and distinguishing elements of the past (and present), preserved themselves from the vice of anachronism; the vice of imposing the distinctive aspects of one's own age on a preceding one.[36] The historicists accused the classicals of this vice but were themselves the more guilty. Rather than being conscious of the distinctiveness of their own age (and others), and thereby transcending them, the Historical Schools were highly 'situated' historically. The truth is that the GHS coincided exactly with the Second Reich, and its *raison d'être* was defined by it: the reconciliation of all sectors of society to a united German state under monarchical autocracy.[37] 'Schmoller's work and with it the whole historical school was to fall into oblivion in Germany soon after his death [in 1917]' (Schefold 1987).

4.5 Does anti-economics have a nationality?

National anti-economics complains that economics makes a claim to be cosmopolitan but in fact is national. We might reverse the question: does anti-economics have a nationality, or is it cosmopolitan? An answer is apparent. Anti-economics is a citizen of the world, but it has a favoured domicile: France.[38]

A national distaste for economics was detected in France from the mid-nineteenth century. 'Political economy until now has had little vogue in France, and on the contrary theories that have made war on it have easily found ardent, sincere and numerous partisans, even among the classes who have received a careful education' (Chevalier 1849, p. 13). In 1880 the Italian historian of thought Luigi Cossa avowed 'Political Economy has never been popular in France, and is called *littérature ennuyeuse* even among cultivated people' (Cossa 1880, p. 182). A century later one student of French intellectual life maintained 'French intellectuals in general had little interest in the study of economics – as an independent discipline it had no recognised existence before the early 1950s' (Judt 1986, p. 182).

This distaste was correlate with ignorance. Taine regretted that issues in economics 'are considered in England and America as so important that not even a barely educated man is a stranger to them. There are only three classes in political economy in Paris, and I do not know of any others in France' (Taine [1893] 1903b, p. 141). Seventy years later Pierre Mendès-France (Prime Minister 1954–55) wrote 'when a Frenchman writes on what is the subject of this book, with the purpose of explaining the usefulness of economics, it is with considerable measure of embarrassment that he faces his Anglo-Saxon readers... since knowledge of economic processes varies from country to country. This inspires a certain fear that the present book may, on many points, seem elementary and "obvious" to our Anglo-Saxon readers' (Mendès-France and Ardant 1955).

And this distaste expressed itself in repulsion: since 1945 there have been three waves of anti-economics.

In the 1950s the polymorphous André Marchal hailed the 'criticisms addressed to all sides of economic science' by French authors (Marchal 1953). He acclaimed the identification of 'la crise de la pensée economique' (Denis 1951), the complaints of 'byzantine refinements which reduce each year the real part in economic teaching' (Charles Morazé in Denis 1951, p. 6), 'the abuse of verbalism' (Maurice Allais), and the calls for a 'science économique humaine'.

In the 1970s *l'Anti-Économique* (1974) of Jacques Attali and Marc Guillaume was made known to 'vast numbers' in France by the publicity of the mass-media (Kolm 1978).[39] These vast numbers comprehended certain exceptional elements: Attali enjoyed for many years the generous patronage of President François Mitterrand, who 'having studied economics with Jacques Attali' had 'an interesting vision of this science' (Defarges 1994).[40]

In 2000 came another wave, centred this time on student agitation against their syllabus, but not lacking in textual complements. In the 1990s *structuralisme* had finally discovered economics, and the anti-texts in this wave were provided by Pierre Bourdieu (1998, 2000), a sociologist/anthropologist of structuralist orientation, who pressed Polanyi's vision of the 'embeddedness' of the economic in the social.[41]

The explanation of the French attraction to anti-economics is a matter on which we will only offer a few remarks by French authors. Chevalier, in the manner of rationalist *philosophe*, blamed it on an unfortunate French preference for imagination over 'cold analysis'. Marchal seeks the answer in a concern for right rather than utility: 'One knows that the whole history of France has been dominated by the aspiration, not to a greater welfare, but to a more perfect *justice*' (Marchal 1953, p. 79). Others seek the answer, not in morality in general, but in specifically collectivist morality. 'The immense majority of our people consider economic freedom as radically immoral. It scandalises them in the fullest sense of the word' (Villey 1946, p. 30).

5
The Totalitarian State and the 'Economist-Scoundrels'[1]

This chapter pursues anti-economics into a new terrain: the totalitarian state. All species of anti-economics we have examined thus far were located in the liberal, 'bourgeois' order of the nineteenth century. These species of anti-economics amounted to challenges to that order, but were in large measure frustrated or constrained.

In the twentieth century the adversaries of the liberal order had rather more success in their confrontation, and on certain occasions, the political dynamic of liberalism was obliterated. On those occasions forces formerly in exile from power, or under constraint, now came to power. These forces faced a novel prospect: the state was now theirs. And they faced a new challenge. Whereas previously their task was simply to destroy, their task was now to create. The outcome of anti-liberal forces hurled into power was 'constructivist totalitarianism'.

Constructivist totalitarianism was 'constructivist' in that it bestowed supremacy on a vision of how the world must be contrived. But constructivism was more than a vision, however grandiose, precise, and immutable. Constructivism was characterised by an imperative: realise or die. Here we arrive at the characteristic ruthlessness of the ideology; constructivism was ready to destroy any freedom or right to achieve its vision. Every department of life was to be directly subordinated to the purpose of construction; no department of life could exist which was not. Thus constructivist totalitarianism upheld the annihilation of any prerogative exempt from the claim of construction.

Under constructivist totalitarianism economics faces the same predicament as every form of inquiry. It will be welcome if it contributes to realisation of the vision, and treated as intolerable if it retards it. Since any sort of knowledge may conflict with the constructivist programme, all species of knowledge are cultivated only by the grace and favour of political authority. Nevertheless some departments of learning may be granted that favour, as their success may further construction. Thus branches of knowledge may exist, be nurtured and thrive under constructivist totalitarianism.

Will economics obtain a dispensation, or will it be seen as an obstruction to construction? There are three characteristics of the *Grande Tradition* which may predispose it to be denied dispensation.

1. *Consumer sovereignty.* The vision of constructivist totalitarianism is derived and validated without any deference to individual wants. This disregard of individual wants by constructivism is in fundamental conflict with the Tradition.
2. *The economic problem.* The vision of constructivist totalitarianism is derived and validated without any reference to, or concern for, the 'economic problem'. Constructivist totalitarianism declines to recognise the existence of constraints and costs. The conviction of constructivist totalitarianism that everything is possible if willed is in fundamental conflict with the pre-eminence that the Tradition affords the economic problem.
3. *Economic liberalism.* The vision of constructivist totalitarianism is to be implemented without any regard for individual economic prerogative.

Yet circumstances have sometimes blunted the edges of these three predisposing considerations. First, constructivist totalitarianism may not (for a time) flout human economic wants, even if it is validated without any reference to them. Indeed, constructivist totalitarianism may for a time have more success in meeting basic material wants than its alternatives. Second, constructivist totalitarianism may not (for a time) flout the economic problem, even if it does not recognise it. Thirdly, the Tradition is not simply identifiable with economic liberalism. The Keynesian revolution, for example, was not antagonistic to certain illiberal macroeconomic policies of the Third Reich.

There is, therefore, no necessity of war between economics and constructivist totalitarianism considered in the abstract: constructivist totalitarianism is too broad a category to make such a conflict necessary. We will find, to corroborate, that while Stalinism doomed economics, Nazism ignored it

The singular feature about the anti-economics of constructivist totalitarianism is not some supposed necessity of anti-economics, but the means by which it will choose to pursue it. The ruthlessness of constructivist totalitarianism now means that anti-economics may be lethal. Thus the most distinctive feature of the anti-economics of constructivist totalitarianism lies in the most notorious feature of constructivist totalitarianism.

5.1 Stalinism

Soviet Union 1929–38[2]

Stalin's Soviet Union provides the most brutal episode of anti-economics in its history. The story begins in the late 1920s.

The late 1920s was a period of deep disequilibrium between the practice and theory of the Soviet state. The state was dedicated to the destruction of capitalism and the realisation of socialism, under the command of the Communist Party. In practice the economy was a version of capitalism, and 65 per cent of national income was accounted for by non-state enterprises. Further, this version of capitalism was managed by persons outside the Party. The officials of the state planning agency (Gosplan), the Supreme Council of the National Economy (VSNKh),[3] and the People's Commissariats of Finance (Narkomfin) and Agriculture (Narkomzem) were almost completely non-Party, save for the two most senior positions in each. Not only were the officials in these organs generally non-Party, they included a number of economists who belonged to the Tradition: Leonid N. Yurovskii, Nikolai D. Kondratiev, and Alexksandr V. Chayanov.[4]

Leonid N. Yurovskii (1884–1938) was 'one of the most brilliant men' (Jasny 1972, p. 209) among the managers of the NEP economy. He had studied in Berlin and Munich where he obtained a doctorate on Russian grain exports (Barnett 1994a). In 1917 he was made the head of the Statistical Department of the Ministry of Food Supplies. In the wake of the Bolshevik seizure of power he declared, in a remaining opposition newspaper, that starvation is not an enemy that can be vanquished by the Red Army and paper money. Having made himself *persona non grata*, he left Moscow to become head of the Saratov Institute of Economics. During those years he wrote *Ocherki po Teorii Tseny* (Studies in Price Theory), a neoclassical exercise in agricultural and industry economics, drawing on, among others, Pareto, Jevons, Walras, Marshall, Fisher, Gossen, Böhm-Bawerk, Clark, Cournot, Cassel and von Thünen.

In May 1922 Yurovskii returned to Moscow as Head of the Currency Section of Narkofin. There he would be in a delicate position. He had been attacked in *Pravda*. And Lenin was about to organise the destruction of *Ekonomist*, which had published remarks critical of the regime by B.D. Brutzkus (1874–1938), an agricultural economist. Lenin told Stalin: '**the entire** staff of *Ekonomist*, are the most ruthless enemies. The lot – out of Russia. This must be done at once' (Lenin 1996b, p. 169, bold in original). Two days later the editorial staff of *Ekonomist*, with Brutzkus, were incarcerated in a Cheka prison, prior to their deportation (Wilhelm 1993, p. 345).

Yet the urgency of the financial situation necessitated the appointment to the Currency Section of a competent economist rather than an aspirant revolutionary, and Yurovskii's appointment was approved by the Politburo.[5] The next three years were his most productive. Yurovskii 'masterminded the 1922–4 currency reform' (Barnett 1994b, p. 664) that created a new, credible store of value and means of exchange, the '*Chervonets*', that underlined the achievement of price stability. He recounted this currency reform in *Currency Problems and Policy of the Soviet Union* (1925).

Throughout the immediate post-Revolution years, Yurovskii had significant contact with Nikolai D. Kondratiev (1892–1938). Kondratiev was born in central Russia in 1892, the eldest of 10 children, of peasant parents. In 1905, before his fourteenth birthday, he joined the Social Revolutionaries (SRs), the political vehicle of peasant discontent. For his activities among the SRs he was expelled from teachers' college, arrested and spent seven months in prison (Barnett 1998).

In 1910 Kondratiev enrolled in the law faculty at St Petersburg and studied economics under Tugan-Baranovski. His academic interests were broad, but their ultimate centre was the predicament of the Russian peasant. In October 1917, at the age of 25, Kondratiev briefly became Kerensky's Minister for Food Supply. In the wake of the events of 25 October 1917 Kondratiev was arrested, and then released in time to run unsuccessfully as an SR candidate for the ill-fated Constituent Assembly. From 1919 he sought to coexist with the Soviet regime, and devoted himself to analysing its economic problems.

In 1920 Kondratiev founded the 'Conjuncture Institute', located in Narkomfin, which may claim (with the NBER) to be the first institute devoted to the study of business cycles. In that decade he travelled abroad, and met Irving Fisher, L. von Bortkiewicz, and Keynes. At home he directed a staff of 50, including Eugen Slutsky who joined the institute in 1926, and published significant work there on the statistical interpretation of time series and business cycles. The former SR now discarded the *dirigisme* of the Provisional Government and became a definite, if circumspect, market advocate. Indeed, in Barnett's analysis, 'Kondratiev was one of the most consistent and unflinching of the pro-market group' in Russia in the mid-1920s (Barnett 1998, p. 83; also Barnett 1995).

Kondratiev had a close association with Aleksandr V. Chayanov (1888–1937), an agricultural economist, playwright and novelist. Chayanov was the author of *Opyty Izucheniya Izolirovannogo Gosudarstva* (Essay on the Study of the Isolated State) (1921), written under the obvious inspiration of von Thünen, but is remembered for his thesis that the peasant household's optimisation decision was distinct from that of the capitalist firm. Jevonian in his approach, he was decried as an 'Austrian' by Marxists. He was, in truth, seeking to go beyond both standard neoclassical economics and historical relativism, by venturing a universal economic form (the peasant household) distinct from the familiar commercial firm.[6] He found an intellectual collaborator in H.L. Makarov (1887–1980), who later, in less fortunate times, was to be his cell mate.

Inevitably Yurovskii, Kondratiev and Chayanov were in a vulnerable situation.

That their analysis strayed well out of the confines of Marxist doctrine had potential to offend, even when it was concerned with the *problems* of capitalism, such as the business cycle. Thus Kondratiev's prediction, on the basis of the 'long wave', that the contemporaneous 'decline' in capitalism would cease in the 1940s offended some watchdogs of the Revolution. Kondratiev was interpreted as saying: 'we are dealing with an essentially perpetual movement of capitalism, first upwards and then downwards, and that it is not appropriate to dream of social revolution yet' (quoted in Klein 1999, p. 151).[7]

The non-Party status of such economists caused offence. Thus one denunciation of Kondratiev complained that at one institute of economics 'Communists put in rare and timid appearances' (quoted in Jasny 1972, p. 201). Others complained that 'development of the science known as "economics of industry" proceeds in almost complete absence of Marxist cadres' (Jasny 1972, p. 33).

The relative liberalism of these economists also caused offence. Kondratiev and Yurovskii favoured broad indicative planning over precise prescription. One Central Committee member flung in Kondratiev's face the dire accusation that Kondratiev et al. had favoured 'general regulatory principles' over quantitative targets (Jasny 1972, p. 176). The more usual complaint was that 'plans had not been meticulously directive enough'. Rather than prepare 'meticulously directive' plans for others, as demanded by the prominent Bolshevik Valerian Kuibyshev (1888–1935), 'economists' advice under the circumstances tended to bring out the constraints upon political leaders' freedom of action' (Smolinski, 1971, p. 139).

The vulnerability was exposed by the tumult and distress created by crash collectivisation and industrialisation. In 1927 there were massive increases in investment, and a grain crisis at the close of the year. Stalin was convinced that an acceleration of industrialisation was required. Further to the Fifteenth Party Congress of December 1927 he announced a campaign against better-off peasants, and a drive for collectivisation. A very broad range of opinion – 'Right', 'Left', and non-Party – mounted 'passionate, persistent and authoritative' criticism of these policies (Davies 1989, p. 61).[8]

Kondratiev's 1927 paper 'Critical Remarks on the National Economic Development Plan' had scoffed at proposals for rapid industrialisation by a senior Party economist (Kondratiev 1998, 3, p. 296). In the journal of the Conjuncture Institute Kondratiev's deputy, Albert L. Vainshtein (1892–1970), became 'one of the most forthright critics' of the new programme (Davies 1989, p. 75).[9] In 1928 Yurovskii advocated a reduction in industrialisation goals as the only means to avoid inflation and shortages.

Stalin's consolidation of power, and the very failure of his new adherence to crash industrialisation, made these criticisms intolerable. In 1928 the Conjuncture Institute was transferred from Kondratiev's control, and then quickly abolished. In 1929 Yurovskii was removed as head of the foreign currency section of Narkomfin. By 1929 Chayanov had 'climbed down' with a public expression for support for collectivisation (Jasny 1972, p. 201).

The campaign against Kondratiev and his company extended to the methods that these people used. Statistics and mathematics were a signature of

Kondratiev and other non-Party organs, and in the spring of 1930 the teaching of mathematics and statistics in economics was drastically curtailed, despite bitter protests by students (Smolinski 1971, p. 151). Mathematical methods were damned as 'a "scientific" cover for fascism' (Davies 1989, p. 483). 'The limited predictive value of mathematical models was then used by their opponents as "conclusive" proof of their uselessness, even though the planners own "non-mathematical" predictions missed the targets by wider margins than the budding econometricians crudest forecasts' (Smolinski 1971, p. 149).[10]

In June 1930 Kondratiev, Yurovskii, Chayanov and Makarov were arrested on charges of sabotage and subversion. Stalin took a keen interest in their interrogations, and instructed the head of OGPU to 'Run Messrs Kondratiev, Yurovskii, Chayanov etc through the mill... interrogate them as strictly as possible' (Stalin 1995, p. 196). Kondratiev was interrogated by Yakov Saulovich Agranov, 'one of the most feared sadists of the Lubyanka' (Barnett 1998). Kondratiev 'confessed' to joining a non-existent party, the Toiling Peasants Party (TPP), as did Yurovskii and Chayanov. Their confessions on the imaginary TPP ran to script: the TPP met regularly to plan an armed insurrection, which, with the help of foreign forces, would restore capitalism, and install a government headed by Kondratiev. Chayanov's particular duty was to advise the TPP on 'how to disrupt the entire economic life of the country in the event of foreign intervention' (Lih et al. 1995, p. 193).

Stalin ordered the publication of a brochure – 'Materials on the Case of the Counter-Revolutionary *Toiling Peasants Party*' – that contained the transcripts of the interrogations of Kondratiev, Yurovskii, Makarov, Chayanov, and other arrested persons made from 27 July to 2 September 1930. The publication was widely distributed among party and state officials (Lih et al. 1995, p. 192).

Stalin also wanted a thorough investigation of the Commissariat of Finance and Gosbank. To Molotov he wrote 'it's obvious even to the blind that Yurovskii directed Finance's measures... the leadership of Gosbank and Finance has to be replaced with people from OGPU and the Worker-Peasant Inspection once these latter bodies have conducted some inspecting and checking up by punching people in the face... definitely shoot two or three dozen wreckers from these apparaty, including several dozen common cashiers' (Stalin 1995, pp. 200, 210).[11]

The execution of Kondratiev, Yurovskii and other 'economist-scoundrels', Stalin told Molotov, was absolutely necessary (Barnett 1995, p. 437). Stalin savoured the prospect of trial: 'how about Messrs Defendants admitting their mistakes and disgracing themselves politically, while simultaneously acknowledging the strength of the Soviet Government and the correctness of the method of collectivisation? It wouldn't be a bad thing if they did.' Yet Stalin hesitated: 'Hold off on the question of turning the Kondratiev affair to the courts. The matter is not completely without risk' (Stalin 1995, p. 218). In the event, secret OGPU courts sentenced Kondratiev to eight years' solitary confinement for 'Kulak-Professor' crimes. Yurovskii, Makarov and Chayanov received eight years each.

Kondratiev and Yurovskii were kept alive to incriminate others. Yurovskii was presented as a 'witness' in the trial of the so-called Industrial Party of December 1930 in which 'several engineers were accused of having organised a vast network of sabotage and espionage for the benefit of the French High Command' (Jasny 1972, p. 85). Kondratiev made an appearance as the (recanting) leader of the 'TPP' in the 'Menshevik Trial' of 1931, in which 14 Menshevik economists and administrators were accused of treason.[12] Menshevik observers interpreted Kondratiev's conduct as amounting to a 'full capitulation' to the interrogators of the Lubyanka, but that he was not as 'completely broken' as other defendants.

Kondratiev and his allies also served as folk-devils to personify the menace of 'Neo-narodnism' (that is, a championship of peasant interests). A campaign of vilification was launched against Kondratiev and 'Kondratievism'. Yurovskii, Kondratiev, and Makarov were 'open defenders of the Kulaks'; 'agents of world capitalism' (Jasny 1972, p. 32) who deliberately prepared wrong plans; who conveyed falsified (that is, true) data of the Soviet Union to 'foreign bourgeois institutions'. These accusations were compiled by dutiful party cadres into a special volume, a kind of festschrift of defamation; *Against Kondtratievschina, the Class War in Economic Theory* (of the Young Guard Library of the Young Communist League), and *Kondratievschina* (of the Agrarian Institute of the Communist Party).

In confinement Kondratiev was permitted to read, write and correspond, and at first remained mentally active. Later in the 1930s, still not 40, he went into a mental and physical decline. His naive (desperate?) pleas for release were refused. The Great Purge of 1937/8 doomed him. On 17 September 1938 he was shot. Yurovskii was released in 1934, and sought work as accountant and (anonymous) translator. He was re-arrested in 1937 and shot on 17 September 1938, the same day as Kondratiev. Chayanov was released in 1934 and granted permission to work in an agricultural institute in one of the geographical extremities of the Soviet Union. He was forbidden to have any contact with other members of the institute, and, in any case, was expelled in November 1935. In a written plea to its director he avowed that he 'wholly denied his former theory' and ' had brushed away all last remnants' of the 'petit bourgeois ideologist' he once was. 'I give myself in full disposal to Government and Party' (quoted in Bukhonova and Chilikova 1997). This tragic document afforded him no shelter. He was re-arrested in March 1937, sentenced on 3 October 1937 to the 'highest form of punishment', and shot the same day.[13]

The destruction of Soviet economics was not an isolated event: it was merely one point in a vast campaign of persecution of expertise that arrived with the confirmation of Stalin's power, and the frustrations he experienced in using it. From 1928 Taylorist management theorists had been 'baited', and killed (Beissinger 1988, p. 97); in 1929 the Academy of Sciences was purged; in 1930 came accusations that five prominent historians were preparing for a monarchist *coup d'état* (Davies 1989, p. 116), followed by a wave of dismissals and expulsions of historians; perhaps 7000 engineers had been arrested by spring 1931 (Davies 1989, p. 117), the Bolshevisation of physics was attempted; from 1940 orthodox geneticists such as Nikolai Ivanovich Vavilov were suppressed.

The destruction of Soviet economics went beyond the *Grande Tradition* and encompassed economists who by any normal criterion would be considered within the bounds of Marxist orthodoxy.[14] Thus the fundamental target was not this or that sort of economics, but *any* sort of economics at all. In keeping with this goal, one young Bolshevik economist patronised by Stalin, K.V. Ostrovityanov, announced that the Communist economy did not contain any material that political economy could study (Davies 1989, p. 160). In his *Economic Problems of Socialism in the USSR* Stalin himself made it plain that economics had nothing to do with economic policy.[15] 'Problems of the rational organisation of productive forces, the planning of the national economy, and so forth, should not be the subject of political economy but rather should be the subject of the economic policy of executive organs' (quoted in Beissinger 1988, p. 151); 'To foist upon political economy problems of economic policy' said Stalin 'is to kill it as a science' (Stalin [1952] 1972, p. 75).[16]

1930 saw the end of anything like economics for at least a generation in the Soviet Union. The perfect intellectual degeneracy of what passed for economic study in the succeeding generation has been described by a witness, Aron Katsenelinboigen:

> In the mid-1950s, discussions took place with the economics faculty of Moscow State University concerning the understanding of the law of 'planned proportional development' mentioned by Stalin in the work *Economic Problems of Socialism in the USSR*. These discussions were reduced to clarifying the grammar of this law. Some thought that the words 'planned' and 'proportional' should be separated by a comma, others that the second word must be put in parentheses, and still others that the words must be written out without any punctuation marks.
>
> (Katsenelinboigen 1980, p. 15)

Post-war Poland, Hungary and Czechoslovakia

The experience of economics in the Soviet Union in the 1930s was replicated in other countries where Stalinism triumphed after 1945. As in the Soviet Union the special position of the economic in Marxist ideology made the treatment of economics something of a leading indicator of Stalinist repression. This is well illustrated by the so-called 1948 'trial' of the Polish Central Planning Office (CUP).

The Polish CUP was established in 1945 and staffed with 'a substantial number of able economists of the younger and middle generations'; 'It became a centre of independent economic thought, in which the analytical methods of Western economics were applied... [the] language of modern economics...was used in the CUP' (Drewnowski 1979, pp. 24, 29). The CUP was also a 'stronghold' of the Polish Socialist Party (PPS), that was nominally in coalition with the communist Polish Workers Party (PPR), but was in 1948 in the process of being destroyed.

On 18 and 19 February 1948 a 'conference' between PPR and PPS on the CUP took place in the Council of Ministers' office, chaired by the Prime Minister. The conference assumed the form of a trial. The prosecutor in the 'trial' was the PPR Minister for Industry, Hilary Minc, who was soon to supervise the crash industrialisation of Poland.[17]

In the words of one witness to the trial, Jan Drewnowski,

> The trial of the CUP was the first full-scale presentation of the Stalinist mode of public life in Poland. For the first time we were told that modern economic science should be called 'bourgeois economics'... For the first time too, quotations from Marx, Lenin and Stalin were used out of context as magic formulae guaranteeing victory in debate... The beginning of Stalinism in Poland may be considered to be the so called 'CUP Trial'.
> (Drewnowski 1979, p. 33)

On 20 March 1948 came the verdict: all heads and chiefs of the CUP who were not members of the PPR were to be dismissed. The now derelict CUP was permitted to linger for one year, and was then abolished. All CUP archives were shredded; the institution was to be an unfact.

The campaign against economics did not end with the CUP. Hilary Minc declared the 'need to lead Marxism into the universities'. As a consequence, recalls Drewnowski (1979, p. 42) 'eight academic economists alone, known to me personally' were arrested and imprisoned for several years. 'The number of economic administration staff arrested at that time was, of course, incomparably greater. I do not even try to estimate it'. '*All* professors of economics lost their chairs', and were forbidden to lecture, give seminars or supervise.[18] The 'policy of humiliating economics' extended into institutional matters. The doctoral degree in economic administration was abolished; the Central School of Commerce in Warsaw was renamed, and a philosopher of law placed at its head. Drewnowski concludes: 'This is how Stalinism began in Poland' (Drewnowski 1979, p. 40; Porwit 1998, pp. 87–8).

In Hungary, too, the beginning of Stalinism was the end of economics. In 1949 all economists in the Hungarian Academy of Sciences were deprived of their membership. Other disciplines in the Academy were badly purged, but no discipline grouping comparable in size to economics was so totally extirpated (Péteri 1991). As one historian has written, 'Few other academic fields within the humanities and social sciences suffered so radical a *Gleich-schaltung* in the late 1940s. Except for a few professors in statistics and accountancy, the whole university professoriate was replaced by new communist cadres during the so-called university reform of 1948–49'(Péteri 1996, p. 367). The renowned Hungarian Institute for Economic Research was closed down (Péteri 1996). The sole and long-standing Hungarian theoretical economic journal, *Közgazdasági Szemle* (Economic Review), was discontinued in 1949 (Péteri 1997).

Czechoslovakia followed a similar path. With the communist coup of February 1948, Karel Engliš, the best known Czech economist of the time, was immediately relieved of his teaching positions, and exiled to his home village. Josef Macek, the second most prominent economist of the time, fled Czechoslovakia in December 1949, following media attacks on him, and just prior to his planned arrest.[19] Jan Novotny, founder of the post-war University of Economic Sciences, was demoted with a salary cut of 50 per cent, and emigrated in 1948. By 1952 all 'bourgeois' professors of economics had been expelled from universities, the Czech Economic Society had been disbanded, the National Economic Institute closed, and Novotny's University of Economic Sciences brought to an end (Albrecht 1999, 2000).

5.2 Nazism

The Third Reich makes a contrast with Stalinism. Anti-economics was integral to Stalinism. It was peripheral to Nazism.

The advent of National Socialism in 1933 badly damaged the human capital of economics in Germany as 'all economists who were of Jewish descent and/or had given political expression to their socialist or liberal convictions were expelled from the country' (Rieter and Schmolz 1993, p. 91). But these expulsions were on account of the economists' descent or politics, not their economics. The regime did ban, dismiss, interrogate, torture, and execute some of those who remained, but never on account of any offence caused by their economic views. The principal professional organisation of economists (the Verein für Sozialpolitik) was disbanded, but this was a consequence of the general policy of *Gleichschaltung* ('bringing into step'). Further, economists were not one of those professional groups (such as lawyers or teachers) subject to the contempt of the SS and the Reich leadership: and their discipline was not tainted by any association with a proscribed political party (as sociology had been tainted to some degree by association with the Social Democratic Party).[20]

The truth is that National Socialism had little interest in purely economic issues, and under the cold shade of this indifference economics subsisted and grew.[21] This is illustrated by the fact that Walter Eucken, the leading personality of the Tradition in the Third Reich, published his general treatise on principles in 1939, and was to see it through four editions by 1944.

This indifference was partly a matter of circumstance, and partly a consequence of ideology.

The matter of circumstance was the apparent economic success of the Third Reich. For about 10 years after 1933 there was little frustration in economic policy; often no gap between promise and achievement. There was no failure requiring scapegoats.

With regard to ideology, the economic had a very marginal place in Nazi ideology in massive contrast with Soviet socialism.[22] The basic stuff of National Socialist ideology was biology not economics, and here lay the great contrast with Marxism, where the economic was at the root of the theory. Over half of Stalin's library, for example, was composed of economic works, many with Stalin's notes and annotations.[23]

All this led to economics appearing insignificant and irrelevant in the Third Reich. And irrelevance was one of the less vulnerable situations.

A danger did lie in the potential for a fascist 'counter-economics' to emerge and displace the Tradition. The materials for the formation of such a counter-economics were there: the inheritance of the German Historical School (especially the identification of Judaism with capitalism by Sombart [1911] 1951), and the revival by Othmar Spann of a 'romantic' economics in the flavour of Adam Müller. Yet nothing significant materialised (see Röpke 1935). Even its well-wishers recognised this. Thus Sombart said of the would-be creators of such a counter-economics:

> The intentions of these writers are obviously the very best: their main point, the abandonment of the old 'Liberal' theory, is certainly excellent. When I read their writings, however, I often have the impression that the leaders of the 'new direction' lack complete insight into the problems of their subject. They are not quite sure of the main point. They do not know what the old Liberal theory really was, or what it led to, or wherein the old and new science of economics really differ.
>
> (Sombart 1939, p. 58)[24]

Rather than the development of a fascist counter-economics, the Third Reich saw a robust revival of the Tradition.[25] As a surprised Sombart put it in 1939: 'In fact, we are witnessing in Germany today the strange spectacle of the old Liberal economics, long pronounced dead, intruding once more with its law-making and schematisations, its obsolete learning disguised in new dress' (Sombart 1939, p. 59):

The leader of this revival was Walter Eucken (1891–1950). While his initial training had been in the Historical School, by the early 1920s he was working on the quantity theory of money, and the ideas of neoclassical theorists such as Böhm-Bawerk and Wicksell. Thus 'Eucken's works mark the return to (neo)classical theory in German economics' (Molsberger 1985, p. 195).

Eucken gathered into a seminar at Freiburg University sympathetic thinkers, including Franz Böhm (1895–1977) (at Freiburg 1933–38), Adolf Lampe (1897–1948), and Constantin von Dietze (1891–1973), a professor at Freiburg who had dissolved the Verein für Sozialpolitik rather than have it brought into conformity with Nazi notions. This seminar became the nucleus of the 'Freiburg School', that had three leading contentions:

1. *The methodology of economics.* The German Historical School's attraction to historicism and aversion to theory should be discarded (Eucken 1938, 1940).
2. *The autonomy of economics.* Economics should adopt a new posture of confidence in public policy formation. The deference of the GHS to non-economic considerations, as well as to political currents, was repudiated. The 'dethronement' of economics was protested. Economics was to be valued, and to value itself.
3. *The problem of special interests.* Special interests had warped economic policy.

Two contrasting solutions to this last problem seemed to present themselves. The first solution was the corporative state, explored and initially favoured by Erwin von Beckerath (1889–1966), his distinguished student Heinrich von Stackelberg (1905–46), and even (for a time) Franz Böhm. In a corporative state a formal juridical representation of all economic interests would prevent the exploitation of the state apparatus by vested interests. It would simulate the perfect market that neoclassical theorists analysed. As one of their number claimed in 1934 a 'corporative market produces the same result as perfect competition'.[26]

The second solution was the anti-monopoly state, favoured by Eucken. In this state one of the constitutional duties of the state would be the elimination of monopolies and anti-competitive practices.

By the early 1940s the former advocates of the corporative state had forsaken it, and had came to concur with Eucken. Stackelberg, for example, 'became a determined critic of every form of the planned economy. In a paper which he read to a small circle in 1943 . . . he elaborated this criticism from a mathematical point of view. He had come to the conclusion that the competitive order is the only principle by which the economic problems of our time can be solved' (Eucken 1948, p. 134). Stackelberg's last book *Grundlagen der Theoretischen Volkswirtschaftslehre* (1944) was, in Kenneth Boulding's judgement, 'on a par with the most simon-pure representation of the Chicago School'.

Thus it might be said that, after two generations of dormancy, the *Grande Tradition* suddenly re-emerged to grow in a totalitarian regime without interference. Here is an irony: while Kondratiev and his circle were dedicated to peaceful coexistence with the Soviet State,[27] but were executed on account of supposed conspiracy against it; the members of the Tradition in the Third Reich were (until a late date) free from persecution, but were in determined conspiracy against the Nazi state.

Following the anti-Jewish pogrom of 9 November 1938, Lampe, von Dietze, Eucken and Gerhard Ritter (a historian) formed what was later to be called the Freiburger Kreis. These four were to be the nucleus of three cells of the German Resistance; the 'Frieburg Konzil'; the 'Frieburger Bonhöffer Kreis'; and the 'Arbeitsgemeinschaft [working party] Erwin von Beckerath'. The 'Arbeitsgemeinschaft' was a discussion circle of economists that included, in addition to Böhm, Stackelberg and von Beckerath, Erich von Preiser (1900–67) and Günter Schmölders (1903–91),[28] the 'political economy specialist' of the 'Kreisau Circle', another ideological wing of the German Resistance (Roon 1971, p. 141). The 'Freiburg Konzil' was a generalist discussion group. The 'Freiburger Bonhöffer Kreis' linked Eucken and his academic colleagues to active conspirators, including Carl Goerdeler, who led the abortive attempt to assassinate Hitler.[29]

The Freiburger Kreis and its remaining extensions disintegrated in the wake of the events of 20 July 1944. Eucken was interrogated but, to the 'astonishment' of his fellow conspirators, not included in the huge sweep of arrests by the time they were suspended on 1 November 1944. Franz Böhm eluded arrest thanks to a name confusion. Dietze and Lampe were imprisoned, and saved from execution by the timely approach of the Red Army. Professor Jens Jessen (1896–1944), the editor of *Schmoller's Jahrbuch* and an economist with connections with the Freiburger Kreis, was not preserved by such good fortune and was executed on account of his close involvement in the 20 July conspiracy.[30] It was in these months that Himmler spoke of the need of a show trial of 'industrialists and economists' (Speer 1981, p. 111).

This belligerent posture of the leading members of the Tradition in Nazi Germany towards the regime distinguishes it from the posture of most other learned and professional groups.[31] Almost before the war had ended, certain retrospects on the Third Reich accused the learned and professional classes of Germany of being badly implicated in the catastrophe. Thus Wilhelm Röpke (1899–1966), who had been an economist at the University of Marburg before being driven into exile in 1933, wrote in the spring of 1945:

> There is scarcely another class in Germany that failed so fatally as that of the intellectuals in general...it was from the universities that most of the other intellectuals drew the disintegrating poison that they then distributed, duly packed and processed, to the mass of the people...the almost inexpiable guilt of many German university professors in preparing people's minds for the Nazi hordes, and later...to swallow its absurdest theories and even sing their praises.
>
> (Röpke 1960, pp. 346–7)

Later research gives little reason to soften this indictment. Investigations into medicine, psychiatry, law, history, archaeology, ethnography, geography, philosophy, theology, psychology, psychotherapy, and natural science have brought to light the animated and sometimes deadly allegiance that a section of each these categories gave the Third Reich, and the facile accommodation to Nazi ideology in each category of many more.[32] Whatever the undoubted range of responses, and whatever the vivid exceptions, the central tendency of the learned and the professional classes was one of ideological cooperation.[33] *La trahison des clercs.*

The Tradition did make a definite contrast to such a tendency of collaboration.[34] Why it made such a contrast is inevitably uncertain.

It may be that the source of this contrast lies in characteristics that are incidental, rather than essential, to the Tradition. Thus it may that it was the Christian devotion of the Kreis that was the formative influence on their actions, as its members sometimes suggested. 'I could neither live nor work if I did not believe that God existed' (Eucken in 1942, quoted in Rieter and Schmolz 1993, p. 105). Yet Christian allegiance in the abstract cannot be a complete explanation; German theology (with celebrated exceptions) proved less than impervious to Nazi ideology.

It may be that the source of the contrast lies in the offence that rationalistic, scientific neoclassical economics would take at the irrationalism that Nazism drew so much energy from.[35] Certainly, on occasion during the Third Reich, Eucken took upon himself the role of defender of reason. In October 1933, for example, Eucken published a paper entitled 'What is the Point of Thought?' that poured scorn on emotionalism, relativism, and irrationalism, and 'made him a *bête noire* for Nazi students' (Nicholls 1994, p. 64). But, however much neoclassical economics honours reason, and however much Nazism dishonoured it, it is also true that a commitment to neoclassical economics could be combined with a commitment to National Socialism. Thus before 1939, certainly, Stackelberg was committed to both. A commitment to neoclassical economics could also be combined with a commitment to Fascism (Luigi Amoroso). It could also be combined with a commitment to Communism; thus Leonid V. Kantorovich shared a totally neoclassical approach with a perfect (and sincere) subscription to Soviet Marxist-Leninism (Katsenelinboigen 1981).

Finally, it might be that the source of the belligerence of the Tradition to the regime lies in its sympathy and consciousness of the three principles mentioned at the beginning of the chapter: consumer sovereignty, the economic problem, and economic liberalism. Any valuation of these could only sit awkwardly with a toleration of political servitude.[36] The degree of dissonance of economic liberalism and political illiberalism is a matter of debate.[37] Yet what it is not arguable is that Stackelberg's embrace of economic liberalism broadly coincided with his disaffection with National Socialism.[38] The same can be said of Beckerath and Jessen.[39]

Part III

6
'The General Contagion of its Mechanic Philosophy'[1]

This chapter turns to irrationalist anti-economics; anti-economics provoked by the deductive, quantitative, scientific aspect of economics; anti-economics that is based on a mistrust of reason, and built on a faith in the non-rational.[2]

Irrationalist anti-economics crosses political boundaries; it has a Right form, and a Left form, but its most important expression is an essentially apolitical 'artistic' form. In its Right form, irrationalism sees scientific reason as destructive of good social order. In its Left form, irrationalism sees scientific reason as constructive of an oppressive social order. Finally, in its 'artistic' form an esteem of rationality is held to be harmful to personality, or even a product of damaged personality. Rationality is detrimental to 'creativity', stretching from fancy through imagination to finally reach the capacity for sympathy.

The Right form of irrationalism emerged in the wake of the French Revolution, and manifested itself in a corresponding form of anti-economics. The 'artistic' form of irrationalist anti-economics burgeoned about a generation later, in the early nineteenth century. The Marxist faith in science precluded a Left form of irrationalist anti-economics until after the mid-twentieth century, when the decline of Marxism allowed an eruption of irrationalist anti-economics on the Left.

The chapter ends with a demonstration of the way in which the irrationalism of many anti-economists, and the rationalism of economists, is manifested in the differing attitudes of the two groups to education; anti-economists generally were hostile to education, while economists were favourable towards it.

6.1 'The Jacquerie and the march of the mind'

From the vantage point of the Right in 1800, it would have appeared that the Enlightenment's project of progress through truth, obtained by reason, had proved a calamity. This project had not achieved truth, but revolution.

Autonomous, independent science, unguided but presuming to guide, was now seen as socially disruptive, and the Right now felt a pull towards anti-science. Thus Maistre denigrated Bacon, Coleridge submittted that it would take 500 Newtons to make one Shakespeare (Levere 1981, p. 26), and Cobbett declared he would learn more meteorology from 'some old shepherd' than any 'philosopher'.

The clash of conservative irrationalism with political economy's maintained commitment to the hopes of the Enlightenment is portrayed in Peacock's *Crotchet Castle* of 1831. The novel is set in rural England, with the violent 'Captain Swing' disturbances of rural labourers as the background. Gathered in Crotchet Castle for a weekend of disputation are a party of ideological antagonists. Reverend Folliot is a classics scholar, MacQuedy is a political economist. They tussle over the 'march of the mind'; Folliot is scathing, MacQuedy avid. The novel concludes with Crotchet Castle besieged by a mob of Captain Swing incendiaries.

FOLLIOT   Here is the Jacquerie. Here is the march of the mind with a witness.

MACQUEDY   Do you not see that you have brought disparates together? The Jacquerie and the march of the mind.

FOLLIOT   Not at all, sir. They are the same thing, under different names.
(Peacock [1831]1924, p. 199)

There are three paths by which the Reverend Folliot might have held 'the march of the mind' and the 'Jacquerie' to be the same thing.

1. Rationality is creative of truth and thereby destructive of the social order

There are false but useful propositions that cannot be rationally believed. There are socially useful fictions and illusions. The suggestion is ancient. That religion, for example, is a useful illusion was maintained by both Gibbon's Roman magistrates and Voltaire. The same sentiment is expressed by Mishan, in his case against economic growth, regarding normative codes and religious belief.

The repeated re-examinations...of fundamental questions about religion, ethics, crime, etcetera, with their unavoidable inconclusiveness, serve further to weaken the moral props of an already disintegrating society and to destroy a belief in divinity that once gave hope and comfort to many.
(Mishan 1969, p. 118)

But the doctrine of useful illusions and destructive realities has barely ever been squarely deployed by anti-economics. Perhaps the closest example is Galiani's complaint of the physiocrats that in saying that the high price of grain was beneficial they were not saying anything 'stupid', but something 'very seditious', since the kingdom rested upon the exploitation of the peasantry.[3]

What comes closest to the doctrine of destructive realities in contemporary anti-economics is the modern unease at an autonomous science possessed of its own rude dynamic. The aspiration behind this unease is to tame science; to put science in its place, so that it supports the 'norms' and 'values' of society, and is thus part of the community. Indeed, 'science' should be 'ideological' and community mythological. This vision of scientific function is rarely presented so: rather it is presented as ridding science of alien values. In truth, these misgivings about autonomous science are born of an actual (if unacknowledged) sense of the vulnerability of these 'norms' and 'values' to critical inquiry. Norms and values have just been substituted for heaven and hell. Such an aspiration to a tame science, observant of some approved set of norms, can be found in modern anti-economics (see Pusey 1991).

2. Rationality is destructive of truth and thereby destructive of the social order

There are true and useful propositions that cannot be rationally believed. Reason, unable to reach such useful truths, consequently forswears them, at a cost. And even if reason could so reach them, the incapable mass, unable itself to appreciate the reasons in favour of certain true and useful propositions, must forswear this truth, unless they accept the authority that can appreciate those reasons. But since the insistence on reason destroys authority, it must destroy any credit previously given by the mass to such truth. Thus reason (science, *philosophes*, intellectuals) is destructive of useful truth.

This thesis finds a classic illustration in the conviction of the Enlightenment as culpable for the French Revolution. The anti-economist Barruel included political economists among those *philosophes* whose rationalism corroded useful trust in political and religious authority prior to 1789:

> Quesnay and his adepts had especially taken to heart the instruction of the people... [and] that it was necessary to establish, especially in the countryside, free schools, where the children would be formed for different occupations...
>
> I fear that... the books and teachers sent by these philosophers yield the peasant less laborious than theoretical. I fear that they will make him lazy, vain, jealous, and soon reasoning seditiously, and finally rebellious.
> (Barruel 1800, pp. 379–81).

3. Scientific reason is destructive of social order

Here the claim is that a scientific reason cannot give credence to socially useful propositions. The prominent anti-economist Samuel Taylor Coleridge exemplifies the position. He believed the scientific reason embraced by the Enlightenment was empirical, abstract and mechanical, and each attribute was blameworthy in its social consequences.

Scientific reason is empirical.   The Enlightenment was inclined to an empiricism of commonplaces and an elevation of common sense, and political economy shared this inclination and elevation.[4] But to Coleridge empiricism did not penetrate beneath the surface. Thus Coleridge dismissed Newton as 'a lazy Looker-on on an external World' (Levere 1981, p. 26), and his optics as 'exceedingly superficial'. To Coleridge the empiricist tendency also had a subversive quality; anyone, Coleridge complained, could now presume to judge policy. Tom Paine found fame with his revolutionary *Common Sense*, but what society needed, held Coleridge, was not an abundance of corset makers deploying their common sense, but a caste of seers penetrating by their intuition deep beneath the surface. Regrettably, political economy contained nothing but the 'simplest common sense' (Coleridge 1956, 5, p. 442).

Scientific Reason is 'mechanical'.   The Enlightenment treated the world as a machine; a structure composed of parts. The development of analytic chemistry in the later eighteenth century, including the Daltonian chemistry which Coleridge despised, exemplified 'the mechanic philosophy'. As did economics: 'the political economy of the present and preceding century partake in the general contagion of its mechanic philosophy' (Coleridge 1972, p. 28). Unfortunately, the mechanic philosophy inspired a subversively liberal view of society.

> Can it then be the result of accident, that the Political Dogmata, the principles of which are notoriously affirm'd and supported in the writings of Locke... need only borrow a few terms from the mechanic philosophy to become a fac-simile of its doctrines? The independent atoms of the state of nature cluster around a common centre and *make* a convention, and that convention *makes* a constitution of Government; then the makers and the made make a contract, which ensures the former a right of breaking it whenever it shall seem good to them.
>
> (Coleridge 1956, 4, p. 761)

To Coleridge the world was a whole, but analytical methodology encouraged it to be, almost literally, torn apart.

Scientific reason is abstract   Here we touch upon the pre-eminent Right objection to scientific method. The Enlightenment, and political economy, had maintained that the only significant realities were general realities: the detail of time, place, history and culture were to be purged from consideration. Thus political economy, says Coleridge, is 'a science which begins with *abstractions*' (quoted in Morrow 1990, p. 102). To Coleridge's mind this abstract political economy had doleful consequences for governance:

> The physiocratic system promises to deduce all things, and everything relative to law and government, with mathematical exactness and certainty, from a few individual and self-evident principles...By this system...the observation of Times, Places, relative Bearings, History, national Customs and Character, is rendered superfluous: all, in short, which according to the common notion makes the attainment of legislative prudence a work of difficulty and long-continued effort, even for the acutest and most comprehensive minds.
>
> (Coleridge 1969b, p. 212)

The responsibility for the excesses of the French Revolution lay in a mule-monster 'composed of 1. Abstract reason and 2. Bestial passions' (quoted in Morrow 1990, p. 112). And political economy was part of the abstraction that fathered the monster:

> all the *epoch-forming* Revolutions of the Christian world, the revolutions of religion and with them the civil, social and domestic habits of the nations concerned, have coincided with rise and fall of metaphysical systems...At the commencement of the French Revolution, in the remotest villages every tongue was employed in echoing and enforcing the almost geometrical abstractions of the physiocratic politicians and economists.
>
> (Coleridge 1972, p. 16)

Coleridge expresses here what was to be a leading sentiment on the Right in the aftermath of the French Revolution; abstractions are 'ideological', and therefore disturbing.

From the French Revolution on, the anti-liberal Right was on guard against abstract method in economics, or anything else. Abstraction was prone to take away those differences in humanity on which the social order was built. Abstraction led towards simple conclusions, and simple conclusions make for simple ('radical') judgements. Abstraction discounted the complexity that prevented simple conclusions. A counter-rhetoric of complexity would prove useful for opportunist conservatives who wished to strike a wise posture of practical subtlety in the face of the world's intricacies, and to cast the economist as the terrible *simplificateur*.[5]

In exile in 1816 Napoleon growled 'If there were a monarchy made of granite, the abstractions of the economists would be enough to grind it to dust' (quoted in Herold 1955, p. 93). In the same year as Napoleon spoke, there formed at Cambridge a conservative circle around the clergymen William Whewell (1794–1866) and his close friend Richard Jones (1790–1855). Greatly admiring Coleridge, Whewell and friends were on a 'crusade against utilitarianism, atheism and radicalism', not to mention what Whewell called 'liberal revolutionism'. The error of these disturbing doctrines was traced to a narrow abstraction, and a remedy entrusted to broad inductions. The abstract methodology of Nassau Senior prompted Jones to a popular exposition of induction, which he thought would be 'useful to young persons and teach them not to talk and decide but to be modest and hold their tongues' (quoted in Williams 1991, p. 138). The 'visionary' Ricardian theory of rent would be disposed of by Jones's historical critique, *Essay on the Distribution of Wealth and on the Sources of Taxation* of 1831 (Rashid 1979). Whewell hoped this book would *'faire époque'* in economics and inaugurate an economics with sound empirical foundation. Whewell was not opposed to theory, or science, or mathematics; but the end result of this methodologising was the factual stew of Jones's *Essay.*

Later in the century an opposition to abstraction was favoured by the German Historical School (Schmoller, for example). Werner Sombart, perhaps the 'last' member of the GHS, articulated at length a hostility to isolating method in economics and the natural sciences, upon which he blamed the 'dissolution of European culture' (Ringer 1969, p. 388).

The Right's hostility to abstraction fathered a kindred hostility to mathematics in economics throughout the nineteenth century. *Blackwood's Edinburgh Magazine* (Fetter 1960, p. 89), Comte (Mauduit 1929, p. 92), the Sismondian Eugène Buret (Buret 1840, p. 15): all voiced their hostility to mathematics in economics at a time when there hardly was any. Ingram and Roscher reiterated the hostility.

This anti-liberal Right hostility to quantification can be paired with a liberal Right hostility, as fifteen years of Napoleonic despotism led some liberals to fault quantitative method. Napoleon hated political economy, but loved statistics. Say hated Napoleon and loved political economy, and it is not surprising to find Say distrustful of statistics. Say was precedent for the tendency for continental Liberals to believe that 'statistical' and 'state' were tied up by more than etymology. Quantitative methods were a tool of constructivist conceit, and so, whereas the anti-liberal right feared abstraction might question state prerogatives, the liberal right feared quantification might extend them. French liberals were aghast at quantitative methods used by, for example Walras (see Breton 1986), and argued against mathematical economics with arguments that are perfectly familiar today. Certain Austrians concurred. They anticipated the anti-mathematical strictures of several twentieth-century liberal anti-economists, such as Murray Rothbard.[6]

6.2 The illogical song

Romanticism

The Right's fear of science as destructive of social order was soon followed by a Romantic fear that the stress of science (and political economy) on rationality was destructive of personality and personal relations. To the Romantics it was good to feel, and any attempts to reason us out of our feeling are bad. This tendency of thought was expressed in a number of particular doctrines.

The most moderate expression of this belief in feeling was that rationality alone was insufficient mental equipment for life. In 1847 Toussenel urged 'A bit more love, and less science... "For it is not enough to have faith to save the world", said Christ, "it requires love"' (Toussenel 1847, pp. 264–5). Seven years later Dickens chastised political economy in a similar vein. In 'all the relations of this life' he declared 'there must enter something of feeling and sentiment... something which is not to be found in Mr McCulloch's dictionary... political economy is a mere skeleton unless it has a little human covering and fitting out, a little human bloom on it, and a little human warmth in it' (Dickens 1854, pp. 553, 558).

Advancing beyond the mere insufficiency of pure reason, the anti-economists also asserted that reason was far less important than feeling. Thus Comte proclaimed 'individual happiness and public welfare are far more dependent on the heart than on the intellect' (Comte 1875, 1, p. 11). Therefore reason should be subordinate in the presence of feeling. 'Feeling must control reason' announced Comte (1875, 1, p. 351). The 'logic of feelings' was to superintend the 'logic of reason'.[7] In the same vein Saint-Simonians urged society to be led by those 'particularly endowed with a capacity for sym-pathy. We most certainly do not claim that men who are to be given the responsibility of leading society should remain strangers to science, but science takes on a new character in their hands' (Enfantin [1828] 1972).

Regrettably, argued anti-economists, reason had subverted feeling. In the words of Robert Southey 'In came calculation, and out went feeling' (quoted in Williams 1967, p. 25). It was on these grounds that the poetry of Byron, Shelley and Wordsworth formed a common front against political economy.[8] The English novel was not excluded from this alliance. In *Hard Times* (1854) Charles Dickens pressed the notion that utilitarian reason (exemplified by political economy) is in a state of contest with the 'tender light of fancy' (Book II, Ch. 9).[9] Dickens wrote, 'My satire is against those who see figures and averages, and nothing else – the representatives of the wickedest and most enormous vice of this time' (Dickens [1854] 1990, p. 275). (This is underlined by the alternative titles of the novel, 'A Mere Question of Figures', 'Two and Two are Four'.) And political economy is one of 'the representatives' of this 'wickedest and most enormous vice'.

The vice of figures and averages corroded virtues, especially charity. Thus Dickens has Gradgrind (who had named two of his younger sons Adam Smith and Malthus) 'writing in the room with the deadly statistical clock, proving something no-doubt – probably, in the main, that the Good Samaritan was a Bad Economist' (Dickens [1854] 1990, p. 160). Dickens here articulates a favoured notion of Romantics: that calculation makes for less noble or elevated behaviour. Thus Wordsworth implores, 'Give all thou canst; high Heaven rejects the lore/Of nicely-calculated less or more' (Wordsworth 1922, 3.43). Marx speaks of 'icy egotistical calculation' in the *Communist Manifesto*, and in *The Jewish Question* 'calculation' and 'egotistical' are treated synonymously. Sismondi complained that 'the calculating mentality extends to children . . . it stifles the progress of the mind, artistic taste, letters and sciences; it corrupts the office holders of a free government' (quoted in Epsztein 1966, p. 115).[10]

Environmentalism

The Romantic objection to rationality has flared and flickered in the two centuries that have passed; but since 1970 it has found a renewed and intense expression in contemporary environmentalism.

Environmentalism has given new life to the Romantic notion that truths are 'to be apprehended and known as much by our feeling natures as by our intellectual powers', to quote the New Age anti-text *The Mystic Economist* (Hamilton 1994, p. 6). Feeling, rather than obstructing discovery, aids it. Coleridge had long before declared 'Deep thinking is attainable only by a man of deep feeling'.[11] Environmentalism has also revived the notion that rationality, calculation and maximisation may weaken morally meritorious commitments; in particular, meritorious commitments to the natural environment. The effort to put a sum on the value of nature may have a corrosive effect on the valuation. Steven Kelman in *What Price Incentives? Economists and the Environment* explains

> Were people constantly faced with questions such as 'How much money could get you to give up your freedom of speech?' or 'How much would you sell your vote for if you could?' the perceived value that the freedom to speak or the right to vote have would soon become devastated, as, in moments of weakness, people started saying 'Maybe it's not worth *so much* after all'.
>
> (Kelman 1981b, p. 74)

The very act of putting a price tag on 'the priceless' must cheapen it.

The environmentalist rejection of rationality goes beyond the argued corrosion it has on values; it extends to the claim that the irrational is somehow a valuable part of human identity. Thus in *The Mystic Economist*

It is not just the wilderness out there that we want to preserve but the wilderness within, the deep ground of being that has been progressively buried beneath layers of rationality, materialism and alienation since the time of the scientific-industrial revolution.

(Hamilton 1994, p. 10)

Regrettably, 'Modern economics relentlessly reinforces this alienation from the self' (Hamilton 1994, p. 167).[12] Consequently, 'practitioners of economics tend to display an extreme form of obsessive rationality involving suppression of their feeling natures and a deep split between their intellectual and emotional selves' (p. 6).

The logical song

Did political economists see 'figures and averages and nothing else', as Dickens claimed? Ricardo might be a useful test, as he would appear to epitomise the calculating tendency. Ricardo was once presented with a defence of Irish reliance on the potato on the grounds that potato crop failure was only occasional. He rebutted it thus:

The argument that the failure of the potato crop is only occasional... appears to me defective. Judging by my own feelings, if for five or six or seven years of easy competency with respect to food, I had to endure one year of famine and to witness the sufferings of my family and friends for that one dreadful year, I would rather that I had never been born.

(Ricardo 1952b, p. 238)

Rather than that economists see 'figures and averages, and nothing else' it may be retorted with more justice that anti-economists saw 'feeling and sentiment' and nothing else. Thus Macaulay wrote of Robert Southey, 'He judges of a theory... as men judge of a picture' (Macaulay [1830] 1865). Rather than a proposition being judged on its logical character, it was judged on its psychological accompaniments; whether it uplifted or depressed, whether its form was beautiful or ugly. Critics have passed the same judgement on Adam Müller: 'Müller led on by his pleasure in words, was very little concerned how far he believed the truth of his own phrases' (Bramsted 1967, p. 38).[13] Is this criticism of the literary mind completely obsolete?[14]

And rather than urge economists to put 'a little human bloom' on their doctrines, there may be more justice in appealing to anti-economists to put 'a little human bloom' on their own thoughts. The anti-economist is, often, not plump with charity. Toussenel's plea for 'a bit more love, and less science', for example, is set in the midst of raging against Protestants, capitalists and Jews.[15]

6.3 'The master tool of corporate enslavement'

Whereas Right irrationalism sees science as subversive of authority, Left irrationalism sees it as constructive of authority. Left irrationalism condemns science and expertise as tools of social control, holds scientific authority to be an extension of political authority, and sees technical experts, including economists, as the maintenance staff of the technology of power.

This Left hostility might be called Rousseauian, in that it was originally articulated by Rousseau. His notions obtained great notoriety, but little issue. It was not until the mid-nineteenth century that there arrived again the possibility of a resurgent Left opposition to science. By that time the Romantic movement, and its heirs, had already pressed a struggle of art against science. Almost simultaneously, and correlate, bohemianism presented a struggle of art against the social order. If art is against science, and if art is against the social order, then science is cast as the ally of the social order. Thus a Left anti-science in the mid-nineteenth century might have seemed imminent.

Yet the politicised left of the nineteenth century did not adopt Rousseauian–Romantic anti-science. Marx despised bohemians as the bourgeois at play, or as the politically unreliable 'jetsam and flotsam' of society. Revolutionary science was a more reliable tool than revolutionary art. In particular, Marx trusted 'materialist' science to subvert religion, and other ideals.[16]

It was only after the mid point of the twentieth century had passed that the Left's pro-science posture declined to the point of disappearance. Now any left posture on science is almost always Rousseauian. In the words of the author of *Against Economics*, '*science*' is a '*European capitalist institution*' of which '*human emancipation demands the almost total rejection*'; it is '*the master tool of corporate enslavement*', 'a cruelly misanthropic, misogynist and warlike force that has fostered only the terrifyingly oppressive climate of Big Brother and Organised Intolerance – *an adjunct of imperialism* . . . [etc.]' (Kanth 1997, p. 43). The functionaries and models of the IMF and so on are now all part of the bad Big Brother (see for example Cypher 1993).

6.4 'Schools for All'

This chapter has dealt with a fundamental fracture between irrationalist anti-economists (be they Right, Left or artistic) and the economists. There is a reagent for revealing this fracture: education. The political economists were supportive of education: they believed education was constructive of a good social order, and beneficial to personality. The anti-economists were, with some exceptions, hostile to education.

The economists and education

Adam Smith was one of the earliest advocates of state supported mass education.[17] In the *Wealth of Nations* he advocated the provision of education for common people to counteract the negative effects of division of labour on the mentality of the labourer. Thus education is formative of character. Turgot shared Smith's attraction to mass education, and in sympathy Condorcet in 1792 presented a scheme for schools for those of ages 6–10.

The next generation of classical economists put still more stress on education. Malthus believed it was a duty to 'provide instruction of the people'. He thought that such education would make for better life decisions, and less distress and so be constructive of a good social order. 'As concerns the education of the poor in particular, the radical theory of popular instruction is Malthusian in origin' (Halévy [1928] 1949a, p. 244). Pre-eminent among the long list of charities that benefited from Ricardo's patronage was Joseph Lancaster's scheme to relieve a constraining teacher shortage by training older children to instruct younger ones. In 1818 Henry Brougham with James Mill established an infant school movement under the slogan 'Schools for All'.

But the political economist most distinctively associated with education is William Ellis (1800–81). He was a co-author with John Stuart Mill of essays on political economy, and a convinced Ricardian. He was dismayed by the 'the deplorable ignorance of the population'. With William Lovett, the Chartist, as his co-director, he established seven 'Ellis Birbeck' schools. These dispensed with corporal punishment, were low cost, and non-sectarian. The questioning style was to be a hallmark of their method.

> Mr Ellis always made the boys reason for themselves as far as possible, his questions merely suggesting the course which their reasoning should follow...thus, they were not taught the definitions dogmatically, but were led to invent and agree to them.
>
> (A contemporary observer quoted in Sockwell 1994, p. 158)

It was these schools that were subject to slanderous caricature by Dickens (and others) as Gradgrind schools.[18]

Further, the political economists did not rely only on market forces to provide education. McCulloch believed that 'one of the most pressing duties' of government is to provide 'elementary instruction for all classes'. Senior held 'that it is as much the duty of the community to see that the child is educated as it is to see that it is fed; that unless the community can and will compel the parent...to educate the child, the community must do so' (quoted in Levy 1970, p. 185). J.S. Mill avowed 'I hold it, therefore, the duty of government to supply...pecuniary support to elementary schools, such as to render them accessible to all the children of the poor' (Mill [1848] 1965b, V, xi, 8, p. 950).

The anti-economists and education

There was a strong tendency for anti-economists to disdain education.

In *Du Pain et du Bled* Linguet denigrated the physiocrats' proposals to teach peasants how to read and write on the grounds that it would make them querulous, and resentful of their unfortunate station in life (1774, pp. 297–301). To Bonald, 'the people needed education for religion, morals and health, but not for literacy' (Beik 1956, p. 80). Comte's own attitude towards education and schooling was not warm. He wished that up to the age of 14 children should be educated at home by their mothers, and over the following 7 years they were to be instructed by 'priests'.

Coleridge groused 'it may be a justifiable expedient, but per se, the conception of public Infant Schools seems to me most miserably mistaken' (Coleridge 1969d, p. 311).[19] Wordsworth was similarly dubious of the value of education for the lower classes (see Todd 1957). Hazlitt mocked proposals to educate the children of the poor on the grounds that it would encourage them to read bad books (Winch 1996, p. 308). Cobbett heaped scorn on the proposals to educate the poor on the same grounds (Cobbett 1835, p. 297). Alison pressed the 'demoralising' aspect of literacy further. Whereas Say and Malthus believed education reduced crime, Alison believed the experience of France taught the opposite: 'in the whole eighty-six departments ... it has been found that, with hardly one single exception, the amount of crime is *just in proportion to the degree of instruction which prevails*; and that it [crime] is nowhere so prevalent as in those towns and departments where education has been carried to the highest pitch' (Alison 1840, 2, p. 320). Ruskin spoke 'lightly' of the three Rs, and proposed that even education in reading be made optional.

Economists, therefore, were forthright advocates of education; while many (though not all) of their leading adversaries were opponents of education.[20] But, in yet another testimony to the perversity of anti-economics, economists have been censured for not sufficiently supporting education. Inglis writes, 'When they came to discuss what children should be taught, they were hardly less narrow-minded than Hannah More' (Inglis 1971, p. 393). This is an indecently misleading comparison. Consider Hannah More's own description of her syllabus: 'My plan for instructing the poor is very limited and strict. They learn of week days such coarse works as may fit them for servants. I allow no writing' (quoted in Owen 1964, p. 92). It is Ruskin, and his company, who are properly bracketed with Hannah More.

7
Moral Economy[1]

'Moralism' is the doctrine that morality is the supreme and necessary resource for the comprehension and solution to the world's problems. It is in moralism that economics finds one of its most uncomprehending, gloomy and malevolent adversaries. This enmity is fated on account of economics' attraction to science, and moralism's repulsion from it. To science the world will be made better by knowing more; to the moralist the world will made better by becoming more moral. So whereas to the scientist economics is a system of knowledge, to the moralist economics should be 'but a system of conduct and legislature' (Ruskin quoted in Groenewegen 2000, p. 5).[2] In as much as economics has thrown its lot in with science, the claims of economics, however logically drawn from its premises, and however circumstantially true, will be without significance to the moralist. And until economics forsakes science, the moralist will be disaffected and confounded by it.

Economics as a scientific endeavour can never prosper in a mental climate permeated by moralism, and it is no coincidence that economics emerged in the eighteenth century when moralism was at bay. It was only early in the nineteenth century, heralded by Robert Southey's appeal for a 'moral economy', that moralistic anti-economics swelled with the resurgence of moralistic, anti-scientific cosmologies.[3] Yet in that century moralism did little battle purely on its own account, but instead made itself effective in alliance with other forces, often political. In the nineteenth century moralistic economics was a weapon of the Right. The Left, despite its bitter sense of injustice, was, as inheritor of the eighteenth century, confident in its ability to win its battles on scientific terrain. We venture that it was only in the later twentieth century that Marxism lost its confidence (or interest) in winning in terms of science, and the Left turned to moralism, and the subordination of the scientific. This shift was followed by a revival of the anti-liberal Right's old ethic of *'richesse oblige'* in such modern guises as 'corporate responsibility'. The Left and the Right are now conjoined in their attachment to moralism. Thus at the opening of the twenty-first century moralism remains a glowing forge of anti-economics.

The chapter begins with an elucidation of the grounds of the quarrel between the economist and moralist. It then examines the genesis of the quarrel in the nineteenth century, the annexation of the moralistic critique by the Right, and its extension to the Left since the mid-twentieth century.

7.1 The moralist and the scientist

The moralist's cosmology

The moralist thesis rests upon a certain cosmology, that a pure form can be summarised under three headings.

1. The universe is morally saturated (moral immanence)

Every action has a certain degree of moral worth (or unworthiness). Further, persons tend either to worthy actions, or to unworthy actions. Crudely put: people are divided into the good and the bad.

2. Morality and immorality are powerful (moral moment)

Good and evil are a power for good and ill. Good things must come from persons seeking to do good, or systems designed to do good. Good things come from good intentions. Conversely, bad things come from bad intentions: poverty, for example, is to be explained by some sort of robbery, theft, or wrongdoing.

The doctrine of the power of good and evil finds a companion doctrine in the thesis of the power of ideals, or 'ideologism'. In this doctrine the shapers of history are held to be 'ideals': ideologies and faiths. The turbulence of events is explained by the conflict between different ideologies and faiths. Knowledge, positive knowledge, is merely an inert atmosphere in which events take place. To ideologism history is a record of the war of 'religions'.

3. Morality must ultimately prevail (moral optimism)

The moralist is a 'moral optimist' in that good can and will win the battle against wrong. Righteousness can win the day if only it puts its troops to the field.

There are several implications of this optimism.

1. People can be made good; thus the moral reformationists such as Comtians and Saint-Simonians.
2. Wrongs are redressable. Injustices can be 'corrected'. The wrongdoer can be brought to justice. Indeed, every injustice can be corrected, and no wrongdoing need be accepted as beyond redress and reparation.

3. The good are fortunate. Or, at least, they will be fortunate. So the righteous will triumph, the meek will inherit the earth, the expropriated will expropriate the expropriators, and so on. Correspondingly, the bad are (or will be) unfortunate: they are consigned to perdition at the hands of God or nature or history.

Six conflicts with the scientific cosmology

The moralist cosmology can easily be paired with a scientific cosmology that would substitute 'rationality' for 'morality'. Thus the scientific cosmology holds that the world is saturated with rationality, rationality is powerful, and ultimately rationality will prevail. These two cosmologies are not congruent, and collide at six points.

1. The source of the world's banes. Whereas to the moralist wrongdoing is the problem, to the scientist ignorance is the problem.[4] Whereas the moralist discounts ignorance, the scientist discounts wrongdoing. And each faults the other for the consequences of their position. To the moralist, science, by neglecting evil, has thereby abetted it.[5] To the scientist, moralism, by neglecting ignorance, has thereby abetted it.

2. The reach of the world's banes. In the minds of moralists the problem of evil extends to knowledge; that is, some knowledge is evil, or at least corrupting. In the mind of the scientist the problem of knowledge extends to morals: that is, some good and bad are unknown.

3. The source of the world's remedies. The moralist's remedy is better morals; the scientist's remedy is more enlightenment. And, as betterment springs from the love of good, the moralist believes we should love not just good, we should love the love of good, so as to nurture the love of good. This love of the love of good is characteristic of the moralist. The scientist believes that, as good things come from the love of knowledge, we should not just love knowledge, we should love the love of knowledge. This esteem of the relish of knowledge is characteristic of the scientist.

While the moralist is optimistic about good defeating evil; the scientist is optimistic about giving reason to mystery. Whereas to the moralist life's great activity is the crusade against, and judgement upon the wrongdoer, to science life's great activity is the extension of knowledge. To the moralist, science is at best a distraction from, and at worst a solvent of, his crusade.[6]

In its stance on the remedy of the world's ills moralism is once again accompanied by ideologism. Like moralism, ideologism scoffs at knowledge as a source of progress. Ideologism worships at the 'cult of culture', which has science removed from any responsibility for human achievement. Ideologism does *not* appeal for science to replace ideology. It is nihilistic about the possibility of science. It appeals to economics to abandon the pretence of science, and to admit to itself its foundation in ideology, faith and values. Thus, unlike moralism, ideologism does not see science as an abstraction, but as a pretence. Whereas moralism sees science as diversionary and distracting, ideologism sees science as non-existent.

4. The reach of the world's remedies. To the moralist, morality assists knowledge. To the scientist, knowledge assists morality.

5. The location of personal distinction and superiority. To the moralist persons are distinguished from one another by whether they are good or bad, rather than knowing or ignorant. To the scientist persons are distinguished by whether they are knowing or ignorant, rather than good or bad. The moralist chastises people for being bad; the scientist scolds people for being irrational. And each is vexed by the other's source of self-esteem. The scientist resent the moralist's presumption of righteousness; the moralist resents the scientist's presumption of objectivity.

6. The relationship, or lack of it, between what is and what ought to be. The moralist and the scientist are deeply divided over an epistemological thesis variously known as the 'fact/value divide', the 'positive/normative distinction', or 'Hume's fork'. This thesis is a thesis of irrelevance.

'Normative truths are irrelevant to the truth of positive claims'.

The distinction slights moral moment.[7] It makes a gate that bars the entrance of morality into science, and amounts to dismissing the moralist as an irrelevance. It effectively bids the moralist to be silent on matters which seem to be of great significance. The moralist, however, believes in the significance of their values, and believes they have a purchase on events.

In fact, the moralist is entitled, by his/her own premises, to reject the distinction since, by the moralist's own premises, the state of the world is shaped by the relative strength of good and evil. Thus to explain why things *are*, it will be informative to know what *should be*. Therefore the notion that the 'is' be explicable and predictable independent of the 'ought' falls away; knowledge of the 'ought' and the 'is' are joined. As Ely put it, 'What exists now as a mere matter of course was once a future ideal, or, to use more technical language, the "Is" includes what was once "ought-to-be"' (Ely 1891, p. 102).

The scientist will, however, remain confident in the distinction, and will, with justice, hold little store by wishful theses about the power of morality that are required to threaten it. However, this victory of the scientist may lack sheen. Truth as mere truth, is not quite the prize it may seem. There is trivial truth, passing truth and shallow truth. The scientist is presumably seeking to avoid shallow, contingent or trivial truth. If such important truth is to be obtained without morality then a 'significance form' of the positive/normative distinction is required.

'Normative truths are irrelevant to the significance of positive claims'.

In affirming this version of the distinction the scientist is affirming that there exists a great realm of positive truth which retains significance under distinctly different value systems. This realm of positive truth is something we can discuss, agree upon and put store by, despite our enduring moral disagreements. In seeking to discover this realm, morals are not being discounted or ignored; on the contrary, values will be served by the discovery of this realm.

In denying this distinction, the moralist is maintaining that there is no significant portion of positive truth to which persons under significantly different value systems would attach significance.[8] The moralist, therefore, puts us in mind of a hypothetical seventeenth-century Christian who might allow black magic to be positive knowledge, but would never allow it to be knowledge that the righteous would wish to know. Or, to illustrate in more modern terms, its puts us in mind of the environmentalist who allows that economics comprehends positive knowledge of certain constructs (such as GDP), but would deny that such knowledge holds any significance to the morally enlightened.[9]

The scientist may retort that truths about human nature must be of significance under different value systems on the grounds that we are stuck with human nature. But this moralist denies 'human nature'. The moralist has faith in the plasticity of human behaviour to moralising, and therefore sees propriety in no way beholden to truths regarding current human behaviours.

7.2 The moralist against the economist

The economist is not a moralist[10] There are several elements of the moralist's cosmology to which the economist cannot adhere.

Every action has a certain degree of moral worth (or unworthiness). The economists' typical disclaimer of any expert moral knowledge means that they, as economists, could not affirm this. Their 'atheism' with respect to social justice is typical of this disclaimer (Hayek 1976).

Persons tend either to worthy actions, or to unworthy actions. The uniformitarian presumption by economists regarding self-interest does not accommodate divisions of humanity into good or bad. It was in this vein that Bentham averred that all men are equal in their cordial devotion to themselves. If self-interest is bad, we are all bad. Further, the favoured reductionism of economics tends to bring everything down to prices, rather than different mores, to explain actions: the tax evader evades tax because they face different incentives from the non-evader.

Good things come from good intentions, and bad things from bad intentions.
The economists' cosmology denies such a significance of intentions to do
good or ill. Good things happen without them being intended by the good;
Smith's 'invisible hand' is the leading example of this. Indeed, in the competitive market system most things, whether good or bad, come about without
anybody intending it. This is because prices in competitive markets are not
shaped by the intentions of the good to achieve a 'good' price, or the bad to
achieve a 'bad' price. Prices are not shaped by any intention about prices at all,
since price is entirely beyond the control of any actor.[11] As prices are critical
in economic activity we are left with the conclusion that reality in general is not
'intended'.[12] And since it is only intended actions that are governed by the
'ought', the explanation of the 'is' seems not to require the 'ought'.

The source and remedies of the world's banes. To the economist the ultimate
problem is what Senior diagnosed to be Ireland's ultimate problem:
'IGNORANCE' (see Black 1960, p. 23). The ultimate remedy is enlightenment. By contrast, the moralising anti-economist believes the remedy lies in
improved morality. A pure articulation of this position comes from the anti-
economist R.H. Tawney (1880–1962).[13]

> What is needed for the improvement of society is not so much that men
> should have profound information as to the possible result of their actions,
> but that they should have a keen sense of right and wrong, that they should
> realise the conceptions of 'right' and 'wrong' apply to *all* relations of life.
> (Tawney 1972, p. 30)

Tawney's words display the moralist's elevation of moral sensibility over
mere 'information', and their identification of the source, and remedy, of
the world's banes.[14] 'The heart of the problem is not economic', wrote
Tawney, 'It is a question of *moral relationships*' (quoted in Martin 1985,
p. 85). 'There is no such thing' he added 'as a science of economics, nor ever
will be. It is just cant' (Tawney 1972, p. 72).[15]

The location of personal distinction. The moralising anti-economist believes
personal superiority (or inferiority) lies in values. This position is manifested
in the 'value gap' thesis that is popular with anti-economists. The thesis
states that economists do not think differently from non-economists on
account of knowing more. They think differently on account of their valuing
differently. Thus neoclassical economics is a 'sub-species of the philosophy
of liberalism with…one ultimate value, which is "freedom"' (Carroll 1992, p. 7).

7.3 Moralism resurgent

It is not coincidental that economics germinated in the eighteenth century
when moralism was in recess. During the Enlightenment the contentions of

moralism were discounted or refused. In epistemological terms, the relevance of moral truths to factual truths had been denied by Hume. In cosmological terms, a moral saturation of the universe (moral immanence) was diluted with the advance of toleration, and a withering of the sense of evil (Macfarlane 1987, pp. 100–3).

> The word 'evil'... begins in the second half of the 18th century to be used as a synonym for dyspepsia and diarrhoea, and turns up in advertisements for 'anti scorbutic drops', guaranteed effective against 'scurvy, leprosy, ulcers, the evil, fistula, [and] Piles'.
>
> (Delbanco 1995, p. 76)[16]

Satan in the eighteenth century becomes the sleek, cynical, witty Mephisto.[17]

The political economists shared this sense of distance from evil. By our standards they seem to have had an illusory sense of security about it. Smith's teacher Francis Hutcheson taught that all humanity was endowed with a moral sense, and that purely malicious conduct is unknown (see Fiering 1976, p. 207). Hume in the same vein maintained that 'absolute, unprovoked, disinterested malice has never, perhaps, place in any human breast' (quoted in Fiering 1976, p. 210). To Smith 'the most hardened violator of the laws of society' is not altogether without compassion ([1759] 1979, p. 9).

The political economists' loss of a sense of evil was congruent with their view that the springs of action were banal in moral terms, and not susceptible to moral approval or disapproval. Montesquieu's monarchy was powered by honour, not virtue. To the economists the economy was powered by neither virtue, vice, nor honour.

This decline in moral immanence was accompanied by the corrosion of moral moment, and the significance of moral agency, under the new scientific cosmology. The clockwork universe of the scientific revolution seemed to have no power for good or evil. The social mechanism turned devoid of any will of its parts.

The decay of a moralist cosmology meant the political economists, in keeping with the Enlightenment, were not interested in moral reformation. Ignorance was the problem, not iniquity.[18] The great remedy was to be enlightenment, and political economy was to be one part of it. With some justice, therefore, Rousseau complained in 1750 that while the ancients talked of morals, the moderns talked only of money.

The advent of the nineteenth century saw a revival of moralism. On the excited margins of the Right, moral immanence made a spectacular resurgence through the resurrection of a literal belief in Satan. Maistre set the example with his invocation of Satan in the French Revolution. Several of the most significant Right anti-economists of the nineteenth century subscribed to such a belief of Satanic immanence. As Carlyle said, 'the very Devil is in it' (Carlyle [1849] 1899a, p. 356).

Coleridge had a sincere and heartfelt belief in the existence of Satan, although he disclaimed any personal acquaintance. Ruskin believed 'to see the Devil *clearly* is in the 19th Century all that less than Saints can hope for' (Watson 1972, p. 68).[19] 'Emerson is said to have angered Carlyle, on a visit to London, for not believing in the Devil, and he showed him slums, gin-shops and finally the House of Commons, asking him at every turn: "Do you believe in a devil noo?"' (Watson 1973, p. 252). To Richard Oastler the New Poor Law was 'fiend-begotten', its sympathisers the 'anti-Christ', and 'political economy' just one of the guises of 'the Demon'.[20] Sombart, a self-identified twentieth-century heir to Ruskin and Carlyle, also revealed in his anti-economics a literal belief in Satan.[21]

The emotional underlay to this revival of moral immanence lay in a new mood set by the revulsion and euphoria evoked by the savage and extraordinary close of the eighteenth century. Complacency gave way to urgency. The age of taste gave way to an age of feeling. The criteria of judgement became warmer. The Augustan axis, with the 'imposing' at one pole and the 'paltry' at the other, gave way to more charged, and less controlled, responses of delight and disgust. Whereas the Enlightenment attended or dismissed, the new century condemned or embraced.[22]

This renewed belief in moral immanence was reinforced – and made important – by the decline of mechanical cosmology between the eighteenth and the nineteenth centuries. Whereas, the eighteenth century saw the social world as an impersonal system, a clockwork, the nineteenth century baulked at such a depiction. The machine was the great metaphorical adversary of the romantic mood. In Carlyle the 'mechanical' is gimcrack, and anything which operated without the imprint of a personal will was 'mechanical'. Democracy was mechanical; constitutionalism was mechanical.

The nineteenth century was drawn to see the world as a stage, rather than machine. The world is a plot line, rather than a process; a drama of actors rather than the operations of a system. Burke's presentation of the events of the French Revolution as a piece of theatre is an inaugurating illustration of this (Carlson 1991). This 'dramatic vision' lent itself to moralism, as a moralist interpretation of the world is impossible without individual choices being significant; without the world being shaped by individuals making worthy or unworthy decisions. The economist's vision, where the market is not the result of an individual will, will remain alien to those absorbed by the dramatic vision.

It is not surprising that those beholden to the dramatic vision both moralised the market, and used dramatic form to convey their morals. In the 1840s and 1850s the 'condition of England' novels, of which *Hard Times* is the greatest example, exploited the novel form to urge various anti-market morals. These novels include a number of specimens of anti-economics. In *Hard Times* the dismal Dr Gradgrind names two of his younger sons Malthus and Adam Smith. *Michael Armstrong the Factory Boy* by Frances Trollope ('quite the worst-written early Victorian novel in print', Jefferson 1972, p. 194) tells of a diabolic factory master, Elgood Sharpton, whose Deep Valley Mill produces a human misery '*incomparably more severe*, than ever produced by negro slavery' (Trollope [1840] 1968, p. 186). 'The political economists of the nineteenth century' we read 'ought to erect a statue to Elgood Sharpton' (Trollope [1840] 1968, p. 120).

But the great epitome of a moral tale is not *Michael Armstrong the Factory Boy*, but *Capital*. One critic has said of *Capital*, 'Unless we grasp it as drama, and in fact as one of the most dramatic books of modern times, we shall comprehend neither the powerful influence that it has exerted upon history nor its basic underlying significance. It is, moreover, drama in the tragic mood' (Tucker 1972, p. 204).[23] *Capital* is, indeed, a 'romance plot'.

There emerges in *Capital* a vision of a class divided society as two great class-selves at war – the infinitely greedy, despotic, exploiting, vicious werewolf-self of capital (Kapitalseele) on the one hand, and the exploited, enslaved, tormented, rebellious productive self of labour on the other.

The interpretation of *Capital* as a dramatic form is underlined by the way Marx presents himself at certain points as a kind of Shakespearean chorus (for example, Marx [1887] 1954, p. 172). Marx was fascinated by Shakespeare. His son-in-law recalled 'His respect for Shakespeare was boundless. His whole family had a real cult of the great English dramatist.' Eleanor Marx recalled that Shakespeare 'was the Bible of our house, seldom out of our hands or mouths' (quoted in Halle 1965, p. 33). Marx believed Timon of Athens' diatribe about gold 'excellently depicts the real nature of money'. As one critic notes, 'There is no critical distance; there are no qualifications. Shakespeare's text is, as far as Marx is concerned, a presentation of the truth' (Watts 1990, p. 28).

To his children Marx taught his moral fables in a literally dramatic manner. Hans Rockle was a 'a magician who kept a toy shop, and who was always "hard up". His shop was full of the most wonderful things ... And though he was a magician, Hans could never meet his obligations either to the devil or to the butcher, and was therefore – much against the grain – constantly obliged to sell his toys to the devil' (Eleanor Marx quoted in Halle 1965, p. 33).

A Righteous Right

The reappearance after 1789 of a belief in the power of moral agency lent itself most easily to the anti-liberal Right, as it suggested the world was needful of some supreme moral authority. A natural development of this suggestion was to suppose that such an authority would be exercised in economic questions by an ancillary moral authority; a 'moral economy'. Thus there emerged in the early nineteenth century among Right anti-economists an aspiration to supplant an 'immoral economy' with a moral one.

Villeneuve-Bargemont announced an ambition to 'remoralise' political economy. Joseph Droz, a sympathiser of Villeneuve-Bargemont, wrote in 1841 'political economy well conceived will always be the auxiliary of morals' (quoted in Epsztein 1966, p. 121). Coux complained that 'The contempt of moral wealth' is 'one of the distinctive characteristics of the school of Adam Smith', and demanded that political economy no longer 'exempt itself' from the issues of right and wrong (Coux 1832, p. 45).

In England it was the Tory Robert Southey who demanded a 'moral' economy, to replace the old 'political' economy of advantage and guile. It was conservative William Whewell who baptised Richard Jones's counter-economics, 'the *ethical* school' (Schaffer 1991, p. 224). Frances Trollope's censures of political economy's moral sightlessness were accompanied by a distinct solicitude for the traditional land-owning class. Dickens' political position shifted distinctly towards the right from the 1840s in the wake of his discovery and burgeoning admiration of Carlyle: *Hard Times* was dedicated to Carlyle (Goldberg 1972). The burning moralism of Carlyle and Ruskin was accompanied by a far Right stance.

Nineteenth-century English political economy sought to deflect the furies of Right poets, 'condition of England' novelists, and sages by stressing the distance between political economy and justice. Senior, and Mill less distinctly, contended that moral truths are one thing and factual truths are another.[24] The mistake of Wordsworth and others was to miss this. 'The distinction between "is" and "ought" statements is essential, though difficult to sustain, in any scientific discourse which concerns men in society. In Wordsworth the two levels of discourse are fused' (Winch 1970, p. 19).

Later in the nineteenth century the English economists also advanced the fact/value divide in 'reverse form', so that positive truths were held to be irrelevant to the truth of normative claims (Cairnes [1873] 1965). This reverse formulation may be seen as a peace-offering by orthodox economists to those who had been offended by claims that the morality of laissez-faire can be justified by reference to political economy. In either form, ordinary or reverse, the stress on the fact/value distinction was a manoeuvre by economists to make economics a smaller target for moralism.

But the classical economists' attempt to deploy the fact/value distinction to protect economics from attack became a provocation to attack itself; this square distinction between fact and value was dismissed as a pretension to objectivity.[25] The 'ideologism' of Schmoller rejected any objective character of economists. In Schmoller's opinion, 'the smaller part of the teachings of political economy consists of scientifically established propositions; the larger part of dogmas which are believed by some and rejected by others according to party sympathies' (quoted in Dawson 1890, p. 2).[26]

The German Historical School did not hesitate to speak on both fact and value, and indeed had little regard for the difference. In Schmoller, 'social and economic studies were fused with the framing of policies for social reform, with little or no regard to any distinction or demarcation between positive and normative and, the nature of the economist's "authority" in the one field as compared with the other' (Hutchison 1964, p. 43).

All the sober-minded 'historical schools' of the later nineteenth century favoured a moralistic anti-economics. These were paternalist in philosophy, and that philosophy lent itself very easily to a vision of society as morally saturated: society was a mass of bonds and duties.[27] As a consequence, practical political economy to Ingram amounted to a 'generally accepted code of social duties', and Toynbee, Foxwell (and Tawney) shared this picture. Since justice underlies duty they were logically led to conclude, 'At the basis of economics lies the question, What is just?' (Lilly and Devas 1904, p. xx).[28] And if justice is part of the province of knowledge for economists, then economists are entitled to speak as economists on justice. Economics, proclaim Lilly and Devas, is 'a chapter in the Philosophy of Right'.

The Left leaves science for justice

Nineteenth-century moralism, therefore, was a resource of the Right, not the Left. It was the Right, not the Left, that made a figure of menace of Satan; the Left of the nineteenth century were inclined to make a hero of Satan, as he represented rebellion.[29] It was the Right not the Left, who saw appeals to morality as complementary to their stress on order, and their deprecation of licentious liberty.

Marx, certainly, rejected some fundamental contentions of the moralist cosmology (see Polanyi 1962; Tucker 1972, pp. 14–16). Despite his own surging indignation, he shunned moral immanence: he avoided moral judgements; he did not even convict capitalism of injustice, or of denial of right (Tucker 1972, p. 19). He was contemptuous of moral moment. He scorned the love of the love of good that it implied. He rejected the notion that good (or bad) comes from people willing good (or bad). But he was, undeniably, a moral optimist, and one of an extreme kind. Marx saw nineteenth-century society as a hateful feasting of predator upon prey, but was convinced that the outcome would be just: the guilty would be vanquished. He displayed his grim satisfaction at the prospective triumph of good in a bloody metaphor involving the *Vehmgericht*: the secret tribunals of medieval Germany that arrogated many of the functions of government. 'If a red cross was seen marked on a house, people knew that its owner was doomed by the Vehmgericht. All the houses of Europe are now marked with the mysterious red cross. History is the judge – its executioner is the proletarian' (Tucker 1972, p. 15). Yet Marx believed the good would come without anyone intending it: a kind of invisible hand in justice. The proletarian revolutionary is not 'good'; he is in Marx's metaphor an 'executioner'; not an office associated with goodness, or a wish to do good.

To Marx, therefore, morality would not be the world's deliverer; the revolution would be. And part of that revolution (he hoped) would be his own *Capital: a Critique of Political Economy*. This would deal a 'blow to the bourgeoisie from which they will never recover' (Marx and Engels 1983, p. 93). Its method, Marx said, would be 'completely scientific' (quoted in O'Malley 1976, p. 49).

Marx's rejection of morality in favour of science was, certainly, expedient for a revolutionary. Science is radical; but morality is conservative. Science announces 'you can', morality says 'you may not'. Science was for revolutionaries, morality was for governesses. Morality says that it is wrong to steal from your employer, but Marxist science proves that your employer steals from you.

But, beyond expediency, Marx as an inheritor of the Enlightenment shared its conviction that science was progress, and moralising was not. And as a dissident from the Enlightment he believed that morality was not universal and absolute. Such an Enlightenment commitment to science with a historicist commitment to moral relativity did not coexist only in Marxism. It was preserved in elements of the American Left in the first half of the twentieth century who were confident science would make for progress if only backward 'moral codes' didn't get in the way. We see this in the declaration of the anti-economist Clarence Ayres, 'All established morality is nonsense of the creation-myth type' (Ayres 1935, p. 40). In a similarly hostile vein, Commons wrote that the 'objective world of rights and duties' is a 'metaphysical notion' that arises in man only when rationality leaves him and the 'savage in him takes possession' (quoted in Biddle and Samuels 1997, p. 304).

Thus at the opening of the twentieth century the Left anti-economists elevated science over morality, while the Right did the reverse. Correspondingly, the Right disdained the fact/value distinction, while the Left tended not to make it a target. But by the mid-twentieth century a noteworthy reverse was taking place. From the 1950s a disdain for the fact/value divide became a familiar item with the Left (see Hutchison 1964, pp. 44–5), and its explicit defence now came robustly from liberal sections of economics (for example, Friedman 1953, pp. 3–7).

The most eminent landmark in the transition is Gunnar Myrdal and his *Political Element in the Development of Economic Theory* (1929 [1953]), written in the 1920s and translated into English in the 1950s. It was Myrdal who brought 'ideologism', so popular with the German Historical School, into mainstream contention and Left endorsement.

To Myrdal, values will always decide the question. It is values that make the blade, whatever be the factual handle. The inevitablity of values directing conclusions meant the whole aspiration of economics to be science must be rejected.[30] And for that reason there should be no Nobel Prize in economics. It was, indeed, 'urgent' said Myrdal 'to put an end' to the Prize (Myrdal 1977, p. 52).

The inevitability of values directing conclusions also meant that anything purporting to be 'positive' economics can only be rationalisations of political valuations. Myrdal, however, did *not* contend that so-called 'positive' economics should be cleaned of political rationalisations. Rather, cleaning is declared impossible and undesirable. Thus Myrdal's thesis is distinct from the well-known Left protest (for example, Marx's 'Afterword' [1887] 1954, pp. 22–9) against political economy as a rationalisation of plutocracy. To Myrdal's mind the proper task facing positive economics is not to clean itself of its politics, but to come clean about its politics. Every economist should display their values, formerly hidden beneath scientific camouflage, and allow others to respond to what they now see.[31]

Myrdal's denial of a significant 'positive' economics distinct from economic norms is generally advanced dogmatically rather than argued (for example, Heyne 1978). For this reason, ostensible reasons for the denial are vague.[32] Nevertheless we may hazard some hypotheses as to the popularity of the denial. First, the Left was no longer confident that science was on its side. Science was not subversive; the threat that it had posed to religion, and therefore the social order, had been exhausted. Science had became 'bourgeois science'. With respect to economics, the appeal of science was weakened by the fact that neoclassical economics was, by any ordinary usage of the term, so obviously more 'scientific' than Marxism. Science was now an adversary. Marx himself was now to become 'humanistic', and the curators of his posterity did not trouble to press his scientific credentials. Quite the opposite (see, for example, Thomas 1976 and Amariglio 1987). More generally, his exegetists no longer see themselves as representatives of the Enlightenment. Again, quite the opposite (see MacIntyre 1981).

Second, the wish to efface a fact/value divide might be traced more speculatively to an imbalance between the plenitude of facts among economists and the paucity of facts among anti-economists. This imbalance became painfully great in the post-war era with the quantitative revolution. Left anti-economics, we suggest, countered by asking, 'What of your facts? They are meaningful/interesting/significant only conditional on values'. The denial of the fact/value divide made powerless the enemy's arsenal. The denial was, thus, the 'equaliser'.

7.4 The judges judged

The economist versus the moralist

The cosmology of the moralist is so vast as to defy any summary appreciation. But it should not be permitted to escape a few evaluative remarks.

The sources of the world's banes and remedies

Is the cause of economic problems moral? Does their solution require an improved morality? Or, to be specific, can economic hardship be ascribed to a lack of morality, and its elimination to a moral improvement? Toynbee told his working-class audiences, 'Remember the material change you want can only be got by the development of higher moral qualities' (quoted in Kadish 1986, p. 209). A century later living standards are higher than Toynbee or Tawney would have dared predict; but whether higher moral qualities had anything to do with it is highly arguable. That it has had much to do with the 'information' that Tawney so disparaged seems unarguable.

Party lines

Is economics a matter of party sympathies, as Schmoller and Myrdal proposed? Is it (as the favoured formulation of this thesis in the latter third of the twentieth century goes) 'right wing'.[33] Several studies have been done on the party sympathies of economists in the United States, and shown this to be false. A 1989 study found that 63 per cent of academic economists described themselves as 'liberal' and only 20 per cent as conservative ('The American Enterprise' 1991).[34] A 1996 survey (Blendon 1997) indicated that economists are much less given to 'right wing' explanations of why the economy is not doing better than the general public (Table 7.1).

Table 7.1 On Why the US Economy Is Not Doing Better

	General public (%)	Economists (%)
Too big Federal deficit	77	32
Too many people on welfare	70	11
Too much foreign aid	66	1
Taxes too high	61	18
People place too little value on hard work	59	18
Too many immigrants	47	1
Too much regulation	42	23
Too much affirmative action	18	2

Even more significantly, surveys have indicated that economists cannot be fitted into a either a Right or a Left view. A 1992 survey compared the responses to 30 economic questions of delegates to the Democratic Convention, delegates to the Republican convention and US economists (Fuller et al. 1995). The correlation between the responses of Republican delegates and those of economists was −0.02. The correlation of responses of Democrat delegates with those of economists was 0.24, but was statistically insignificant. Further there is no linear combination of Republican and Democrat responses which yields a statistically (or quantitatively) significant correlation with economists' responses; indicating that economists cannot be considered merely a mixed population of Republicans and Democrats. The economists' positions cut across party sympathies.[35]

Fact/value divide

Are there any positive contentions that retain significance under a wide variety of value systems? There surely are. Consider the contention that a minimum wage will cause significant unemployment that will be concentrated on those with the least human capital. And let us suppose this contention is true. Which value system, currently entertained by any sizeable audience in the West, would entitle one to declare such a truth insignificant, without interest, and meriting neglect?

Value gap thesis

Are economists separated from anti-economists by differences in normative principles, rather than positive contentions? Milton Friedman has judged this value gap thesis to be a rhetorical stratagem of anti-economists to avoid debating critical positive issues (Friedman 1967, p. 87). For, if values do indeed determine economists' policy positions, then there is no need to rebut their claims on positive questions. One can merely impute unacceptable values as the foundation of their policy recommendations (an easy thing to do) and the battle is won. In Friedman's mind anti-economists conjure up this spurious 'value gap' to evade the strength of economists' positive contentions, and to hide the weaknesses of their own. A normative superiority is conjured up because there is, in reality, a positive inferiority.

Yet it must be allowed that as long as economics has values, it must be possible that a value gap exists. And economics obviously does have values; it is obviously not exhausted by its positive content. It obviously does have a normative content that does not lessen its attraction to the scientific cosmology or repulsion from the moralist one.

The composition of this suite of the values of the *Grande Tradition* is arguable. We will venture here that economics values pre-eminently these things: reason, well-being, and freedom.

The Tradition in economics values reason. This value amounts to an attachment to good argument, a pleasure from understanding why, an itch from not knowing why. Without this mental sensitivity there would be no Tradition: the whole labyrinthine apparatus of economic theory is owed to it.[36]

The Tradition in economics also values the state of a person being pleased; a state of 'well-being'.[37] A critical feature of this value is that the living Tradition has placed almost no quasi-moralistic restrictions on what states of being pleased are valuable. Elevated and base; gross and refined; solid and frivolous; 'self-centred' and 'social'; worldly and unworldly; all these pleasures are valued.

Finally, the Tradition is also attached to freedom; the so-called 'negative freedom' of political philosophers; the freedom from coercion and constraint. This attachment should not be overstated. The political economists cannot be caught avowing an attachment.[38] Such an attachment cannot be considered very prominent among all who have contributed to the subject; strictly scientific contributors have included communists, fascists and Nazis. And, economic liberals frequently fault economists for being insufficiently attached to freedom. Yet, freedom is probably at least in part an ultimate value, even if economists would be more comfortable to call it 'choice'. The Tradition's absence of quasi-moralistic restrictions on what states of being pleased are valuable reduces to an attachment to freedom. And economists' disinclination to truck with 'meddlesome preferences' also amounts to an attachment to freedom. This attachment of economists to freedom, at least as an ultimate value, is typical of their peers in the liberal societies in which economics grew.

This value triad of the Tradition can come into conflict with other value systems.

First, the triad may conflict with value systems with fewer elements. The threefold composition of the Tradition's values distinguishes it from libertarianism, which, by contrast has one value; freedom. The threefold composition distinguishes it from constructivist ameliorationism of welfare states that value well-being and reason, but not freedom. It distinguishes it from Spartan 'republican' philosophies that value freedom and reason, but not well-being. It distinguishes it from pragmatic but intellectually under-developed societies that value well-being and freedom, but not reason.

Second, the value system of the Tradition comes into conflict with value systems with different elements. Despite its relative complexity, the triad of values is obviously not a complete statement of the good. It excludes humanity, equality, beauty, nature, and values of personality. The Tradition has never denied the existence of other 'good things'. But it has implicitly taken the values of reason, freedom and well-being to be pre-eminent to the others. All other values retreat before reason, freedom and well-being.

Third, the value system of the living Tradition comes into conflict with value systems which flatly deny its values. Reason, well-being and freedom may seem commonplace desiderata, but have at all times been candidly despised by a few, and subject to an implicit contempt by many more.

The truth is that there has long been a value-gap between economists and some anti-economists; we will see throughout Part III the values of reason, well-being and freedom being slighted. The existence of this gap beckons an evaluation of the values of economists and anti-economists, an impossibly forbidding task. Yet it is possible to register the (discouraging) truth that however strenuous is the moral aspiration of the moralist anti-economists, that aspiration is not matched by achievement. The moralising of moralisers is not always impressive; sometimes it is repulsive. Ruskin and Carlyle's own vile notions of 'just conduct' with respect to civil unrest in British colonies will be noted in Chapter 8. Wagner's strange brand of morality may be discovered in his exaltation of *Machpolitik*, and his recommendation of infanticide to preserve the 'fitness' of the human race. Myrdal's much 'laboured' value premises allowed him to be an advocate of forced sterilisation of the genetically inferior sub-strata (Carlson 1990, p. 91).[39]

Yet, for all these strictures, the moralist is not an entirely unsympathetic figure. One may make a different contrast: not between the moralist and the scientist, but between the 'moralist' and the 'connoisseur'. The moralist is dark, estranged, judgemental, caustic, impolitic, gross, rejecting, uncomprehending, disturbed, dissatisfied. The connoisseur is sunny, social, appreciating, ironical, politic, refined, accepting, understanding, calm, contented. The first is grave and intensely felt, yet crude; the 'prophet'. The second is comfortable and sophisticated; the *'philosophe'*. The first (dare we say it?) is the anti-economist, and the second is the economist. But the first may, as a social type, possess a usefulness, lying in their gravity. And the second may not always possess a usefulness. The connoisseur-*philosophe* seeks to cope with things by knowing about them. But might it sometimes be wrong always to try to 'understand'? Might it sometimes be futile to try to assimilate through comprehension all evil and misfortune? Might it sometimes be better to leave them as dark mysteries, and simply to feel?

8
The Religion of Love
and the Science of Wealth

One of the most popular strokes of anti-economics is the claim that economics amounts to a doctrine of selfishness. Economics at best condones selfishness. More likely it insinuates it. Indeed, say its critics, it has praised it. Worst of all, by abetting egoism, economics has corroded any general sense of regard for others, and therefore cleared a path for inhumanity and cruelty.

In this chapter we will outline the emergence of this stream of anti-economics in western Europe in the aftermath of the French Revolution. We will argue that it was at the opening of the nineteenth century that egoism became a preoccupation of thought, and the notion of egoism as the great bane of human existence received a sudden charge. Correspondingly, the notion that altruism, philanthropy and compassion are the great deliverers of mankind received a great stimulus. Under this world view, economics received a predictable damnation that has endured to this day.

We shall contend, however, that economics never pled for selfishness. It has never affirmed that 'selfishness is good'. The Tradition has often defended economic freedom, never selfishness. We further contend that, contrary to myth, economics has been an ally (even a leader) in several philanthropic causes.

And yet, we will argue, there is a genuine conflict between economics and the partisans of altruism. Economics is plainly not a humanitarian movement. It denies a key humanitarian precept that 'regard for others is *all* the good'. It is this denial that is the true field of contest between economics and its philanthropic adversaries.[1]

8.1   The discovery of egoism

The Enlightenment background

A repugnance towards selfishness is presumably of ancient provenance. Yet by 1776 a respectful estimation of the uses of this apparent vice was no great novelty (Mandeville [1732] 1924). Hume and Smith, the pre-eminent moralists of the eighteenth century, beheld this clash of opinion and, in the reconciling spirit of the age, averred that egoism was no vice, and that neither was altruism (on Hume see Halévy [1928] 1949a, p. 14). Put simply, it was the world's portion of self-interest that built the world, and it was the world's portion of altruism that helped share it out.

There were eighteenth-century dissidents from this complacency about egoism. The 'communist' Étienne-Gabriel Morelly (1716–81) stormed against 'cupidity' in *Code de la Nature* (1755). 'The only evil I perceive in the universe is avarice. All others – whatever name they are given – are only shades, degrees of that' (quoted in Durkheim 1967, p. 82). Rousseau lamented that his typical contemporary's 'self-love augments in the same proportion as his indifference to the remainder of the universe' (quoted in Keohane 1978, p. 457). But Morelly and Rousseau were dissidents. And, balancing these dissidents, there were other *philosophes* who elevated self-interest to a pitch of glory that economists of the period never approved, or condoned. Claude-Adrien Helvétius (1715–71), for example, extolled self-interest to a degree that disgusted Turgot.

There were also, very occasionally, eighteenth-century censures of economics on account of its stance towards acquisitiveness. Linguet, for example, faulted the physiocrats for pandering to avarice (Boss 1976). But at the same time economists were also faulted for being *too benevolent*. To Galiani, for example, it was the *benevolence* of the economists that was a problem (Faccarello 1998). It was their benevolence to the peasantry that threatened to undermine the social order. [2]

Overall, the tendency of eighteenth-century thought, in comparison with the nineteenth century, was to be at peace with human nature, in both its selfless and selfish aspects. Human nature was not a problem, and so economics' own acceptance of human nature could not be reprimanded for exacerbating a problem, or obstructing its solution.

The aftermath of 1789

In 1789 the complacency about the issue of egoism and altruism in society began to dissolve. Almost a century of preoccupation with egoism and altruism began.

One indication of this emergent interest was the coinage of new words to describe selfishness. In France *égoïsme* prior to the late eighteenth century was a literary allusion, referring to obtrusive references to oneself. The *Dictionnaire Historique de la Langue Française* records that it was from 1789 that 'it indicates the excessive attachment to oneself'. In 1793 *égoïste* (egotistical) is recorded as coming into being.[3] Complementing the term *égoïsme*, the Saint-Simonians had by 1827 added the term *individualisme* (Bestor 1948, p. 282) and by 1829 *exploitation*, in the sense of 'turning to account for selfish purposes'. (The *OED* records the earliest English usage of exploitation in this sense at 1844.)[4]

The English usage of egoism and egotism in their sense of selfishness also dates from about 1800. Prior to that 'egoism' referred to the philosophic doctrine that there was no proof for the existence of anything but one's own mind; and 'egotism' indicated the obtrusive use of the pronoun 'I'. The earliest usage of egoism in the new sense recorded by the *OED* dates from 1800, and registers its novelty: 'affection . . . was lost in selfishness or according to their new word Egoism'. English had long possessed a suite of words to describe kindred concepts. 'Self-interest' and 'self-love' dated from the seventeenth century. But neither of these two has the pejorative impact of egoism. Indeed, 'self-love' is defined by the *OED* as 'Regard for one's own well-being, regarded as a natural or proper relation of a man to himself.' 'Avarice' and 'cupidity' date from Middle English but the ideas they represent are distinct from egoism. Egoism need not be manifested in an 'eagerness for wealth' (that is, avarice); and, strictly speaking, an 'eagerness for wealth' need not be a manifestation of egoism.

Matching the new coining of egoism were new coinages indicating their opposite. 'Selfless' dates in English from 1825. *Altruisme* appeared in 1830 in France (from Auguste Comte) and in English in 1853.

'Egoism', and its companion terms, were coined by their professed enemies to facilitate their condemnation, and in the early nineteenth century condemnation was profuse. The Saint-Simonians declared, 'By naming egoism, we have put our fingers on the deepest wound of modern civilisation' (Enfantin [1828] 1972, p. 20). Comte announced that positivism was 'even more severe than Catholicism' in its condemnation of egoism (Comte 1875, 1, p. 13). The disquiet about egoism was not restricted to anti-liberals. Benjamin Constant feared that modern (that is, post-Napoleonic) war would be motivated by egoistic principles, unlike previous wars, and would be all the more horrible. De Tocqueville in *Democracy in America* ([1835] 1945) also displayed a sensitivity to the egoism in modern society.

This preoccupation with egoism was not restricted to prose critics. Since the Directory, the French world of letters was absorbed by the spectacle of thrusting ambition (Epsztein 1966, p. 46). In English literature, Jane Austen's novels, usually seen as journeys in self-discovery, have also been interpreted more precisely as turning on a relation between self-knowledge and selfishness (Watts, 1990, pp. 127–42). At about the same time as Austen was writing, the critic (and anti-economist) William Hazlitt was absorbed in metaphysical and social issues of self-regard ([1825] 1902). Literary historians have also noted 'the extent to which Russian writers from the 1840s to the 1860s were concerned with the problem of "self love". The theme is evident, for example, in Herzen's *Who is to Blame?*, Turgenev's *Rudin*, and Tolstoy's *Family Happiness* and *The Cossacks*' (Scanlan 1999, p. 552). Dostoevsky's 1864 *Notes from Underground* also contains an attack on egoism.

Not all this attention to egoism was hostile. The Romantic fascination with the individual, genius and solitude was not inimical to self-assertion.

There were, indeed, protests against the protest against egoism. A moderate specimen is Stendhal's (1783–1842) *Souvenirs d'Égotisme*. (*Égotisme* was a neologism put into currency by Stendhal.) An immoderate specimen is Max Stirner's (1806–56) brazen celebration of individual self-assertion against any claims of society, *Der Einzige und sein Eigentum* of 1845 (The Ego and His Own).[5] And later in the century Nikolay Gavrilovich Chernyshevsky (1828–89) advocated egoism as the most natural and desirable spring of human behaviour.

Neither did economists join in the campaign against egoism. One explicitly praised the utility of 'self-love'. In the fifteenth chapter of the first edition of *An Essay on the Principle of Population* Malthus writes:

> It is to the established administration of property, and to the apparently narrow principle of self-love, that we are indebted for all the noblest exertions of genius, all the finer and more delicate emotions of the soul, for everything, indeed, that distinguishes the civilised from the savage state; and no sufficient change has as yet taken place in the nature of civilised man to enable us to say that he either is, or ever will be, in a state when he may safely throw down the ladder by which he has risen to eminence.
>
> (Malthus [1798] 1993, pp. 117–18)[6]

Here Malthus is comparing self-love to a ladder; a highly useful tool, or faculty; like sight or imagination. But is Malthus identifying *selfishness* with a useful tool? No. Self-love is not selfishness: self-love is a regard for one's well-being, selfishness is a disregard for the well-being of others. A regard for one's well-being is consistent with a regard for others. Indeed, Malthus claims that regard for one's well-being is the basis of a regard for others.

> Nothing that has been said tends in the most remote degree to undervalue the principle of benevolence. It is one of the noblest and most godlike qualities of the human heart, generated, perhaps, slowly and gradually from self-love; and afterwards intended to act as a general law; whose kind office it should be to soften the partial deformities, to correct the asperities, and to smooth the wrinkles of its parent.
>
> ([1798] 1993, p. 120)

Nevertheless, it is significant that no economist of significance before or since has troubled to give such prominent esteem to 'self-love'.[7] But the stresses of the times pressed Malthus to take a position; the attitude to the self and to others was now the focus of a critical dispute. In this dispute, Malthus was not going to admit any censure of a regard for the self. And he was not going to admit any priority of regard for others over a regard for one's self. Compassion was now to be treated warily by Malthus and economists. For most of the nineteenth century, political economists were to be watchful for 'mistaken humanity' and unthinking charity. The older complacency about human nature had given way. So whereas anti-economists felt the problem lay in an undue regard for oneself, the political economists felt a greater danger lay in well meaning, but misdirected, actions born of a regard for others.

The triple alliance against egoism

A preoccupation with egoism emerged in the wake of the French Revolution partly because the Revolution seemed to discredit the Enlightenment's favoured positions, including its trust in self-interest. An assault on self-interest also served the new post-Revolutionary ideological postures; the anti-liberal Left, the anti-liberal Right, and the 'religion of love'.

The Left

The anti-liberal Left saw egoism as destructive of the collective existence they were seeking. They identified 'egoism' with 'modern liberty'; the autonomy, independence, and prerogative of the individual. They had been hostile to these before 1789 (for example, Rousseau), but the opposition was muted owing to the alliance of the anti-liberal Left with the liberal Left in their struggle with the Right. The end of the old order meant that the adversary of the anti-liberal Left was no longer kings, who interfered with others; but the bourgeoisie, who did as they pleased with their own. Private property, not public property, was the new enemy, and a name for the new-found adversary was 'egoism'. One example of the good use to which the new term could be put was by Jacques Roux, a leading figure of the *enragés*. Demanding legislation against speculators in 1793 Roux asked, 'How much longer will you permit these rich egotists to go on drinking from golden goblets the purest blood of the people' (quoted in Welch 1984, p. 25). In February 1794 Maximilien Robespierre declared in his 'On the Principles of Political Morality', 'We wish in our country that morality may be substituted for egoism.'

The Right

The anti-liberal Right saw egoism as destructive of the order they were seeking to preserve. Order consisted of ties: the ties of those below to those above, and the ties of those above to those below. Egoism spelt the end of those ties. Thus the counter-revolutionary historian Augustin Barruel believed individualism and self-interest were behind the Revolution (Godechot 1971, p. 42). In the same vein, Coleridge described self-interest as the 'Quality Cousin of Jacobinism' (quoted in Morrow 1990, p. 113). The Saint-Simonians considered egoism to be part of the destructive 'critical age' of the sixteenth to eighteenth centuries. Sismondi in his *Fall of the Roman Empire* explained the survival or collapse of states in terms of the selfishness or selflessness of their inhabitants. States populated by the selfish were defeated: those populated by persons dedicated to the interest of the whole survived.[8] Comte agreed with Sismondi that modern Europe lacked the ancients' critical attachment 'to the united body of their fellow citizens'. Comte in 1824: 'Europe lives politically only by violence... these means can maintain society for some time, but if they do not soon unite with a moral plan, a force of sentiment, egoism will finish it by dissolving all' (quoted in Mauduit 1929, p. 30).

The religion of love

A third source of ideological energy that reacted violently to the presence of self-interest was the religion of love, and its particular form, the cult of compassion.

The religion of love enjoins us to love others. But it asserts more than simply the goodness of loving others. It also asserts the supreme utility of loving others. The religion of love, then, contends that benevolence is the principal solution to the world's problems. All you need is love.

As compassion is born of what most pains love – suffering of the loved – the religion of love is constantly accompanied by the cult of compassion: an ethic that exalts the value of tenderness towards suffering. In this cult, pity and sympathy become important duties of mankind. They, too, are not only good, but useful.

The cult of compassion had been launched well before the nineteenth-century protests against egoism that are discussed here. By its close the Enlightenment had already been thoroughly moistened with 'sweet fraternal tears'. Sympathy and fellow-feeling were *à la mode* by the mid-eighteenth century. Thus the immediate great popularity of Adam Smith's *Theory of Moral Sentiments* from its date of publication in 1759.

But, undeniably, the eighteenth century gave less room to the cult of compassion than the nineteenth. The perseverance throughout the eighteenth century of certain cultural paradigms (the Augustan, the Stoic, the classic) and their values (reason, dignity, restraint) were enough to keep the fellow-feeling of the eighteenth century rather gentlemanly, if not genteel.[9] Theirs was emotion without commotion; a sentiment without passion. The Enlightenment's single unrestrained, intense, and 'low' alternative to the classic – the lampoon – gave still less room to the cult of compassion, as the satirical is plainly antithetical to the sincerity and gentleness of pity.

The Augustan edifices of the eighteenth century were demolished by recurring waves of romantic sentiment. The key antipathy of the Romantic was control, including emotional control. And the Romantic's key source of knowledge was his individual, solitary vision; no 'impartial spectator' judiciously assimilating all society's interests, but one engrossed by the particulars that touch his self. Cultural historians have recorded the consequent new hankering for 'men of greater sensibility and feeling than the eighteenth century with its Robert Walpoles and Bernard de Mandevilles and its Popes and Chesterfields' (Roberts 1979, p. 60). Literary critics have noted how Romanticism extended the appropriate domain of pity, allowed the common man to be the object of tragedy, and made the acceptable depth of pathos deeper. Pity was no longer the 'charming pity' (*pitié charmante*) of the neoclassic taste; 'tears' became 'sobs'.

Borne strongly by new Romantic currents, the cult of compassion swept across the divide between the ideologically Left and the ideologically Right. The cult carried some concerned with order (the Right), and some of those hostile to it (the Left). It encompassed the 'Left Christianity' that was enormously popular during the July Monarchy,[10] and the 'Christian socialism' of Frederic Denison Maurice (1805–72) and Charles Kingsley (1819–75) that arrived in the aftermath of 1848. But the religion of love also included the authoritarian Saint-Simonians and Comte. Comte: 'Love is naturally the one universal principle' (1875, 1, p. xi).

However, the religion of love was distinguished from many familiar, political, manifestations of the Right and Left through its solution of the problem of egoism. To the Left of the Enlightenment and their nineteenth-century inheritors, the solution was political: revolution. Thus Rousseau, Morelly and Mably all held that selfishness was a problem, but that communism was its solution. By abolishing property, egoism could be neutralised. Godwin held the same, and Marx, in a similar way, believed that selfishness would be eliminated by revolution. Selfishness in the mind of these authors was not an innate disposition, but only a behavioural strategy optimal under capitalism.

To the Right, by contrast, there was no overthrow of authority that could change naturally sinful man into virtuous man. Yet the solution of the traditional Right was as political as that of the Left: submission to established authority. Traditionally this submission was to an established church. Thus whereas to the Left the solution was revolution, to the Right it was orthodoxy. When religious orthodoxy became a less viable solution, in post-Christian western Europe in the late nineteenth century, the state was increasingly substituted as a secular church.[11] The state was to become an 'ethical agency' and no less than 'the greatest moral institution for the education of human kind'.[12]

The religion of love, in contrast with both the Left and Right, saw the root solution lying in a change in man's nature. It repudiated the Right's solution through submission to authority, and judged as refuted the Left's hope of reforming man through a revolution of political institutions. It was in sympathy with the new Romantic sensibilities that sought to stare into the human heart rather than contemplate the cause and effect of the social contrivance. It was correlate with the gathering strength from the early nineteenth century (after its effective extinction in the eighteenth) of tragic drama, with its presumption that in the failings, and strengths, of human nature lay the seat of mankind's destiny.

But how to cleanse man's tainted heart? By religion. Comte and Saint-Simon held that it was the decline in the old religion that accounted for the noxious growth of egoism.[13] 'Egoism finally succeeds devotion' proclaimed the Saint-Simonians 'as atheism replaces godliness'. And to the religion of love it was the advent of a new sort of religion that would reverse this growth. Man would be reformed by inculcation, exhortation and example as fixed in a new rite and a new priesthood, as elaborated by Comte and the Saint-Simonians. Even those who had no fancies of contriving new cults had great hope in the power of religion to secure social betterment: to Sismondi, religion was 'the most sublime of the social sciences' (1834, p. 4).

The religion of love was confident about the power of such a reformulated and revived religosity to reform man. History revealed that man had once been better. And recent history, some Comteans maintained, showed that now he was again improving. For example, to Frederic Harrison, the Comtean anti-economist, the decay of bribery in British public life illustrated such a moral improvement.

8.2 Economics as the science of venality

The religion of love, with no offence to logic, saw egoism as its adversary. With more doubtful logic it identified political economy with that adversary. It did so on several grounds.

1. Political economy teaches an ethic of self-interest

Villeneuve-Bargemont (1784–1850) dismissed the school of Smith as 'egotistical'; the Saint-Simonians complained that political economy sought of 'the new [social] science to reduce it to the narrow confines of individualism' (quoted in Halévy 1949a, p. 52). The 'social Catholic' Charles de Coux was more belligerent. He contended there were two types of political economy: the anti-Catholic (that is, orthodox political economy), and the Catholic. Anti-Catholic political economy 'addresses itself exclusively to human cupidity' (Coux 1830). Catholic political economy, by contrast, was founded in sacrifice.

In the mid-nineteenth-century English-speaking world the proposition that political economy fostered greed was put baldly by the anti-economist and slavery advocate, George Fitzhugh: 'no writings, since the promulgation of the Christian dispensation, have exercised so controlling an influence on human conduct as the writings of these authors [of political economy]. The morality which they teach is one of simple and unadulterated selfishness' ([1854] 1960, p. 54).

The notion that political economy fosters greed is also the key to understanding John Ruskin, perhaps the most fanatical of all enemies of economics.

I know no previous instance in history of a nation's establishing a systematic disobedience to the first principles of its professed religion.

The writings which we (verbally) esteem as divine, not only denounce the love of money as the source of all evil, and as an idolatry abhorred of the Deity, but declare mammon service to be the accurate and irreconcilable opposite of God's service. ([1862] 1967, p. 61)

To Ruskin the error of political economy lay in it 'considering the human being merely as a covetous machine'. No precepts of any worth could be derived from such an assumption, for Ruskin professed an extreme altruistic code. To Ruskin it is the moral duty of any superior to treat their subordinates as their children, quite literally.[14]

Ruskin's example incited similar sentiments in the English Historical School of the late nineteenth century. It was Ruskin's adherent Arnold Toynbee (1852–1883) who in 1883 spoke of 'the bitter argument between economists and human beings'. Foxwell in 1885 complained 'We have been suffering for a century from an acute outbreak of individualism unchecked by the old restraints and invested with almost a religious sanction by a certain soulless school of writers. The narrowest selfishness has been recommended as public virtue' (quoted in Koot 1977, p. 565). R.H. Tawney may also be mentioned.

Complaints about political economy were not restricted to France and England. From the mid-nineteenth century these same complaints were articulated in the so-called Old German Historical School. In 1848 Bruno Hildebrand accused Smith of adopting a egoistic theory of human conduct in his *Die Nationalökonomie der Gegenwart und Zukunft*. In 1853 C.G.A. Knies (1821–98) undertook 'a thorough going critique' of the assumption of egoism (Philipovich 1912, p. 174), while exempting Smith from censure regarding such assumption, in his *Die Politische Oekonomie von Standpunkte geschichtlichen Methode* (Philippovich 1912, p. 171). The 'new' German Historical School from 1870 onwards concurred with the Old on the issue of egoism: 'The new school...demands above all the abandonment of the premise that man in his economic action is influenced only by egoism' (Adolf Held 1877, quoted in Philippovich 1891, p. 224).[15]

2. Political economy insinuated an ethic of self-interest, even if it did not preach it

The Comtean anti-economist Frederic Harrison (1831–1923) condemned political economy as a 'tissue of degrading nonsense' (quoted in Adelman 1971, p. 176) on the ground that it matter of factly described the operation of self-interest, without simultaneously condemning it. This amounted to its exoneration. He explained with an analogy:

A body of political writers who undertook to systemise the laws of government on the assumption that men crave only for place and power, and who rigidly excluded from their view questions of religion, education, morality, society and industry – might construct a science of the British constitution, and a number of hypothetical laws of politics, including the laws of rotten boroughs, of bribery, patronage, and place hunting... But such men could hardly complain if they were accused of lowering rather than elevating political morality, of systemising corruption, and reducing venality to a science.

(Harrison 1865, p. 373)

In the late twentieth century the same indictment includes the charge that the study of economics actually makes people more self-seeking. This draws on evidence that economics students are more likely to 'free ride' in experiments than non-economics students. Anti-economists have seized this research to assert that 'practitioners of the dismal science are a pretty selfish bunch' (Gittins 2001).

3. Political economy denied the existence of altruistic motives

A favoured theme of anti-economists was that man had a selfless dimension. Thus Harrison writes 'Perhaps no single case can be found of one capitalist or one workman whose industrial conduct is never influenced by some motive derived from custom, public opinion, sense of duty or benevolence' (Harrison 1865, p. 361). And Leslie claimed, against 'a system that takes cognisance only of individuals', that the most powerful motive to the accumulation of wealth was 'conjugal and parental affections' (Leslie 1888, p. 196).[16]

Some anti-economists went so far as to adopt a serene confidence in the basic selflessness of man. Consider again the anti-economist and slaver George Fitzhugh:

Man is, by nature, the most gregarious, and therefore, the least selfish of animals. Man loves that nearest to him best. First his wife, children and parents, then his slaves, next his neighbours and fellow countrymen. But his unselfishness does not stop here. He is ready and anxious to relieve a famine in Ireland, and shudders when he reads of a murder at the antipodes. He feels deeply for the sufferings of domestic animals, and is rendered happy by witnessing the enjoyments of the flocks, and carolling birds that surround him. All men are philanthropists, and would benefit their fellow-men if they could... Our happiness is so involved in the happiness and well being of everything around us, that a mere selfish philosophy, like political economy, is a very unsafe and delusive guide.

(Fitzhugh [1854] 1960, pp. 129–30)

Other detractors of political economy had no wish to paint such a prettified portrait of human conduct: egoism was a problem not a pseudo-problem. But they would have sympathised with a related complaint.

*4.　Political economy, in denying the possibility of selfless impulses,
denied the possibility of future improvement based on the utilisation
of those impulses*

Even if political economy did not praise egoism, and even if it did not foster
greed, its cynicism about selfless motivations prompted the rejection of any
scheme for improvement premised on selfless motivations.

The terrible proofs

The case against political economics extended beyond its supposed praise of
selfishness. It extended to political economy's supposed denigration of selfless attempts to relieve suffering. The case extends to an accusation of cruel
tolerance of suffering, and barbarous obstruction to its relief. Malthusianism
and the New Poor Law, and the political economists' responses to workplace
regulation, were taken as decisive proofs of this accusation.

Malthusianism

To the Religion of Love, Malthus was the clinching proof of the brutal
egoism of economics.[17] In Malthus they could flourish an explicit attack on
charity or any assistance for distress. Thus Saint-Simonians, in pressing the
case against political economy, asked, 'Do not Malthus and his students
prove that charity should refuse misery help and shelter? (Enfantin [1828],
1972, p. 130). And Antoine Frédéric Ozanam (1813–53), founder of the Society
of St Vincent de Paul, wrote:

> Malthus and Bentham have taught us these ignominious doctrines that
> reduce all human economy to a calculus of interests, who suffocate the
> family of the poor for not having enough food to nourish their children,
> who close the refuges of the indigent and the orphaned, who dry up the
> sources of alms giving, and throw magnificent contempt on all the
> splendid institutions of charity.
>
> (Ozanam 1865, 8, p. 314)[18]

Malthus's writings provided, in particular, two verbal treasures that anti-
economists were to cherish and flaunt.

1.　Nature's feast.　In the second edition (1803) of the *Principle of Population*
the following passage appeared.

> A man who is born into a world already possessed, if he cannot get
> subsistence from his parents on whom he has a just demand, and if the
> society do not want his labour, has no claim of *right* to the smallest
> portion of food, and, in fact, has no business to be where he is. At
> nature's mighty feast there is no vacant cover [setting] for him. She tells

him to be gone, and will quickly execute her own orders, if he do not work upon the compassion of some of her guests.

([1803] 1986, p. 697)

Although Malthus removed these words in the third (1806) edition the passage was quoted with some triumphing for the remainder of the nine-teenth century by anti-economists; by Blanqui, Proudhon, Toussenel, George, and Southey. Pierre-Joseph Proudhon (1809–65) after quoting it, provides his own terrible summarising epigram: 'Here we have the necessary, fatal conclusion of political economy . . . Death to he who does not own' (1846, p. 24). Leroux, just to drive the point home, quoted it three times in his *Les Malthusians*. And, not suprisingly, Leroux misquoted it:

> A man who is born in a world already possessed if the wealthy do not need his labour, is truly redundant on earth. At the great feast of nature, there is no place for him. Nature commands him to go, and she will not hesitate to execute this order herself.
>
> (Leroux 1849, p. 54)

This misquotation omits Malthus's reference to the claim that the poor have on their parents. And the redundancy of labour to 'society' is turned into redundancy with respect to the 'wealthy'.

More grossly the authors of an anti-Malthusian tract provide this 'quotation': 'the poor are uninvited guests at the banquet which nature spreads for her more favoured children: and from which she bids them BEGONE!' (Introduction to Marcus 1839, p. 6). But the anti-economists needed neither large nor small improvements to the original: the accurate quotation was grist enough.

2. *Children and parish assistance.* In chapter 8 of Book IV of the *Principle of Population*, Malthus summarises in four paragraphs how he would 'gradually abolish' Poor Law relief. The first and fourth read:

> I should propose a regulation to be made, declaring, that no child born from any marriage, taking place after the expiration of a year from the date of the law; and no illegitimate child born two years from the same date, should ever be entitled to parish assistance.

> With regard to illegitimate children, after the proper notice had been given they should on no account whatever be allowed to have any claim to parish assistance . . . The infant is, comparatively speaking, of no value to the society, as others will immediately supply its place. Its principal value is on account of its being the object of one of the most delightful passions in human nature – parental affection. But if this

value be disregarded by those who are alone in a capacity to feel it, the society cannot be called upon to put itself in their place.

(Malthus [1803] 1986, pp. 515–17).

This passage was subject to some slight softening after the second edition: instead of the infant being of 'no value' to society, it was of 'little value'.

This passage, too, was a prize for anti-economists. The proposal to leave children to private charity would seem to risk the worst: hungry children and no private charity. And the justification of the proposal turns on the chilly presumption that a child's life is of purely instrumental value. ('The infant is, comparatively speaking, of no value to the society, as others will immediately supply its place'.)

Malthus's passage was accurately quoted by Southey in his anonymous review (Southey 1803). But it is then immediately subjected to misrepresentation. Southey summarises: 'If you ["the miserable, poor people of England"] beget children, he says to them, they must perish for want.' This is a blatant distortion: it ignores that Malthus denied any expectation of infants perishing from want, owing to the presence of private charity: 'If this system were pursued, we need be under no apprehensions whatever, that the number of persons in extreme want would be beyond the power and will of the benevolent to supply' (Malthus [1803] 1986, p. 517).

But Southey's misrepresentation was just a prelude to a more fantastic misrepresentation by French and English authors: that Malthusianism recommended the management of the problem of population by the killing of the newborn. The anti-economists intended this accusation quite literally. To Leroux 'infanticide at public expense has been publicly called for by the disciples of Malthus' (Leroux 1849, p. 104).[19] Malthus, says Toussenel, declared positively 'society can refuse a child a right to live' (1847, p. 62). Toussenel explains that Malthusians favour 'that a national award be given to mothers who sacrifice the fruit of the womb; and they want that mothers can visit the remains of the children in sumptuous cemeteries where they can breath the souls of the children amidst the smell of roses' (1847, p. 62).[20]

Wherein arose this myth of an 'annual massacre of infants' (Leroux 1849, p. 107)? The source is the *Book of Murder!* (Marcus, 1839).[21] This was a reprint of a paper by one 'Marcus' that was 'printed for private circulation' in 1838. Marcus begins by commending Malthus for drawing attention to the problem of overpopulation, and then advances his own solution to the problem: the extinction of surplus infants by deadly gas. This would be carried out by an association with legislative sanction. Mothers were to be consoled with the prospect of interment of their deceased children in beautiful cemeteries (or 'Infants' Paradise') decorated with plants and flowers, and which were to be the 'scene of recreation of all classes'.

Anti-economists, including Carlyle and Engels, made good use of Marcus and his sick proposals to besmirch the Malthusian population theory, 'the crudest most barbarous theory that ever existed' (Engels [1844] 1973, pp. 199, 219). But who was Marcus? He was not a political economist.[22] Several libraries record 'Marcus' as the pseudonym of Matthew Livingston Davis (1766–1850), a scoundrel journalist, who in 1826 was committed for trial over swindling several million dollars. Davis's chief claim to memory is as the 'only intimate friend and associate' of Aaron Burr (1756–1836; vice president of the United States, 1801–5), of whom he was an 'adoring friend, a zealous henchman, and an unwise biographer'.

How does Davis come to write the *Book of Murder!*? The connection would seem to be his master Aaron Burr. Burr was 'a disciple' of Bentham (Halévy 1949b, p. 297), and while in England in 1808 Burr had proposed to Bentham that an invasion of Mexico be undertaken, that would leave Burr as emperor, and Bentham as legislator. Perhaps more significantly Burr also met in 1808 William Godwin, who had not yet become an adversary of Malthus, and had publicly toyed with infanticide as a remedy for the population problem.[23] Did Burr devise the scheme of *Book of Murder!*? Did he even write it himself? Davis was custodian of Burr's papers upon his death in 1836. And Burr 'occasionally gave evidence of mental aberration' (Sherman 1929, p. 318). Perhaps a person who could imagine himself Emperor of Mexico could also concoct the 'Infants' Paradise'.[24]

The New Poor Laws

An easy extension of the culpability of Malthusianism was a culpability for the 'New' Poor Laws of 1834 that reduced poor relief. This was common meat of anti-economists of the early Victorian period. But one may provide an example from 1998; from John Gray's *False Dawn: the Delusions of Global Capitalism*. The New Poor Law was, says Gray, based on the denial of the supposition that the community at large shared a responsibility for the welfare of a given individual. And it was strict to the point of cruelty. Gray calls upon Eric Hobsbawm to bang the indictment home. 'There have been few more inhuman statutes than the Poor Law Act of 1834' says Hobsbawm. And 'middle-class liberal economists' were its authors (Hobsbawm quoted in Gray 1998, p. 10).

Workplace legislation

Climbing boys. In 1818 the passage through the House of Lords of a bill to restrict the use of boys as chimney-sweeps was obstructed by James Maitland, the eighth Earl of Lauderdale (1759–1839). He objected to the bill on the grounds that (i) any restriction should be left to voluntary compliance and (ii) any restriction could multiply fires: 'He could not suffer his humanity to run headlong with him'.

It was Coleridge's view that the bill would 'have been quietly assented to, had it not afforded that Scotch Coxcomb, the plebeian Earl of Lauderdale, too tempting an occasion for displaying his muddy three inch depths in the Gutter of his Political Economy' (Coleridge 1956, 4, p. 854).

Political economy has not since been spared censure on account of chimney-sweeps. In 1971 a popular historian, Brian Inglis, construed the absence of any record of expression of Ricardo on the Bill as indicating Ricardo's opposition to it. Lauderdale, argues Inglis, was not 'publicly repudiated by Ricardo'. And, Inglis goes on to note:

> Ricardo was assiduous in his attendance at Westminster, and it was rare for a debate on any subject related to the economy to go by without a speech from him; but he had not intervened in the debate on the factory bill, or in the debate on the climbing boys. And although he did not explain why, the reason can be inferred from the premise that was constantly appearing in his writings at the time: that the legislature must not be allowed to infringe the rights of the owners of property.
>
> (Inglis 1971, p. 166)

Factory Acts.   The classic reference of the humanitarian objection to economists is their alleged opposition to legislation for relieving the plight of those labouring in the nineteenth-century's dark satanic mills.

> British historians of the Industrial Revolution are unanimously of the opinion that early factory reform was achieved in the face of strong hostility from economic experts of the day. It does not matter whom we consult: Toynbee, Trevelyan, the Hammonds, Cunningham, Clapham; the classical economists are always depicted as unalterably opposed to the Factory Acts.
>
> (Blaug 1958, p. 211)

8.3   Economics, selfishness and humanity

Economics and selfishness

So we arrive at the critical question. Are economists apologists for selfishness?

The truth can be stated concisely. Economics has never 'pled' for selfishness; it has never recommended, praised, or expressed thanks for it. It is a complete misrepresentation of political economy to presume that it supposed that selfishness was good.[25] Classical political economy merely claimed that certain good things do not require selflessness. In particular, national wealth does not require selflessness; the prosperity of the typical citizen does not require that the typical citizen loves his neighbour as himself. What this prosperity did require, according to political economy, was a strong measure of economic freedom. It is economic freedom that the political economists, rightly or wrongly, recommended, praised and expressed thanks for, not selfishness.

The partisan of selflessness may reply that the distinction between economic freedom and selfishness is over fine. Is not economic freedom a licence to pursue self-interest? This query is reasonable. But to give logic its due, to license the pursuit of self-interest is not to commend self-interest; it is to judge licence to be a better policy than non-licence. In any case, the mere licence of self-interest cannot be equated with the actual pursuit of self-interest, since it is an entirely true, if trite, observation that almost all persons are not 'self-interested' in their economic conduct: they are often motivated by the welfare of those in their peer or family group. So although their action in the market is in no way motivated by a concern for their market counter-party, their motivation to go to market is often more than self-interest.[26]

The humanitarian critic may reply that the system of economic freedom is, nevertheless, not a system of altruism, and this reply is worthy. There is nothing in the economist's theory of the free market that makes impossible one billion perishing from lack while one million revel in profusion. However, the real question for the friend of humanity is not whether the market system constitutes a system of benevolence, but whether it serves benevolence better than the alternatives. The point here is that insofar as economic freedom does give licence to self-interest, the market advocate will argue that the market gives less licence to such self-interest than market regulations often have.

Yet, the humanitarian critic may persevere, market regulations need not serve selfish purposes, even if sometimes they have. Can we not conceive of constraints on economic freedom that make the market mimic a more altruistic system? In supporting the free market are not economists effectively opposing such constraints? In fact, economists do not oppose such constraints: economists approve of the welfare state, as is shown in repeated surveys of economists. One such survey indicated that only 17 per cent of US economists disagree with the proposition 'the redistribution of income within the US is a legitimate role for government' (Fuller et al., 1995). If economists look doubtfully on trying to mimic benevolence by market regulation it is not through any lesser benevolence, but a lack of the optimism which most have about the attainability of their goals.

Economics does not apologise for selfishness: and neither does it insinuate selfishness.

Anti-economists (for example, Gittens 2001) have flourished studies (for example, Marwell and Ames 1981) that conclude that in Prisoner's Dilemma games economists play the non-cooperative solution (in which one party 'gains at the expense of the other') more frequently than non-economists.[27] But experiments with the Prisoner's Dilemma games leave unclear whether participants play the cooperative solution from (i) experiencing a disutility from not cooperating or (ii) not understanding the game. Experiments in which the understanding is not at issue have pointed to quite different results. Consider the experiment in which $10 notes are planted in classrooms. Economics students were found more likely than non-economics students to return these notes; 56 per cent of such notes in economics classes were returned, while only 31 per cent of notes left in non-economics classes were returned (Laband and Beil 1999).

Anti-economists have also brandished survey research that concluded that, of all academic disciplines, economists were the least generous to 'large charities such as United Way and viewer supported television' (Frank et al. 1993).[28] This conclusion, however, has little relevance to the issue. When one thinks of 'charity' a *television station* does not leap into mind. Neither does the United Way, which is more a community services association than a foundation for the benefit of the poor or helpless.[29]

A further embarrassment for the thesis that economics insinuates selfishness is the evidence that professional economists are less likely than sociologists to cheat on their dues to their professional societies. A 1994/5 US study of 892 economists, sociologists and political scientists suggests that 38 per cent of sociologist with incomes above $40,000 reported an income below that (and so paid a lower fee to their professional society) but only 23 per cent of economists did so (Laband and Beil 1999; see Table 8.1).[30] This data does not imply that sociologists are any worse than economists: the fee structures of the professional societies of sociology and politics provide a greater incentive to cheat than the economists' society. Nevertheless, the data does rudely deflate any suggestion that economists are less public minded than their counterparts in other disciplines.

Table 8.1 Percentage of US Academics who Apparently Cheat on their Subscription to their Professional Societies

	Economics	Sociology	Political science
Income $40,000 or above	22.8	37.7	26.8
Income above $50,000	33.5	50.5	25.2

The charge of egoism made against economics can be much better made of several conspicuous members of the party of protest against egoism (and economics).

John Ruskin: 'A profoundly self-centred man, he must be assumed to have had an almost unequalled gift of sweeping aside facts that his pride or self-love encouraged him to disregard; while his was the type of sensitiveness that if, sufficiently exasperated, often flashes out in cruelty' (Quennell 1949, p. 62).

Comte: an 'ungrateful, self-centred, and egocentric personality' (*Encyclopedia Britannica*).

Economics with humanitarianism

If economics does not preach or insinuate selfishness, has economic doctrine nevertheless discouraged selfless attempts to relieve the suffering of others?

The political economists held that humanity and benevolence are worthy of esteem in certain, but common, circumstances. The best proof of their belief is their practice.

The philanthropy of Smith, Thornton and Ricardo was extensive. Smith's first biographer states that he 'gave away large sums in secret charity' (Rae [1895] 1965, p. 437). The impressive charity of the monetary theorist Henry Thornton (1760–1815) has been noted by historians of philanthropy. Between 1790 and 1793 Thornton gave £20,408 to charity, while his other expenses came to £6,964; thus charity absorbed almost 75 per cent of his total outlays (Hayek 1939, p. 25).[31] Ricardo was one of the leading British philanthropists of his lifetime. In the village attached to his estate he established a dispensary that treated 225 patients per annum, rebuilt an almshouse for eight 'poor persons', and established a school for 250 children (Weatherall 1976, p. 96). He subscribed to many charitable causes including Persons Confined for Small Debts, the Marine Society, the Jews' Hospital, the Waterloo Subscription, Extreme Distress at Spitalfields, the Poor of the Parish of St George's Hanover Square, and the Gloucester Magdalene Asylum. Ricardo's first vote in Parliament was in favour of the formation of a committee of inquiry into the criminal law with a view to reducing its severity. He voted for the Abolition of Punishment by Whipping Bill, and for the resolution in favour of the abolition of capital punishment for a number of offences.[32]

Neither, contrary to Toynbee's assertion, was Ricardo lacking in sympathy for the poor. Regarding a manuscript by Francis Place on the Poor Laws he wrote:

> [Place] has stated the case of the poor with great force, and I think in many respects with great justice. He tells you what their complaints are against the rich, the chief of which is a want of sympathy with their distress, and oppressive laws.
>
> (Ricardo 1952b, p. 61).

Ricardo's last letter to Maria Edgeworth addressed itself to Ireland:

> You have been so long subjected to misrule as hardly to be in a fit state to be reclaimed by common means. Coercion and severity have proved of little use, and I hope the system of indulgence, kindness and conciliation will now be tried.
>
> (Ricardo 1952b, p. 295)

The New Poor Law

The anti-economists' counter-example to the apparent benevolence of the political economists would be the New Poor Law. But whatever its faults, the New Poor Law was, contrary to Gray, premised on the assumption that the community did share a responsibility for the welfare of any given individual. And 'middle-class economists' specifically supported that premise. Thus J.S. Mill writing on the New Poor Law justifies it with these words:

> Apart from any metaphysical considerations respecting the foundations of morals or of the social union, it will be admitted to be right that human beings should help one another; and the more so, in proportion to the urgency of the need: and none needs help so urgently as one who is starving. The claim to help, therefore, created by destitution is one of the strongest that can exist.
>
> (Mill 1965b, V, xi, §13, p. 960)[33]

Senior concurred with Mill: it is the 'duty of the community', he asserted, to see that children are fed, and 'that unless the community can and will compel the parent to feed the child . . . the community must do so' (quoted in Levy 1970, p. 185).

Further, anti-economists such as Gray are wrong to the point of absurdity to describe the New Poor Law as among Britain's most inhuman statutes. Did the New Poor Law prescribe that all persons (and their families) receiving relief wear a badge bearing a large 'P'? Did it require the whipping of labourers who refused to work at wages set by Justices? Did it impose a life sentence of being 'fed on bread and water and refuse meat, and caused to work by beating, chaining or otherwise' on those who had been twice convicted for refusing to work for 'bare meat and drink'? Did it require that any servant leaving their master without his permission be branded with an 'F' on his forehead? All these were the statute laws of Merrie England concerned with the management of the poor and 'idle'.[34]

Other historical episodes that supposedly show political economy opposing irresistible humanitarian measures reveal, in truth, something quite different.

The climbing boys

Political economy cannot be described as opposed to the restriction on the use of boys as chimney sweeps.

Henry Thornton was a Vice-President of the Society for Superseding the Necessity of Climbing Boys. Henry Brougham voted in favour of legislation (Phillips 1949, p. 27). But what of Ricardo? Inglis argues thus: there is no record of Ricardo expressing his opposition to Lauderdale; therefore he agreed with Lauderdale. On this strange logic most of the inhabitants of the United Kingdom could be inferred to agree with Lauderdale; indeed, most members of the Society for Superseding the Necessity of Climbing Boys could also be inferred to agree. It is true that Ricardo did not vote in favour of the 1818 Bill. But he could not have voted for it, for he was not a Member of Parliament until 1819. It is true that no vote in favour is recorded of Ricardo at the successful passages of Bills through the House of Commons in February and March in 1819: but no vote could be recorded since Hansard did not record how MPs voted. (This was the standard practice of Hansard of the period: Cannan, 1894, p. 249.) But we do know that the March 1819 Bill passed the House of Commons 'without opposition'. If Ricardo disagreed with it, why was he not heard? He was not an MP to keep his disagreement to himself. Despite all this, Inglis plainly insinuates that Ricardo opposed the Bill. It all speaks of the determination of Inglis to convict Ricardo of inhumanity no matter what the lack of evidence.

The Factory Acts

The classical political economists (both British and French) were not hostile to factory legislation in the abstract. They tended to favour regulation of the factory labour of children and youth, and tended to oppose such legislation for adults (see Blaug 1958; Fetter 1980; O'Brien 1975; and Staum 1998, p. 110). Thus Mill, Torrens, McCulloch and Senior supported the 'Althorp Act' (1833)[35] that restricted the daily hours in textile mills of those aged 13 to 17 to no more than 12. But the struggle over the 10-Hours Bill, that would restrict the maximum hours of adult women and children to 10, found political economists mostly in opposition. Torrens, Senior and Mill were opposed,[36] McCulloch was undecided.

Political economy did not add distinction to itself through its general opposition to the 10-Hours Act of 1847. Sympathetic twentieth-century commentators have judged as weak what should have been political economists' strength: their analytic performance. But their opposition should not be interpreted as political economists attempting to frustrate what the great mass of distressed factory hands implored. An 1848 survey of 502 female operatives in Lancashire by a factory inspector indicated that 46 per cent of female workers wanted to work longer than 10 hours (West 1983).

Slavery

Not only have economists not been opposed to many humanitarian measures, the values of economists are complementary to humanitarianism. The great enemy of brutality is freedom, and the great ally of cruelty is freedom's antithesis, violence. Economists opposed cruelties based on force: capital punishment, flogging, slavery, war (see Fetter 1980).

For this reason economics was associated with one of the great humanitarian movements of the eighteenth century: the repudiation of slavery. Historically speaking, this movement was a novelty. The Greco-Roman world had rarely articulated any hostility to slavery. Plato had wished for slave laws more severe than were known in his own society (Morrow 1939).

Christianity tolerated slavery. It was only in the late eighteenth century that an abstract opposition to slavery emerged,[37] and the classical economics that emerged in that period spoke for this opposition with almost a single voice. Smith had impugned the efficiency of slavery in the *Wealth of Nations*, and condemned its injustices in the *Lectures on Jurisprudence*; Josiah Tucker faulted its costliness (Pocock 1985, p. 163). Condorcet and Du Pont had successfully campaigned for the abolition of French slavery in February 1794, and Say threw odium on the 'vicious system of production' that was a usurpation of violence over intelligence (Say 1865, p. 208). Ricardo publicly spoke against the 'the infamous custom, the shocking system' of slavery; Brougham dismayed slavers by making trafficking a transportable offence in the Felony Act of 1811; McCulloch argued that slavery was 'productive of the worst effects' (1843, p. 1044); Thomas Perronet Thompson was a lifelong anti-slavery crusader (Fetter 1980); Senior condemned slavery in his *Edinburgh Review* review of *Uncle Tom's Cabin*; and John Elliot Cairne's *Slave Power* of 1862 became an anti-slavery classic.[38]

Indeed, the support which economics lent to the abolition of slavery was the occasion for one of the great outbursts of anti-economics; Carlyle's *The Nigger Question*. It was in this tract that economics was first hailed as 'the dismal science', a 'dreary, desolate, and indeed quite abject and distressing one'. What so maddened Carlyle about political economy was the fact that it had, with philanthropists, championed the end of slavery in the West Indies. To Carlyle the 'unhappy wedlock of Philanthropic Liberalism and the dismal science' had given birth to 'dark extensive moon-calves, unnamable abortions, wide coiled monstrosities', such as 'Black Emancipation' (Carlyle [1849] 1899a, p. 354).

Economics against humanitarianism

Yet political economy was not a humanitarian cause. If it was sometimes in coalition with humanitarianism, it was sometimes anti-humanitarian. Thus Senior in 1860 complained that 'the wise precautions of the present poor law are to a great extent counteracted by the mistaken humanity of charitable people' who 'are, with the best of motives . . . continually increasing the number and resources of the hospitals, which compete with each other in offering the freest possible medical care to all who come' (Senior [1860] 1962, pp. 27–9).[39] This sort of anti-humane posture, not infrequently found in nineteenth-century political economy, is utterly obsolete: since the mid-Victorian period there has been a revolution in humanitarian sensibilities, that has been shared by the tendency of economics no less than the tendency of general opinion in society.

But there remains a conflict between the economist and the humanitarian. There is something incompassionate about the economist. He is not, as Bagehot said of Senior, a 'melting lover of his species'. This conflict between the economist and the humanitarian turns on the same questions that separated the political economist from the philanthropist: Is a regard for others all the good? Should compassionate sentiment be the supreme guide? Economics answers in the negative. If economics does not deny a potential value to altruism, neither does it take it to be always valuable, or the only value. If it wordlessly accommodates the tender feelings that are the motive force of so much human activity, it has never elevated kindness into the paramount guide for action; or allowed that pity should conquer all.

This conflict between economists and humanitarians over the standing and utility of benevolence obtains a great significance given the huge and ever waxing contemporary popularity of the humanitarian ethic. This is a contest in which economics will always be at a deep rhetorical disadvantage, always cast as Scrooge against the Spirit of Christmas.

Nevertheless, there are at least three considerations weighing in favour of the economists' rejection of the pre-eminent value and significance that the humanitarian affords humanity.

1. *The supply of humanity is limited.* This limit means that the indiscriminate charges to that supply that are implied by the supremacy of humanitarian impulses are wasteful of humanity. We should, instead, take care to 'economise on love'. Further, this limit on the supply of humanity gives an instrumental value to non-humane behaviours. To adapt an earlier writer, it is not to a butcher's selflessness that we must appeal if we are to furnish our tables. It is these less than selfless motives that put the world in motion. Selflessness is not 'all the good'.

2. *The power of humanity is limited.* It is not in the power of humanity to accomplish all things. In this vein Locke once averred that the discovery of quinine had done more good for the world than all of its charity. Economists agree with Locke that love alone will not remedy malaria or many other ills. It was the limited power of pure humanity that was the leading premise in the classicals' case against the humanitarian ethic. According to Malthusian doctrine humanity could not alleviate poverty.

3. *Other values conflict with humanitarianism.* Justice may sometimes conflict with humanity, even if it often complements it. Reason may also be antagonistic to humanity, as sympathy may be born of weak-mindedness. Thus Jevons once asked why does the suffering of animals receive more concern from the English public than the murder of Australian Aborigines? Reason may, additionally, be antagonistic to humanity since suffering itself may be born of weak-mindedness. Thus distress may flow from a foolish action or judgement. Or from a foolish emotional self-management, to the extent that our emotional lives can be managed well or ill.

Economics against pseudo-humanitarianism

If economics is sometimes in conflict with humanitarianism, we would venture that the real conflict lies elsewhere. It is not a genuine humanitarianism that fires the crudest structures against economics. It is instead a false humanitarianism – that may be called 'pseudo-humanitarianism' – that transforms compassion from the source of good to the good itself. In this pseudo-humanitarianism of sensibility the good is implicitly assumed to have been achieved by a rich experience of sympathy, even if the suffering still remains. Pseudo-humanitarianism is the leading, if unstated, part of the creed of the compassion traffickers amongst anti-economists.

In the contest with pseudo-humanitarians, economists are actually in league with humanitarians, since pseudo-humanitarianism is in reality non-humanitarian. It supposes 'his tears matter more than the distress that bade them follow' (Stafford 1987, p. 43); it amounts to an uncoupling of sentiment from action; it reduces to a 'feeling without kindness'. The Reverend Thomas Mozley (1806–93), a leader writer for *The Times* in the mid-nineteenth century, is an illustration. He expressed at length what seems to be a genuinely felt sympathy for the agricultural poor, and exhorted his readers to feel likewise (Mozley 1843). But he was also resolved that nothing should be done: 'Nothing but the deepest and bitterest poverty will subdue the uneducated classes' (quoted in Roberts 1977, p. 161). To Mozley, to feel for the poor was proper *and* sufficient. The feeling completed the duty of the rich to the poor. The poor, it seems, were an unfortunate but necessary sacrifice, rather like fallen soldiers in a necessary war. One salutes them but one does not discontinue the war.

The disconnection between sentiment and action secured by pseudo-humanitarianism can even reduce to a paradoxical 'feeling with *un*kindness'. It is pseudo-humanitarianism that may account for the strange spectacle of economists being reproved for their lack of compassion even when their rigorous policies are in a considerable measure approved. The New Poor Law is an example. The pressure to change the Poor Law was widespread, and certainly did not exclude many of the friends of feeling, who agreed that it needed reform (Coleridge, Southey and, 150 years later, Polanyi).[40] The offence of economists, it seems, was not that they reformed but that they did not 'feel'. Thus Lucy Aikin (1781–1864), a historian and editorial collaborator with Southey, complained 'There is a pseudo-science called political economy which dries up the hearts and imaginations of most who meddle in it' (quoted in Viner 1963). Yet this very same Aikin was a vigorous critic of the leniency of the old Poor Law, and of any 'excess' charity to the poor.[41]

The disconnection between sentiment and action in pseudo-humanitarianism has on occasion even counselled the preservation of privation in order to nurture and experience benevolent feelings. Thus in the 'The Old

Cumberland Beggar' Wordsworth argues that beggary should be not be eradicated, as the political economists advocated. It should instead be preserved so as to nurture the sympathetic faculty, and to give the mass of the population the opportunity to enjoy the pleasant feeling of being charitable (Wordsworth 1947).

Even if we neglect such anti-humanitarian consequences of pseudo-humanitarianism, its key doctrine of the intrinsic good of feeling (that some good is secured by a rich experience of sympathy, even while the suffering still remains) will seem an utterly inadequate and delusive doctrine to any cause for the public welfare. It is foreign to economics. And economics is seemingly right to reject the intrinsic value of feeling. What did Toynbee's working-class audience want more: sympathy or action?[42]

Yet common precepts of decent personal relations do not reject the intrinsic good of sympathetic feeling. On the contrary: the merit and propriety we attach to commiseration with others' suffering (and congratulation on the occasion of others' joys) reflect, in part, a belief that such fellow-feeling is right in itself, independent of its consequences.

There is, therefore, over the intrinsic value of sympathy a disagreement between economists and the lay public. And this disagreement can throw light on the poor reception of economics by lay audiences. Leslie Stephen in *The Utilitarians* compares James Mill and Samuel Taylor Coleridge. 'If we were to apply the rules of ordinary morality', says Stephen 'it [the comparison] would be entirely in Mill's favour'. Mill supported a large family, was an industrious and effective functionary in the administration of India, and completed a suite of works which were sufficiently significant in their own day to be recalled in the next century. In far more comfortable circumstances, Coleridge was incapable of managing his family, produced a spray of fragments (a few brilliant), and in later years was embroiled in drug addiction. Yet 'Coleridge died in the odour of sanctity, revered by his disciples and idolised by his children: while Mill went to the grave amidst the shrugs of respectable shoulders, and respected rather than beloved by the son who succeeded to intellectual leadership.' Stephen explains: 'the amiable and kindly, whose sympathies are quickly moved, gain an unfair share of regard in life and afterwards. We are more pleased by an ineffectual attempt to be kindly, than by a real kindness bestowed ungraciously' (Stephen [1900] 1950, p. 37).

8.4 Anti-economists against the religion of love

We have seen how the anti-economists of the religion of love drew a great distance between themselves and economists. Yet numerous *anti*-economists were also often distant from the religion of love. The Left and the Right rejected it. Further, the Right's rejection of the religion involved a brutality which was no part of the economists' rejection.

The Left rejected the religion of love on the grounds that it tended to conserve the social order. Thus Marx rejected philanthropy because it purported to relieve the working class without the overthrow of the existing order (Marx [1847] 1963, p. 106). More generally, the Left would have to be cautious of any system of attachments, as they could potentially be conserving. Thus the 'brotherhood of love' of the Saint-Simonians was rejected by the Russian radical theoretician and anti-economist so admired by Marx (and Lenin), Nikolay Gavrilovich Chernyshevsky, who preserved in the latter part of the nineteenth century a strident philosophy of self-interest that seems to arrive directly out of the eighteenth (see Woehrlin 1971, p. 226).

The Right also rejected the religion of love, but on the grounds that it disturbed social order (Radcliffe 1993). Philanthropy spelt a *lack* of attachment, and thereby a hostility to order. To be drawn in all directions by brotherly love is to fail to fall into orbit around any larger satellite. Thus Burke, Coleridge, Southey and Wordsworth disliked philanthropy, as did Carlyle who saw it as enemy of order. Man is not lovable; he needed more to be ruled than loved.

The Left and the Right also rejected the cult of compassion. The Left was wary of pity since pity is in many ways a moderating phenomenon, and therefore stabilising. And the Tories, contrary to mythology, had no more compassion than the economists. On the contrary, they had less. We will illustrate by reference to slavery, capital punishment, 'the conditions of the working class' and the Irish famine.

Slavery was condoned by Coleridge (in his maturity) and Wordsworth, and unabashedly defended by Carlyle, Ruskin, Alison and (until 1833) Cobbett.

Wordsworth wrote a sonnet in praise of capital punishment (Wordsworth 1841). In his youth Wordsworth complained of the 'idle cry of modish lamentation' over the execution of Louis XVI, and the attachment of so much importance to 'the personal sufferings' of a single individual (Wordsworth 1974a, 1, p. 32).

The 'conditions of the working class' did not necessarily awake any Tory sympathy. In 1833 Coleridge faulted wages for being too high. And he took the occasion to censure the political economists for their 'maxim' that high wages encouraged the supply of labour.

> Every man in Manchester, Birmingham, and in other great manufacturing towns knows that the most skilful artisans, who may earn high wages at pleasure, are constantly in the habit of working but a few days, and of idling the rest. I believe St Monday is very well kept by the workmen in London.

> (Coleridge 1969c, p. 231)

On these grounds Coleridge complained that 'the lives and properties of millions of men' are staked on a 'a maxim of modern political economy'.

Whereas the seamstress attracted the sympathy of many (including Ruskin) Carlyle had not much for them apart from scorn.

Thirty-thousand outcast needlewomen working themselves swiftly to death... British charity is smitten to the heart, at the laying bare of such a scene; passionately undertakes, by enormous subscription of money, or by other enormous effort, to redress that individual horror... but here perhaps is the saddest thing of all... In high houses and in low... no real needlewoman 'distressed' or other, has been found attainable in any of the houses I frequent. Imaginary needlewomen, who demand considerable wages, and have a deepish appetite for beer and viands, I hear everywhere.

(Carlyle [1850] 1898, p. 28)

Whereas Ricardo had proposed a 'system of indulgence, kindness and conciliation' towards the Irish, in the January 1848 issue of *Blackwoods'* the anti-economist Archibald Alison grumbled about the 'unheard of munificence' showed by 'British liberality' to famine stricken Ireland.

Has crime decreased, and industry improved? Has attachment to the British government become universal, and hatred of the stranger worn out in consequence of the leniency with which they have been treated, and the unparalleled generosity with which their wants have been supplied? The facts are notoriously and painfully the reverse.

(Alison 1850, p. 393)[43]

We will finish with Tory attitudes to misery in another troubled British possession, Jamaica, and 'the Governor Eyre case'. In October 1865 a rioting mob in Jamaica destroyed a court house and killed 18 persons. Governor Edward James Eyre declared martial law, and within four weeks British troops had killed or executed 586 blacks and flogged another 600.[44] Liberal opinion in Britain was outraged, and J.S. Mill formed a Jamaica Committee to press for charges to be laid against Eyre. In response to this 'small-loud group... of Nigger-Philanthropists', Carlyle and Ruskin created an Eyre Defence Committee, with the explicit support of Charles Dickens and Charles Kingsley. Carlyle pronounced himself to be 'heartily sorry' for Eyre. Kingsley declared Eyre's methods to be a glorious example of 'modern chivalry' (Ford 1947–48).

A historian of Tory paternalism has written:

The paternalists, with their compassionate pleas that property do its duty, formed a striking contrast to the economists... This contrast has led many historians to see in paternalism a source of later collectivism, one leading to the welfare state... That the Tory social conscience led to such a government is a myth too long held, one that a reading of Tory periodicals should end.

(Roberts 1977, p. 169)

9
Crusaders and Consumers

From offence at the selfishness of individual human beings, we turn to offence at the selfishness of humanity.

Economics has tended to judge any social system by the degree to which it supplies human satisfactions. Any offence that anti-economists have taken at this criterion of judgement we have thus far passed over. This chapter reverses that neglect. This chapter turns squarely towards a shaft of anti-economics that declares the state of human satisfaction to be a radically insufficient criterion of judgement of any social philosophy. According to this species of anti-economics, reverence for the good must often debar the service of human comfort and ease. According to this species of anti-economics, economics, by falsely identifying the defence of the good with a search for human comfort and ease, has facilitated various offences against moral values. Above all, by recognising nothing to be good or valuable unless it provides comfort and ease to humanity economics has approved of the degradation of the natural and cultural environment. This species of anti-economics, therefore, embraces the antagonism of the environmental movement to economics, and a parallel animosity of the partisans of art to economics. We confront, in other words, the complaint that economics has an ethical system in which 'the market' is the only criterion.

We will argue that this objection to economics gained a charge from the decline in Christian theism. The most effective vehicle of opposition to the supremacy of human satisfactions has, historically speaking, been religion. It is religion that has divided the world into the sacred and mundane, and demanded the abnegation of human will in the presence of the sacred. It was only in the deistic Enlightenment that the claims of the sacred shrivelled, the room for the worldly grew, and economics germinated. But the end of the Enlightenment saw a reaction against this worldliness, and a reawakened longing for the sacred. The Christian revival in considerable measure satisfied this, but with the decay of Christianity from the late nineteenth century, anti-worldly sentiments sought compensation in sacralisations of nature and art. These substitute religions have since anathematised economics on account of the supremacy of human satisfactions that economics supposedly assumes. In the mind of these substitute religions their conflict with economics is the conflict of the coming Kingdom with the Reign of Mammon.

9.1   The sacred versus the civilised

The pursuit of happiness

Religion is popularly identified with a belief in the existence of supernatural beings, yet theorists of religion often prefer to identify 'the sacred' as the critical constituent of any religiosity (for example, Eliade 1959). The sacred is understood as the antithesis to the 'profane'; the mundane, the worldly, the ordinary, comprehensible. While the mundane is familiar and commonsensical, the sacred is a marvel, awe inspiring, peculiar and incomprehensible. While the mundane is open to all, the sacred is restricted, even forbidden, and violation of these restrictions is an abomination. And while the sacred has unarguable claims upon the mundane world, the mundane world has no claims in reply. In the face of the sacred, humanity is to submit, and to sacrifice, to forgo, and to deny its will.

The tendency of historians of religion is to believe that the history of the sacred reveals a gradual contraction of its reach. Traditional pre-literate religions believed the fragments of the sacred to be dispersed throughout the natural world: sacred groves, mountains, rivers. Judaism and Christianity concentrated the sacred in God, and left its appearance on earth to enclaves in space (the Church) and time (miracles). The rationalistic tendencies of the Enlightenment completed this tidy up so that in deistic Christianity the sacred was compacted into a single point, God, distant and removed from our earthly existence. Two well-known critics of economics, and advocates of 'bionomics', have described this situation with regret: 'As the Enlightenment proceeded even the immediacy of God disappeared... "God" was no longer seen in and through the creatures but was viewed as standing outside them and above them, known to exist only by reason. The creatures functioned quite autonomously without God' (Daly and Cobb 1989, p. 384).

The Enlightenment's companion project was to destroy the claims of the earthly representatives of God to manage the world. The world was now given over to human wishes, only loosely constrained by any unworldly Christian values. The ultimate good had been doing as God wished; it was now seen as doing as you pleased, and no irreconcilability between the two was admitted.

A temperate hedonism was, therefore, characteristic of Enlightenment thought. There was an interest and even esteem for worldly satisfactions; they were now worth thinking about. 'Comfortable' assumed its modern, familiar meaning of ease.[1] *Philosophes* composed treatises on 'happiness'.[2]

The citizens of the new American state dedicated themselves to the 'pursuit of happiness', and their ideological equivalents in England subscribed to a felicific calculus.

Among the leading Enlightenment advocates of the worthiness of comfort and ease were the economists. A range of economists sought to legitimate luxury (that is, 'refinement in the gratification of the senses'), including Nicholas Barbon, Bernard Mandeville, Jean-François Melon and David Hume (Berry 1994; Steiner 1997). 'Civilisation' was used by Smith as synonymous with economic development. Say recommended 'comfort' (using the English) as the goal of life. The French should import this English word 'comfortable', said Say, and it was so borrowed.[3] Say disposed with a shrug of those who disapproved of his esteem of comfort.

I have heard deplored the introduction in our customs of coffee, chocolate and one thousand other superfluities that our fathers did well without. They also did without shirts; the habit of washing did not spread until the 14th century. It was only under the reign of Henri III, King of France, that one began to dine with forks. America was discovered when we had not yet glass in our windows. Is it not better that we have acquired the need for these than have the merit of knowing how to do without them?

(Say 1840, p. 54)

The attainment of 'pig wash'

The mild and tranquil hedonism of the Enlightenment was not to live undisturbed long into the next turbulent century. The Romantics aspired to neither comfort, utility nor even 'happiness'. The various forms of Christian revival in the first half of the nineteenth century also spurned any such aspiration. But perhaps the purest, bitterest and most brutal antipathy to the bland hedonism of the eighteenth century was expressed in the de-Christianised religiosity of Thomas Carlyle. The 'light comfortable kind of "wine-and-walnuts" philosophy' of utilitarianism was, he declared in 1850, a 'Pig Philosophy'. The tenets of this philosophy were:

1. The Universe, so far as sane conjecture can go, is an immeasurable Swine's-trough, consisting of solid and liquid, and of other contrasts and kinds; – especially consisting of attainable and unattainable, the latter in immensely greater quantities for most pigs.
2. Moral evil is unattainability of Pig's-wash; moral good, attainability of ditto...It is the mission of universal Pighood, and the duty of all Pigs, at all times, to diminish the quantity of unattainable and increase that of attainable. All knowledge and effort ought to be directed thither and thither only; Pig Science, Pig Enthusiasm and Devotion have this one aim.

(Carlyle [1850] 1898, p. 316)

The representative of Carlyle's 'Pig Science' was, unavoidably, political economy. Carlyle complains that as far as McCroudy (that is, J.R. McCulloch) is concerned 'The Universe' is 'a huge dull Cattle-stall and St Catharine's Wharf: with a few pleasant apartments upstairs for those who can make money' (Carlyle [1850] 1898, p. 282). But 'Is not political economy useful? And ought not Joseph Hume and MacCulloch to be honoured of all men?' 'My cow is useful', replies Carlyle 'and I keep her in the stable, and feed her with oilcake and "chaff and dregs", and esteem her truly. But shall she live in my parlour? No; by the Fates, she shall live in the stall' (quoted in Groenewegen 2001, p. 81).

Carlyle believed the end of man was not comfort, but work. There was, he said, a 'sacredness' in Work (the capital is Carlyle's).[4] His veneration of work only heightened his conflict with Enlightenment. The Enlightenment did not see work as an end. To the mind of the Enlightenment 'labour' was 'toil' (see, for example, Smith [1776] 1937, p. 30), and 'toil' was the opposite of ease. Work would obtain consumption, but what consumption it procures may be rationally judged not worth the work that procured it. Thus, speaking in defence of 'idle Negroes', Ricardo wrote 'Happiness is the object to be desired, and we cannot be quite sure that, provided he is equally well fed, a man may not be happier in the enjoyment of the luxury of idleness than in the enjoyment in the luxuries of a neat cottage and good clothes' (quoted in Halévy [1928] 1949a, p. 320).

Carlyle's judgement of the ignobility of comfort and the nobility of work found significant popularity among social critics in Germany at the close of the nineteenth century (Breckman 1991). One such was the anti-economist Werner Sombart, who appears to have had a genuine loathing of the material aids to life: to Sombart the British soldier's safety-razor was a proof of British degeneracy. Sombart adopted the word '*comfortism*' to designate the materialism he so detested. To Sombart the proper aspiration of man is to connect to his environment, not to manipulate it for his convenience. Happiness and comfort were offences against the good; since the good lay in resistance and strength in the face of unease. To Sombart, therefore, heroism was the great achievement of human existence, war was its occasion, and honour (not 'happiness') was its reward.[5]

In nineteenth-century England doubts about the value of material comfort were aired by Ruskin, and entertained even by such muscular Victorians as Walter Bagehot. But it was in the inter-war period of the twentieth century, with the popular newspaper sermonising of W.R. Inge (a Dean of St Pauls) against 'consumptionism', that this sentiment appears to have burgeoned (Wiener 1979). The attack on consumption was pursued in the mid-twentieth century by J.B. Priestley and F.R. Leavis (Leavis 1963, pp. 46–7), whose elevation of 'creativity' can be treated as an artistic pair to Carlyle's esteem of 'work'. Be it Carlyle or Leavis (or Sombart), the sheer inanimate, vegetating, passivity of consumption was a cause for offence.[6]

An antipathy towards 'comfortism' or 'consumptionism' is familiar in the contemporary world, although it is now styled as a contempt of *consumerism*. The roots of the contemporary contempt remain as they were in the past. But by the late twentieth century the most powerful focus of objection to the pursuit of comfort was new; it was that its pursuit entailed the destruction of 'nature' which possessed an inherent good, independent of any service with which it may supply humanity.[7] It was in the late twentieth century that there swelled the doctrine that in the face of nature humanity must submit, sacrifice, forgo, and deny itself. It is nature that has been made sacred.

9.2 Nature's temple

The death of God and the birth of Gaia

Economics was born in a period in which nature was not holy. To the Enlightenment, nature lacked a sacred or even mysterious character. Nature was an impressive and effective facility for our earthly existence. 'Nature is a great economist' said the celebrated eighteenth-century naturalist Gilbert White (1720–93) (Worster 1994, p. 9). The 'classic spirit' of that century held that nature was best when civilised, tidied up, and harnessed to productive use, in the manner of a beehive. Ricardo displays this sensibility in writing to Malthus while Malthus holidayed in Wales, 'I expect that your eye will be quite weary of the bare mountains of Wales and you will hail with pleasure the more fruitful country of England' (Ricardo 1952a, p. 107).[8]

At the height of the Enlightenment, Rousseau had already rejected his period's 'lordly' attitude to nature. But a consequential repudiation awaited the arrival of Romanticism. The nucleus of the new Romantic sensibility was an aversion to *control*; and that was complemented by an attraction to abandon, movement, profusion, life. The Romantic sensibility consequently nurtured a cult of life, and nature. The Romantics promoted a seeping of the sacred beyond its narrowly restricted deistic boundaries into the natural world.[9]

Historians of the environmental movement have offered up Wordsworth as the personification of the new Romantic veneration of nature (Bate 1991). Wordsworth's credentials as a kind of Romantic ecologist are several; his campaign in the 1840s to preserve the Lake District from man-made encroachment; his recommendation that the Lake District be made 'a sort of national property'; his commendation of the fact that in the Lake District the hand of man was 'incorporated and subservient to the powers and processes of Nature'; and, above all, his sometimes rapturous psychic state in receiving nature.[10]

John Stuart Mill, as an admirer of Wordsworth and assimilator of all the currents of his age, reproduced similar sentiments. In his *Principles of Political*

Economy Mill commends, in a now much-quoted passage, the communion of the soul with nature: 'Solitude in the presence of natural beauty and grandeur, is the cradle of thoughts and aspirations which are not only good for the individual, but which society could ill do without'. Mill goes on to express repulsion at Ricardo's 'fruitful country':

> Nor is there much satisfaction in contemplating the world with nothing left to the spontaneous activity of nature; with every rood of land brought into cultivation, which is capable of growing food for human beings; every flowery waste or natural pasture ploughed up, all quadrupeds or birds which are not domesticated for man's use exterminated as his rivals for food, every hedgerow or superfluous tree rooted out, and scarcely a place left where a wild shrub or flower could grow without being eradicated as a weed in the name of improved agriculture.
>
> (Mill 1965b, IV, vi, §2, p. 756)

Finally, Mill adds, there really are enough human beings in the world anyway.

Nevertheless, the cult of nature was not at its most potent form with the Romantics. Not all Romantics participated in it. Of those who did, some (like Wordsworth) were orthodox Christians. And, however much Mill admired nature, the grounds of his admiration rested purely on the instrumental value that nature had to mankind.

It was the sudden decline in the prestige of Christianity in the last third of the nineteenth century which provided the occasion for the sacred to brim over its deistic boundaries and gush into the natural world.

Historians of religion tend to agree that in 1870, or thereabouts, God died.[11] Thus in place of the early nineteenth-century religious revival there arrived, at about 1870, a religious waning. A proximate stimulus of this waning were the advances of biology and biochemistry. This advance lent itself to an aggressive atheistic materialism in which the sacred was treated with contempt. But this materialism was not the only response to the implication of the new life sciences. For the new life sciences, in exploding Christianity, did not destroy the sacred, only its compression in a God or Church. The new life sciences amounted to a cosmological supernova that blew spiritual debris across the universe. The 'diffused sacred' of older religions was, thereby, resurrected. One manifestation of this resurrection was the interest in spiritualism that absorbed, for example, the eminent life scientist (and strenuous anti-economist) Alfred Russel Wallace (Coleman 2001a).[12]

But for our purposes, the most significant manifestation of the newly diffused sacred was a worship of nature.[13] This is articulated at length in Hippolyte Taine's essay of 1868 'Sainte Odile et Iphigénie en Tauride'. Taine writes there that when we contemplate woodland we feel 'things are divine'; in this 'great natural temple' the young trees form the 'columns of a cathedral', and the bogs have the air of a crypt: 'If one wishes to know in what consists true religious sentiment, it is here that one must come.' He concludes: 'to see is to pray'; 'the divine is on the earth' (Taine [1868] 1903, p. 80).

Another 'nature as cathedral' text is supplied by John Muir (1838–1914) founder (in 1892) of the Sierra Club. In 1869 he declared of the Sierra Nevada 'No description of Heaven that I have ever heard or read seems half so fine ... perched like a fly on the Yosemite dome I ... humbly prostrate before the vast display of God's power, and eager to offer self-denial and renunciation with eternal toll to learn any lesson in the divine manuscript' (quoted in Cronon 1996).

To worship one needs a church, and it is not coincidental that the sentiments of Taine and Muir corresponded with the birth of the National Park movement. In 1872 legislation was passed to create the world's first such park, Yellowstone National Park in the United States. This was followed by similar legislation in Canada, Germany, Sweden, France and Australia.[14] At about this time the United Kingdom saw the creation of the first organisations dedicated to preserve nature; the Commons Preservation Society 1865 (Britain's first 'environmentalist' society), the Lake District Defence Society 1883 (headed by the Wordsworthian Hardwicke Rawnsley), the National Trust for Places of Historic Interest and Natural Beauty 1895, the Royal Society for the Protection of Birds 1889, and the Fauna and Flora Preservation Society 1903. And 1877 is the date of the *OED*'s first recorded usage of 'pollution' in the sense of environmental destruction, rather than the older more general sense of defilement.[15]

To summarise our thesis: in the late nineteenth century there was a precipitation of the sacred upon nature. This may seem to overstate the religious aspect of the modern reverence of nature, but environmentalists do not always recoil from such a characterisation. Thus one anti-economist environmentalist writes: 'Some people accuse the conservation movement of campaigning with quasi-religious fervour. But if religion means a return to the deepest spiritual and moral values, a reconnection between ourselves and our source in the natural world, is that not a cause for celebration?' (Hamilton 1994, p. 11). Two other well-known ecological economists, Herman E. Daly and J.B. Cobb (a theologian), write by way of a prefatory remark to their environmentalist anti-text 'We are both Christian theists, and we want to show how our belief supports the biospheric vision' (Daly and Cobb 1989, p. 376).

Declarations of the 'rights of nature'

The sacralisation of nature facilitated or energised three distinct theses which in coalition constituted the creed of the renewed environmental movement of the late twentieth century.

1. *Environmental naturalism*. Man should live more 'naturally'. Nature is to be the touchstone of all decisions, and is to be revered and honoured by the way man lives. Put simply, we should live more like animals. As D.H. Lawrence urged, 'Be a good animal' (quoted in Cohen 1993, p. 224). Or as the founder of Earth First declared, 'We believe we must return to being animal' (quoted in Cronon 1996, p. 20). Like animals we should do without technology, markets, impersonal relations and rationality. We should 'live simply', and think simply, too.
2. *Environmental apocalypticism*. Nature is vulnerable to fatal damage by man's civilisation, with dreadful consequences. This environmental apocalypticism may be interpreted as the expression of a dread of the 'pollution' of the sacred by the 'impurities' of the mundane. The mundane has radically defiled the sacred, and so threatens the mundane order by the destruction of sacred energies that underpin that order.
3. *Biocentrism*. Nature has an objective and intrinsic value. It has a value independent of the service with which it provides mankind. Trees have rights. So do rocks.

All three are the sustaining doctrines of a number of environmentalist anti-texts that maintain that 'purely economic reasoning results in the destruction, rather than the protection of nature': *The Bankruptcy of Economics: Ecology, Economics and the Sustainability of the Earth* (1999) by Joseph Wayne Smith et al.; *The Mystic Economist* (1994) by Clive Hamilton; *The Economy of the Earth* (1988) by Mark Sagoff; *For the Common Good* (1989) by Herman E. Daly and John B. Cobb; *Creating Alternative Futures: the End of Economics* (1978) by Hazel Henderson; and *Small is Beautiful: Economics as if People Mattered* (1973) by E.F. Schumacher.

Whether these three theses of environmentalism are truly in conflict with economics is more arguable.

Environmental apocalypticism is a thesis of particular fact, not general principle. That economic growth damages nature is entirely consistent with core economic principles.

Environmental naturalism is an ethical injunction which economics does not affirm, but which the liberalism of economics both accommodates and dismisses. Any desire to live 'more naturally' is accommodated as individual 'preference'; any desire for others to live more naturally is disregarded as a 'meddlesome preference'.

Biocentrism is another ethical injunction which economics does not affirm, but upon which the liberalism of economics puts limits. The extent to which economics limits biocentrism depends on which of the three forms its non-affirmation of biocentrism will take. These three possible forms we may call 'atheism', 'agnosticism' and 'toleration'.

'Atheism' can be defined as a denial of the existence of the intrinsic value of nature. Such a denial was advanced by Leon Walras.

Any being that is not human is a thing. The thing is an impersonal being, that is to say a being that doesn't know itself, that does not own itself, that is not at all responsible for its conduct, nor susceptible to merit and demerit. By this reason things are at the discretion of persons. For all time it is a right and a duty for the latter to contribute to the former regarding their end, the accomplishment of their destiny. It is why we burn the wood of the forest, why we eat the fruits and animals of the land, why we turn rivers from their course. And if it was useful and possible to pierce the earth right through, to drain the seas, to draw closer the earth and the sun it would be permitted or else commanded, for this only[,] it is for all time a right and a duty for us to subordinate the end of things to our will, their blind destiny to our moral destiny. Thus on one side the impersonal *nature*; on the other side *humanity*. Reason submits the first to the second.

(Walras 1860, p. xi, emphasis in original)

'Agnosticism' can be defined as a denial of the knowability of the intrinsic value of nature. Agnosticism does not deny the existence of intrinsic values, it denies the existence of any significant knowledge of intrinsic values.

The agnostic position dismisses human claims to knowledge of intrinsic values as illusions; they are not reflections of intrinsic value, but of human delight. Thus animals beautiful to the human eye are (illegitimately) awarded an intrinsic value; animals which are rare (and so have a subjective scarcity value) are also awarded a spurious intrinsic value. Agnosticism pursues the suspicion that human satisfactions are latent in the supposed recognition of intrinsic values even in the cathedrals of nature. In this vein William Cronon has argued that nature, as it is found in National Parks, is a human contrivance to satisfy human yearnings.

Far from being the one place on earth that stands apart from humanity, it [the wilderness] is quite profoundly a human creation...As we gaze into the mirror it holds up to us, we too easily imagine that what we behold is Nature when in fact we see a reflection of our own unexamined longings and desires.

(Cronon 1996, p. 7)

In this agnostic view every putative recognition of intrinsic value betrays signs of a human longing. The appeal of wilderness is an appeal to a front-iersman fantasy. You used to shoot buffaloes. Now you dance with wolves.

This agnostic position, without denying the existence of intrinsic values, brandishes the seeming paradox of a group of human beings (environmentalists) deciding what is the objective value of things independent of subjective human opinion. Without denying the existence of intrinsic values, the agnostic position contends that our ignorance of these values must, and should, leave our conduct unaffected by their existence.

But neither atheism nor agnosticism seem a satisfactory position. Walras's view that no action can be wrong as long as it pleases humanity is shocking.[16] And while agnosticism puts us on guard against the temptation to elevate our pleasures into the world's duties, nevertheless the thesis that it is impossible to recognise extant intrinsic values seems pessimistic. Economics, however, is neither agnostic or atheist about any intrinsic value of nature.

'Toleration' is the best description of the position of economics on biocentrism. Economic doctrine does not affirm an intrinsic value of nature, yet economics supports social mechanisms that allow persons to affirm in action that nature has an intrinsic value. The major social mechanism is market patronage; if persons do affirm intrinsic values, then the market will accommodate. But, the affirmation of intrinsic values accommodated by the social mechanisms favoured by economics extends beyond 'the market'. They include also the provision of 'public goods', (that is, goods whose benefit is non-excludable and non-rival, such as the light of a lighthouse). Any environmentalist sentiment that the very existence of a species, or habitat, is valuable will fall into the category of public good, as the benefit derived from the preservation of its very existence is both non-excludable and non-rival. Thus the provision by law of national parks and protection of species are interpretable as the provision of a public good, and therefore as consistent with economics.

The biocentrist will be dissatisfied with toleration. They will protest that there is no reason to suppose that such accommodation of the affirmation of intrinsic values by the market and public goods will lead to a rightful amount of affirmation. And this protest has good grounds. There is nothing in economic doctrine that is inconsistent with the contention that a 'welfare efficient' system of markets and public goods is unduly insensible to the intrinsic value of nature.[17]

But economics 'will only tolerate toleration'. Economics denies that the rights of nature should be enforced over the common opinions and wishes of humankind. Democracy, in other words, trumps nature. The critical insinuation of environmentalism is that nature trumps democracy (see Lewis 1992, p. 40). Thus environmentalists object to the 'democratic' character of economics. One relatively open handed reproof of this democratic orientation is provided by the environmentalist Clive Hamilton in his anti-text: 'Consumer sovereignty is the foundation stone of the Western political system and that is why economists, the ideologists of that system, defend consumer sovereignty so vociferously' (Hamilton 1994, p. 187). Here we see economists being identified with democracy ('the Western political system') and being cold-bloodedly faulted for the identification.[18]

Autocracy in Arcadia

Peter Self (1919–99) provides a more extensive illustration of the reluctance about democracy felt by anti-economists who are dedicated to elevating certain eternal values above the reach of an insensible populace and market.

Peter Self was the principal officer of the Town and Country Planning Association, the twentieth-century version of the older, semi-utopian Garden Cities Movement that advocated the creation of small self-contained communities that 'would combine the amenities of urban life with the ready access to nature typical of rural environments'.

In his anti-text *Econocrats and the Policy Process* (1975), Self argues that the processes of government have been warped by what he terms 'econocrats', economists who 'attempt to turn economics into a master science of human values, capable of disclosing and quantifying these values according to some objective criterion of value known to the economist' (Self 1975, p. 7).

To Self, cost-benefit analysis is the embodiment of econocracy (Self 1975, p. 7). To Self, the injury that cost-benefit analysis does to good policy lies in the fact that it is concerned only with 'individual preferences' – that is, how much people are willing to pay in a market-type situation. Self believes, uncontroversially, that the market sometimes does not place ideal valuations on things. More controversially Self believes that it is the role of the state to override market valuations. Thus Self opposes cost-benefit analysis because it undermines this overriding role. Rather than engage in cost-benefit analysis, says Self, the state should facilitate 'planning'.

Evidently, Self's contrast between 'planning' and 'cost-benefit analysis' reduces to a contest between 'planners' seeking to plant and cultivate human life in shapes and patterns that accord with planners' visions, and cost-benefit analysts responding to the tugs and pulls of human likings and loathings. To put the contrast another way, planning is autocratic, while cost-benefit analysis is democratic. And Self does not shy away from making the contrast in similar terms. To Self the political base of cost-benefit analysis is 'populist-democratic', and is correlate with what he calls 'political populism', the programme that 'seeks to maximise direct decision making of the electorate, thereby limiting the discretion of elected representatives and converting them potentially to no more than mandated delegates' (Self 1975, p. 106). To Self the rise of cost-benefit analysis since the Second World War is linked with the rise of political populism. In the 1940s, says Self, political populism was in disrepute and cost-benefit analysis did not exist. Since then political populism and cost-benefit analysis have both surged. Both, in Self's view, are to be regretted.[19]

9.3 The heathen as the philistine

Environmentalists claim that economics' use of human satisfaction as the sole criterion of judgement is disrespectful of the value of nature. We now take up the claim that economics' use of human satisfaction as the sole criterion of judgement is disrespectful of the value of art. We take up the thesis that economics is an accomplice of an abhorrent philistinism.

Ruskin put the grievance very concisely when he complained that political economy condoned the fact that pornographic lithographics were better business than the paintings of Tintoretto: 'The modern political economists have been without exception incapable of apprehending the nature of intrinsic value at all' (quoted in Grampp 1973, p. 369).[20] One may also instance as examples of aesthetic antagonism towards economics Matthew Arnold's aloof disdain for political economy, or the publication in F.R. Leavis's *Scrutiny* in the 1930s of some exercises in anti-economics (Kitchin 1933). Yet the notion that economics is an accomplice of philistinism has received no extended articulation; there seem to be no artistic anti-texts. More common, perhaps, is the diatribe against the economic, rather than economics as such.[21] In this diatribe, art creation and wealth creation are cast as fated adversaries, and art creation is judged the righteous victor.

This perceived antagonism between economics and art is expressed in its purest form when art assumes the sacred, and the economic the profane. We maintain that such a resolution to sacralise art, and have humanity submit to it, is a historical expression of the discharge of the sacred from the perimeters of a faltering Christian orthodoxy. Art at the beginnings of the modern Western world was in the service of religion, not a religion. Art was a means, not an end, of worship. The artist was an artisan and was wholly identified with worldly society (Gimpel 1969). The various holy fools of Christendom did not paint, or compose.

With the advent of the Enlightenment, art did not withdraw, as the sacred did, to the edges of the world, but remained united with the world. To the Enlightenment, commerce did not pollute art.[22] Neither did technology: the advancement of the sciences was believed to coincide with the advances of the arts (see Hume [1777] 1985). There was one culture. As Taine put it, every scientist composed verse, and every poet wrote science. Thus Smith was a member of the largely literary and artistic London society, the Club, and the author of *Lectures on Rhetoric and Belles Lettres*. The analyst of the wealth of nations saw no inconsistency with professing on beauty. 'That utility is one of the sources of beauty has been observed by every body' (Smith [1759] 1974, p. 179). To the Enlightenment, the useful was beautiful and the beautiful was useful.

The Romantic tendency rejected the Enlightenment's association of utility and beauty. The basic Romantic aversion to control lent itself to a refusal of any notion that art be subservient to anything, including any requirement that art be of utility. A tension between utility and beauty was now perceived; utility was not one of the sources of beauty; it was one of the sources of ugliness. 'Nothing is truly beautiful unless it is useless; everything useful is ugly ... The most useful place in a house is the lavatory' (Théophile Gautier quoted in Bell-Villada 1986, p. 437). There was no merit for beauty in utility; the merit of beauty lay in its beauty. Thus the notion of 'art for art's sake' originated with the Romantics.[23] The Romantic impulse, therefore, constituted a fairly advanced stage in the transition from art for the glory of God, to art for the glory of the god of art.

For the remainder of the nineteenth century art for art's sake remained a powerful lure, often embraced, but sometimes repulsed. Art historians have recorded how several leading lights of Romanticism (Hugo, Lamartine, George Sand) rejected art for art's sake from their middle years (Gimpel 1969, p. 105).

It was in the later nineteenth century, coincident with the decay of orthodox Christian belief, that there came a renewed embrace of the sacralisation of art. It was with the 'death of God' that art as a substitute-sacred found a revived strength to face down and scorn the claims of a mundane world. By 1866 the phrase 'art for art's sake' was given a new impetus in English by Rossetti. Matthew Arnold's religious speculations of the 1870s have been commonly interpreted as amounting to the aestheticisation of religion, and the sacralisation of art (see Livingston 1973). It was in this period that John Ruskin observing storm clouds breaking over Chamonix and revealing the mountains behind 'all fire in the light of the sunset', had a 'God as Beauty' experience, to match the 'God as Nature' experience of Taine. 'It was then only beneath those glorious hills that I learned how thought itself may become ignoble ... when compared with ... the prostration of all power – and the cessation of all will – before and in the Presence, of the manifested Deity. It was then that I understood that all which is the type of God's attributes ... is in the pure and right sense of the word BEAUTIFUL' (Daley 1997, p. 95).

Manifestations of 'art as sacred' include:

- The belief that the artist is not merely the instrument of the divine, but divine (see Gimpel 1969).
- The doctrine that the value of art is greater than the value of anything else.
- A posture of alienation towards the world. This posture may be merely one of detachment, where art is a sanctuary. Or it may be squarely aggressive, as in the scandal seeking art-quack of the late twentieth century.

The sacralisation of art facilitated three theses that are inimical to the economic.

1. *Artistic puritanism.* Art is damaged by 'the world'; including civilisation, economic development, and living standards. The promotion of technology and the promotion of art were now (contrary to Hume) antithetical.[24] The Industrial Revolution served as an opportune proof of this thesis, as it was easily convicted of being a great uglifier.

(Southey's 'The Manufacturing System' is an early example of the use of the Industrial Revolution to censure economic development on account of its cost to beauty.)[25] A less historically contingent proof rested on the thesis that the provision of mass satisfactions (that is, consumerist culture) was necessarily anti-art. Mass production was, for example, supposedly achieved by the elimination of aesthetically superior craft production (Ruskin). The accompanying improvements in man's material circumstances were never allowed to mitigate this censure. Thus F.R. Leavis in *Two Cultures?* (1963, pp. 45–6) pours scorn on the notion that improvement in material conditions might excuse their 'creative' cost. 'The human soul' proclaimed Lawrence 'needs actual beauty even more than bread' (quoted in Williams 1967, p. 201).

2. *Bohemianism.* Art is the touchstone of judgement, and should be honoured by the way man lives. This reduces to living life like a modern painting: strangely, unaccountably, defying utility and reason.

3. *Aestheticism.* Art has an objective,[26] intrinsic and supreme value. While Christianity had given art only an instrumental (if objective) value, and the market gives art only an instrumental (and subjective) value, aestheticism bestows an intrinsic and objective value on art. Art is now to serve no purpose (except itself). Art does not have to answer to anything; it is its own justification.

Puritanism and bohemianism are conducive to a hostility to the economic. But it is in aestheticism where the conflict with economics is deepest. Economics, certainly, does not affirm that 'Art has an objective and intrinsic value'. It does not affirm that art has value independent of what people are willing to sacrifice for it. It does not 'privilege' artistic values. Economics does not assert any wrong is done if the world leaps for joy at the sight of the immolation of the Hermitage Gallery.

Since art would seem to have an intrinsic value this position seems unsatisfactory, and makes economics vulnerable to the contention that it is 'philistine', even 'immoral'.

One defence of economics is a table-turning manoeuvre. This would begin by observing that not only art has an intrinsic value; the state of human satisfaction, too, has such a value, regardless of the service (or harm) it does art. Yet the cult of art is reluctant to recognise this truth, and this fact is betrayed by the inhumanity of some of its partisans. The callousness of some landmarks in literary modernism has been noted by critics.[27]

A more fundamental defence of economics against the charge of philistinism is that the social mechanisms that economics favours allow the affirmation in action of intrinsic aesthetic values. The social mechanisms allow that individuals may recognise intrinsic values, recognise they have claims on them, and respond in action. This affirmation in action lies not just in market patronage of art, but also the preservation and creation at public expense of art that has an 'existence value', and thereby constitutes a 'public good'.[28] We conclude that the non-affirmation of artistic instrumental values does not preclude the accommodation of intrinsic values.

The anti-economist will retort that there is nothing in the social mechanism favoured by economics to suppose that the right degree of affirmation is given to art. This is true; these mechanisms may give too little (or too much) affirmation, and economics does not deny it. What economics does deny is that an inappropriate amount of affirmation would be the licence for over-riding public preferences. It does deny that 'Art has an intrinsic value that must be accommodated regardless of the wish of general mankind'. Economics is, as its enemies have complained, 'democratic'. Whatever wrongs are done in the spirit of democracy, economics implicitly denies that this wrongdoing is licence to ignore or discount the wishes of the public. It is this posture that has earned it the sanctimonious reprimands of anti-economists that it is in the grip of 'moral relativism' (Hamilton 1996), 'antinomianism' (that is, a self-exemption from moral law), and a blindness 'to the moral function of public law' (Sagoff 1988).

A baleful lesson of history is that moral law has been infinitely better served by attending to human satisfactions than to the decrees of those blessed, in their own mind, with an unusual insight into the 'moral function of public law'. Nevertheless, if moral law *does* indeed counsel the discount, in certain situations, of human satisfactions then economics *is* to be censured by moral law. However, even if moral law does so counsel, this does not imply that economics is without use, or even without great use. It would imply only that economics is less than some ultimate piece of wisdom that would tell everything about anything that one would ever want to know. And certainly economics is less than some ultimate piece of wisdom. So is mathematics. And medicine. And ecology. And art criticism. Or any other valuable piece of learning there has ever been.

10
Rival Gospels of Wealth

From the grievance that economics has been beholden to wealth creation, we turn to a grievance that economics has been of insufficient service to wealth creation. In this chapter we take up the charge that economics has misdirected society's ambitions for the realisation of its material potential. Economics, complain critics, has advocated the invisible hand as a means to prosperity. In truth, these critics claim, wealth is to be reached by a different path. The teachings as to what that path is are various. One doctrine, that we might call the 'Conquest of Nature', maintains that wealth lies in harnessing the unharnessed powers of nature. Another, the 'Gospel of Technology and Engineering' teaches that technological and scientific knowledge is the road to unprecedented prosperity. A third, the 'Gospel of Labour' preaches work and a work-ethic as the answer to material wants.

In historical terms all these gospels have their roots in the Enlightenment. Thus whereas most anti-economics can be interpreted as a contradiction in some dimension of the Enlightenment, this genre of anti-economics represents a survival of Enlightenment. All have been preached with enthusiasm over the two centuries since the close of that epoch.

10.1 The conquest of nature

Man has won

The aspiration to conquer nature germinated in an epoch when man knew he was weak, but believed he might be strong. It was in the seventeenth century that there arose the view that wealth is not a matter of divine gift or human theft, but a question of harnessing the forces of nature. In Descartes' words we should 'render ourselves as the masters and possessors of nature and contribute to the perfection of human life', and we could do so by proper scientific method.

The Enlightenment inherited a Cartesian rationalistic current that was committed to the conquest of nature, even to the point of hoping to conquer death. Yet there was another wing of the Enlightenment that was more hopeful of human nature than the seventeenth century, but less hopeful in the power of reason, and that correspondingly saw the remedy of mankind's predicament less in the conquest of nature and more in the cultivation of social intercourse. This wing comprised the creative seed of classical economics, and classical economics refused the conquest of nature.[1]

In Smith, labour is a matter of gathering and preparing for human use the productions of nature; humanity is 'parasitic' on nature, rather than its 'master'.[2] The classical economists, more generally, tended to see labour and nature cooperating in the production of wealth: land is the mother and labour the father.[3] But the key point is that to the classical economists the productivity of human labour depended not upon its effectiveness in mastering, grappling, or unlocking the power of nature, but within its social organisation; its division of labour, sustained by market exchange. This outlook is well illustrated by Smith when he nominates 'the two greatest and most important events recorded in the history of mankind'. What are they? The invention of writing, the wheel, the lever? To Smith these two events are the discovery of America, and the passage to India by the Cape of Good Hope. These two events created a world market, 'by uniting, in some measure, the most distant parts of the world, by enabling them to relieve one another's wants...and to encourage one another's industry' (Smith [1776] 1937, p. 590).

The rejection of the market almost impels abandoning the thesis of the productivity of labour as dependent on a division of labour sustained by market exchange. It is not surprising that in nineteenth-century anti-economics the conquest of nature reappeared in a number of forms. So, for example, Henry Carey subscribes to the conquest as the path to abundance, as did his follower Robert Thompson (1844–1924). In his anti-text Thompson declares, 'This history of human economy is the story of man's transition from the savage's subjection to nature, to the citizen's mastery of her forces' (Thompson 1875, p. 29).

But the most consequential revival of the conquest of nature was in Marxian economics. Man, in Marx's words; 'opposes himself to Nature...in order to appropriate Nature's productions in a form adapted to his own wants'. Capitalism 'is based on the dominion of man over Nature...It is the necessity of bringing a natural force under the control of society, of economising, of appropriating or subduing it on a large scale by the work of man's hand, that first plays the decisive part in the history of industry' (Marx [1887] 1954, pp. 173, 481). Further, socialism, it seems, will only perfect that dominion. Engels in the *Anti-Dühring* hails the change in man's relation to nature that will come with the advent of socialism: 'man's environment, which up to now have dominated man, at this point pass under the dominion and control of man, who now for the first time becomes the real conscious master of nature' (Engels [1894] 1947, pp. 420–1).

The Marxian vision of the triumph of man over nature is presented vividly in a Bolshevik science-fiction utopia *Red Star* ([1908] 1984) by Alexander Bogdanov (1873–1928). Bogdanov was a leading intellectual light of Russian Social Democracy, and a member of the Central Committee of the Bolshevik party in the years 1905–1907. In the wake of the failure of the 1905 revolution, Bogdanov composed his tale of an earthling who is kidnapped, and transported to Mars, where he discovers that a Bolshevik revolution had taken place on the planet centuries before. The Martian world now enjoys a perfect material abundance, but is overshadowed by a constant struggle between the Martians and their natural environment. A Martian spokesman elaborates:

> True, peace reigns among men, but there cannot be peace with the natural elements. Even a victory over such a foe can pose a new threat. During the most recent period of our history we have intensified the exploitation of our planet tenfold, our population is growing, and our needs are increasing even faster. The danger of exhausting our natural resources and energy has repeatedly confronted various branches of our industry...We can triumph as long as we are on the offensive, but if we do not permit our army to grow, we will be besieged on all sides by the elements...So far, however, man has won.
>
> (Bogdanov [1908] 1984, pp. 79–80)

Bogdanov has, effectively, expanded the class struggle so that it amounts to a never-ending war between humanity and nature.[4]

Red Star, it has been said, was Stalin's favourite novel (Graham 1993, p. 62). The novelistic poses of 1908, therefore, became revolutionary actions after 1917. 'Praise of nature, declared Maxim Gorky "is praise of a despot"'.

> Under Stalinism, official art and propaganda painted wild nature as the enemy of the working class, calling on all Soviet citizens to help it tame the wilderness and make it serve the needs of the proletariat. Novels, paintings and posters showed heroic Soviet workers damming rivers, draining marshes, felling forests and dotting the tundra with factories. Every good Marxist was expected to support the struggle of 'collectively organised reason against the elemental forces of nature'.
>
> (Cartmill 1993, p. 219)

More prosaically, Stalin in *Economic Problems of Socialism* expressed the hope that 'having come to know the laws of nature, reckoning with them and relying on them, and intelligently applying and utilizing them, man can restrict their sphere of action, and can impart a different direction to the destructive forces of nature and convert them to the use of society' (Stalin [1952] 1972, p. 3).

The conquest of nature paradigm was not the preserve of specifically Marxist socialism. In Raymond Williams's judgement 'if you read the typical case for socialism as it became standard between the wars, it is all in terms of mastering nature, setting new horizons, creating plenty as the answer to poverty' (Williams [1982] 1995, p. 45). Neither was an aspiration to master nature the preserve of socialism, of any kind. It was a common premise of post-war development economics. In 1951 the UN Department of Economic Affairs' *Measures for the Economic Development of Under-Developed Countries* (authored by, among others, W. Arthur Lewis and Theodore W. Schulz) stated that 'Progress occurs only where people believe that men can by conscious effort master nature' (quoted in Frankel 1992, p. 227).

In 1982 Raymond Williams commented 'and still today we read these triumphalist arguments about production'. He adds 'They are a bit less confident now'. But not always less confident. Writing in the same year as Williams, Balogh in *The Irrelevance of Conventional Economics* (Balogh 1982) praised, with no lack of confidence, 'that tremendous watershed in history, the establishment by the human race through science and technology of its practical domination over the natural environment'. That eighteenth-century watershed, sends Balogh into raptures:

> Man's capacity to exploit his physical environment and harness its elemental forces to his purposes was unrecognizably transformed. The vicious stranglehold of primitive stagnation, abject poverty, debilitating sickness and ignorance was to be finally broken, the stultifying incubus of primitive fears and magical superstitions thrown off, thereby unleashing the productive forces of man's long dormant ingenuity . . . The face of the earth, little changed since the invention of the plough and the wheel, was transformed.
>
> (Balogh 1982, p. 31)

10.2 The triumph of energy

But Balogh's own excitement over man's 'capacity to exploit his physical environment' was by 1982 no longer typical of the conquest of nature paradigm as it had become popularly interpreted. That popular interpretation was driven by an excitement over the notion of energy.

This excitement can be traced back to the development of the physics of energy in the mid-nineteenth century. This in essence amounted to the concept of energy and the first and second laws of thermodynamics (the conservation of energy, and the inevitable dissipation of energy available for work). These 'came to be regarded as fundamental to the explanation of physical reality' (Harman 1982, p. 61).

With the development of the concept of energy, science gave the world a thrilling prospect: the existence of a thing (energy) which made every wheel turn, which could be used but not destroyed, and which might be bottled up, and also 'tapped', 'unlocked', and even unleashed. The notion of harnessing nature now had an exact and impressive scientific imprimatur.

Frederick Soddy (1877–1956) is one of the better known anti-economists who saw the science of energy as the basis of a new political economy. He was awarded the Nobel Prize for physics in 1921 for his work on atomic structure. He believed, however, that 'the world's real problem was faulty economics, not a faulty chemistry, and for the second half of his nearly eighty years economics replaced chemistry as the centre of his economic life' (Daly 1980). He expressed these views in *Cartesian Economics* (1922) (that is, economics that subscribed to Descartes' programme for the mastery of nature) and *Wealth, Virtual Wealth and Debt* (1926).

Soddy believed that 'the flow of energy should be the primary concern of economics'. Regrettably, it is not of even minor concern to economists. Soddy complains that 'there has been a long divorce between natural and human knowledge. The effect on economics, essentially a subject with the closest relations with the world of facts and physical realities, has been singularly disastrous' (Soddy 1926, p. 25). If economists had understood the physics of energy they would have appreciated that the impossibility of a perpetual motion machine implied the 'absurdity' of interest income (1926, p. 106). 'Is it any wonder that such crude confusions, such triumphs of mental instincts over reason, experience and common sense have produced a general sterility of constructive thought? ... When I sit and warm my hands, as best I may, at the little heap of embers that is now Political Economy, I cannot but contrast its dying glow with the vainglorious and triumphant science it once was' (1922, p. 8). Economists, added Soddy, should no longer be tolerated in universities, as they 'wittingly suppress rather than propagate the truth' (quoted in Martinez-Alier 1987, p. 142).

The truth was, according to Soddy, that under current technology energy was coal, and those countries that had plenty of coal would prosper, and those that lacked it could not. Thus Great Britain developed, but Ireland stagnated. 'Cartesian economics' said Soddy, 'is capable of diagnosing instantly the root of the Irish trouble' (1922, p. 11). But new technologies for the exploitation of energy promised new wealth: 'if atomic energy is ever tapped an outburst of human activity would occur such as would make the triumphs of our times seem tawdry, and primitive humanity's struggles for energy as the fantastic memory of some horrid dream' (Soddy 1926, p. 30).

A cult of energy similar to Soddy's was found in the American 'technocracy' movement of the 1930s.[5] The leader of this semi-craze/semi-ideology was not a Nobel laureate, but a self-educated, failed floor-polish vendor by the name of Howard Scott (1890–1970), whose 'disrespect for economists, with the sole exceptions of Veblen and Mitchell, was profane and profound' (Chase 1933, p. 7). In the depths of the Great Depression, Scott explained his philosophy to a shaken American public in 'Technology Smashes the Price System' (Scott 1933). 'What is wealth, real wealth?' asks Scott. 'The economists vary in their definitions but in general the word is applied to all objects possessing value. Marshall the famous British economist defined value as the measure of desire.' But the truth is, 'It matters not a rap what men think wish or desire. We are face to face with a law of nature. The law of Conservation of Energy has a perfectly definite social implication.' That is that 'physical wealth is not measured in terms of labour, goods, or money, but in terms of energy. And with the discovery of that truth, the bankers, the industrialists, the Marxists, the Fascists, the economists, the soldiers and the politicians are a thing of the past' (Scott 1933, p. 129). Regrettably, 'It has been our great misfortune that in our disaster the only people that we have looked to for guidance...have been the economists', who can only offer the price system. The economists' price system should be replaced by an energy system, in which the allocation of non-tradeable energy certificates equally to all members of society would be exchanged for consumer goods in accordance to the energy requirements of their production.

The capitulation to nature

In the post-war period the notion that wealth is a matter of tapping the energy resources of nature has been resurrected, but from a quarter absolutely distant from Scott's engineers, and with a thesis absolutely opposed. It has been resurrected by the environmentalist movement.

To environmentalists, too, wealth creation is essentially a matter of the exploitation of natural resources. To environmentalists, consumption of energy is, it seems, the sine qua non of wealth creation. To environmentalists too, economists are blameworthy for their ignorance of physical laws (see Common 1995). To environmentalists too, the laws of thermodynamics, so important to Soddy and Scott, have a huge import for our economic existence (see for example Daly 1980). It is fitting for 'ecological economists' such as Herman B. Daly and Juan Martinez-Alier to memorialise Soddy with sympathy.

But the inference that environmentalists have drawn from their energy theory of wealth is entirely different from those arrived at by Soddy and Scott. Environmentalism agrees with Soddy and Scott that 'The conquest of nature is the means to create wealth'. But whereas the inference of Soddy and Scott was 'Therefore, conquer nature', the inference of the environmentalists is 'Therefore, do not create wealth'.

Further, the environmentalists make a very different assumption from Soddy and Scott about the magnitude of energy. The latter took energy to be effectively infinite, with appropriate technology. Environmentalists take it to be finite with any technology. Thus wealth creation is a matter of the consumption of natural resources, but only a finite amount can be created. So whereas to Soddy and Scott the vigorous exploitation of natural resources was the long-run hope of mankind, now it will spell its long-run doom. And whereas previously the economists were convicted of being oblivious to the hidden springs of abundance, now they are rebuked for being oblivious to the shrinking pools of succour.

One instance of the green indictment of economics that draws on the conquest of nature paradigm is found in the helter-skelter prose of the indefatigable anti-economist Hazel Henderson (b. 1933).[6] In 'The Finite Pie: the Limits of Traditional Economics in Making Resource Decisions' (see Henderson 1978) we find several of the themes of Soddy and technocracy: the pre-eminence of the laws of thermodynamics, the poverty of economics in the absence of those laws, the notion that all economic activity is a gift of the sun, the meaningless of the 'price system'.

> Spaceship Earth and its natural cycles powered by the sun, contain information on the values of these matter and energy exchanges in the biosphere, and . . . economics must repair to the physical and biological sciences to obtain this essential baseline data on the accuracy of its own models. Unfortunately, human perceptions of value, i.e. prices, with which economists deal, are notoriously inaccurate because they are based on (1) our subjective, imperfect observations of the objective world and our resulting unrealistic expectations of the availability of its resources, and (2) our subjective evaluation of what is important to us, or 'valuable'.
>
> (Henderson 1978, p. 48)

One also finds in Henderson the environmentalist inversion of supremacy of energy, so that energy is valuable on account of its limitation rather than its power. And economists are rebuked for missing this. 'Economists, hypnotised by their elegant equilibrium model of free market supply and demand, cannot readily handle the possibilities of absolute scarcity on the supply side.'[7]

10.3   The gospel of technology and engineering

If wealth is a matter of harnessing the forces of nature, then it becomes imperative to know how to make a harness. The conquest of wealth leads on, therefore, to the gospel of technology and engineering. The gospel states that technological progress has been the critical key to all progress: or, in the characterisation of technocracy: 'science and technology could redeem mankind from his burden of labor' (Aikin 1977, p. 43). Consequently, in the words of Veblen, '"social research" means, in good part, industrial research of a very objective and even mechanical character, if it is to mean anything substantial' (quoted in Aikin 1977, p. 23). Regrettably, economics disclaims any technological knowledge.

Not only has economics disclaimed knowledge of the key to wealth, it has advocated as means to wealth what is actually a bar: a piece of social organisation, the market and property. The gospel took offence at the market as it took offence at anything cultural. The gospel of technology was not merely an overexcited elevation of technical possibility; it is a denigration of what is the opposite of technology; culture. To the gospel, technology is uniting, rational, enabling; while culture is dividing, non-rational, and disabling. 'Only social organisation, lagging behind changes in technology as it did, blocked the road to redemption' (Aikin 1977, p. 43). Veblen (and Scott and Soddy) saw the market as cultural block; exchange is just parasitism or vandalism; a system of private wealth and public poverty. Even more, money is seen as a cultural block; both right-wing technologism and left-wing technologism share a hatred of money. The root of this hatred is that money is powerful but not technological, and thus a perversity, an offence to science, an irrationality. Something so powerful must at least conform to laws of science, and not violate them.

'Technology decides everything'[8]

Veblen hoped for a 'Soviet of Engineers' to smash the price system, and replace the parasitism of management and ownership. His hopes in the United States were disappointed. But in the Soviet Union something like a Soviet of Engineers came to pass. The gospel of technology and engineering was seized: technology was to make the new society; the age of electricity is the age of socialism said Lenin. Correspondingly Lenin's main advisers on economic planning were electrical engineers. Among the two hundred scientists, engineers and agronomists put in charge in 1920 of drawing up Russia's first long-term plan of economic development there were virtually no economists. The plan was sent for final approval to the All-Russian Congress of Electrical Engineers (Smolinski, 1971, pp. 138–9). 'For decades economists were excluded from planning. The Planning Commission was – like the whole country – led by engineers' (Sutela 1991, p. 29). Eighty-nine per cent of the last Politburo of the Soviet Union received their education in technical areas (Graham 1993, p. 73).

10.4 The gospel of work[9]

If nature is to be harnessed then we need to make a harness. We are led to the gospel of work, that preaches that the way to riches is by labour. In the words of the Marxist historian Christopher Hill 'It *was* by hard work and labour discipline that England won its industrial lead over the rest of the world' (Hill 1964, p. 34).

The gospel of work and the Tradition actually share some common ancestry in seventeenth-century Puritanism (that held that goods things can only come through work), and in the commonplace Enlightenment salutes to physical labour. Certainly, the predecessors of classical economics were congenial to the gospel of work. Pre-classical thought was strongly inclined to a 'backward bending labour supply'; so when work was most needed and productive, there would be least of it.[10] This pre-classical posture constitutes a critical feature of the gospel of work: it holds that, not only is work necessary, it cannot be bought by incentives. It requires sanction. This sanction could be internal ('a new ethic') or it could be external.

In a significant doctrinal innovation classical economics rejected a negative elasticity of work to the wage. Hard work can be summoned by offering sufficient reward for labour, and any amount of sloth can be induced by an insufficient one. 'Our ancestors were idle for want of a sufficient encouragement to industry' (Smith [1776] 1937, p. 319).

The Tradition therefore treats the gospel of work as, at best, superficial. Hard work is not sufficient for wealth. And insofar as it is necessary, the Tradition has never made the provision of 'hard work' something that required either compulsion or reform in human character. Contrary to Hill, it would hold there is no 'urgent necessity of imposing a new ethic' of work on the inhabitants of pre-industrial societies, such as Africa. One may contrast how the gospel of work treats the reluctance of indigenous Africans to work outside the traditional economy with how the Tradition treats it. Whereas Hill blames 'cults and taboos that teach the African that work is degrading', the Tradition makes it 'the result of the hidden costs associated with working for European employers. These hidden costs included the risk of dying while at work; the cost of transporting oneself over long distances of treacherous terrain; the fear that wives would be lost if left behind for any time; the fear of being subjected to inadequate and strange food, poor housing, and degrading and brutal working conditions, and the fear of being cheated of one's earnings' (Ellis 1981, p. 253).

From almost its beginning the Tradition has been faulted by anti-economists for not heeding the necessity of sanction if mankind is to labour. Coleridge objected to the 'maxim of political economy' that 'the desire of bettering their condition will induce men to labour even more abundantly and profitably of servile compulsion'. But, objected Coleridge, 'The love of indolence is universal or next to it.' On the basis of their maxim, political economists 'stake the tranquillity of an empire' (Coleridge 1969c, p. 231).

Thomas Carlyle made essentially the same complaint about economics in furious and bitter terms in 'The Nigger Question'. This essay is the occasion of one of the most celebrated explosions of indignation at economics. The subject of his ire was the predicament of the white landowner in the West Indies subsequent to the abolition of slavery. Carlyle presents the landowner's difficulty as follows: 'He himself cannot work; and his black neighbour, rich in pumpkin is in no haste to help him. Sunk to the ears in pumpkin, imbibing saccharine juices, and much at ease in the Creation, he can listen to the less fortunate white man's "demand", and take his own time in supplying it' (Carlyle [1849] 1899a, p. 352). At this point Carlyle has political economy enter. If there was a labour scarcity in Jamaica then political economy recommends, says Carlyle, the immigration of labour to Jamaica.[11] But immigration will turn Jamaica into an Ireland; so an island of rich lazy persons is made an island thick with poor lazy persons. The 'devlish' sloth remains. 'What say you to an idle Black gentleman, with his rum bottle in his hand...no breeches on his body, pumpkin at his discretion, and the fruitfulest region of the earth going back to jungle round him...?', asks Carlyle (Carlyle [1849] 1899a, p. 356). Carlyle knows what to say:

> No Black man who will not work according to what ability the gods have given him for working, has the smallest right to eat pumpkin, or to any fraction of land that will grow pumpkin, however plentiful such land may be; but has an indisputable and perpetual right to be compelled, by the real proprietors of said land, to do competent work for his living.
>
> (Carlyle [1849] 1899a, p. 355)

The calls for compulsory labour were not restricted to the anti-liberal Right. The anti-liberal Left was just as enthusiastic, although they were more motivated by a wish to put masters into work than former slaves back to work. Point 9 of the 10-point programme of the *Communist Manifesto* calls for 'Equal liability of all to labour. Establishment of industrial armies, especially for agriculture.' *Der Zukunftsstaat* (The Future State), a highly influential prescription for the transition to socialism written by Carl Ballod (1864–1931) and praised by Lenin, advocated a system of labour conscription covering all males between the ages of 17–26, and all females between 15–21. With the advent of Bolshevik power Lenin enthused about labour conscription; he said it was better than the 'guillotine' (Smolinski 1967, p. 112). It was at this time that Lenin was ordering 'the imprisonment of workers who blatantly violated labour discipline' (Beissinger 1988, p. 29). Trotsky envisaged whole segments of the labour force subject to military discipline: 'labour armies', 'the highest degree of intensity' of discipline, and coercive measures including blacklists, penal battalions and concentration camps. Trotsky's vision reached its greatest realisation with Stalin's constitution of a slave labour force, variously estimated between 1.5 million and 5.5 million in size by the close of the 1930s (Rosefielde 1996; Wheatcroft 1996).

Indeed, a doctrine of 'wealth through slavery' is only the perfection of the gospel of work. And such a doctrine had Marxist precedents. Both Marx and Engels ascribed huge productive power to slavery. 'Without slavery North America, the most progressive of countries, would be transformed into a patriarchal country... Cause slavery to disappear and you will have wiped America off the map of nations' (Marx [1847] 1963, p. 94). To Engels 'The introduction of slavery... was a great step forward. It was slavery that first made possible the division of labour between agriculture and industry on a considerable scale... Without slavery, no Greek state, no Greek art and science; without slavery, no Roman Empire. But without the basis laid by

Greece and the Roman Empire, also no modern Europe' (Engels [1894] 1947, p. 270).

Economics, by contrast, has argued that slavery impoverished a nation. By destroying all incentive it made labour inefficient, slothful, and delinquent. It was on account of the economists' opposition to slavery that certain anti-economists have entered into the ledger of claims against economics the ruin supposedly brought by the abolition of slavery.[12] Thus Byles in *Sophisms of Free-Trade and Popular Political Economy Examined*, paints in vivid hue the ruinous effects on the West Indies of emancipation:

> Slave labour is abolished and prohibited throughout the West Indies ... Plantations are abandoned to the Jaguars and other wild beasts: mills and machinery silent and decaying, roads obliterated by the rank growth of the jungle; dykes that fenced large and fertile districts against the sea left to ruin ... The blacks ... are fast relapsing into their original barbarism.

Who is to blame for this relapse? 'Not a "gay science", I should say, like some we have heard of; no, a dreary, desolate, and indeed quite abject and distressing one: what we may call, by way of eminence, the *dismal science*' (Carlyle [1850] 1899a, p. 354).

(Byles 1904, p. 102)[13]

Part IV

11
The 'Unconquerable Private Interests'[1]

The types of anti-economics examined in Parts II and III are 'public'; they are hostile to economics on account of some supposed offence to public life. In this chapter we turn to a species of economics which is the diametric opposite, that is 'private'. We turn from anti-economics that springs from a sense of offence at the harm done to the state of the world, to an anti-economics that springs from a sense of offence at the harm done to the state of oneself. We turn, from 'ideal' (that is, ideological) enemies of economics to the 'interested' enemies of economics. We turn from the seemingly high-minded and conscientious objections of supposedly disinterested observers, to the less pretentious, but not always less noble, objections founded upon a doughty concern to defend one's own estate. We turn towards the familiar conflict between economics on the one hand, and the 'special pleading' of 'vested interests' on the other.

We will argue that the particular policy reforms that the *Grande Tradition* favours will *always* be opposed by some on interested grounds, and the policies that the Tradition considers ideal will always be opposed by *all* on interested grounds. We conclude that while various forms of ideal anti-economics will flare and wane, interested anti-economics is the interminable and untiring adversary of economics.

We go on, however, to argue that the greatest importance of interested anti-economics lies not in its operation as distinct and independent from ideal anti-economics, but in its operation in conjunction with ideal anti-economics. We maintain that in spite of the contrast between ideal and interested economics, each gains significance through its collaboration with the other.

11.1 The disharmony of interests: an argument

Market liberalisation

For perhaps the greater part of its life the Tradition has been attracted to economic liberalism; a programme to maximise national wealth through the elimination of impediments to the freedom of markets. Even though the advent of neoclassical and Keynesian analysis has cooled this attraction, there remains the belief that for many segments of the economy impediments to the freedom of markets should be minimised.

That economically liberal reforms *may* attract an 'interested antipathy' is a commonplace, and has long been felt by economists. Such antipathy is vividly portrayed by Smith in discussing the 'restraints on imports' imposed by law in eighteenth-century Britain:

> The member of parliament who supports every proposal for strengthening this monopoly, is sure to acquire not only the reputation of understanding trade, but great popularity and influence with an order of men whose numbers and wealth render them of great importance. If he opposes them, on the contrary, and still more if he has authority enough to be able to thwart them, neither the most acknowledged probity, nor the highest rank, nor the greatest public services, can protect him from the most infamous abuse and detraction, from personal insults, nor sometimes from real danger, arising from the insolent outrage of furious and disappointed monopolists.
>
> (Smith [1776] 1937, p. 438)

That economically liberal reforms *must* attract an 'interested antipathy' is a distinct and stronger proposition, but it is one that may be easily sustained on the following assumptions. Suppose economic liberalism maximises wealth. And suppose policies are never imposed that make everyone worse off. Then one may argue:

- Regulations which make everyone better off cannot exist (economic liberalism).
- Regulations which make everyone worse off will not exist (who would want them?).
- Therefore, regulations make some better off and some worse off, and so the elimination of regulations must make some worse off and some better off.
- Therefore the elimination of regulations will be opposed by some.

This argument's conclusion is simply a generalisation of many particular conclusions familiar from microeconomics: that liberalisation always has losers to set against winners. Some examples:

- The de-monopolisation of output markets harms output sellers as a class (and benefits output buyers as a class). And de-monopolisation of input markets harms input sellers as a class (and benefits the input buyers as a class).

- The elimination of subsidies harms the subsidiser (taxpayer) and benefits the subsidee (buyer and seller).
- The elimination of tariffs harms the import producing factor, and benefits import using factor or consumer.
- The toleration of speculation, fortuitous circumstances aside, will *either* benefit the producer and harm the consumer, *or* benefit the consumer and harm the producer.

Economic liberalism, it seems, is doomed to be contentious on purely interested grounds.

Nevertheless the necessity of an interested and rational hostility to economic liberalism has not been widely granted by economists. On the contrary, there is an implicit optimism that opposition to economic liberalism is based either on ignorance, or on the presumption of a small and overbearing minority. Smith is an illustration. There is an Enlightenment serenity about Smith's assurance that liberalising the grain trade would somehow benefit everyone. In his mind, any extension of opposition beyond an insolent few must be a matter of superstition. Such a belief in the basic popularity of economic liberalism (as long as it was understood) was doubtless encouraged by political economists' belief that economic liberalism was on the side of the consumer (that is, the majority), and against the predatory producer (the minority). In truth, even within the standard framework of competitive markets, particular measures of economic liberalisation (such as grain deregulation) need not be in the interest of the consumer, and may be costly to them by the common measure of consumer welfare.

The necessity of opposition to the Tradition's policies can be extended to the Tradition's recommendations in matters of public finance. Economic liberalism in this circumstance may be interpreted as a commitment to the maximisation of national wealth subject to a public finance constraint (that is, a constraint to spend so many dollars) under the assumption of competitive markets. This scenario has produced a number of precepts, beginning with a recommendation of taxing pure rents. At least since the time of Ricardo, economists have argued that certain taxes do not have an impact on national wealth, and some do, with a resulting partiality of economists to those taxes which do not. In the Ricardian model these were taxes on rent and luxuries. This implication of political economy for the treatment of rent can provide an 'interested' explanation of the *froideur* faced by political economy in Oxford: 'A "science" that could produce a theory of exploitation of this kind with its plain sight on a major source of college revenues could scarcely expect cordiality. The Heads of College who could inform a Royal Commission as late as 1852 that College rents rolls were their own affair could hardly be enamoured of Ricardianism' (Checkland 1951, p. 53). And was only Oxford unenamoured of Ricardo? Richard Jones's 447-page attack on

Ricardian rent theories, *An Essay on the Distribution of Wealth*, was printed at the expense of the University of Cambridge (Jones [1831] 1956, p. xli).

11.2 A harmony of interests: a thesis

Every measure of economically liberal reform will always be opposed by some interest. A distinct proposition can be additionally advanced: the completely free market will always be opposed by *every* economic interest. On the odiousness of the free market there will be agreement amongst the interests. So while there is disharmony over every measure of economic liberalism, there is harmony over the undesirability of the liberal regimen.[2]

The reason why every interest opposes the free market is simple: barring fortuitous circumstances, for *any* economic interest one cares to nominate, there is always a regulation/intervention that will improve that interest's position relative to what it would enjoy in the free market. No one, in other words, has a 'vested interest' in the completely free market. The completely free market is optimal for no interest.

Free trade is never *optimal* for any interest. Free trade certainly will be improving for some interests but it is never optimal. In a pure exchange model, for example, fortuitous circumstances aside, the consumer goods owner will always find some tariff (or bounty) better than free trade, as the tariff (bounty) shifts relative prices in favour of the good with which they are relatively well endowed. In a Ricardian model, the export sector's fixed factor which benefits from the abolition of a tariff will benefit still more from an export subsidy. In a two factor Heckscher–Ohlin model, factor owners will always benefit from some tariff/bounty (as it shifts product prices in a manner favourable to the factors of which they are relatively well endowed).

The abolition of a wage minimum is never actually optimal for any capital interest; a wage maximum imposed to exploit monopsony power will be superior. *Free immigration* is never optimal to any capital interest: the subsidisation of immigration (or taxation of emigration) is superior. *The abolition of a rent maximum* is never optimal to any landowner: a rent subsidy, in addition to the abolition of a maximum, is superior.

Thus, contrary to Marxist mythology, laissez-faire is not a capitalist bliss point; it is a point where no capitalists (or labourers) want to be.

The only special circumstances whereby a free market is actually optimal for any interest is when there is an interest whose endowment is strictly representative of the endowment of the economy; that is, it is a miniature replica of the economy as a whole. In the pure exchange economy this would be the consumer whose vector of goods is a scalar of the vector of the whole economy. In the Stolper–Samuelson two good/two factor model this is the interest whose capital/labour ratio equals the capital/labour ratio of the economy as a whole. These special circumstances seem unlikely to be fulfilled.[3]

Thus the free market is never the optimal policy regimen for any interest. What every interest cherishes is preference and privilege, not the free market's cold equality before the law. There is no vested interest to support the free market. Whatever friends the free market has are false friends, and its true enemies are all-embracing. The vocation of the free market advocate is a universally unpopular one.

11.3 Interested anti-economics appraised

We have argued the pervasiveness of interested anti-economics. But what of its merit?

The criterion used to evaluate the merit of ideal anti-economics in previous chapters was logical value: was their case true or reasonable? This criterion is not easily used here. Interested anti-economics rarely has intellectual constructions of any significance. It is true that interested anti-economics may find genuine inadequacies in arguments of the Tradition; the raw bias of interested anti-economics does not preclude this possibility. Nevertheless, either on account of their incapacity, or because of the difficulty in persuading the public that they 'trade for the public good', they have typically pressed on their enemy with the machines of war contrived by the 'ideal' adversaries of economics. Therefore, if interested anti-economics is to be evaluated at all it must be evaluated in terms of utility, and of justice.

The disutility of interested anti-economics, on the theory outlined, is obvious. It reduces national wealth. The injustice of interested anti-economics is also not hard to argue. For the presumption in considering the opposition of 'vested interests' to economic liberalism is that such interested anti-liberalism is a matter of a minority of the better-off defending an income that is obtained by a regulation at the expense of the average person. Interested anti-economics, it can easily be argued, offends equity.

The defence of aristocratic privilege in *Ancien Régime* states serves vividly the characterisation of interested anti-economics as inequitable. The opposition (amounting to covert insurrection) against Turgot's Six Edicts in 1776 was a matter of privileged classes defending their privilege. The opposition to the 1807–1808 ministry of Karl Stein and Karl von Hardenberg (1750–1822) (Simon 1955, pp. 16–19) that emancipated the peasantry and attempted to impose taxation on nobles was sourced in the same aristocratic resentment. Southey's 'On the Economical Reformers' is a defence of ancient sinecures.

Yet it is possible that the interest which is served by a regulation may *not* be a rich minority. The members of this interest may amount to a numerical majority. 'The vested interest' may be 'the people'. Further, even if the interest which is served comprehends only a minority, that minority may be considered a deserving minority by some moral systems. Within the standard framework, for example, it is possible that a regulation may serve a poor minority by the ordinary measures, that in an egalitarian moral system would be judged a deserving minority. Considered in the abstract, therefore, interested anti-economics need not offend equity.

Whether, in the circumstances, regulation *would* serve such a poor and suffering minority will be variously estimated. A considered answer would lead deep into thickets of theoretical and factual controversy, and, given the bounds of this book, we cannot follow. We will constrain ourselves to recording that in the mind of one anthropological observer the introduction of minimum wage regulation led one especially poor and suffering minority, the Australian Aborigines, 'into the gates of hell'.[4]

11.4 The interests of an interest

The previous section has presented a model that concludes that economics will always be dogged by interested opponents. Yet that model of interested anti-economics suffers from three arguable assumptions.

1. The argument assumed the truth of the tenets of economic liberalism. The theory has assumed that perfectly free markets maximise wealth; that interventions cannot make everyone better off, but only give to some by taking more from others. But the assumption is arguable. Neoclassical welfare economics provides a familiar suite of causes as to why free markets may not secure wealth maximisation: externalities, natural monopolies, informational issues. Nevertheless, the familiar case of welfare economics against the perfectly free market does not tell against the conclusion of the preceding arguments. It can be reached by a reformulation of premises thus: deviations from the precepts of neoclassical welfare economics that make everyone better off cannot exist; deviations from the precepts that make everyone worse off will not exist; therefore deviations make some better off and some worse off; therefore their removal will make some better off and some worse off. Conclusion: precepts of neoclassical welfare economics will always be opposed by some interest. The general point is that in the neoclassical framework, regardless of whether we allow externalities, natural monopoly and so on, the pursuit of the public interest will be opposed by some private interests.[5]

2. The argument assumed that the Tradition is concerned only about wealth maximisation. Contrary to this assumption, economics is also concerned about wealth distribution.[6] But allowing for this concern only increases the interested antagonism towards economics. One important example is the antagonism of Ricardian political economy to rent, and its insinuation that rent is an ill-gotten gain.[7] This offended all who depended on rent, comprising not only the most powerful political class and the Church of England, but also the bodies responsible for higher learning in the Kingdom.

3. The model assumes that the only thing that interests an 'interest' is wealth.
This assumption is false. But allowing for non-material interests will only
increase the scope of interested opposition. Thus the intellectual authority
of economics diminishes the voice of other disciplines (management, sociology) covetous for influence in policy formation; and has reduced the
prominence of demi-savants who wish to have their thoughts heard. The
philosophes feel reduced by the suggestion that they are not equipped to
comment on economic affairs. The churches feel reduced by the contraction
in their pastoral role, and indeed their presence in the socio-political structure.[8]

In summary, these objections to the model of interested anti-economics do
not give any warrant to dilute its conclusions. Indeed, they give grounds to
strengthen them: economics faces powerful interested enemies.

11.5 Vested ideals

Complementarities

Ideal anti-economics has been contrasted with interested anti-economics.
But contrast does not mean disconnection. The real significance of
interested anti-economics does not lie in its operation independent of ideal
anti-economics. A greater significance derives from its joint operation, or
complementarity, with ideal anti-economics.

Economic history suggests that successful opposition to economic liberalism
is typically the conjunction of a interested objection with an ideological
opposition. Thus the protectionism of imperial Germany suited economic
interests; but it also suited the agrarianism of conservative ideologues. The
simple moral is that an ideal opposition in league with interested opposition makes a formidable force. Thus it is no surprise that worldly covetous-
ness has been a motive even in highly 'ideological' political convulsions:
the Reformation, the French Revolution, the Russian Revolution, the Third
Reich; all these involved massive theft, through legislated (and unlegislated)
larceny.

In the history of anti-economics two such complementarities of ideological
and interested objections may be mentioned.

1. The controversy over grain trade liberalisation in France in 1770. This was
probably the first outburst of anti-economics. Opposition flared first in
the 'mutiny' of the 'police' (that is, grain trade regulators). The grain trade
regulators had 'ideal' objections to political economy. But they also had
interested objections: the 'police' benefited from regulations (Kaplan 1976,
p. 223). They were sometimes corrupt, and they enjoyed their importance
and position: 'The behaviour of some administrators betrayed a bitter
resentment over the fact that the liberal regime had undercut their authority

to govern locally, without, however, relieving them of the obligation to maintain order' (Kaplan 1976, p. 212)

2. *Tithes and the Church of England.* The Church of England contained tendencies hostile to political economy that were strong up to 1832, and lingered in weakened form somewhat longer.[9] The objections of these tendencies were in part ideal, but the ideal hostility was complemented by a sense of threat to the material position of the Church arising from political economy.

Tithes were an ancient source of income for the Church, but by the end of the eighteenth century they had become widely unpopular. The most serious opposition to tithe income came from political economists. In the *Wealth of Nations*, Adam Smith attacked tithes as a 'very great hindrance' to agricultural development (Smith [1776] 1937, pp. 367, 788–9). Ricardo condemned tithes as 'a very burdensome, and a very intolerable tax', which inhibited not only agricultural production but also manufacturing, as the consequent rise in corn prices increased the cost of labour (Ricardo [1817] 1951, p. 178). The political economist MPs Joseph Hume and Henry Brougham took up the cause against tithes 'that exasperated the country in an unparalleled degree' (quoted in Evans 1976, p. 122). The political economists did not have the campaign against tithes to themselves; it embraced a wide range of radical constituencies, most far more impassioned in their criticism than economists. Yet it was with a forgivable exaggeration that some anti-economist churchmen complained of the 'fertile source of odium raised against the Church' (Banfield 1843, p. 58) by the opinions of political economy, and declared the urgency of securing 'the venerable fabric from the effects of the shock that it had received from the political economists of the Ricardo school' (Banfield 1843, p. 54). In the same vein a paper defending 'Ecclesiastical Revenues' by the Reverend Edward Edwards (sometimes identified as author of the anti-text by 'Piercy Ravenstone') spat fire against the Ricardian analysis of tithes ('singular', 'delusive', 'utterly destitute of foundation', and 'a vulgar error of a corps of theorists and projectors . . . who feel . . . contempt for the common sense and experience of all the rest of the world' (Edwards 1823, p. 529).[10] This resentful opposition of the Church was not purely verbal: in 1831 Nassau Senior was forced to resign his chair in political economy at King's College London, a Church of England foundation, on account of his recommendation that some of the tithe income of the established Church in Ireland be transferred to Catholics.

Superstructures and substructures

While interested anti-economics is connected with ideal anti-economics through their conjoint operation, interested anti-economics is also connected through its animation and nurture of ideal anti-economics. Material interests hostile to economic liberalism have every incentive to foster sentiments that are hostile to economic liberalism, and will do so through all the arts of the advocate; repetition, argumentation, suggestion and association. Thus state broadcasters have a material incentive to foster a cult of art; armies have a material incentive to foster nationalism; welfare agencies have a material sentiment to foster 'the religion of love'; juridically incorporated trade union structures have a material incentive to foster anti-liberal legalism; import replacing trade associations to nurture patriotism.

There is, in summary, a causal linkage running from interests to ideals. And since, as we have argued, interested anti-economics is ever present, almost every variety of ideal anti-economics will receive perpetual charge and stimulus from interested sources. Economic liberalism is almost fated to face a conjunction of material and ideal anti-economics.

But there is another causal linkage running from ideals to interests. Ideals can nurture and forge material interests. Ideals, in order to fulfil/accommodate its sentiment, will commonly create institutions that will in turn possess material interests. Thus sentiments helped create the grain 'police' in eighteenth-century France; the cult of art helps create state broadcasting bodies; the religion of love helps create welfare agencies; nationalism creates armies; religious sentiment creates churches; anti-liberal legalism creates juridically incorporated trade union structures. Indeed, sentiments can nurture and forge 'vested interests' without actually creating an institution or corporation. Nationalist inspired tariffs *create* import competing industries, which then have every material incentive to oppose economic liberalism. Apartheid prohibitions on non-white employment create (by immigration) a white skill group that faces income loss if those prohibitions are removed. Once created these constituencies have perfectly material motives to nurture the sentiments which support them.

In summary, ideal anti-economics nurtures interested anti-economics, while interested anti-economics nurtures ideal anti-economics. We conclude that interested anti-economics is bound up with ideal anti-economics, each sustaining the other so as to make a formidable alliance.

12
'The Infallible Dicta of the Holy Mother Church of Political Popery'[1]

This chapter turns from objections to what economics asserts, to objections about how these assertions are tendered. This chapter turns to the grievance that economics adopts an authoritarian consciousness in dealing with the public; lecturing those who listen, ignoring those who dissent,[2] and brandishing authority in the face of any who persist in dissent. This chapter turns to the grievance that economics deserves no such authority, and that the public has erred in conceding even a partial authority. In the minds of this criticism economics should forgo its presumption of a right to the public's intellectual allegiance, and ought instead to engage in dialogue and debate with those who disagree (see, for example, Manne 1993).

This thrust of anti-economics has an undeniable rhetorical appeal. Any profession is vulnerable to censures on account of its alleged conceit. The hauteur of the professional in the face of the lay person is disagreeable, for hauteur is disagreeable. The lay person defends their right to form their own opinion, and to have their own opinion respected.

But we will contend that the anti-economists' representation of the relation of economics to the public is, in large measure, a parody, a travesty, a complete falsification. We will contend, rather than speaking *de haut en bas* the leading creators of economics have sought to meet the public mind. We will assert that, rather than arrogate any claim on the public, there has been a greater risk of economists (both historically and currently) trimming their professions to ingratiate themselves with the public. We suggest that, rather than irrationally accepting too much authority of economists, the public has accepted too little, to its cost. Finally, we contend that in large measure all these strictures against economists are much more appropriately directed against anti-economists.[3]

The true grievance of this specimen of anti-economics, we suggest, is not that economists possess an unjustified authority, but that economists possess any authority whatever. For the authority of economists is their 'power'. And if economics has no authority, it might as well not exist. To destroy economists' authority is effectively to destroy economics.[4] Thus the grievance over authority may be seen as a strategy to effectively destroy economics that conveniently saves on the necessity to present a substantive case against it.

12.1 Authority: the attack

Anti-economists advance three censures regarding economists' authority.

1. Economists' authority is neither warranted nor rational. It is not warranted because they are no better judges of the truth than the public. And it is not rational because they have provided no evidence to the public that they are better judges.
2. Economists intend their authority as 'non-rational authority'. By invoking authority rather than arguing their claims, they take advantage of the public's mental docility to have their doctrines accepted unthinkingly; in bandying authority they have implicitly asked persons to subordinate their own judgement to economists. They have, therefore, betrayed the commitment to reason that they claim to uphold.[5] The heterodox economist J.S. Nicholson (1903, p. 565) expressed this sentiment when he complained that free trade economists oppose 'the arguments of the living to the opinions of the dead'.
3. Economics' authority is invoked to reduce the breadth of debate and the consideration of alternative views. There should be greater pluralism than presently exists in the benumbing presence of economic dicta. In this spirit Robinson complained in 1829: 'What can I gain by speaking to the Ministry ... who cannot do other than obey what the apostles of this Political Economy dictate? In the House of Commons discussion has ceased; and the most decisive proofs are laughed down by the simple assertion – they are contrary to Political Economy ... The infallible dicta of the Holy Mother Church of Political Popery supersede and suppress everything that can be offered by reason and evidence' (Robinson 1829, p. 510; 1827 p. 411).[6]

That economists' authority is neither warranted nor rational has been argued by anti-economists on three grounds:

- the denunciations of renegade economists
- the disagreement amongst economists
- the erroneousness of forecasts of economists.

Renegades

There is no dearth of persons who have been educated as economists, but have later foresworn their peers, and furnished denunciations of their old guild (Blaug 1998; Leontief 1982; Schumacher 1973; Ormerod 1994; Mathews

1991). These denunciations are relished by anti-economists, and they are not ill-advised to do so. Renegades from a putative authority may bear novel information which discredits that authority; they are, indeed, especially privileged to bring such novel information.[7] But, in fact, no novel information is brought, just the old charges repeated in new mouths, whose utterances are then gratefully quoted by anti-economists (for example, Hall 1990). Thus, ironically, the flourishing of renegades by anti-economists amounts to an argument from authority; renegades are invested with authority that the auditor is presumed to accept.

Disagreement

Controversy among economists has repeatedly been used as an argument that economists lacks authority. 'A science they call it, though cannot yet agree among themselves upon their definitions, and differ as widely in most of their conclusions. Yet it is a science forsooth!' (Southey 1831, p. 279).[8]

But this lack of consensus has been exaggerated. A 1990 survey of 1350 US economists (Alston et al. 1992) revealed that on the following propositions it was more likely than not that three randomly polled economists would all take the same position.

- Tariffs and import quotas usually reduce economic welfare
- A large federal budget deficit has an adverse effect on the economy
- Cash payments increase the welfare of recipients to a greater degree than do transfers in kind of equivalent cash value
- A minimum wage increases unemployment among young and unskilled workers
- Fiscal policy has a significant stimulative impact on a less than fully employed economy
- A ceiling on rents reduces the quantity and quality of housing available
- Effluent taxes represent a better approach to pollution control than pollution ceilings.[9]

Yet, undeniably, on many economic issues there is no such consensus. What are the implications of this lack? Anti-economists seem to reason as follows: any discipline that inculcated its members with a body of truths would have unanimity in its members' judgements, since truth is one. There is not unanimity in economics, therefore, economists are not inculcated with truths. This is a valid inference. It is also a shallow one. A deeper inference would be that economists are not inculcated with any unconditional doctrine, be it true or false. What economists are inculcated with is not doctrine, but guides (models, stylised facts, classic episodes), which are often ambiguous by themselves, and point directions only in conjunction with user, and in ways that will vary with user. There will, therefore, be no unanimity. The relevant question is whether guides are reliable in tendency.

If the economists' guides are reliable in tendency, then the discipline will have an authority, and one that is located in the *tendency* of opinion. Consider some event (say, a stock-market crash). Suppose that whenever this event occurs there is a probability in excess of 0.5 that it would have been forecast to occur by a given forecaster. It is not difficult to see that the probability of a majority of a group of forecasters predicting the event will be greater than the probability of a single forecaster. As the number of forecasters rises, the probability of a majority predicting the event approaches 1. Indeed, as long as the probability of a single forecaster predicting the event (when it does occur) is in some small degree in excess of 0.5 then, as the sample grows, the probability that a majority will have forecast it (when it does occur) approaches 1. We are, therefore, permitted to use the following logic: 'If a stock-market crash occurs a majority of forecasters would have predicted it to occur. A majority of forecasters have not predicted it to occur. Therefore a stock market crash will not occur.' There is in this circumstance a reliability about the tendency of opinion. It is the *tendency* of opinion among economists that commands an authority.[10]

A critical feature of the authority of the tendency of opinion is that it does not require a 'consensus' of opinion. If an event would have been forecast with a probability of 0.6, then whenever the event occurs the profession would have been split 60:40 in its forecasts. But nevertheless (for any large number) the majority of the profession is highly likely to make the correct prediction, and therefore have authority.

Thus a lack of consensus may coexist with authority. A lack of consensus is no proof of authority's non-existence.

Forecasts

A supposed lack of predictive success has been used to discredit the authority of economists, on the grounds that the strongest evidence of a lack of knowledge is the predictive failure of the supposed possessor of knowledge. When many favoured predictions of some discipline that supposedly possesses knowledge are falsified, more than those predictions are discredited; the discipline is itself discredited, and revealed as a bad picker. Thus anti-economists concerned to destroy the authority of economists serve their goal well by making severe judgements of the accuracy of economists' predictions. 'Some sceptical people have kept records of economists' predictions and tested them against actual outcomes. These studies have repeatedly shown that economists' forecasts are consistently wrong' (Hamilton 1994, p. 1).[11]

Claims that 'economists' forecasts are consistently wrong' are very misleading for the lay audience for which they are intended. Table 12.1 reveals that OECD forecasts of a central macroeconomic variable, real GDP, are (i) correlated with GDP outcomes, and (ii) better correlated than a naive forecast that assumes future growth will be the same as current growth.

Table 12.1   Correlation of OECD Forecast in Year t of Real GDP Growth in Year $t+1$, 1968–95

	USA	Japan	Germany	France	UK	Italy	Canada
OECD forecast	0.86	0.69	0.56	0.68	0.61	0.59	0.72
Naive forecast	0.19	0.62	0.40	0.51	0.32	0.24	0.39

Note: Naive forecast in t of real GDP growth in $t+1$ = real GDP growth in t.
Sources: Row 1: Pons (1999); Row 2: World Bank, *World Development Indicators*; IMF, *International Financial Statistics*.

Even more germane to the issue of authority is the fact that the forecasts of economic models outperform those of the public.[12] We conclude that the attempt to disprove the authority of economists in macroeconomic variables fails. The predictive outperformance of the public proves that economists' authority is rational.

But how *much* rational authority is established by this outperformance is uncertain. A competent astronomer can predict eclipses to the minute, but the most celebrated economists cannot predict stock-market falls to the year. From this type of comparison we conclude that economists' predictions provide at best a weak *proof* of superiority of knowledge, regardless of any superiority they may actually have. Thus the model in which a public rationally invests authority in an economic expert and confidently heeds advice does not apply. However much economics may know, the depth of its rational authority is modest.

Instead of economists trying to persuade the public that they know the right policy, they have sought to persuade the public *of* the right policy. This, historically, has been the way economists have often proceeded. From Ricardo's letters to the *Morning Chronicle*, through Keynes's radio broadcasts on the BBC to Friedman's television programmes on the PBS, they have sought to argue directly with the public.

12.2   The public and the economists

Economists, complain anti-economists, presume a right to the public's intellectual allegiance. In truth, a survey of 250 years of the attitude of economics to public opinion reveals that the Tradition has variously held public opinion to be an ally to be marshalled, a potentate to be courted, or even an irrelevance to be ignored. But it has never assumed any right to the public's acquiescence.

No estates in knowledge

The historical genesis of economics in liberalism bequeathed to it a bias against the brandishing of authority. The founding experience (and myth) of liberalism was the struggle against the authority of *Ancien Régime* societies. This struggle was primarily against political authority. But it was also a struggle against intellectual authority, often embodied in religious oversight of sacred and secular knowledge.

The defining political principle of liberalism that formed in the struggle against *Ancien Régime* societies was that ultimate authority lay with individuals; that all the legitimate authority of the state was an authority delegated to it by individuals. The plausibility of this principle was supported by a key epistemological tenet of liberalism: there are 'no estates' in knowledge, and each individual is the best judge of his own situation. It was on this tenet that it was argued that the obviously advantageous delegation of individual authority to some sovereign state could be assured. And it was from this tenet that there flowed an esteem for the 'commonsensical' commonplace; a resource shared by all. The tenet implied an attraction to, or at least tolerance of, discussion. And *a fortiori* to a refusal to defer to intellectual authority.[13]

The correlation of economic liberalism with political liberalism left economic writers in pre-revolutionary France predisposed to conflict with a political/intellectual authority. Thus Sebastian Vauban's (1633–1707) *Projet d'une Dixme Royale*, of 1707(?) offended Louis XIV, and was 'pilloried' by Parliament. In 1707 Pierre de Boisguilbert was exiled from Rouen for several months on account of his economic tract *Détail de la France*. In 1734 Jean-François Melon's (1675?–1755) *Essai Politique sur le Commerce* won him some celebrity with the public and notoriety with the royal authorities. The *Essai* was suppressed. The book's open and critical discussion of government policy was not much to the taste of a ministry or a king who felt that such matters were best left to the decision of those suited to rule by their education and birth. All this was in accord with the notion that the formulation and examination of policy making was not a public matter, but the prerogative of the king and whoever he admitted (Hofman 1993, p. 43). The public was not entitled to air any 'opinion' on government policy.[14]

The prerogative of political authority to assume intellectual authority was questioned by the physiocrats. They elevated common sense to 'evidence'.[15] They sought to distinguish 'public opinion' from the jabber of the street: the public opinion they sought to persuade was 'discussion among experts and professionals competent to judge'. In their view 'public opinion assumed a critical function, guiding the king in the performance of his duties'. But the monarchy was doubtful about unsolicited guidance; Mirabeau's *Théorie d'impôt* of 1760 resulted in his imprisonment and exile from Paris for three months.[16] The physiocrat Nicholas Baudeau was briefly exiled in 1763 and again, for two and a half months, in 1776 following the fall of Turgot.[17]

The eighteenth-century French economists in seeking to bring policy formulation into the public sphere, on the basis of a belief in the equal capacity to judge issues form another contrast to their adversaries in the policy battles of the 1760s. Galiani and Necker slighted the notion of enlightened public opinion. Necker: 'the multitude of men is quite wild. It is eager to love and to hate' (Faccarello 1998, p. 138).

English eighteenth-century economists shared their French counterparts' doubts about the pretensions of established authority. In the *Wealth of Nations*, for example, Smith disparaged the endowed universities, argued that medical degrees were no more than a barrier to entry, and opposed established religion.[18]

The national clerisy

In the wake of the French Revolution Necker's view of public opinion seemed more persuasive than that of the physiocrats, and the notion of enlightened public opinion was at a discount. Counter-revolutionary authors blamed public opinion for subverting the monarchy. And where authority had not been destroyed it was slipping: in early nineteenth-century England Tories were disturbed by the declining prestige of the unreformed House of Commons and the law; the encroachment on the established Church by Dissenters and other religious minorities; and the turbulence in the medical and legal professions created by upstart challenges to their older institutions and norms (Webb 1992). Beholding this disorder, and in the mood of reaction against liberalism, intellectual authority took to the field again.

The supple intellect of John Henry Newman advocated traditional religious authority. Newman, a mild anti-economist, went so far as to equate the 'liberalism' that he detested with the doctrine that each man could decide questions for himself. Auguste Comte provided a vast, baroque vision of a revived authority, invested in a scientific 'priesthood' to which the public would unquestioningly submit. Standing between orthodox religion and unorthodox scientism was Coleridge. His strange fusion of religion and science produced an epistemology that scorned the mere common sense favoured by the Enlightenment: 'All the positive Institutions and Regulations, which the prudence of our ancestors had provided, are declared to be erroneous ... and the whole is delivered over to the faculty, which all men possess equally, ie the *common* sense or universal Reason' (Coleridge 1969b, p. 213).[19]

Rather than common sense, what was needed, said Coleridge, was a class of seers. He championed the public endowment of a national intellectual class that would instruct the rest of the nation, and faulted Smith's 'pernicious' criticism of such public endowments.[20]

As a kind of Enlightenment survival and bearers of a persevering liberalism, English classical economists of the early nineteenth century were generally immune to this attempted relegitimation of authority. The one partial exception was John Stuart Mill who, as an assimilator of new currents, felt an attraction to some form of national intellectual leadership. Yet Mill never bandied authority; he wrote the *Principles of Political Economy* to win the public's mind by argument, and in that he had a smashing success.

In any case, political economists were sensitive to how little authority they had to flourish. Therefore, instead of economists trying to persuade the public that they knew the right policy, they tried to persuade the public *of* the right policy. Ricardo, for example, gave 107 speeches to the House of Commons, and addressed the public through speeches and journalism.

Rather than political economists, it was anti-economists who sought to intimidate by bandying authority in the face of objectors. Laying paradox upon paradox, the anti-economists could even flourish the authority of political economy. Thus the well-known anti-economist George Poulett Scrope championed his own remedies for industrial distress, on the grounds that they are 'IN CONFORMITY WITH THE SOUNDEST PRINCIPLES OF POLITICAL ECONOMY' (Scrope 1835, p. 6). Such bluster was never heard from any economist of significance.

Further, unlike the political economists, the anti-economists abandoned argument in preference to two techniques of persuasion that dispense with argument and provide condemnation without cause.

Reflex discreditation. Reflex discreditation occurs when an argument, rather than being considered, is summarily rejected on the grounds that its advocate is an 'economic rationalist; 'neoliberal ideologue'; 'neoclassical' or 'bourgeois economist'. Thus rather than meet argument with argument, argument is dismissed on the grounds that its provenance is tainted and delegitimating. An early notice of the phenomenon of 'reflex discreditation' in anti-economics occurred in 1823. In that year Ricardo complained that 'the words "political economy" had of late become terms of ridicule and reproach. They were used as a substitute for an argument' (quoted in Cannan 1894, p. 412).

Rhapsody. The 'exalted expression of sentiment, an extravagance of idea or expression without connected thought or argument'; the frenzied war-dance; the theatric exhibition; the clamorous accusation and terrible judgement: these spectacles are familiar to any student of anti-economics. Carlyle is a celebrated example from the past. His jangling soliloquies entranced huge audiences. But, as one of his critics has judged, 'through Carlyle's prose the nerve of proof – in the readily understood and familiar sense of straight forward argument – simply cannot be traced' (Holloway 1953, p. 3). Carlyle expected the populace to obey at his command, and to believe at his command.

Politic economy

By the mid-Victorian period the project of recreating some form of anti-popular authority was expiring.[21] As this aspiration to anti-popular authority was anti-liberal in genesis, its expiration might be considered harmless to political economy. But in the event this project was displaced by something far more detrimental to political economy and its authority; a kind of authority of the populace. The extension of the franchise during the late nineteenth century moved the populace into the centre of the political terrain, and the rule of public opinion so feared by early nineteenth-century liberals seemed in danger of realisation. Critically, this populace could not be taken to be sympathetic towards political economy. So whereas in the eighteenth century 'public opinion' was seen as an ally to political economy, 'public opinion' was now dubious of political economy.

It was the thesis of W.H. Hutt (1899–1988) that political economy in the new circumstances of late Victorian England attempted to preserve its remaining authority by deferring to the new, looming public opinion. Hutt claimed that in the wake of the Great Reform Act of 1867 'several outstanding economists were obviously affected by popular sentiment, by the desire to retain authority and influence, and by the course of politics' (Hutt 1936, p. 179). To preserve their station in the face of shifting public sentiments, Hutt contends, economists adjusted their public presentation to find favour with the public. They adapted tactical silences over doctrines that the public would reject, and abandoned doctrines which would discredit them in the public eye: 'economists had to compete with their opponents for the acceptance of their authority. They tended to become *politic* economists: they refrained tactfully from stressing truths that would offend or not be readily believed by those who trusted them' (Hutt 1936, p. 185).[22]

Hut singled out J.S. Mill as an 'outstanding economist' especially affected by 'the desire to retain authority'. Condescending of the populace rather than contemptuous, Mill's sense of superiority extended to a confidence in his power to shift public opinion in the direction he desired. But, 'in attempting to find out "the mode of putting a thought which gives its easiest admittance into minds not prepared for it by habit", in his readiness to sacrifice "the non-essential in order to preserve the essential", and in his desire to give "a more genial character to Radical speculations", he suffered a subtle and unconscious corruption of his intellectual purity' (Hutt 1936, p. 183).[23]

Beyond the 'tactful' concealment of unpopular opinions, came the actual tacit revision of doctrine. Even such an (apparently) unshrinking disputant as John E. Cairnes seems to have unwittingly judged doctrines in terms of public reception. 'Political Economy and Laissez-faire' (Cairnes [1873] 1965) is a case in point. Cairnes is concerned to repudiate any allegiance between political economy and laissez-faire. But how does he proceed to this conclusion? In our reading he orientates himself by the following syllogism:

The public is against laissez-faire
Therefore laissez-faire is wrong
Political economy is right
Therefore political economy is against laissez-faire.

If only political economy rejected laissez-faire then political economy would win the people.

The upshot, in Hutt's analysis, is that by about 1870, instead of economists sitting in judgement of propositions advanced by the public, it was the other way around. Instead of economists waving their opinions in the face of the public, the public's disbelief was waved in the face of economists. Public opinion was the gauge by which the validity of economic opinions would be measured. The public's belief or disbelief was now insinuated as a mark of truth or falsehood. This came about, ironically, through the aspiration of political economy to be a pre-eminent actor in public affairs, for 'those who will lead, must also, in a considerable degree follow' (Burke [1790] 1968, p. 128).

It may, therefore, be said that about 1870 there was the possibility of English political economy developing, as it largely did in Germany, into a passive accompaniment of political currents. In this development Mill would have done in England as Roscher did in Germany; personally admiring Ricardo, but in fact disarming and neutralising the *Grande Tradition*. And Mill did indeed do this to some degree, and the English Historical School did emerge with the help of his patronage; Leslie, Foxwell and Cunningham.

But the development of a German-style English Historical School was frustrated by a contrary development: the emergence of an autonomous scientific economics pioneered by the neoclassical economists, Jevons, Marshall and Edgeworth. Ambitious in science, the neoclassical lacked the ambition of the classical political economist to be an actor in public affairs. Turgot was no longer the model, von Thünen was. Problem solving was no longer pre-eminent, science building was. 'Truth', said Marshall, 'is the only thing worth having' (quoted in Maloney 1985, p. 52). Further, this new autonomous scientific economics had a confidence in its own specialist criterion for judgement that the public could never share. There was no possibility that the public's belief and disbelief would now be insinuated as the mark of truth or falsehood. 'Politic economy' was in retreat.

At the close of the nineteenth century, the disappearance of 'politic economy' from the leadership of English economics is illustrated by Marshall's protest against protectionism and 'tariff reform'. Whereas the English and German Historical Schools tended to favour a moderate protectionism (then gaining in public popularity), Marshall led a public struggle against protectionism (Coats 1968). And he sought to invoke the authority of economics against protection by very publicly expressing his and his colleagues' opposition to protection. The historical economists were greatly offended by this slight to public sensibility. In Foxwell's view Marshall's behaviour

> has had the defect which so many of us foresaw at the time of putting economists out of court altogether. We are now hopelessly discredited: in fact political economy seems to me to have fallen back in public opinion to the position it held about the [18]70s. I hoped that the more realistic and liberal tone of the work of the last generation would have gained for English economists something of the respect which German economists enjoy in the world of affairs.
>
> (Foxwell quoted in Coats 1964, p. 102)

Foxwell, and the German economists, did not very long enjoy respect. But the triumph of the science-building imperative in economics after the late nineteenth century did not spell the end of all impetus to 'politic economy'.[24] The mass public remained a potentate. The Enlightenment presumption that the public was an ally to be marshalled remained illusory. Material considerations biased the public against the Tradition: the public was a heap of vested interests, each (paradoxically) opposed to the public interest. And the purely ideal motives of the public also found the Tradition an awkward, discomforting and unfitting thing. Legislation for minimum wages, maximum hours and equal pay; all of these are part of every sensible citizen's vision of a decent society. Yet all stick like a bone in the throat of anyone who has absorbed the core of the Tradition. There therefore remains a reward for anyone who can mould this awkward, discomforting and unfitting creature into a socialised, tame and padding accomplice of society's proprieties.

In fact, the emergence of quasi-scientific neoclassical economics has allowed new ways of so taming this awkward and unfitting creature. The first way of taming is the elevation of scientific technique over other considerations, so that method becomes the reference point of all affirmation. In this way economics becomes all style and no substance, all ritual and no worship, a religion of good taste, permeated by 'ironic belief'; a sort of harmless economic Anglicanism, practised in tranquil sanctuaries at one remove from the rude hubbub of the world (see Wiles 1979–80).

A second method of 'breaking in' untamed economics lies in the elevation of the model over doctrine, which is also characteristic of neoclassicism (see Niehans 1990). Models can be built to perform any feat one may wish. Neoclassical models can justify deregulation. They can also be contrived to justify regulation. Indeed, a neoclassical economist may be operationally defined as someone who can supply an optimising rationale for any regulation one cares to conceive.[25] It is true that more ingenuity in neoclassical economics is required to justify a regulation than its abolition, but ingenuity is not something neoclassicals lack.

The result is that there remain forces and resources in modern economics to forge a politic economy.

The paradox is that the politic economy that wins the popularity of the public serves them ill. One may compare the rapturous reception of the politic Necker with the unpopular, awkward and brusque Turgot that he vanquished. And compare how feeble and meretricious were the policies of Necker with those of Turgot. Or one may contrast Marshallian economics with the German Historical School. Under Marshall, English economics did perhaps fall back in public opinion. It certainly lacked the delightful 'respect which German economists enjoy in the world of affairs'. Schmoller was often favoured with invitations to meet Kaiser Wilhelm II (Barkin 1970, p. 9). Most important of all, German lecture theatres were flooded with students keen to absorb the economic wisdom of the Historical School of the day (Lindenfeld 1997, p. 282). Perhaps economics has never been so popular anywhere as it was in Germany in that period. And perhaps it has never anywhere been so bad. For this popularity was purchased at the cost of a renunciation of the 'uncongenial' theoretical core of economics, and that amounted to a programme of intellectual disarmament which had two catastrophic consequences. The German hyperinflation of 1922–23 is directly attributable to the precepts of the Historical School that had 'proved' the falsehood of what we call 'monetarism'. The ineffectiveness of German economists in dealing with the Great Depression is also attributable in part to the intellectual impoverishment of the Historical School.

13

'Economists, Glory to You and the Jews!':[1] a Postscript on Anti-Semitism and Anti-Economics

This chapter argues that there exists a correspondence between anti-economics and a now infinitely discredited ideological force, anti-Semitism. We will argue that, during its first 150 years, anti-economics found in anti-Semitism its own döppelganger, sometimes out of sight but never far distant, moving and swaying with the roll and pitch of anti-economics.

13.1 The logic of the homology

The preceding chapters have distinguished a number of types of anti-economics: a Right anti-economics and a Left anti-economics, both based on an offence (for different reasons) at the market; a nationalist anti-economics based on a offence at universalism (or 'cosmopolitanism'); an anti-individualist anti-economics based on a offence at self-interest; a materialist anti-economics based on an offence at worldly materialism; and an irrationalist anti-economics that takes offence at rationalism.

In each species of anti-economics, economics is identified with the offending phenomenon (the market, universalism, self-interest, rationalism and so on) and, consequently, an anti-economics is generated. One may infer that if some other thing, 'x', can be identified with the same offending phenomenon (the market, universalism, self-interest and so on) then the same sensibilities that generate an anti-economics, will also generate an 'anti-x'. But what other thing might be equated to the market, universalism, self-interest and so on?

It is incontestable that, rightly or wrongly, Jewry has been frequently identified by both Jew and gentile, by anti-Semite and philo-Semite, with all these offending items: the market, universalism, self-interest, rationalism and materialism.

We conclude that, in the presence of this stereotyping, certain forms of anti-Semitism and certain forms of anti-economics will occur as a pair. So Right anti-economists will see Jews as subversives, or usurpers. Left anti-economists will see Jews as potentates of the social order. Nationalist anti-economists will see Jews as curdling the national spirit. Anti-economists of the religion of love will see Jews as epitomes of greed. Materialist anti-economics will see Jews as morbidly charmed by wealth. Irrationalist anti-economists will see Jews as the vessel of a 'lifeless' rationalism.

Is this conclusion confirmed? Is there any evidence of this pairing of anti-economics and anti-Semitism?

Paired antagonisms

Right anti-economics

Certain Right anti-economists saw Jews as trespassers, or usurpers, of the old social order. Bonald, the most significant anti-economist of the Restoration, felt 'an almost medieval hostility towards the Jews' (Ages 1974, p. 33). His 'On the Jews' (1806) branded Jews as usurers, and accused them of contriving scarcities in Moravia, Bohemia and Austria from which they profited. Worse still the Jews are 'enemies' of Christianity, who will succeed in defeating Christianity unless their designs are recognised and confounded. Regrettably, wrote Bonald, imprudent liberalisations of old economic and social prohibitions are permitting Jewish infiltration and control.[2]

At about the same time Cobbett complained of 'Jew-devils' (Cobbett [1830] 1967, p. 412) being part of the subversion of the old order. In 1805 he charged that Great Britain was possessed of a 'system' that was ruining it; 'the system by which the ancient Aristocracy and the Church have been undermined; by which the ancient gentry of the kingdom have been almost extinguished, their means of support having been transferred, by the hand of the tax gatherer, to contractors, jobbers and Jews' (Osborne 1984, p. 87). In Cobbett's view, Jews, by fostering the commercial spirit had transformed the City of London into a 'Jewish wen' (wen = tumour). With their new wealth they arrogated the position of the old nobility. David Ricardo was instanced as an example of this distressing process: 'Baring assists at the Congress of Sovereigns, and Ricardo regulates things at home' (quoted in Halévy 1949b, p. 53).[3] Oastler also favoured the theme of Jews undermining the old order. Rothschilds and Jews are the 'Slaughter House Masters' who had 'usurped the place of our Old English merchants' (quoted in Persky 1998, p. 638).

Left anti-economics

Certain anti-economists affiliated to socialist movements held that Jews were potentates of the contemporary social order. To Toussenel the Jews were the 'Kings of the Age'. 'Europe is entailed to the domination of Israel. This universal domination, of which so many conquerors have dreamed, the Jews have in their hands' (quoted in Lichtheim 1968, p. 320). In the same vein Leroux announces, 'The true successor of Napoleon is the Jew.' Similar themes were pursued by Marx. The Tsar Nicholas I and Emperor

Francis Joseph both could not exist without Jewish support: 'Thus we find every tyrant backed by a Jew, as is every Pope by a Jesuit' (quoted in Silberner 1953, p. 7)

The identification of the market with the social order was extended to the phenomenon of imperialism by the anti-economist J.A. Hobson. Hobson's theory of the Anglo–Boer War was, in its original formulation, anti-Semitic. The 'Jew-Imperialist' had 'fastened on the Rand...as they are prepared to fasten upon any other spot on the globe...making their gain not out of the genuine fruits of industry...but out of the construction, promotion and financial manipulation of companies' (quoted in Mitchell 1965, p. 355). Political power would consolidate their economic power, and using 'the wider and ever growing Jewish control' of the press they manipulated the 'slower-witted Briton' into pursuing a war of annexation in southern Africa (see also Silberner 1952; and Allett 1987).[4]

Nationalist anti-economics

Some anti-economists saw Jews as alien to the body politic.

Carlyle asked, 'A Jew is bad; but what is a shameless Jew, a Quack-Jew? And how can a real Jew...try to be a Senator, or even a citizen, of any country, except his own wretched Palestine, whither all his thoughts and steps and efforts tend – where in the Devil's name, let him arrive as soon as possible, and make us quit of him!' (quoted in Kaplan 1983, p. 527). Thomas Carlyle could stand outside the Rothschild residence and 'savour the just punishment that would one day be meted out' to their likes (Kaplan 1983, p. 527). Carlyle, we might finally note, used the term 'anti-Semitism' twenty years before it was supposedly first coined in the 1870s (Gross 1991).

In a nationalistic vein, Proudhon complained of 'this race which poisons everything, by meddling everywhere without ever joining to another people'. He had plans for the Jews still more drastic than Carlyle's. 'The Jew is the enemy of the human race. One must send this race back to Asia or exterminate it' (quoted in Lichtheim 1968, p. 322).

Anti-Semitism was also a tendency of the nationalist historical schools of the late nineteenth century. 'Schmoller and Wagner both vented their concern over Jewish penetration of German society in public' (Lindenfeld 1997, p. 284). Cunningham vindicated Edward I's expulsion of the Jews in 1290 on the grounds that 'the incompatibility of the temperament between Christian and Jew rendered it impossible for both to live at peace under the same political and municipal institutions' (Cunningham 1896, p. 91).[5]

Anti-individualist anti-economics

Karl Marx gave what is, perhaps, the most condensed identification of Jews with self-interest in a paper of 1843 that is usually known by the name, 'On the Jewish Question':

What is the profane basis of Judaism? *Practical* need, *self-interest*. What is the worldly cult of the Jew? *Huckstering*. What is his worldly god? *Money*. Very well: then in emancipating itself from *huckstering* and *money*, and thus from real and practical Judaism, our age would emancipate itself ... In the final analysis, the *emancipation* of the Jews is the emancipation of mankind from *Judaism*.

(Marx [1844] 1963, p. 34)

Marx once predicted that the emancipation of the Jews in the ordinary civil sense would turn gentiles into 'beggars' and 'proletarians' (quoted in Silberner 1953, p. 7).[6]

Materialist anti-economics

Some anti-economists identify Jews with a 'doctrine of possession'. Sombart claimed 'Jews differ from the Christians, whose religion has tried to rob them of all its earthly joys. As often as riches are lauded in the Old Testament they are damned in the New' (Sombart [1911] 1951, p. 221). Borrowing and adapting an argument from Weber about capitalism and Protestants, Sombart alleged that Jews see 'material well-being' as a symbol of God's pleasure.

Irrationalist anti-economics

Some anti-economists have identified Jews with rationality, and faulted them for it. Sombart made it the leading trait of Jews: 'Rationalism is the characteristic trait of Judaism as of Capitalism: Rationalism or Intellectualism – both deadly foes alike to irresponsible mysticism and to that creative power which draws its artistic inspiration from the passion world of the senses' (Sombart [1911] 1951, p. 206). In Sombart's view Jews suffer from 'an over-rating of mere knowledge' (Sombart [1911] 1951, p. 258).

The gospel of work

The gospel of work implies that economics has erred in pressing the market as the great road to prosperity. It is work, says this gospel, that will bring material rewards, not buying and selling. That Jews do not 'work' and only buy and sell is an anti-Semitic contention easily found in Cobbett, Proudhon, Sombart and others. To Cobbet, Jews cannot do manual work and so have turned London into a centre of commerce. To Proudhon:

The Jew is by temperament an anti-producer, neither a farmer nor an industrialist nor even a true merchant ... He knows but the rise and fall of prices, the risks of transportation, the incertitudes of crops, the hazards of demand and supply. His policy in economics has always been entirely negative, entirely usurious; it is the evil principle, Satan, Ahriman, incarnated in the race of Shem.

(Quoted in Silberner 1953, p. 4)

Sombart decries as characteristically Jewish the elevation of brainwork over 'hard bodily work' (Sombart [1911] 1951, p. 260).

To summarise: anti-economics has often been paired with anti-Semitism. We confidently venture no such collection of anti-Semitic quotations can be made from economists of equal stature. Yet not all the anti-economists examined in this book were anti-Semites.[7] The Saint-Simonians were anti-economists and yet were animated philo-Semites. Comte, too, was philo-Semitic.[8]

A coincident antagonism

Perhaps more telling would be the verification of another implication of the hypothesised correspondence between anti-economics and anti-Semitism; if economics is identified with the market (or universalism, self-interest, rationalism and so on), and if Jews are identified with the market (or universalism, self-interest, rationalism and so on), then economics and Jews are identified with each other. Anti-economics and anti-Semitism become a single, fused antipathy.

Has there been a single, fused antipathy?

One manifestation of a fused antipathy would be the feeling that there is something objectionably Jewish about economists. There are a few such stray remarks to that effect. Josiah Tucker was dubbed by some of his adversaries Josiah ben Tucker ben Judas Iscariot, on account of his support for the admission of Jews into the trade with Turkey, and for his support of the naturalisation of Jews as British subjects (Shelton 1981, p. 84; Rashid 1982). The *Poor Man's Guardian* calls Joseph Hume a jew-peddler (Silberner 1952, p. 33) Cobbett describes the political economists as 'Scotch Jews'.[9]

Another manifestation of a fused antipathy would be the feeling that there is something objectionably Jewish about economic doctrine. In John Wilson's mind political economy was 'mapped out' by 'the genius of the Jew' (Grampp 1976, p. 548). Engels says that the favourite science of the Jewish *commerçant* is political economy (Engels [1845] 1858, p. 312). More specifically, certain anti-economists have identified *homo economicus* with *homo Judaica*. The Irish nationalist and anti-economist John Dillon wrote that 'economic man' is epitomised by Shylock. Hobson states that the foreign Jew 'is the nearest approach to the ideal economic man ... he is almost devoid of social morality' (quoted in Allett 1987, p. 103). Webb makes the same identification in expressing her objections to Jewish immigrants. The Jew

> is deficient in that highest and latest development of human sentiment –
> social morality ... the immigrant Jew ... seems to justify by his existence
> those strange assumptions which figured for *man* in the political economy
> of Ricardo – an Always Enlightened Selfishness, seeking employment or
> profit with an absolute mobility of body and mind, without pride, without

preference, without interests outside... the existence and welfare of the individual and the family.

(Webb 1968, pp. 155–6)

The most significant manifestation of fusion is treating economists and Jews as one and the same. Such a treatment is found in Leroux. His polemic against economics is entitled *Malthus et les Économistes* (1849). This tract, supposedly concerned with Malthus and economists, begins with a part entitled *Les Juifs Rois de l'Époque* ('The Jews Kings of the Age'), which opens with a 20-page tirade against Jews. With barely a pause for breath Leroux moves on to Malthus.

But it is in Toussenel that the fusion of the two hate objects is most vivid, concentrated and conscious. Toussenel's *Les Juifs, Rois de l'Époque* (1847) is judged by historians a significant event in the history of modern anti-Semitism. A century later a littérateur and Vichy collaborator was to publish a study of Toussenel in which he approvingly contended that the anti-Semitism of Toussenel was 'exactly the attitude of Adolf Hitler in *Mein Kampf*' (Thomas 1941, p. 14). *Les Juifs, Rois de l'Époque* is also a significant anti-economist tract. Entangled in its tumult of abuse of Jews is abuse of economists, J.B. Say, the *Journal des Économistes*, and chairs in political economy. This inclusion is not incidental. In its closing pages, he declares: 'Economists, glory to you and the Jews! For they are the Jews, note well, the true Jews of Juda, who run almost everywhere the trade in human flesh' (Toussenel 1847, p. 177).

13.2   Conclusions and qualifications

To conclude: there may be a homology between certain forms of anti-economics and anti-Semitism. As long as Jews are identified with the market, self-interest, rationality and so on then anti-economics will be paired with anti-Semitism, as the general accusations against economics are those against the Jews.

But it is not our contention that there is a *necessary* homology between all anti-economics and anti-Semitism. The homology requires that Jews be identified with the market, rationality and so on. But Jews need not be so identified, and there is nothing in the premises of anti-economics that requires such an identification. In any case, any contention of a necessary homology shatters on the existence of philo-Semitic anti-economists, and anti-Semitic economists.[10] This lack of any necessity of the homology between anti-Semitism and anti-economics is underlined by the fact that anti-Semitism disappeared from anti-economics by the mid-twentieth century. While this could be explained simply in terms of the atrophy of anti-Semitism (if there is no anti-Semitism then it cannot coexist with anti-economics), it is significant that even in places where overt and active anti-Semitism persisted in the post-war period, such as the Soviet Union, the harrying of economic science appears to have had no anti-Semitic aspect (Katsenelin-boigen 1981, p. 46).

Neither is it our contention that the anti-Semitism we have examined is identifiable with the anti-Semitism that made itself infamous in the twentieth century. The anti-Semitism that we have examined in this chapter was generally 'cultural', and not biological. Jewish culture was held to bear certain undesirable traits, but other societies may acquire and bear these traits in the same measure. Thus Sombart held 'Scotchman and Jews are interchangeable' (see Harris 1942). In this sort of anti-Semitism a gentile may be openly classed as a 'Jew' on account of their opinions and actions (for example, Leroux 1849, p. 17). Thus an anti-Semitic writer of this school, Auguste Chirac (1803–85), can say of Leon Say (1826–96), a Huguenot and propagator of the economic doctrines of his grandfather Jean-Baptiste Say, 'This Jew is a Protestant' (quoted in Glasberg 1974, p. 67).

14
The Not-so-Puzzling Failure of Anti-Economics

Over the past two centuries a ragged, crashing, fantastic cannonade has been loosed against economics with the purpose of destroying it. But whenever the din subsides, what is seen to be its impact? Nothing. Its projectiles have smashed fruitlessly around their target. The deadly barrage has been an uncompensated failure.

This failure of anti-economics presents questions. What is the location of the failure? What is faulty with this purportedly lethal engine of war? Must it have failed? Or might one conceive a successful anti-economics in place of the unsuccessful? Finally, if the criticism of anti-economics must fail, must *all* criticism, beyond that normally practised by economists themselves, fail? Does the current practice of 'normal criticism' exhaust all useful criticism? Or is there a culture of criticism that is comprehended by neither anti-economics nor economics?

In this chapter we advance some hypotheses as to why anti-economics has failed, and why it must fail. We also argue that there exists a suite of critical practices which avoid the destructive ambitions of anti-economics, yet are neglected by the routine criticism of economists of their craft.

14.1 The apparatus of criticism

To locate a failure of anti-economics we need a chart of the process of criticism. One may imagine the process of criticism as consisting of three logically consecutive operations: *representation* (of what economics says); *examination* (of the truth, utility, significance, intelligibility, falsifiability of what it says); and *evaluation*, or the judgement of the worth of what it says. We argue that anti-economics criticism is inadequate in all three operations.

Inadequate representation

Anti-economics is marred by absurd misrepresentations of economics.[1] A student of anti-economics will struggle to find any boundaries to its fatuities. Even if one is to restrict oneself to those authors taken more seriously by the wider world, it is possible to discover jewels of unaccountable absurdity.

- 'Adam Smith advocated the soak-the-rich policy of progressive income taxation' (Rothbard 1995, p. 467).[2]
- 'Hayek...had certainly never been much troubled by epistemological worries' (Myrdal 1977, p. 52).[3]
- Keynes's *How to Pay for the War* is a militarist document (Waring 1988, p. 44).[4]
- 'The Spirit of interference...constitutes the very essence of modern [that is, classical] political economy. Everything is to be done by the state, nothing is left to the discretion of individuals' (Ravenstone 1821, p. 3).
- The 'French economists' asserted the 'absolute illegality of interest' (Ruskin 1905, 17, p. 271).
- The physiocrats included d'Alembert, Diderot, and la Harpe (Robison 1798).[5]
- 'In general, very few economic papers test hypotheses' (Hall 1990, p. 99).

Misrepresentations are not restricted to doctrinal specifics: general doctrines of economics are also misrepresented. Thus it is asserted that economics 'plead selfishness', whereas no significant economist (with the arguable exception of Malthus) has asserted the superiority of selfishness over self-lessness. Or that economists are 'right wing', to which attitudinal survey responses put the lie. Or that economists 'believe in the market', in the sense of taking it as a normative first principle.

These misrepresentations are not restricted to the doctrinal: misrepresentations of character are also worth pausing over. Here, of course, classical economists are presented as cold, hard, blinkered (see Clark 1969 for one widely-read example). A relatively restrained example is Polanyi's reproof of Ricardo's 'icy unconcern' for the predicament of the poor. That Ricardo's temperament is foreign to the post-Romantic world is undeniable; it might be truly said of Ricardo, as was said of Thornton, that he was 'affectionate but passionless'. And the same may be truly said of all classical economists who came to maturity in the eighteenth century. Yet 'passionless' is not 'icy', and neither is 'affectionate'. Ricardo, as already noted, was a significant benefactor of 'the poor and helpless' (Weatherall 1976, p. 113).

Complementing these unfavourable misrepresentations of economists are favourable misrepresentations – amounting to sheer indulgence – of the vicious opinions of anti-economists. Thus Carlyle's brutality is somehow mysteriously transmuted into a superior moral vision.[6] A similar feat is achieved for Ruskin.[7] So, for example, in a work that summarizes 300 papers on Ruskin (Cate 1988) the Governor Eyre affair is mentioned precisely once.

Inadequate examination

That the examination of anti-economics was inadequate was the conclusion of the preceding chapters, and there is no benefit in repeating those arguments for that thesis here. But whatever they lacked, the contentions of anti-economists dealt with in previous chapters at least possessed a dignity sufficient to make them worthy of appraisal. What has not been stressed so far is the capacity of anti-economists' examinations to be asinine.

Malthus's population doctrines, in particular, attracted inopportune theoretical claims, fanciful speculation and foolish inference.

- *Fanciful speculation.* The thesis of Alison's anti-Malthusian *The Principles of Population and their Connection with Human Happiness* is that human happiness is guarded by a divine Providence that will not permit food shortage to trouble an expanding population. According to Alison we can see this Providence silently toiling to ensure food ample to meet needs: for, unheralded, a new supercontinent is emerging from the coral reefs of the Pacific ocean:

  While man in the old world is pining under the miseries which its wickedness created... an insect in the Pacific is calling a new world into existence, and countless myriads of happy animals are labouring to extend the continents... At least twenty five million square miles, capable of maintaining five times the whole present inhabitants of the globe in affluence and plenty, are there in the course of creation, and slowly but certainly... to rise by alluvial formation above the level of the deep, or to be elevated by the internal fire into the Alps and the Andes of a future world!

  (Alison 1840, pp. 499, 502)

- *Foolish inference.* T.E.C. Leslie sought to rebut Malthus's allusions to supposed American fertility by reference to a decline in vigour and fecundity in American families. Leslie's evidence for such a decline? 'the vastly greater proportion of diseases of the digestive organs in the United States than in Great Britain, the premature fading of American women, and what dentists report of the frailty of American teeth' (Leslie 1888, p. 136).

- *Naive theorising.* On the basis of the interval between each generation, Ravenstone believed he could demonstrated that 75 years was the shortest time for population to double from natural increase (Ravenstone 1821, p. 39).

The anti-economics literature outside of Malthusianism also exhibits a crass (impudent?) disregard for the factual truth. Linguet's discourse on the toxicity of bread is matched by equivalent inanities of successor anti-economists today. Thus: 'The long-term pattern of the Industrial Revolution was to institute a lower financial standard of living and declining conditions of life' (Saul 1996, p. 116). We sympathise with the critic who declared that one anti-text 'appears to me to break a world record, that of the number of factual falsehoods' (Kolm 1978, p. 641).[8]

But it is not our charge that asininity was characteristic of their contentions. Most were not so.

Several were true. The crucial defect in their advocacy here was not their contentions' lack of truth, but the inadequacy of their justification. An illustration is anti-economists' criticism of Senior's argument that a 10 per cent reduction in the length of the working day would annihilate the profitability of manufacturing. Senior's argument was scorned by anti-economists. And they were right to do so: Senior's case rested on an implicit self-contradiction in his premises. But none pointed out Senior's error. As Schumpeter said of Marx's response to Senior, 'in all the pages of vituperation that he bestowed upon it, he failed to adduce the decisive criticism which he does not seem to have perceived' (Schumpeter 1954, p. 486).[9]

Another example of anti-economists' criticisms that were true, but inadequately justified, were their strictures against Say's Law. A rejection of Say's Law was one of the shared themes of anti-economists. In the United Kingdom, Tory organs of opinion aired attacks on Say's Law. Thus Scrope in the *Quarterly Review* in 1831 wrote:

> The economists have nowhere committed greater errors than in discussing the relations of the demand to the supply of commodities. They insist, that there can be no falling off in the general demand for goods, because, all business merely being the exchange of goods, the general demand is measured by, in fact consists of, the general supply. We have shown, however, that ... a general increase in the propensity to save, as compared with that to spend, would ... occasion *a general glut*.
>
> (Scrope 1831, p. 23)

In 1829 David Robinson exclaimed, 'According to the economists ... an enlargement of production, even if it were a thousand times greater, could not cause a general excess of commodities, or reduce the rate of profit. Speak of the ravings of madmen!' (Robinson 1829, p. 672). Galt in *Blackwood's* in 1822 'extolled the benefits of wartime government expenditure' (Gordon 1965, p. 440), and the *British Critic, Monthly Review* and Coleridge concurred.[10] To Ruskin, Mill's notions of Say's Law were his 'most curious' error (Ruskin quoted in Groenewegen 2000). Theophilus Craster in his *A View of Manufactures, Money and Corn Laws, Adverse to Every Theory of the Economists* declared 'Individual economy doubtless is not only laudable, but necessary. But in the case of a rich country DIFFUSION is clearly no less its duty than its interest' (Craster 1840, p. 18). Edward Stillingfleet Caley (1802–62) shared similar views (see Dutton and King, 1985). Later in the nineteenth century, Robert Scott Moffat in *The Economy of Consumption. An Omitted Chapter in Political Economy* maintained that 'the tendencies of accumulation . . . are normally always in excess of the demands of industry' (1878, p. 222). In 1887 a retired Birmingham manufacturer William Lucas Sargent (1809–89), wrote in his anti-text that if a nation 'consume too little, capital will be unduly increased and overproduction and gluts will result' (Sargent 1887, p. 342).

The Left in Britain had disputed Say's Law sixty years before J.A. Hobson's *The Physiology of Industry: Being an Exposure of Certain Fallacies in Existing Theories of Economics*. Hodgskin is one example (Thompson 1984b, p. 170).

In France hostility to Say's Law also crossed political boundaries. While the aristophile Sismondi disputed Say's Law (Sismondi [1827] 1991, pp. 104–7), under-consumptionism became popular with French socialists in the 1830s and 1840s, and was adopted by the revolutionary (and anti-economist) Auguste Blanqui. In his view 'under-consumption was the root of business stagnation. Restore to the worker "what had been stolen from him for the pockets of capital". His improved means of purchase would spur production; this in turn would bring prices down and wages up. Consumption would rise in proportion to production' (Bernstein 1971, p. 205).

In Germany under-consumptionism was advocated by Johan Karl Rodbertus (1805–75). His student Adolf Wagner believed 'it was possible for governments, through fiscal policies, to influence the course of the national economy' (Ascher 1963, p. 296). The German Historical School 'closely examined the ambiguities of Say's Law' (Hutchison 1988, p. 530)

In the United States, Henry Carey in his *Principles of Social Science* summarily rejected Say's Law, and opined 'where saving is most practised, society is stagnant' (Carey [1859] 1963, p. 61). The labour activist George Gunton (1845–1919) advanced under-consumptionist doctrine in his anti-text, *Principles of Social Economics Inductively Considered and Practically Applied with Criticisms in Current Theories*. 'Instead of parsimony, on the part of the great body of consumers, promoting the use of capital in production and the growth of industrial prosperity in the community, it tends to prevent it' (Gunton 1891, p. 79).

To summarise, it would appear that almost every anti-economist believed that aggregate demand had a significance that the classical economists had not allowed for. In this belief the anti-economists were right.[11] But it was not wrong for their objection to Say's Law to fail. The arguments were too crude; they failed to grapple with the arguments of, say, J.S. Mill (1965b, III, xiv) in favour of the Law. In their nihilism they overdid it; they refused the theorising of the Tradition that contained the elements that would articulate their intuitions about effective demand and help bring out the weaknesses in the classical theory (as Keynes was to do). While their negative contentions were justified, their positive contentions were exaggerated. In seeking a knock-out blow, they failed to land a punch.

Inadequate evaluation

Inadequate in representation, and examination, the fundamental deficiency of anti-economists lies in evaluation.

Adequate valuation is already made difficult by improper representation and examination. Anti-economists do not know what economics says, and they do not appreciate what is central in what it says. Thus the triumphing by anti-economists over the travails of the Phillips Curve (MacIntyre 1981, p. 85), as if the Phillips Curve was at the centre of economics, rather than at the periphery.

Beyond the problems created by inadequate representation and examination, the evaluation of anti-economists is marred by their neglect of predictive accuracy as a resource in theory evaluation. Thus well-informed and scientific specimens of anti-economics are still flawed by the presumption that flourishing the falsity of a theory's assumption amounts to a destruction of the value of the theory (Smith et al. 1999). It is as if the notion of 'ideal types' had never been aired; or the uses of instrumentalism never considered; or Friedman (1953) never been read. It is as if they are unaware that all models are false, but nevertheless some predict well.

There is an even more basic flaw in the valuations of anti-economists. They neglect a key truth: that all value is comparative; that all evaluation consists of a comparison of the performance of a model with the next best alternative. If anti-economics is resolved to evaluate economics negatively it must demonstrate more than the mere existence of defects; it must maintain that economics has more defects than some alternative. If the complaint is falsehood the complainant must show, not merely that it is false but more false than the alternative.[12]

This lack of appreciation that all evaluation is a matter of comparison tends to the exaggeration of the significance of criticism even when it is valid. Scrope's vigorous scientific capability provided several effective censures of classical theory. But he overestimated their significance by judging economic theory against absolutes (truth, logical consistency) instead of by comparison with the alternative.

The incapacity of anti-economists to judge the value of what they have done, even when they have achieved something, is drolly illustrated in the case of the anti-economist Simon Gray (fl. 1793–1840). Simon Gray cogently argued against the greatest economic law of them all, the Law of Demand. In 1815 he clearly explained the Giffen good phenomenon that defies the Law (Masuda and Newman 1981), and deserves praise rather than the starchy reprimand he sometimes received from Victorian economists. Yet Gray's judgement was flawed by fatuity. Entitling his first book *The Happiness of*

States (so as to recall *The Wealth of Nations*), then publishing a 500-page puff of it under a false name, and following up with '36 Letters to the Duke of Wellington on Anti-Economism; or the Distress in the Nation caused by the Measures adopted at the Suggestion of the Abettors of the pseudo-Science of Economism'; all this spells a judgement warped by grandiose images of his self and works.

14.2 The origins of dysfunction

The location of the source (or sources) of dysfunction begs the question as to why the dysfunction occurred.

Ignorance

Good criticism of any subject requires good knowledge of the subject. Economists defending their subject from anti-economists have been tempted to charge anti-economists with ignorance of economics.

Comte's knowledge of economics was 'practically non-existent' according to Hayek, and 'exceedingly slender' according to Mill (quoted in Oakley 1994, p. 164). Comte's British devotee and anti-economist Frederic Harrison 'did not, in all likelihood, possess a sound knowledge of classical economic theory' (Ekelund and Olsen 1973, p. 414). 'With the partial exception of Malthus's *Essay*' writes Donald Winch 'there is little evidence that the poets [Southey, Wordsworth and Coleridge] read the works of the leading economists' (Winch 1970, p. 18). And while List 'claimed to have studied the writings of Rousseau, Say, Smith and other political economists' in fact 'his writings betray no trace of direct or indirect influence' of political economists (Tribe 1988, p. 21). Henry George's 'statements with regard to Malthus betray the grossest ignorance of the great economist he tries to deprecate' (Bastable 1884, p. 12).[13] Finally, 'There is no evidence that Carlyle had read any of the classical economists' (Gordon 1991, p. 268).

So, are anti-economists ignorant of economics?

Many are. This ignorance is sometimes betrayed through gaffes. Thus J.R. McCulloch becomes Peter Mculloch (Cobbett); John Stuart Mill, a life-long atheist who never attended a lecture in his life, becomes an 'academic' and 'clergyman' (Coombs 1995); Paul Samuelson's *Foundations of Economic Analysis* becomes a first-year text (Pusey 1991).

Further, anti-economists sometimes concede their ignorance, either unworriedly to the world at large, or privately in discomfit. In 1825 John Wilson, the editor of *Blackwood's Edinburgh Magazine* and ingrained enemy of political economy, found himself committed to lecturing on political economy, and 'turning almost in desperation to friends for assistance in the preparation of lectures which he had berated much and studied little' (Fetter 1960, p. 88).

But, surprisingly, ready public admissions of ignorance seem more common than the private confessions of Wilson's sort. In a debate over

Malthus, Leroux coolly acknowledged, 'I have not read him at all. His whole system is set forth on one page and can be summed up in his famous arithmetical and geometrical ratios. That's enough for me' (quoted in Roche 1971, p. 114). The knowledge of economics of the co-author of one 1970s anti-text amounts, by his own account, to 'only hazy recollections of genial hours with his economics tutors' (Hollis in Hollis and Nell 1975, p. vii). One 1990s author of several *petit riens* in the anti-economics corpus has also candidly granted, 'I must admit to having no competence in economics whatsoever' (Manne 1982, p. viii). Ruskin has also been presented as one such self-confessed economics ignoramus: 'by his own confession his studies of Political Economy have not encroached much on his time' (Ruskin's father quoted in Hilton 1985, p. 247).

On the other hand, Ruskin claimed to have read the *Wealth of Nations* (Groenewegen 2000, p. 3), and certainly had managed to dip into Mill. Further, Comte had read Adam Smith, Say and French physiocrats, and had skimmed *The Principles of Population* (Pickering 1993, p. 128). His British disseminator Frederic Harrison 'made a careful study of Adam Smith's *Wealth of Nations*' (Harrison 1911, p. 271), a book he enthused over in the manner of Comte: 'Adam Smith . . . is not an economist at all.' List almost certainly read Smith and Say: his *National System of Political Economy* contains four quotations from various works of Say, and four from the *Wealth of Nations*, not to mention consideration of Smith's views on certain highly particular subjects (for example, the Treaty of Metheun).[14] Southey had 'borrowed Smith's *Wealth of Nations* from the Bristol Library in November 1793 and his letters reveal familiarity with details of the text' (Eastwood 1989, p. 322). Coleridge told his brother he had 'attentively read' Smith, Malthus and Ricardo (Coleridge 1956, 5, p. 442). Carlyle declared to the political economists, 'For my sins, I have read much in those inimitable volumes of yours – really, I should think some barrowfulls of them.'[15] And he had. In his letters of 1815 Carlyle reports his reading of books 1 and 2 of the *Wealth of Nations*, and in 1817 he describes Adam Smith as the 'most honest and ingenious man of our age'. In 1848 he carefully read Mill's *Principles of Political Economy*, and made markings or marginal comments on 153 pages of it (Carlyle 1980). Finally, Marx had probably read more political economy than any of his contemporaries.

Thus, contrary to the suggestion of several economists, the principal anti-economists of the nineteenth century were not unread in economics. They had at least read some Smith; with the possible exception of shameless Leroux, and even he could (surely) claim to have read his younger brother Jules's 49,000-word attack on Adam Smith that the pair had published in their encyclopedia (Leroux 1841).

But what is the significance of the fact that most anti-economists of the nineteenth century had read Smith? Ignorance of Smith may be a sufficient condition for being a bad critic of classical economics, but it is not a necessary one. The important thing is not reading, but understanding. Their own well-wishers have testified to their lack of understanding. John Sterling, Coleridge's friend, wrote, 'I always lament to find Coleridge talking of Political Economy. He did not understand. He merely attacks & therefore his abuse though often deserved is never satisfactory' (Coleridge 1969d, p. 312).[16]

Madness and psychological inadequacy

The anti-economists of the nineteenth century cannot be said with great justice to be fundamentally ignorant. With more justice it could be said that they were mad.

The least troubled in mind among the anti-economists were the fantasists; those who cannot see the sharp corners and solid objects of life.

William Sewell (1804–74) was a clergyman, a professor of moral philosophy at Oxford, and 'the *Quarterly*'s most prolific advocate of paternalism' (Robertson 1977, p. 157). In 1837 he sought unsuccesfully to have the Christian Socialist Frederic Maurice elected to the Drummond Chair in Political Economy at Oxford (Hilton 1988, p. 47). His two-volume melodrama *Hawkstone* (1845) has an aloof aristocrat first defeat a bloody proletarian uprising in Hawkstone fomented by Catholic priests, and then set about recasting the town as an autarkic Christian community that pays wages and prices implied by Christian duty. Inevitably, political economy appears in *Hawkstone* as a transaction between fools and scoundrels.[17]

Sewell did not merely write fantasy, he lived it. He created 'St Columbia's College' near Dublin, with the intention 'to furnish the Irish gentry with a school on the model of Eton' (*DNB*). By 1847 the project had accumulated a debt of £27,000, that was only paid off by a benefactor on the condition that Sewell sever all connection with the school. Returning to England, Sewell became warden of a second new school, St Peters, near Oxford, which he conducted 'on medieval principals; the fasts of the church were strictly kept, and full services held in the chapel night and morning'. By 1862 this venture, too, was £28,000 in debt. Sewell hastened abroad to elude his creditors.

More tragic than the fantasists were those whose minds' creations were trembling, insecure and chaotic.

Friedrich List was, evidently, a manic-depressive. He spent one summer, 1831, taking the 'spa cure' for this condition. In 1846, the last year of his life, he was 'feverish, restless, indiscreet'; he 'imagined he was being persecuted by a host of enemies' who put his life in danger (Henderson 1983, p. 88).

In 1828 Comte lost his mind for a period of about 9 months; he came to believe that he was a Scottish Highlander, and was confined to the asylum of the pioneer psychiatrist Jean-Étienne-Diminque Esquirol. Various twentieth-century psychiatrists have variously judged Comte to be 'megalomaniac', 'manic depressive' or just plain 'half-crazy' (Pickering 1993, p. 400).

Leroux was subject to manic phases, which a sympathetic biographer has charitably described as 'ecstasies'. 'He had a tendency towards ecstasy that he resisted all his life recalling himself back "to a sense of reality"...in Grenoble he suffered an attack of ecstasy that kept him in his room for several days' (Bukanin 1976, p. 70).[18]

John Ruskin was a grossly disturbed human being who fell conclusively into madness in 1878.

Putting aside sheer madness, psychosomatic illness and depression were common among anti-economists.

'Coleridge was frequently ill, depressed in body and mind' (Levere 1981, p. 27). He suffered jaundice, stomach troubles and indigestion. Byron and Shelley 'frequently fell ill' (Butler 1981, p. 75). From about 1838 Southey suffered 'softening of the brain' (*DNB*). Carlyle, from the age of 23 until his death, complained of nausea, chronic constipation and depression. Throughout his adult life he complained of 'a pain over all organs of digestion', as if a rat was 'gnawing' on him. He slept badly, and claimed that at the age of 25 he went for three weeks without any sleep (Halliday 1950, p. xi). 'The letters of the Carlyles are replete with references to a disintegrating or almost recovering body' (Desaulniers 1995, p. 4). He allowed they had a strong psychosomatic component.

T.C. Leslie's life was shadowed by 'chronic illness' of mysterious provenance, characterised by insomnia and (in Leslie's own words) 'violent and depressing headaches'. This misery was compounded with a 'strong sense of persecution' (Lipkes 1999, p. 138). W.T. Thornton suffered a year long nervous breakdown (Lipkes 1999, p. 120). Arnold Toynbee died at the age of thirty subsequent to a mental collapse (Kadish 1986). In the face of merciless insomnia, large doses of the recently discovered depressant chloral hydrate were applied, but did not succeed in giving Toynbee sleep. In a short while he succumbed to 'brain fever'.[19]

Blanqui 'constantly complained of ailments. They were probably psychosomatic disorders rather than physical defects, for he did not seem to have any organic troubles' (Bernstein 1971, p. 235).

Marx can only be described as mentally afflicted. He suffered headaches, a head that 'buzzed and prickled', 'an obnoxious affection of nerves of the head', a 'chaotic condition of the cranial nerves' that 'assumed serious dimensions', 'nervous derangement', and 'cerebral congestion' (Marx quoted in Nelson 1999a and 1999b). Not to mention episodes where he 'rambled in his speech', fantasised about insanity, and experienced 'unbearable' insomnia where 'he *hardly slept at all*' despite 'even very powerful doses of chloral' (Engels quoted in Nelson 1999b). These mental afflictions were accompanied by physical ones; severe piles, furuncles, carbuncles, great festering boils, a black misshapen swelling the size of a fist, an abscess 'nearly the size of an egg', liver problems, nausea, 'diabolic' pains in his left buttock, severe sciatica, 'almost chronic' coughs, disordered digestive apparatus, gastric fever, pleurisy, bronchitis and ulcerations. 'My sickness' wrote Marx, 'always originates in the mind' (quoted in Nelson 1999b, p. 100).[20]

Finally, what mental turmoil must be betrayed by Charles Kingsley's 'impetuous, restless, nervous' energy that made constant movement 'almost necessary to him' (Houghton 1952, p. 310), driving him to run to hounds on foot, and leap hedges and ditches 'for five hours at a stretch'? [21]

This enumeration of mental inadequacy includes many prominent anti-economists of the nineteenth century. It also excludes many prominent anti-economists. But the inclusions are sufficient to point to an unusual tendency to mental ill-health among anti-economists. It may be replied that a picture of perfect health cannot be drawn of the economists. If Marx and Engels each experienced a nervous breakdown, as they did, (Nelson 1999a and 1999b), then so did Mill and Keynes. But whatever mental ill-health there is in economists there is no comparison to that among anti-economists.[22]

Aggression

If anti-economics is blighted by incomprehension, and still more by mental illness, it is doomed by the character of its essential psychological roots. Anti-economics is not born of a perplexity. It is born of frustration, affront and humiliation.

Frustration

Economics frustrates:

1. *The scramble for wealth.* The market is never the ideal avenue for enrichment. There is always a straighter, smoother less arduous path which will be opened by some state intervention that is in a private interest, but not in the public's. Economics has tended to keep those paths gated.
2. *The struggle for power.* To be effective, political authority needs to be able to claim intellectual authority. Economics can and does menace that claim.
3. *The craving for prestige.* Rival disciplines covet significance. The looming significance of economics casts an obscuring shadow over them.
4. *The striving for a new model society.* Two dreams, both of at least some nobility, are frustrated by economics.
   (i) Economics frustrates striving to realise the common longing for a life of a more connected existence, one denser in social ties; one permeated by social unity. Economics casts doubt on the realisability (or utility) of this 'socialist' dream.
   (ii) Economics frustrates the striving to realise longing for a society without social sanction; one perfectly purified of all coercive relations. Economics casts doubt on the realisability (or utility) of this 'libertarian' dream.

5. *The bafflement of the scientific ingénue.* Economics frustrates those completely unable to appreciate or understand science, as much as art can frustrate philistines.

Affront

Economics also affronts. The moralist is indignant at a scientific cosmology that seems to glide over wrong doing. The humanitarian is offended at a system of thought that does not render unambiguous homage to the sovereignty of suffering from suffering.

Humiliation

Economics humiliates. Economics is not one of the arts of mollification. Properly conceived, economics is concerned to acquire reason, not popularity. It speaks plainly, without seeking to please. This plain speaking may injure self-esteem; inevitably some interests, and societies, are not flattered by its diagnoses.

From frustration, humiliation and affront is born anger and aggression. In this psychological context, anti-economics is not a set of beliefs about economics (each of which is conceivably true or false) it is a matter of feeling, of anger.[23] In this psychological context, anti-economics is just war by other means. This mood of this 'criticism' is captured perfectly by Marx: 'Its object is its enemy, which it wants not to refute but to destroy... Criticism concerned with this object is *hand-to-hand* criticism' (quoted in Tucker 1972, p. 80). Little wonder so much anti-economics is feeble criticism, it is not really criticism at all. It is just a substitute violence. This violence can be found in the language of anti-economics; the comparison of economists with a 'virus'; and Marx's own grimly satisfied comparisons of his criticisms with hand-to-hand combat.[24]

It can be granted that aggression need not forswear logic; one may 'destroy' by refutation. And anti-economics need not be aggressive; Gustav Schmoller pursued his anti- economics with public self-control and decorum. But if the essence of anti-economics does not lie in belligerence, its perfection surely does.

14.3 In defence of criticism

Anti-economics has sought to demonstrate to the world that economics is a bane. But, we have argued, it has failed in its attempt, and we have given some reasons why it failed. The question arises, must anti-economics fail? Might one conceive a successful anti-economics?

It is easy to identify one circumstance where no future anti-economics can succeed: when economics is not a bane. If it is not one it cannot be demonstrated to be one.

Anti-economics has commonly presented one supreme ground as to why economics is a bane: that is, that economics is sympathetic to the market. Anti-liberal anti-economics (both Right and Left), and their allies in nationalism, in the religion of love, and in the cults of nature and art, have all tried to show that economics is a bane on account of its sympathy towards the market.

But the market is not a bane. It is a highly useful contrivance. In seeking to prove economics is a bane on account of its sympathy for the market anti-liberal anti-economics has doomed itself to failure. Linguet, it will be recalled, devoted mental energy to proving bread is a poison. For 250 years illiberal anti-economics has, in effect, been strenuously striving to prove that bread is poison. In the twentieth century, millions, perhaps 94 million (Courtois 1999, p. 94), were killed in one especially determined example of this attempt to prove that bread is poison. Yet no one, we contend, will ever discover that bread poisons. Yet no one, we contend, will ever discover that the market despoils. The illiberal anti-economics that is premised on that thesis must fail.

Liberal anti-economics, by contrast, has tried to show that economics is a bane on account of its failure to sufficiently illuminate the wonder working of the market, and throws only a misleading, false light on it. This liberal anti-economics, too, is doomed to failure. New theories will arrive and will better explain the market, its deeds, merits (and faults), and they will outshine the old; but these theories will never reveal that maximisation, competition, allocational efficiency, market equilibrium are not important parts of the market system.

But to conclude that anti-economics is doomed to fail is not to conclude that there is no room for valid criticism of economics; our objection to anti-economics is not that it is criticism of economics, but that it is *bad* criticism of economics. Economics, certainly, finds the world surprising, and will be in need of criticism (good criticism) until it is much less surprised.

But has it received it? There is one mark that it has: the tendency of the Tradition towards integration. Integration is a mark of rational criticism. Truth is one, but falsehood is many. Truth has only one pole, and all that pushes towards it, pushes towards only one place. Rational 'criticism'; the sorting out of ideas into good and bad, or better and worse; the discarding of the bad bets, and the concentration on the good bets, pushes towards that one place. We conclude that any intellectual formation in which rational criticism is a major force will experience integration.

By contrast, intellectual formations in which rational criticism is only a minor force will not experience an expanding, homogenising development. Their only opportunity for development is disintegration. An intellectual formation in which reason is not a major force has been formed by non-logical considerations. Since illogic is lawless those who happen to agree (on non-logical grounds) on basic ideas cannot be expected to develop them in the same way: with illogic the same premises can yield any conclusion. Disintegration is a mark that rational criticism is a weak force. The only way an intellectual formation in which rational criticism is weak can stop disintegrating is by stopping development completely: fossilisation. Criticism, be it good or bad, finishes, and obedience to some authority becomes everything.[25] To summarise: intellectual formations in which rational criticism is only a minor force will either (i) disintegrate, or (ii) adopt new, plainly non-logical values (traditionalism, charismatism, personal loyalties) which may be tremendously popular, but will not be science.[26]

Marxism may be identified as a disintegrating process after Engels's death.

The 'revisionism' of Eduard Bernstein marked an almost immediate fissure in Marxism. A close friend of Friedrich Engels, Bernstein had been the editor (with Marx's acquiescence) of the journal of the repressed German socialist party, during which time he 'established his reputation as a leading party theoretician and a Marxist of impeccable orthodoxy' (Tudor 1999, p. xvii). But within two years of Engels's death in 1895 he urged socialists to attend to the ideas of the 'extraordinarily ingenious' developers of marginal utility theory; Walras, Jevons, Gossen, Böhm-Bawerk, Wieser and Menger. In his *Evolutionary Socialism* of 1899 the labour theory of value, of working class immiserisation, the ever greater concentration of capital, and the inevitability of crisis are all deemed unsatisfactory (Bernstein [1899] 1993).

Another, quite different, defector from Marxism was Werner Sombart. In 1894 he had reviewed Volume 3 of *Das Kapital* with sympathy (despite significant reservations), and thereby won the approval of Engels, of whom Sombart later wrote a warm obituary. It was at this time that Sombart described himself as a 'convinced Marxist' (Harris 1942), and prior to about 1914 he was widely seen as an academic interpreter of Marx. Class struggle was a true, if incomplete, theory of history. But in his subsequent journey Sombart was to revile Marxist materialism, and elevate faith, nation and caste. The self-described 'convinced Marxist' was to hail the 'conservative revolution' of 1933.

In Russia, Marxism disintegrated not long after it was introduced. 'In Russia... most of the early Marxists soon drifted away from orthodox Marxism – eg Bulgakov, Tugan-Branaovsky, and Struve. Eventually, many of the core Social Democrats [Marxists] also adopted various revisionist stances' (Dovring 1996, p. 66). Pyotr Struve (1870–1944) a youthful Marxist analyst of Russian capitalism, who in 1898 composed the first manifesto for the nascent Russian Social Democratic Workers' Party, soon disaffiliated from Marxism. Struve aimed to preserve 'the grandiose frame of Marx's sociological system' but placed inside it the theorising of the economist Vladimir Dmitriev, who he described as a 'Ricardo elaborated and verified in logic and mathematics'. Mikhail Tugan-Baranovsky wanted 'to cleanse Marxism of its unscientific elements' (quoted in Dreyer 1974, p. 52), and argued that marginal utility 'provides an unexpected confirmation' of the views of Ricardo and Marx. If Tugan wanted to cleanse Marxism of unscientific elements, it might be said that Sergey Bulgakov (1871–1944) wished to cleanse it of its scientific elements. Beginning as a well-trained Marxist economist, Bulgakov became a Orthodox priest, and abandoned Marxism for 'sophiology', a kind of heterodox version of Orthodox Christianity. Bulgakov was broadly complemented by the God-Builders, a literary-philosophical form of Marxism, associated with Anatoly Lunacharsky (1875–1933), which sought to reconcile Marxism to the power of religious sentiment. To the God-Builders, Marxism was not an economic theory, but would become 'the religion of the future'.

Rather than in religion or science, the true future of Marxism within Western Europe lay in Hegelianising philosophy. In the second third of the twentieth century, Marx the materialistic (even positivistic) economist began to be replaced by a 'young' and philosophising Marx. This is reflected in the greatly shrunken attention of Marxists to anything that could be described as economics: in one estimate Leszek Kolakowski's *Main Currents of Marxism* devotes only 10 per cent of its pages to economics. So whereas the Second International tended to view Marxism as an economic theory, *Das Kapital* is, in the judgement of one representative of the modern tendency, '*not* economics' (Carver 1975, p. 8).

The disintegral tendency of Marxism is underlined by its experience in Japan. In the post-war period Japan could boast the 'largest group of Marxian political economists' in any country outside the communist world (Sekine 1975, p. 847), yet its development there was singular and divergent. Its most distinct feature was the 'Uno Marxism' of Kozo Uno that 'through a maze of Japanese abstract nouns' advocated the rejection of both Soviet Marxism and the humanistic Marx of the West. Whatever its merits its influence on Western Marxism was near zero.[27]

Marxism, then, spread but did not homogenise, integrate, or maintain its integrality. The history of Marxism is of it being overwhelmed by whatever matter it seeks to cope with: gradualism, nationalism, science, religion, philosophy.

The history of economics, by contrast, is largely a matter of overwhelming whatever it has sought to cope with. Thus it has been said that mainstream economics has a 'voracious appetite' to consume and digest a miscellany of discrete items (Niehans 1990). A correlate of this is that various national and doctrinal streams (or schools) merge, and boundaries dissolve. There takes place the much regretted homogenisation of economics, and the dissolution of national traditions in economics (see Petridis 1994; Choi 1996; Ikeo 1996; Sandelin and Sinimaaria 1997). The great tendency of the Tradition is to become integrated and whole.[28] We contend this is testimony to the significance of rational criticism in its dynamic.

Critical fields of fire

But there is nothing to suggest that the amount of rational criticism in the Tradition is 'optimum'; there is nothing to suggest there were not detours, wrong turns, wasted opportunities or neglect of good ideas. What were, with hindsight, detours, wrong turns, wasted opportunities or neglected ideas are consistent with efficient use of limited cognitive resources without the benefit of hindsight. But, in any case we make no assumption of efficient use of cognitive resources. Such efficient use is no part of our definition of the Tradition, and we make no denial of non-rational factors or malfunction in the apparatus. Rather than 'efficient' use, we assert that, as purely contingent fact, there has been 'sufficient' use of cognitive resources to prevent both fossilisation and disintegration. [29]

Rather than believing that extant criticism is 'optimal', we think that there is space for cultivation beyond the standard criticism practised by economists.

If we think of the classic occasions of economists' criticism; the discuss-ant's remarks, or referee's report, or seminar commentary; most turn on the conception of a 'beautiful paper' that exemplifies excellence in dexterity and competence in the execution of algorithms or operations required for the purpose at hand. Criticism implicitly consists of a comparison of the actual work with that beautiful paper. This criticism, inevitably, is the criti-cism of those who aspire to the achievement of dexterity. It is the criticism practised by the practitioner; 'constructor criticism'.

We contend that there is a realm of criticism beyond 'constructor criticism', a realm which may be neglected by practitioners. This realm embraces the constituents of the critical apparatus: representation, examination and evaluation.

Representation

One important critical concern is to clarify the subject of research. 'Anyone who has attempted to keep pace with even some small part of the enormous output of theoretical literature must have asked himself at times, what exactly is it *about?*' (Worswick 1972, p. 26). A companion concern is the identification and articulation of the essential contentions of some body of theorising. There is a vast body of reinterpretation of the Keynesian revolution, initiated by Axel Leijonhufvud (1968). There is a distinct (if connected) body of inter-pretation over Say's Law (Kates 1998). Another, if smaller, representational literature concerns what the rational expectations revolution amounted to (Sent 1998).

Examination

'Constructor criticism' includes examination, but is dominated by the measurement of the performer's competence in the use of appropriate algorithms. It is 'technical' in that it is concerned with the 'how to'. But a richer criticism will go beyond the 'competency' that is so much the con-cern of the normal scientist. This richer criticism appreciates that there are other dimensions worthy of examination. Beyond the 'how to' dimension there is the 'what' dimension: examining what has been achieved, beyond (trivially) the execution of the algorithm.

Examination of the 'what' dimension encompasses two tasks. The first task is the measurement of the consequence (or 'importance') of any performance. This traces a given performance's implications and impact, in terms of both light and fruit. This is where one tries to answer the 'so what?' question regarding any performance. This is where one tries to situate a performance among other performances and issues, and follow the extent of its repercussions. An extension of this task involves advancing from what *is* or *will be* the consequence of actual performances, to a judgement of what hypothetical performances *would be* (or would not be) of consequence. Here we come to the 'agenda-setting' aspect of criticism (for example, Leijonhufvud 1998), where the critic advances an opinion as to what performances would be telling, and what would be fruitless.

The second task in examining the 'what' dimension is concerned, not with the consequence of what has been done, but with what can and cannot be done; it is concerned with the capabilities of economics. This examination encompasses the attempts of Robbins and Hayek to delineate the boundaries of possible knowledge. But this sort of task can descend from such heights to more particular questions. For example, part of the 'what's wrong with econometrics' debate includes a concern to determine what can, and cannot be learnt from competently executed econometrics (Mayer 1980; Leamer 1983) or from rationalistic methods more generally (Summers 1991). This literature is characterised by a pessimism about what can be learnt, that contrasts with the optimism of the practitioner 'technician', for whom every problem has a solution, and the only difficulty is incompetents not following the prescribed solution.

Evaluation

The ordering of the value of performances is an everyday part of economics. This ordering embraces both the noise of controversy, and the silent process of canon formation, by which some performances over time fade away, while others gain in brightness.

However, the research culture of economics is tilted against evaluation. There is not much value of evaluation. There is little reward in economics for scholarship, appreciation or connoisseurship.[30] Further, insofar as there is evaluation there is room for evaluation of the principles behind that ordering. As is notorious, theory evaluation in economics is problematic. There is a need to obtain better answers to the basic questions of the 'theory of evaluation':

1.   What does value consist of?
2.   What are its sources?
3.   What are its signs?

These questions are, surely, harder to answer than in other scientific disciplines. And this fact makes it all the more necessary to try to obtain them. The great surge of methodologising in economics since 1970 is an attempt to give an answer to those questions.

There is, in addition, a second opportunity for the development of richer evaluation. This would change the object of evaluation from the theory to the discipline that produces the theory. This goes behind the actual commodities produced, and enters into the factory; to examine the process by which those commodities are made, and examine the good functioning or ill functioning of that process. Here we come to those far-reaching judgements of the health or infirmity of economics, or segments of it (Johnson 1975; Thurow 1983; Krugman 1994; Buchanan 1985).

Explanation

This reveals how things are done; how successful theories are made, or how theories are made successful. So whereas, for example, a dramatic critic might explain the creation of dramatic tension, in economics the critic might explicate the elicitation of assent. This is the field of 'rhetoric' which has burgeoned since 1980. Studies in rhetoric usually have the air of an exposée (as all those ploys and sly stratagems are brought to light), but there is no reason why this must have any destructive intent or outcome.

In conclusion, there is a realm of criticism beyond the realm of 'constructor criticism'. The cultivation of this realm does not spell an adversarial relationship between the critic and the subject. A judge is not, properly, an adversary of the judged. Neither does it spell the yawning division of the profession between actors on one side, and, on the other, a critical chorus to hail or accost (as takes place in literature and arts). Some significant 'actors' in classical economics (Smith, Mill) were natural critics. In the twentieth century Friedman makes a reckonable critic, and Keynes a stimulating one.[31]

Yet the cultivation of this realm of criticism will leave some division between actors and chorus. There will always be consumers and producers. There will always be minds that make superior critics but inferior creators (Schumpeter), and minds that make inferior critics but superior creators (Joan Robinson).

There is, finally, another group in the arena apart from actors and chorus; there is another group that can attend to the critical chorus, and that the critical chorus should attend to: the audience; the wider public. The critic has a capacity to inform and to instruct not just actors, but the wider public. And they have a capacity to inform not only about economics but also the pretended criticism of economics.

Notes

1. The Damnation of Economics

1. One example of vice-regal patronage of anti-economics is Canada's 'Governor General's Award for Non-Fiction'. In 1995 this honour was bestowed upon John Raulston Saul's anti-economic polemic *The Unconscious Civilization* (published in 1996). A taste of Saul's wisdom: 'Over the last quarter-century economics has raised itself to the level of a scientific profession and more or less foisted a Nobel Prize in its own honour onto the Nobel committee thanks to annual financing from a bank. Yet over the same 25 years, economics has been spectacularly unsuccessful in its attempts to apply its models and theories to the reality of our civilisation' (Saul 1996, p. 4). See Pusey (1991) and Cox (1995) for examples of patronage of anti-economics by Research Councils and Broadcasting Corporations.
2. Another example of economists' 'stillness': the economists of 1860 did not join the numerous editorial rebukes of Ruskin's anti-economics tracts (Anthony, 1983).
3. The anti-economist is *not* to be contrasted with the economist. An economist (that is, a person with a specialist knowledge of economics) may be an anti-economist. The true obverse of anti-economist is 'philo-economist': someone who holds that economics is a boon.
4. One may think of economics as a disease (as the anti-economist does), or one may think of economics as diseased. Mark Blaug: 'Modern economics is "sick"... To paraphrase the title of a popular British musical: "No Reality, Please. We're Economists"' (Blaug 1998, p. 13). This second position is not as radical as the first position. Yet, the two can encourage the same consequence.
5. Kanth reveals the essence of the anti-economists when he declares 'the point... is not to criticise economics endlessly, *but to dispense with it altogether*' (Kanth 1997, p. 3). Henderson does the same when she demands that economics must 'simply be swept away' (Henderson 1981, p. 12).
6. The radicalness of the renunciation that is characteristic of anti-economists is not found in Keynes. Recall that Keynes believed classical economics was valid as a special case. Marx, by contrast, could never allow that bourgeois political economy was true as a 'special case'.
7. An example of the identification of economics with the market: the one thing many environmentalist critics of economics 'know' about economics is that economics favours markets (see Kelman 1981a). These environmental critics do not favour the market, and so they decide they do not favour economics.
8. Robert Torrens once wrote: 'And who are the distinguished Economists who support the doctrines of the Manchester School? I know of not one, with the exception of Senior; and he possesses in an unusual degree of perfection the faculty of self-refutation' (quoted in O'Brien, 1977, p. 7).
9. Skousen (1991) is an example of the denigration of economics by a free-market advocate.
10. Thus Senior in 1839 proposed only a gradual reduction in the duty of corn over 12 years. Torrens in 1843 opposed the complete and immediate abolition of the Corn Laws.

11. Engels: 'our economics is essentially Christian' ([1844] 1973, p. 221).
12. To continue, economists have been criticised for being high born (Pusey 1991), and for being low born (see Castles 1984; Fetter 1925). In the 'Inheritor and the Economist' Samuel Ferguson 'casts its Economist as a low-bred English *laissez-faire* fanatic, in contrast with the genteel cultivation of the Inheritor' (Eagleton 1999, p. 99).
13. Friedman (1986), for example, praises the value of economists in general, despite his attribution of great harm done by the ideas of Keynesian economics.
14. Ferdinand Galiani's methodological critique of economics combined a rejection of law-likeness in economic affairs with a confident *a priorism* (see Coleman 1995, pp. 120–2).
15. Comte illustrates the holistic objection: 'The avowal of the economists that their science is isolated from social philosophy in general, is itself a sufficient confirmation of my [negative] judgement; for it is a universal fact in social, as in biological science, that all the various general aspects of the science are scientifically one, and rationally inseparable ... Thus, the economical or industrial analysis of society can not be effected in the positive method, from its intellectual, moral, and political analysis' (Comte [1855] 1974, p. 447). The Comtean anti-economist John Kells Ingram (1823–1907) pursues the thought: 'He who treats every disease as purely local, without regard to the general constitution, is a quack ... These considerations are just as applicable *mutatis mutandis* to the study of society' (quoted in Ekelund 1966, p. 178).
16. For one statement of the holistic critique of economics see Heilbronner (1970, p. 91). Syme (1876) is a nineteenth-century example.
17. A kindred objection is that the economists have mistaken the meaning of wealth. Thus, it is claimed, wealth is not material but 'moral'; it is the social capital of society that makes a society strong (Bonald). Alternatively, wealth is 'life' (Ruskin).
18. We see a disregard for the economic on account of a low esteem of the material in the derision of Leavis (1963) for the 'standard of living', or in Arnold's (1871, p. 42) pronouncement that political economy is 'boring'.
19. A riposte to political economy similar to that of Carlyle's was made by the anti-economist Bonald early in the nineteenth century. 'We know exactly ... how many chickens lay eggs ... we know less about men: and we have completely lost sight of the principles which underlie and maintain societies' (quoted in Cohen 1969, p. 479).
20. The utopian has little interest in the economic system of their future utopia, and thus '*Utopian Economics*' is a book that will remain unwritten. Utopians have no interest in dealing with the economic problem, since they have no appreciation of its existence (see Gordon 1991, p. 161). This is one reason why they are utopian.

2. The 'Wretched Procurers of Sedition'

1. Toussenel (1847).
2. The Abbé Coyer, a leading critic of the Loi de Dérogeance, that regulated the economic activity of the nobility in France, was a popular author with the physiocrats (Kisaki 1979).
3. It was on account of the candid championship of economic privilege that conservatives repudiated the reforms of Turgot. It was, for example, complained that the abolition of the corvée would 'confound the Nobility ... and the Clergy ... with the people' (Stephens 1895, p. 133) The result of emancipating industry would be that 'every manufacturer, every artist, every workman would regard

himself as an isolated being, depending upon himself alone . . . All subordination would be destroyed' (quoted in Stephens 1895, p. 134).

4. The counter-revolutionary author Sénac de Meilhan (1736–1803) exemplifies a conservative identification of economic liberalism with political liberalism. Meilhan admired Turgot and despised Necker, yet 'Sénac de Meilhan assimilated the struggle for liberty of the press to the campaign for liberty of the grain trade, viewing both as manifestations of the same subversive spirit' (Kaplan 1976, p. 611).

5. Certain Revolutionary legislation also bore the imprimatur of the physiocrats; the Revolutionary decree of 29 August 1789, freeing the grain trade, and the land tax established by the Constituent Assembly on 1 December 1790 followed physiocratic precepts.

6. It was Louis XV who dubbed Quesnay his thinker, not Louis XVI.

7. Charles de Coux (1787–1864) was one anti-economist who took up Bonald's theme of the materialism of economics, and blamed on it several economic ills. In his opinion the 'half Protestant, half atheist' followers of Adam Smith were to blame for the 'maximum' of 1793, the assignats and fiscal bankruptcy (Coux 1832, p. 45). Smithians were to blame for these policies (all antagonistic to the precepts of political economy) on account of their elevation of material wealth over moral wealth.

8. Alban de Villeneuve-Bargemont (1784–1850) was another Right anti-economist, similar to Bonald. See Villeneuve-Bargemont (1839, p. 365) for his blame of the 'immense catastrophe of 1789' on (among other things) 'English economic and political theories'.

9. In Italy many chairs in political economy were suppressed in the Restoration (Augello and Guidi 1996, p. 30).

10. The 'ultraroyalist' police were sympathetic to the attempts to resurrect guilds (Sibalis 1988, p. 729).

11. Another lecturer on political economy at the Conservatoire who fell foul of the 'ultras' was Charles Dunoyer (1786–1862) His journal *Le Censeur* was twice closed down, and he was imprisoned in 1817 (Staum 1998).

12. Under the head of 'Right anti-economists' one might also include Jean-Charles-Leonard Simonde de Sismondi (1773–1842), save for his warm personal relations with political economists, including Ricardo. Though commonly seen as 'progressive', Sismondi was attracted to the paternalist trinity of land, church, and locality (see Desroussilles, 1976; and Lutfalla, 1976). Alison wrote in praise of Sismondi in *Blackwood's* (Alison 1845).

13. Charles Fourier was the author of *Political Economy Made Easy*: 'Economists have agreed to *sanction* commercial fraud and cheating with a licensed system of general and individual *lying*' (Fourier, 1828, p. 7).

14. The execution of Louis XVI.

15. 'One must never forget the powerful position held by cameralism as an "entrenched orthodoxy" if one is to appreciate the audacity and liberating impact of the new laissez-faire doctrines taught by the French Physiocrats and Adam Smith' (Epstein 1966, p. 177). Smith achieved renown in Germany only after 1789. The same is true of Italy (Palyi [1928] 1966, p. 188).

16. 'Müller deeply resented Smith's attempts to dissolve the social order into a mechanism composed of individuals as the ultimate social units, and he was convinced that Smith's appeal to and reliance on self-interest would lead to anarchy' (Aris 1936, p. 317).

17. David Robinson on political economy: 'According to their fundamental principles, their own system must be a consuming pestilence to the empire' (1829, p. 678)

18. In eighteenth-century England anti-economics was quiescent but not absent. Adam Smith did not entirely escape: one critic of his economics thought it relevant to accuse him of countenancing sodomy (Thompson 1971, p. 89). Do we see here again the feeling that licence in the market sphere spells licence in other departments of conduct?

19. Johnson disliked Smith. But there is no evidence that this was on account of Smith's economic doctrines (Middendorf 1961).

20. Smith's leniency towards Hume's atheism was rebuked by the Bishop of Norwich's *A Letter to Adam Smith on the Life, Death and Philosophy of David Hume*. It is telling that the most bitter contemporary critic of the *Wealth of Nations*, William Julius Mickle, 'disapproved strongly, on religious grounds, of Smith's association with and open admiration of David Hume' (Rae [1895] 1965, p. 71).

21. Thus the *Anti-Jacobin Review*, an organ of William Pitt and George Canning, declared in 1798 'the views of the French *Economists*...have facilitated the propagation of principles, subversive of the social order, and consequently, destructive of social happiness' (quoted in Rashid 1986, p. 59).

22. C.F. Bastable records this conservative anxiety when he noted of Trinity College that 'when the chair of Economics in this University was about being founded...the then Board of Trinity College...wished to appoint a "safe conservative" to the post! In fact there was an undefined feeling that many existing institutions were incompatible with the results arrived at by economic study' (Bastable 1884, p. 9).

23. In 1822 Lord Castlereagh 'turning towards Ricardo, asked him if he would kindly give the country gentlemen the instruction in political economy of which they stood so sorely in need' (Halévy 1949b, p. 114). William Huskisson (1770–1830), a Tory President of the Board of Trade, was a political economist himself (Huskisson [1830] 1976). Even Disraeli in *Coningsby* (1844) scorned the scorners of Ricardo, claimed free trade for the Tories, and sought to pin protection on the Whigs.

24. In 1825 Sydney Smith thought 'A set of lectures upon Political Economy would be discouraged in Oxford, possibly despised, probably not permitted' (Mallet 1927, p. 215). It was permitted, but not loved: by the close of Nassau Senior's inaugural lecture in the subject in 1826 the entire audience had walked out.

25. 'Those who approached economics as did the writers in *Blackwood's* worked backwards and condemned the processes of the market because they appeared to lead to a break down of the old political and social order' (Fetter 1960, p. 90).

26. Blaming political economy on Rousseau was not exceptional in British Right anti-economics. Thus Patrick Geddes (1854–1932) in his *John Ruskin. Economist* of 1884: 'Five years hence some orthodox political economist will probably still survive to acknowledge his indebtedness for the all important social assumption of his hypothetical science, the "Contrat Social", to its illustrious author, that ingenious metaphysician whom economists have never yet sufficiently honoured, M. Jean Jacques Rousseau' (Geddes [1884] 1973, p. 15).

27. Thomas De Quincey (1785–1859) might be bracketed with his literary associates Coleridge, Wordsworth, and Southey. He combined an extravagant Toryism with an extravagant admiration for the mind and theories of David Ricardo. But despite this admiration of the mind of Ricardo, De Quincey was convinced of the baleful consequences of Ricardo's theory of rent. 'In no instance has the policy of gloomy disorganising Jacobinism, fitfully reviving from age to age, received any essential aid from science, excepting in this one painful corollary from Ricardo's chapter on Rent, Profit and Wages...Separate, the doctrine of rent

offers little encouragement to the anarchist; it is in connexion with other vices that it ripens into an instrument of mischief the most incendiary' (1897, p. 250).

28. See Wordsworth's reference in *Humanity* to

> heartless schools
> That to an Idol falsely called 'The Wealth
> Of Nations', sacrifice a People's health

29. In Wordsworth's opinion Adam Smith was 'the worst critic, David Hume not excepted, that Scotland, a soil to which this weed seems natural, has produced' (1974b, p. 71).

30. 'The correspondence reveals Wordsworth as extremely busy in his efforts to keep Brougham out of a Westmorland seat' (editorial note in Wordsworth, 1974b, p. 140).

31. As far as the Right was concerned, if the market gave too little to labour, it also too gave much to the manufacturers, an ambitious, presuming, and restless interest.

32. Two other maverick political anti-economists merit mention. Henry Drummond, (1786–1860; independent MP 1810–13, 1847–60) was a landlord and 'Tory of the old school' who was 'accustomed to attack the political economists' (*DNB*). But 'scarcely pretending to consistency' (*DNB*) he endowed in 1825 the new chair in political economy at Oxford, and defended the new science at length in his 'Principles of Currency'. He was at least slightly mad.

   Edward Stillingfleet Cayley (1802–62; independent MP 1832–62) announced in the House of Commons his preference for the old 'patriarchal system' over the new 'artificial society'. He favoured protection for agriculture and manufacture, inconvertible currency and legislation against machinery (Dutton and King 1985).

33. That Ricardo threatened the 'Unseen Foundations of Society', was argued by the Duke of Argyll in his anti-text (1893). The doctrine that Ricardianism fathered socialism was favoured late in the twentieth century by another Right anti-economist, Irving Kristol: 'there can be little doubt that this evolution of economic thought [Ricardianism], under the influence of scientism, did much to encourage socialist idealism' (Kristol 1980, p. 208). Franceso Nitti, Italy's Radical prime minister 1919–20, advanced the same opinion in *Catholic Socialism* though on different grounds: the consequentialist ('utilitarian') criteria of political economists had destroyed respect for property. 'The Utilitarianism of Ricardo, Senior Stuart Mill, Bastiat, Rossi, Dunoyer, etc. carried forward to its ultimate conclusions, has produced Socialism' (Nitti [1895] 1911, p. 10)

34. Under the heading of Right anti-economists of late nineteenth-century Britain one might also include Ingram. His well-received and well-known Comtean objections to economics may have received some charge from his political position. He believed that 'superior rank and wealth are naturally invested with superior power'. Similarly, the Comtean anti-economist Frederic Harrison, who held himself given to the popular cause, welcomed 'the legitimate titles of capital to social respect and practical power' as long as capitalists recognised their social responsibility (quoted in Adelman 1971, p. 187). It is worth noting that, on account of his belief in the superior power due superior rank, Ingram held that J.S. Mill's notion of the status of women was 'perverted' (Ingram [1888] 1910, p. 153). Carlyle, too, expressed derision of the feminist sentiments Mill admitted into his *Principles* (Carlyle 1980, p. 89).

35. To illustrate this societarian hankering after the past, we refer to how one 'societarian' anti-economist expresses appreciation of the high employment

aspects of 'statist, paternalist and semi-feudal institutions' (Dow 1992, p. 280). Herman Daly and John Cobb, in what they describe as their 'severe critique of the discipline of economics' assert 'the feudal system was more communitarian than either socialism or capitalism in both theory and practise. It has been badly maligned since the Enlightenment' (Daly and Cobb 1989, p. 15).

36. Polanyi adds, for good measure, that 'the economic theory of the classical economists was essentially confused'; that 'perplexing pseudo- problems' exist 'in nearly every department of Ricardian economics'; and that, with the exception of some special insights classical economics was a 'hopeless attempt to arrive at categorical conclusions about loosely defined terms' (Polanyi [1944] 1957, p. 124).

37. Not all anti-liberal Right thinkers were anti-economists. Joseph de Maistre instanced Vauban as the kind of usefully practical mind that is drawn to political economy. Maistre thought highly of Mirabeau's physiocratic works, and judged Turgot to be 'an excellent man' (Lebrun 1988, pp. 20, 78). In revising the liberal educational syllabus of Tsar Alexander I, Maistre recommended the elimination of many subjects, but not political economy. It was Count Sergey S. Uvarov, the reactionary minister of education of Nicholas I, who from 1811 began the elimination of political economy from Russian schools (see Edwards 1977).

38. Ely Halévy's judgement of 1901 that Adam Smith was 'the most sceptical of Whigs' has weathered well through a century of Smith studies (see Winch 1978). Alexander Carlyle, a resolute conservative and acquaintance of Smith, recorded of him 'that on political subjects his opinions were not very sound' (Carlyle 1861, p. 281).

39. The incongruity of political economy with the *Ancien Régime* was freely conceded by patrons of political economy. William Petty-Fitzmaurice, 1st Marquess of Lansdowne (1737–1805), a prime minister, a radical Whig, a patron of Bentham and an admirer of Adam Smith, declared, 'With respect to French Principles, as they had been denominated . . . founded on the abolition of the old feudal system, were originally propagated among us by the dean of Gloucester, Mr Tucker, and had been more generally inculcated by Dr Adam Smith, in his work on the *Wealth of Nations*' (quoted in Rashid 1986, p. 58).

40. Tom Paine is also testimony to the encouragement that economists gave to critical discussion; to Paine the work of Quesnay and Turgot had diffused a spirit of inquiry through France.

41. It has been argued that anti-economist Thomas Hodgskin (1787–1869) was influenced by the distinction between human institutions and 'the natural order of things' of Book III of the *Wealth of Nations*, where tithes, primogeniture, entails and slavery are condemned (Smith [1776] 1937, p. 360).

42. Burke's famous lament of 'sophisters, calculators and oeconomists' obscures his attraction to classical political economy (Barrington 1954; Pettrella 1963–64; Winch 1996). Burke did believe the 'monied interest' was a significant figure behind the Revolution, and mentions Turgot as representative of that interest (Burke [1790] 1968, p. 213).

43. Carlile's punishment was publicly deplored by David Ricardo. Wilberforce consequently complained that Ricardo 'seemed to carry into more weighty matters those principles of free trade which he had so successfully expounded' (quoted in Castles 1984, p. 21). Ricardo's defence was met with a rebuttal by an Anglican divine, William B. Whitehead in *Prosecutions of Infidel Blasphemers Briefly Vindicated in a Letter to David Ricardo* (1823).

44. Thomas Perronet Thompson (1783–1869, radical MP, proprietor of the *Westminster Review* and author of 100 papers on economics) declared that political economy 'has indeed long been defined to be the science of preventing our betters from defrauding us; which is sufficient to account for its being eagerly pursued on one hand, and vilified on the other' (Fetter 1965, p. 431). In France, Dunoyer was an advocate of class war between productive classes and nobility.

45. 'If there [were] but a few dozens of persons safe (whom you and I could select) to be missionaries of the great truths in which alone there is any well-being for mankind individually or collectively, I should not care though a revolution were to exterminate every person in Great Britain and Ireland who has 500 pounds a year' (Mill 1963, p. 84).

46. One may associate with Say the strange case of Pietro Custodi, a fervent Jacobin of the Italian republics of 1796–99. In 1803–1805 he published an extensive collection of Italian writings on political economy. In publishing them, he felt, he said, like a 'gun dealer who has supplied weapons to an army' (Macciò and Romani 1996, p. 41).

47. One (surely negligible) case where political economy was the stuff of revolution was the Bonnymuir affair of 1820. This was a deluded attempt by 25 Scots armed 'with a gun or two, and two pistols' to overthrow the British government (see Grampp, 1976; Halévy 1949b, p. 83). One of the leaders of the insurrection, John Baird, told the press that one of the reasons for the revolt was 'unjust and impolitic restrictions' on imports, presumably a reference to the Corn Laws that had been one of the targets of mass demonstrations during 1819. Baird's legal defence was conducted by an object of Tory loathing, Francis Jeffrey, the friend of Ricardo and Malthus, and the Whig editor of the *Edinburgh Review*.

3. The 'Apostles of the Rich'

1. Percy Shelley to T.L. Peacock: 'Have you seen Godwin's answer to the apostle of the rich [Malthus]?' (Shelley 1965, 10, p. 234). Hazlitt described the Ricardian doctrine as amounting to 'the divine right of landlords'. Hazlitt's opinion has been retained by Georgists. In a Georgist anti-text F.Y. Edgeworth's reservations about land taxes are explained by the fact that his family 'owned Edgeworthtown, which he would inherit and own as an Irish absentee landlord' (Gaffney and Harrison 1994, p. 104).

2. This Left form of anti-economics is overwhelmingly situated on the anti-liberal wing of the Left. Nevertheless, there is a small contingent from the liberal Left who are so sweeping in the hostility to order that the market itself is censured on account of its use of property relations. Hodgskin was one Left liberal, an anti-collectivist champion of 'natural' over 'artificial' social arrangements, who found in the existence of capital something 'unnatural', contrived, and therefore objectionable.

3. 'The worker appears as the direct descent of the slave and the serf' (Enfantin [1828] 1972, p. 83).

4. 'There grew up under the Restoration a type of empty and subtle science, that dared to take the name of the most beautiful of sciences, and which without heart, without eyes, without ears, pretended however to be the chatelaine of society: it is called Political Economy' (Leroux 1850, 1, p. 184).

5. Rudolf Hilferding puts the same thought as Marx this way: 'Beneath the husk of economic categories we discover social relationships' (Hilferding 1949, p. 186).

6. The term 'plutocracy' made its very first appearance in English and French in the sixteenth century.

7. Books on economics, said Rousseau, 'were good for nothing' (Perrot 1984, p. 248). And Rousseau's views on economic policy were highly antipathetic to physiocracy (Rousseau [1755] 1997a). Yet Rousseau was not an anti-economist: he did not join the agitation against physiocracy. He merely resisted Mirabeau's attempt to engage him in physiocratic ideas. Thus in 1767 he wrote to Mirabeau 'Love me always; but do not send me any more books; do not again ask me to read any; do not attempt to enlighten me if I stray; this is no longer the time for it. One does not become a sincere convert at my age' (Rousseau 1997b, p. 271).

8. As property is an element of order, the Right, whether liberal or illiberal, has been attracted to property. Even the anti-liberal Right, therefore, may find use for political economy. Tsar Nicholas I had Harriet Martineau's *Illustrations of Political Economy* distributed (see Grampp 1976). But property is one thing and political economy is another: under his equally anti-liberal grandson, Alexander III, the censor confiscated the works of Adam Smith (Hunt 1963, p. 131). Even Tsar Nicholas I eventually had Martineau's *Illustrations* withdrawn, and her forbidden from entering Russia.

9. Piercy Ravenstone: 'It was in the armory of her [political economy's] terms that tyranny and oppression found their deadliest weapons' (quoted in Thompson 1984b, p. 63). In the same vein, Bronterre O'Brien (1805–64), the Irish-born Chartist and editor of the *Poor Man's Guardian* (1831–35), described the 'juggle of political economists' as designed 'to cause the few to take from the millions the whole produce of their labour and to accomplish this object . . . by all sorts of sophistry' (quoted in Thompson 1984a, p. 31).

10. The chair in political economy at the College de France was held by Michel Chevalier, a vociferous critic of certain policies of the 1848 Revolution. Chevalier resumed his restored chair of political economy in 1849.

11. Adam Müller had also provided secret political reports to the Prussian state, and once proposed that he anonymously edit two journals to be secretly financed by the Prussian state.

12. A student of Wordsworth's politics writes, 'But there can be no doubt at all that his opinions on major issues such as Catholic emancipation and parliamentary reform would have been substantially the same whatever the politics of his patron' (Todd 1957, p. 158). And Müller had an undeniably unworldly dimension. He converted to Catholicism, and thereby denied himself any employment in the Prussian civil service. But it is by their unworldliness that the unworldly make themselves vulnerable to worldly inducements.

13. Of those economists and anti-economists we have examined so far, the one person of genuinely working-class background was a political economist: Francis Place. Born in poverty, arbitrarily apprenticed by his father, a strike leader at twenty-one, blacklisted and made destitute by unemployment, he ultimately became chairman of the quasi-revolutionary London Corresponding Society. Place constitutes a puzzle to the less complicated anti-economist; and they have sought to explain away his ardent sympathy for political economy (see Inglis 1971, pp. 206–7).

14. Four members of the Political Economy Club in 1823 had university degrees; Malthus, Senior, Charles Prinsep and Henry Warburton. Nine had none. The education of the remainder is unknown. A chi square test indicates that the difference in this proportion from the House of Commons is not significant at the 5 per cent level, although it is significant at the 10 per cent level.

15. The Royal Economic Society was also plainly not representative of the population at large: vastly fewer than 39 per cent of the general population attended the top 23 public schools.
16. The authors of works on political economy in France between 1776 and 1789 have been classified by their status under the *Ancien Régime*: 11.5 per cent clergy, 39.4 per cent nobility, and 49.1 per cent commons (Shovlin 2000, p. 51). In what may have been the first use of the term, Nicholas Baudeau in 1776 remarked that the audience of political economy lay in 'the middle class' (Perrot 1984, p. 248).
17. In a much heralded attack on economists in Australian government (Pusey 1991) it was claimed that a disproportionate number of public servants from the Treasury, and other leading departments, were educated in 'elite private schools'. In truth, a far smaller proportion of officers of either the Treasury or other leading departments attended elite private secondary schools than in comparable elite sections of Australian society.

Secondary Education of Elites in Australia (%)

Education	Business	Union	Politics	Media	Voluntary associations	Academia	Treasury etc.
Private (non-Catholic)	56	6	33	45	47	64	14.9
State	33	83	48	38	34	27	39.1
Catholic	11	11	19	17	19	9	27.9

Sources: Higley et al. (1979, p. 86) for business, union, politics, media, voluntary associations and academia; Pusey (1991, p. 52) for Treasury etc.

18. In 1925 an American railway magnate dismissed professors of economics as either foreign born or sons of foreign born, 'inbred through centuries of oppression' with the spirit of revolt 'latent or active in all of them' (quoted in Fetter 1925, p. 20).
19. In 1990 only 21 per cent of US economists believed the reduction of capital gains tax would increase economic growth; 95 per cent of delegates to the 1992 Republican convention believed it would (Fuller 1995, p. 230).
20. Mill: 'The things to be regretted, and which are not incapable of being remedied, are the prodigous inequality with which this surplus is distributed ... and the large share which falls to the lot of persons who render no equivalent service in return' (Mill [1848] 1965a, I, iii, §5, p. 54).
21. Malthus *did* justify not giving to charity. But this was not to justify poverty. Charity, he believed, would not relieve poverty.
22. Malthus was convinced that incentive had utility. But incentive is not poverty.
23. Marx adds that safety measures and 'strict' working time regulation are required.
24. Schmoller's opening article in the first issue of *Schmoller's Jahrbuch* has been described as a 'paen to Bismarck' (Lindenfeld 1997, p. 231).
25. *The Condition of the Workers in Great Britain, Germany and the Soviet Union* is garnished with 'facts' worthy of Winston Smith's labours in the Ministry of Truth. 'Consumption of perfumes and cosmetics increased by 270 per cent' between 1932 and 1936.
26. *The Australian* 18 August 1997.

27. See Kuczynski 1956.
28. Say: 'I assure you, Monsieur, that I received no personal provocation from him whatsoever. He even offered me a lucrative post in the public service, and it was I who sent in my resignation when he became Emperor, not wishing to share with him in the spoilation of France' (Say 1997, p. 126).
29. Du Pont 'constantly sought office' from the Napoleonic regime, 'often importuning friends with requests of assistance in this matter' (Betts 1987, p. 198). But he never received preferment. Pride made Du Pont avid for office: it also prevented him stooping for it.

4. The Dream of Nationhood

1. See Hodgson (2001) for a recent articulation of the sentiment that general reasoning in economics and nothing are pretty much the same thing.
2. For example, Wolowski (1878).
3. Hume's 'On National Characters' contains a footnote in which he states he is 'apt to suspect the negroes to be naturally inferior to whites'. The modern foes of Hume's reputation grip this remark so tightly that they miss its significance: racism in Hume's thought was a footnote (see Palter 1995).
4. Even before the close of the Enlightenment the uniformitarianism of political economy had been disputed by the anti-economist Ferdinando Galiani. 'In Political Economy a single change makes an immense difference: a canal dug, a port built, a province acquired' (Galiani 1968, p. 59). But Galiani's geographical relativism was no threat to Enlightenment uniformitarianism.
5. The Enlightenment's belief in the progress of knowledge is matched by the nineteenth-century historicists' belief in the lack of progress in knowledge. Thus to Cunningham the history of political economy was not a matter of progress from error to truth: 'A system of doctrine ceased to hold its ground, not because it was refuted, but because there was a change in the social conditions it assumed, so that it had ceased to be relevant to changed circumstances' (Cunningham 1892a, p. 10).
6. The treatment of the nation as an integral social system also throws doubt on the very possibility of economic laws. If *all* economic variables are endogenous then there are no economic relationships, either causal or correlational, as there can be no relationships between two endogenous variables. But the integrality of the nation is doubtful. The common feeling that the purely economic may 'disturb' the political, and the purely political may 'disturb' the economic, suggests that there are two unintegrated systems, one economic and one political.
7. Perhaps the universalist aspiration in France and England was strong enough to defeat any such programme. More exactly perhaps national sentiment in both was experienced as a kind of chauvinist universalism; where each country assumed it would be the template for others.
8. List borrowed the infant industry from Hamilton (Schumpeter 1954).
9. Heinz Arndt quoted in Szporluk (1988, p. 204). Other appraisals of Ranade are provided by Adams (1971) and Kellock (1942).
10. S.V. Ketkar's *An Essay on Indian Economics* (1914) is another manifesto of Indian national economics. To Ketkar 'an Indian economic science' would be an 'organic development' of those 'economic ideas which existed in the country at the beginning of the nineteenth century', before being stamped out by 'the superposition of the Western culture' (Ketkar 1914, p. vii). Chandra (1965, pp. 710–19) provides more details on 'Indian economics'.

11. During the 1920s, a period of nationalist upsurge in China, List was translated into Chinese.

12. It was through the Land League's activities that Dillon's younger brother, John, was to gain great prominence in nationalist agitation, and ultimately obtain in 1918 the leadership of the Irish Nationalist Party.

13. Another 'historical' and 'inductive' anti-text of Irish provenance is Hutcheson Macaulay Posnett's *The Historical Method in Ethics, Jurisprudence, and Political Economy* (1882).

14. The frustration which Great Britain experienced in Ireland with orthodox remedies, made relativistic rebukes of political economy popular with politicians. In 1881 Gladstone condemned those who applied the 'principles of abstract political economy to the people and circumstances of Ireland' as if they 'had been proposing to legislate for the inhabitants of Saturn and Jupiter' (Boylan and Foley 1991, p. 138). Mill, we should note, shared Gladstone's sentiments, but never on account of some supposed Irish character. And for this he was faulted by the anti-democratic essayist W.R. Greg: 'Mr. Mill never deigns to consider that an Irishman is an Irishman, and not an average human being – an idiomatic and idiosyncratic, not an abstract, man' (see Levy and Peart 2001).

15. In Cunningham's judgement Alfred Pigou, Marshall's successor and epigone, was a 'web of pretentious words'.

16. '"All men are created equal". So wrote Thomas Jefferson, and so agreed with him the delegates from the American colonies. But we must not press them too closely nor insist on the literal interpretation of their words' (Commons 1907, p. 1). Schmoller would have wholly agreed, as would Sombart: 'All men are not, as the English would have it, equal' (quoted in Mendes-Flohr 1976, p. 105).

17. Ely had similar views on race to Commons. He thought 'valuable' a book of 1891 *Our Country* (by Josiah Strong) that heralded the approaching triumph of Anglo-Saxons over all 'weaker races'.

18. Ely proclaimed that 'political independence' was the basis of a 'national economy' (Ely 1891, p. 29).

19. Myrdal also had the typical nationalist belief that the economic could not be analysed independently of the social: 'While in developed countries an analysis purely in "economic" terms . . . may make sense . . . in underdeveloped countries this approach is simply not applicable' (quoted in Sovani 1973, p. 224)

20. Adolph Wagner (1835–1917) was a radical nationalist but only moderate relativist. Although he did admit 'historical-legal' categories in economics, he adopted many Millian theses: diminishing returns in land; Ricardian rent; production limited by capital; the wages fund; wages reduced by population growth. He rejected the quantity theory of money, the neutrality of money and the gains from international free trade. He was a founding member of the *Verein* but left after a few years.

21. 'Manoïlesco anticipated the general arguments and even many of the specific points of what twenty years later came to be known as the ECLA . . . doctrine' (Schmitter 1979, p. 34).

22. Thus Luis Escobar: 'the Latin American countries do not have a national theory of development . . . the task of the present social science is precisely to discover those characteristics, which I call "interior" and which are basically "national"' (quoted in Valdes 1995, p. 119).

23. See Hodgson (2001) for one relativist expression of dissatisfaction with the supposedly historical character of Marxism.

24. 'Prior to about 1900, "culture" both in the German and Anglo-American tradition still had not acquired its characteristic modern anthropological connotations . . . it was associated with . . . art, science, knowledge, refinement . . . ' (Stocking, 1968, p. 201). Before 1900, in other words, 'culture' meant 'progress'.

25. 'Precisely from 1600–1776 a very powerful acquisitive drive developed' (Schmoller ([1907] 1991, p. 137).

26. Polanyi's father was a guerilla commander in the Hungarian national revolt of 1848.

27. Karl Bücher: 'Everybody knows how the absolutist state furthered this movement to "a national market, national commercial institutions – everywhere the capitalistic principle", and how not infrequently in the effort to accelerate it gave an artificial existence to what would not flourish on its own strength' (Bücher 1912, p. 138). Sombart: 'Just so does Capitalism appear on the scene; like the Jewish religion, an alien element in the midst of the natural, created world; like it, too, something schemed and planned in the midst of teeming life' (Sombart [1911] 1951, p. 206).

28. The revival of national economics in the developed world has spelt that relativistic anti-economics is now embraced by both Europhiles and Europhobes. Europhiles see economics as a threat to the European way (for example, Gray 1998), and Europhobes see economics as an oppressive manifestation of Eurocentrism (for example, Kanth 1997).

29. One specific manifestation of the cult of culture is the reverence of Asian values. Chalmers Johnson is the most prominent and choleric critic of the application of universalistic economics (and rational choice theory) to Asia (see Johnson and Keehn 1994).

30. Compare Gray's dictum 'laissez-faire must be centrally planned; regulated markets just happen' (Gray 1998, p. 17) with Sombart's claim that capitalism is 'something schemed and planned in the midst of teeming life'.

31. 'Nationalism is a cultural tradition rather than some tribal sentiment left over from premodernity' (Sauer-Thompson and Smith 1996, p. 154).

32. Thus the first chair in economic history in the United Kingdom was filled by George Unwin in 1910, the first chair at Cambridge by J.H. Clapham (1928) and the Economic History Society was chaired by T.S. Ashton. None of these three had the nationalist/collectivist outlook of Cunningham.

33. Syme, for example, is filled out with trivial geographical suggestions: 'When the soil is barren the people are poor; when it is rich they are wealthy' (Syme 1876, p. 214); and lame generalisations about race: 'Some races have a greater aptitude than others for certain modes of taxation; the Teutonic races, for example, favour taxes on property and income more than the Latin and Slavonic races, who prefer personal taxes' (Syme 1871, p. 214).

34. 'Ingram had little understanding of the neoclassical economic defence of free trade' (Koot 1987, p. 57). This ignorance of the Historical School of what they thought they objected to remains in their contemporary equivalents. Gray for example believes that capital mobility will remove the benefits of country specialisation and trade (Gray 1998, p. 82): 'the contrast between this theoretical requirement of unrestricted global free trade and the realities of the late twentieth-century world needs little comment'. What 'needs little comment' is that anyone who could write that 'the effect of global capital mobility is to nullify the Ricardian doctrine of comparative advantage' both in 'theory and practise' knows nothing of economic theory.

35. 'They can be classified as follows: one genuine difference of judgement (about the amount of free enterprise in ancient Rome), one correction of a factual mistake, two misinterpretations of Marshall's meaning invited by the extreme compression of his account, one misinterpretation arising from a misprint, one manipulation of Marshall's meaning by quoting its words out of context, and one infiltration of a rogue word into a plausible one so as to turn it into an absurd one' (Maloney 1976, p. 442). 'One cannot help feeling that Cunningham was grasping at straws' (Kadish 1982, p. 236).

36. The national economists' stress on history and induction was a weak shot anyway. The *a posteriori* method does not imply relativism. And relativism does not necessitate an *a posteriori* method. The vast range of conclusions that pure neoclassical economics can generate is an illustration of the possibility of an *a priori* relativism. What is impossible in pure theory?

37. 'An examination of the birth dates of Reichstag deputies belonging to liberal parties at the turn of the century . . . shows a severe under representation of the generation that came into adulthood in the 1860s and early 70s – a phenomenon not found in other parties' (Smith 1991, p. 90).

38. If the favourite domicile of anti-economics is France, its favoured pied-à-terre is Australia (see Coleman and Hagger 2001). Its presence there is even reflected in the dialect. Although the word 'econocrat' was in use outside Australia in the 1960s, its usage since then appears to have contracted to Australia. *The Australian Concise Oxford Dictionary* contains the term. But neither the second (1989) edition of the *Oxford English Dictionary*, nor the 1998 *New Oxford English Dictionary* contains it.

39. Marc Guillaume had another go at an anti-text in 1986 (Guillaume 1986).

40. Attali was president of the European Bank for Reconstruction and Development from 1991 until his removal in 1993, amid scandal, and press reports that, at cost of more than $1.2 million, the Travertine marble in the EBRD's lobby was replaced with imported Italian Carrara marble on the grounds that the original didn't give 'the right feeling'.

41. Another critic, speaking generally of French intellectual life has written, 'Even today, the French character is more inclined to judge rather than to look and prizes moralistic appreciation above concrete analysis' (Debray 1981, p. 88).

5. The Totalitarian State and the 'Economist-Scoundrels'

1. Stalin to Molotov in August 1930 (Barnett 1995, p. 437).

2. Twentieth-century constructivist totalitarianism was palely foreshadowed by the Napoleonic Empire, and the hostility of twentieth-century constructivist totalitarianism to economics found a pallid parallel there. Napoleon, in Macaulay's judgement, 'hated' economics. In a move to suppress economics and social science, Napoleon in 1803 suppressed the section of the Institut National des Sciences et Arts that was concerned wth mores and politics. He declared this second section constituted 'a type of philosophic Tribunat' [=the Chamber of the Consulate that had opposed Napoleon's designs on power] (Charpentier 1935, p. 90). The other sections (physics and mathematics, and literature and arts) survived.

3. VSNKh was a kind of super Department of Industry.

4. There were also a number of non-Party 'Menshevik' economists who were prominent in the economic administration of the NEP. Vladimir Gustavich Groman (1874–1937) was their leader. A fervent planner during the period of War Communism, Groman later became an advocate of 'equilibrium' and

'balance'. Vladimir Aleksandrovich Bazarov (1874–1939) was a former Bolshevik, and mathematical economist at Gosplan who sought to investigate the Soviet economy using 'models on the pattern of exact natural science', that 'took the conception of equilibrium as his point of departure' (Belykh 1990, p. 577).

5. On Yurovskii's appointment, one Politburo member made the sardonic comment 'I hope he is not a Marxist' (Iurovski 1995).

6. Neither Chayanov, Yurovskii or Kondratiev were beholden to neoclassical economics, but (in Barnett's words) hovered between neoclassical and classical approaches.

7. Slutsky's mathematical representation of business cycles was criticised on account of its stationarity property, since that implied that the economic system would persist, and was not destined to be destroyed by its own internal contradictions (Klein 1999).

8. This broad range of opinion against Stalin's crash industrialisation resisted any imputation of unity. Thus Bukharin in 1928 denounced Kondratiev (Louca 1999) and Chayanov.

9. Yurovskii had already in 1926 ventured against crash industrialisation in 'On the Problem of the Plan and Equilibrium in the Soviet Economic System' published in *Vestnik Finansov*.

10. In 1930 the daily economics newspaper *Ekonimischeskaya zhizn'* ceased to be a general economic newspaper (Davies 1989, p. 122). In 1931 all humanities and social sciences were eliminated from Moscow University (Treml and Gallik 1973, p. 218).

11. In late September 1930 the newspapers duly announced the execution of 48 'supply wreckers' from the Ministry of Trade, six 'wreckers' from consumer cooperatives, and three fire brigade officials.

12. Groman was arrested in July 1930, put to trial March 1931 and sentenced to 10 years, and 'probably died in the camps' (Vronskaya and Chuguev 1989). Bazarov was never put to trial, and vanished in the Gulag. Abraham Moiseevich Ginzburg (1878–193?), a former Menshevik and industry economist in VSNKh, received 10 years.

13. Chayanov's wife was later 'informed' by the authorities that Chayanov had been sentenced to 10 years imprisonment, and had died on 22 March 1939. Makarov was released in 1935, but until 1955 remained in exile (that is, prohibited from the 40 largest cities in the USSR). Vainshtein spent 1930–55 in prison or exile save for a short interval in the mid-1930s (Davies 1989, p. 121). S.A. Pervushin (1888–1966), a cycle theorist at Gosplan and 'first rate economist' (Jasny 1972, p. 4) was, at the beginning of the 1930s, 'condemned by the regime but not executed, although it is likely that he spent a number of years in exile' (Barnett 1996, p. 1008). Slutsky, the most brilliant theorist at Kondratiev's Institute, had much the mildest fate: he transferred to the Institute of Meteorology in 1931.

14. The total embrace of Stalinism's rejection of any sort of economics is illustrated by the 1930 campaign, personally sponsored by Stalin, against 'Rubinism' and 'Mechanism': economics doctrines advanced by devotees to Marx, Lenin and Stalin (Davies 1989, p. 158).

15. Stalin's nominal target in *Economic Problems of Socialism*, L.D. Yaroshenko, was imprisoned from about November 1951 to December 1953 (see Khrushchev 1971, p. 274).

16. The fate of Nikolay Voznesensky (1903–50) may reflect Stalin's resolution to eliminate any autonomous study of the economy. Voznesensky was a 'young

and ardent planner' appointed by Stalin to the Chairmanship of Gosplan in 1938. He had confidence in the capability of rational planning, and had completed an 800-page manuscript on economic management of Communism when in 1950 he was arrested and executed, and his manuscript destroyed (Bullock 1998, p. 1049). These actions may reflect Stalin's hostility to experts who presume to judge matters which are the preserve of 'executive authority'. It may also be significant that Stalin's target in *Economic Problems of Socialism*, L.D. Yaroshenko, was a Gosplan economist and therefore a subordinate of Voznesensky. It is worth noting that that A.N. Kosygin who was Voznesenky's associate and saved from execution only by a mysteriously kind good fortune (Khrushchev 1971, p. 257), sponsored the massive re-establishment of management science in the Soviet Union in the 1960s.

17. The CUP's 1948 plan, by contrast, called for an increase in per capita consumption. Minc's resignation as Industry Minister in 1956 marked the end of the application of Stalinist economic prescriptions to Poland.

18. Oskar Lange (who had made the mistake of defending the CUP during the 'trial' and, in any case, was a former member of the youth wing of the PPS) was given a chair in statistics, not economics.

19. The Chinese Cultural Revolution of the mid-1960s saw a similar crushing of any economic study. The leading journal, *Economic Research*, ceased publication (to resume in 1981) and postgraduate research in economics was halted (to resume after 1978). A characteristic incident of the period was that the manuscript of a history of Chinese economics, by Hu Jichuang, was only preserved from destruction by its concealment. Quite appropriately, Chinese authorities in this period saw fit to republish several times Stalin's *Economic Problems of Socialism in the USSR*.

20. 'Individual sociologists were persecuted and the discipline was "*gleichgeschaltet*", but it was not proscribed as such' (Lepenies 1988, p. 336).

21. Fascist Italy, like the Third Reich, condoned the existence of the *Grande Tradition*. Italian representatives of the Tradition (Luigi Einudi and Constantino Bresciani-Turroni) continued to publish. A follower of Pareto, Luigi Amoroso (1886–1965) was a partisan of the regime, and sought to rationalise corporatist ideology in terms of neoclassical theory (see Keppler 1994).

22. One commentator rightly says of Eucken's sedate *Grundlagen*, 'It is unlikely that the average Nazi Gauleiter would have bothered to read past the first chapter, and even if he had done so, it would have been difficult for him to find much in the book that was objectionable or subversive' (Nicholls 1994, p. 110).

23. Werner Maser considers it 'certain' that in Landsberg prison Hitler was 'told about' Malthus's *Principle of Population*, 'probably by Rudolf Hess' (Maser 1974, p. 263). But Hitler, says Maser, 'stood Malthus on his head', by using overpopulation as the grounds for war.

24. The poverty of 'fascist economics' may also be ascribed to two other reasons. (1) 'More than any other form of political radicalism Fascism sails along with a minimum of intellectual freight – and is proud of it' (Röpke 1935, p. 86). (2) National Socialism was based on the concentration at a single point of supreme cognitive authority; there was no need (or wish) to garner authority from professors.

25. This chapter uses a classification of German economists by Rieter and Schmolz (1993) to identify members of the *Grande Tradition*. They allocate 59 economists in the Third Reich between four categories: 'historical-holistic', 'historical-neoclassical', 'individualistic-neoclassic' and 'macroeconomic and monetary'. We consider members of the last two categories to be members of the Tradition.

26. The highly illiberal corporatist solution to the problem of vested interests complemented a fascist political orientation. Beckerath was favourably drawn to fascist Italy. Stackelberg was an active member of the Nazi party, and a staff-sergant in the SS. His work was praised by Amoroso, who refers to Stackelberg in his pro-fascist writings.

27. The sentiments and tone of a memorandum from Kondratiev to Molotov (in Kondratiev 1998, 3, pp. 171–4) illustrate Kondratiev's reconciliation to the political supremacy of the Bolsheviks.

28. Schmölders's proposed programme of economic liberalisation was more cautious than that which the Freiburg School favoured, reflecting the Kreisau circle's *froideur* towards the economic liberalism entertained by Eucken et al. (Roon 1971, pp. 244–52). Böhm, von Dietze and Jessen also had an entré into the Kriesau circle.

29. Karl Friedrich Goerdeler (1884–1945) was an uncompromising economic liberal, who, as leader of the conspiracy against Hitler, gave considerable thought to economic policy in Germany in the post-war context. In these issues he was advised by the future Chancellor Ludwig Erhard (1897–1977).

30. Jessen's inclusion as a member of the Tradition is problematic on account of his changing doctrinal affiliation. Rieter and Schmolz put him in a mixed catergory: 'historical-neoclassical', although he 'increasingly turned back to traditional economic theory' (Rieter and Schmolz 1993, p. 95). In Günter Schmölder's opinion Jessen shared Nazi ideas 'to some extent down to 1933', but kept *Schmoller's Jahrbuch* 'remarkably free' from Nazi influence, and maintained 'the importance of a competitive economy and the supreme decision of the consumer' (Schmölders 1948, p. 136).

31. 'It seems that as a group, economists were less heavily implicated in the Nazi movement than other professional groups. This was partly because of the Nazi's own relative indifference to economics compared to racial science or even sociology' (Lindenfeld 1997, p. 329).

32. Röpke highlights, in particular, law: 'there were indeed, few faculties of law that were not filled with the spirit of obdurate anti-liberalism, anti-democratism, nationalism, and anti-Semitism' (Röpke 1960, p. 348). He passes judgement on others: 'it was largely historians, archaeologists and art critics who everywhere in the occupied countries of Europe, to the utter disgrace of learning, became mental myrmidons of the Nazis and looted archives and museums' (Röpke 1960, p. 351).

33. For studies of the varied but generally favourable responses of the academy to the Third Reich see, for science, Walker (1989, 1996); for history, Schönwälder (1996); for archaeology, Schnapp and Vigne (1982); for art and art criticism, Petropoulos (2000); for philosophy, Sluga (1989); for geography, Heske (1986); for psychotherapy, Cocks (1997).

34. But nothing is impossible to anti-economics. One anti-economist has the absurdity (or indecency) to assert the 'essential congruity between the Nazi economic vision and . . . the liberal Freiburg School' (Mommsen 1991, p. 159). The basis of this assertion is one Otto Ohlendorf (1907–51), best known as the commandant of 'Task Force D' that murdered 90,000 civilians in the Soviet Union in 1941/2 (Herbst 1982). In 1943 Ohlendorf joined the Economics Ministry, where in various memoranda he contrasted the German economic order with capitalist and Bolshevistic orders. These last two were dedicated to economic efficiency and the 'rationalist method', and thus technology and mass production. This sort of 'rationalist method' might serve to meet consumer demands after the war, but how important

was it to meet consumer demand, asked Ohlendorf? 'I can see economy only in the broader contexts, and not economic contexts, but rather social, that is national contexts... The goods we produce after the war are not so essential: what is essential is that we preserve and develop the substance of our biological values, thus winning the peace' (quoted in Speer 1981, p. 77). Further, complained Ohlendorf, the 'rationalist method', had wiped out 500,000 'handicraft' livelihoods of the 'Mittelstand' (the middle rank), whose 'independence', 'freedom' and 'initiative' Ohlendorf, in the tradition of the German Historical School, saw as in need of protection. Finally, the increased industrialisation associated with technology and mass production would dry up 'the inner wellspring of the German people, the farm population', and destroy 'guarantee of food' (quoted in Speer 1981, pp. 80, 81). This hostility to technology was complemented by Ohlendorf's adherence to the mystical biodynamic farming practices of Rudolf Steiner's anthroposophy.

That this Nazi brew is concocted largely from elements that would make Eucken blanch is evident. Ohlendorf's opinions are more appropriately related to anti-economists, such as Carlyle (see for example Harrison 1994).

35. Lindenfeld's judgement is that economics was less implicated in the Nazi movement 'due to internal trends within the field: the continuing reaction against the historical school, and the growing prestige in the 1920s of analysis rather than holism' (Lindenfeld 1997, p. 329).

36. Historians of the German Resistance have stressed that the members of the Freiburg Kries were far from being politically 'liberal' according to the popular usage and standards of the post-war world. But in our terminology they were twentieth-century instances of the liberal Right; they believed in freedom *and* order. The term they later used to describe their philosophy, 'ordoliberalism', is testimony to their doctrinal position.

37. To say that economic freedom sits awkwardly with political servitude is not to say the two cannot coexist (they can). And it is not to say that there is some 'contradiction' in favouring both economic freedom and political servitude (there is not). But the two sit awkwardly together in that the good reasons in favour of one constitute good reasons against the other. A superficial thinker may favour both economic freedom and political servitude, a less superficial thinker will find it difficult to do so.

38. In 1937 Stackelberg made two attempts to discharge himself from the SS (Konow 1994, p. 160). Fritz Machlup, who was acquainted with Stackelberg, states that Stackelberg later 'became very critical of the National-Socialist regime' (quoted in Konow 1994, p. 161).

39. Röpke stresses the significance of liberalism for the relative immunity of German economics to Nazi ideology. 'If there was any faculty in which a breath of the liberal spirit was to be found, it was in the faculty of economics, and this accounted for the emphasis with which this group of professors fought against the economic doctrines of Nazism' (Röpke 1960, p. 349).

6. 'The General Contagion of its Mechanic Philosophy'

1. Coleridge 1972, p. 28.
2. Irrationalist anti-economics coexists with rationalist anti-economics (for example, Hollis and Nell 1975; Smith et al. 1999; Keen 2001). Rationalist anti-economics rests upon a peculiar overestimate of theorising as a tool of discovery and criticism, and is engrossed by the aspiration to dispose of economics by nothing but

syllogism, or 'mathematical proof', or by snaring it in an 'internal inconsistency' or contradiction. The significance of rationalist anti-economics is not much more than to gratify the prejudgements of the wider audience of anti-economists. It can have little direct persuasive power; their over-refined rationalism is dry grass for the human mind.

3. Peacock has his 'economist' MacQuedy conceding, but without regret, that enlightenment is subversive of order. 'Discontent increases with the increase of information. That is all'.

4. 'Common sense' was given prestige by Bacon and Descartes, the Enlightenment's two father figures. The attachment of Enlightenment economics to a methodology of empirical commonplaces is stressed in Coleman (1996).

5. Bismarck was one opportunist conservative who sought to adopt this wise posture of a practical subtlety in the face of economic 'doctrinaires'. One contemporary admirer of Bismarck reported, 'Again and again he has hushed his academic critics with the rough and ready argument "No theory!". He prefers to judge of society as he sees it and knows it, and not according to principles and *formulae* laid down in books. With him an ounce of fact is worth a ton of theory' (Dawson 1890, p. 26).

6. In the late twentieth century another liberal anti-economist, George Gilder, attempted a romantic political economy in which the rationality and calculation of neoclassical economics will encumber an economy, but faith, fancies and dreams will build it (Gilder 1982).

7. Comte believed 'systematic action of the heart upon the mind is one of the most precious fruits of Positivism' (1875, 1, p. 600).

8. Byron takes five distinct swipes at Malthus in *Don Juan* (cantos xi, xii and xv). To quote just one:

> While Wellington has but enslaved the whites,
> And Malthus does the thing 'gainst which he writes
> (Byron 1982, xii:20)

In *Queen Mab* Shelley writes,

> The harmony and happiness of man
> Yields to the wealth of nations
> (Shelley 1965, 1, p. 100).

Wordsworth's jibes at the 'wealth of nations' have already been noted.

9. *Hard Times* is usually interpreted as a protest against the extinction of the light of fancy by a philosophy of numbers and facts. '*Hard Times*, like all his novels, is essentially a plea for the imagination and the emotions' (Hicks 1937, p. 465).

10. The procedures of instrumental rationality no more privilege egotism than altruism. It makes an egotist a more effective egotist, just as it makes an altruist a more effective altruist.

11. Coleridge blamed Lauderdale's supposed cognitive deficiencies on his supposed emotional deficiencies:

> O when the *Heart* is deaf and blind, how blear
> The Lynx's Eye! How dull the Mould-warp's Ear!
> [Mould-warp = mole] (Coleridge 1959, 4, p. 1129)

12. 'After more than two centuries of domination by rationalism, this new ethic is re-affirming the validity of acting according to the imperatives of our feeling nature rather than always succumbing to the arguments of the intellect. This of course is anathema to economics' (Hamilton 1994, p. 8). Of course.

13. 'Müller is opposed to the clarity of argument...he is waging war on rational thought' (Reiss 1955, p. 27).

14. Literary critics, according to Terry Eagleton, 'are not usually adept at what is normally called thinking' (1999, p. 4).

15. *Plus ça change*...In 1997 one anti-economist introduces his anti-text *Against Economics* with this injunction: *'all you need is love – not economics'*. There is, we may note, no charity in *Against Economics*. Vituperation, bile and insult there are in generous measure (for example, 'most economists, of this bent, *are* idiots'; Kanth 1997, p. 4). But no charity.

16. It is in keeping with his scientific aspiration that Marx was not opposed to mathematical economics, as his unpublished mathematical manuscripts make clear. 'Not a single injunction against mathematical economics can be found in Marx's published or unpublished writings' (Smolinski 1973, p. 1201).

17. Smith, writing in 1776, was not the first to advocate state support for universal education. Historians of education record that in 1768 Barthélemi-Gabriel Rolland (1734–94) proposed universal state supported education (Boyd 1964). See also Green (1964).

18. Another highly negative representation of the Ellis schools is made by Gilmour (1967). What strongly offends this author is that the schools taught political economy.

19. Coleridge: 'I more than doubt the expedience of making even elementary mathematics a part of the routine in the system of the great schools' (quoted in Castles 1984, p. 5).

20. Carlyle delivered an emphatic sermon on the need for universal education in *Chartism*. Southey believed that the Church should provide 'universal popular education', but that censorship should be tightened to compensate for its subversive effect. The *Communist Manifesto* called for 'free and public education for all children', although 'education' is idiosyncratically defined by Marx to be a combination of 'instruction' and 'public labour' (Small 1987).

7. Moral Economy

1. 'MORAL and political economy' were distinguished by Robert Southey. 'The political economists', he complained, 'treat this subject as Machiavelli treated the policy of princes, setting aside all considerations of morals and religion' (quoted in Eastwood 1989, p. 323).

2. In the same vein as Ruskin, the very moral George Fitzhugh complained, 'Political economy is quite as objectionable, viewed as a rule of morals, as when viewed as a system of economy. Its authors never seem to be aware that they are writing an ethical as well as an economical code' ([1854] 1960, p. 54).

3. Significantly, E.P. Thompson's claim that 'moral economy' was an eighteenth-century term is unsupported by any eighteenth-century references (Eastwood 2000, p. 652).

4. Streeten's summary of Balogh's position also illustrates the moralist position: 'wickedness as much as foolishness was responsible for the mismanagement of our affairs' (Streeten, 1970, p. xvii).

5. Herman Daly expresses the moralist fear of the impact of science on morality: 'A World View of scientific materialism leaves no room for purpose, for good and evil, for better and worse states of the world. It erodes morality in general and moral restraint in economic life in particular. As power has increased, purpose has shrunk... scientism leads to debunking any notion of transcendental value and to undercutting the moral basis of the social cohesion presupposed by a market society' (Daly and Cobb 1989, pp. 334, 336).

6. The author of *Against Economics* expresses the moralist's disparagement of the importance of science: 'scientific knowledge is neither a necessary nor a sufficient condition for human emancipation. The latter stems from a moral, spiritual and personal resolve against inequity, oppression and injustice. Ordinary people such as rubber-tappers in Brazil, workers in Poland, and peasant women in India, amongst innumerable others, have heroically shown the way (repeatedly) to resist the depredations of capital and the state without consulting the manuals of science' (Kanth 1997, p. 43).

7. To the moralist anti-economist the positive/normative distinction also offends moral immanence. In their minds the very existence of normative truths appears to be undermined by the distinction; it is a distinction that beckons moral nihilism (Weisskopf 1971, p. 90). This conclusion appears to rest on an assumption that positive truth is the foundation of all objective truth. However dubious this assumption, it follows that if there is no mooring of normative truth to positive truth, then there is no mooring of normative truth to objectivity. Normative truths are now merely subjective; merely true reports of individual psychic states.

8. The scientist, by contrast to the moralist, says there is no significant portion of normative truth which is significant under different world views. Thus the enlightened and advanced societies have no use of the morals of the ignorant and 'backward' ones. And *vice versa*! This moral relativism of the scientist is easily found in Engels (Engels [1894] 1897; Nielson 1983, p. 239).

9. The moralist's belittling of the possibility of significant positive knowledge reflects the morally saturated character of the moralist's cosmology. Not only are people for the good or for the bad; so are tools. Thus the moralist will not allow means to be 'neutral'. Means are on the side of either the good or the bad.

10. Of American academic economists who signed an 'anti-war' petition in the 1960s only 18 per cent had 'moralist' objections, while 40 per cent of sociologists and anthropologists who signed the same petition had such objections (Ladd and Lipset 1975, p. 119). 'The basis for the opposition of sociologists and psychologists differed sharply from that of political scientists and economists. The latter were more likely to indicate "realist" reasons for opposing the war – that is, the belief that we had erred in intervening without viable South Vietnamese allies, that we had miscalculated our chances to win, that we lacked *vital interests* in Vietnam' (Ladd and Lipset 1975, p. 118).

11. In the competitive system the wage rate is not intended by anyone: if the wage is low it is not because any employer intended it to be low, however much the employer might welcome its lowness. An employer can always choose to pay more than the market wage, and forgo profits. But it remains the case that in a system of competitive income maximisation any single intention about the wage would be completely nugatory for the general level of wages.

    The moralist denies that prices are competitively determined: 'Prices are manipulated' (Myrdal 1957, p. 49).

12. However much reality is the *consequence* of intentions, the consequent reality is not intended.
13. Tawney: 'We all respect economics. It is a body of occasionally useful truisms' (quoted in Terrill 1973, p. 66).
14. Contrast Tawney with Stigler: 'we have the answer to the question of how the economist can operate so extensively and easily as a critic of policy when he is not in possession of a persuasive ethical system. The answer is he needs no ethical system to criticize error... He lives in a world of mistakes' (1982, p. 8).
15. Marshall's exhortation to judge schemes for increasing wages by the same order of mind as that which judges the stability of battleships Tawney dismissed as 'twaddle'.
16. The earliest reference to evil as 'disease, malady' that the *OED* records is from 1725.
17. Art historians have recorded how in illustration Satan had by mid-century lost his horn and hooves, and by the close of the eighteenth century was 'increasingly heroic' and 'human' (Hodgson 1974, p. 43).
18. Thus Benjamin Franklin chose to use in his autobiography the word 'erratum' in preference to 'sin' (Delbanco 1995).
19. At the approach of his mental collapse Ruskin came to believe the Devil was on his way to confront him. When at last the 'foul fiend' arrived in person, Ruskin grappled with him and flung him to the floor. Ruskin told John Brown, J.M. Keynes's maternal grandfather, that 'the Devil' had invented political economy (Ryan 1981, p.81).
20. Oastler: 'The Demon called Liberalism who is now stalking through the land scattering absolute want in the richest corn fields, and the deepest distress amongst the busy rattling of our looms – assuming first one name and then another: March of Intellect, Political Economy, Free Trade, Liberal Principles, etc.' (quoted in Driver 1946, p. 295).
21. In 1937 Werner Sombart, after hailing Carlyle and Ruskin, wrote, 'Only he who believes in the power of the devil can understand what has taken place in western Europe and America in the last hundred and fifty years. For what we have experienced can be explained only as the work of the devil. We may distinctly trace the ways in which Satan has lured mankind into his own paths' (Sombart 1937, p. 5).
22. Moralism, defined as 'an addiction to moralising' is first recorded by the *OED* in 1828.
23. Literary critics have vastly more interest in Marx than any other economic writer.
24. Mill: 'All know that it is one thing to be rich, another thing to be enlightened, brave, or humane; that the questions how a nation is made wealthy, and how it is made free, or virtuous, or eminent in literature, in the fine arts, in arms, or in polity, are totally distinct inquiries' (1965a, p. 3).
25. Foxwell believed that the proclaimed 'independence' of political economy of 'any laws of the moral world' made it 'distinctly unmoral'. 'It is not surprising that all that was best in the literary, artistic, and spiritual worlds rose in revolt and ultimately brought about a contempt for economic teaching' (Foxwell 1887, p. 85).
26. Lilly: 'It is not unusual for party politics to be hidden under the mask of economics' (Lilly and Devas 1904).
27. Ingram wished capitalists to become 'social administrators' permeated by 'richesse oblige'.

28. 'At the heart of Schmoller's program was his concern for justice' (Betz 1993–94, p. 334). See Schmoller (1894).
29. Marx sometimes referred to himself as Old Nick.
30. 'Every economist is painfully aware that there exists widespread doubt about the supposed "scientific" character of economics. This distrust, is, indeed, well founded' (Myrdal [1929] 1953, p. xiii).
31. Myrdal, mysteriously but conveniently, exempted his own views from political categorisation. He maintained that his own 'honesty about dishonesty' entitled him to be immune from ideological classification.

> I have since my early youth laboured with the problem of valuations in economic research and, unlike the conventional economists, have endeavoured to reach a clarity about intrinsic value premises that could make my analysis of facts and my policy conclusions rational, although conditioned by the choice of value premises. I therefore felt deeply hurt by being presented in the press of the whole world as simply a 'socialist' or 'radical' economist. (Myrdal 1977, p. 52)

32. A typical presentation of the denial of the fact/value divide runs: 'It is *not* possible . . . to construct a science of economics that is "independent of any particular ethical position or normative judgement"' (Heyne 1978, p. 185). Five authorities favourable to this contention are then cited. The author concedes, 'The citation of names is hardly an argument'. Indeed.
33. William F. Buckley's *God and Man at Yale* is an example of the older tendency in anti-economics that deplored a collectivist political bias in economics (Buckley 1951).
34. In 1968, 68 per cent of US academic economists voted for the Democrat presidential candidate, compared to 58 per cent of university-wide faculty and 43 per cent of the American population (Ladd and Lipset 1975). In 1969 a survey by the Carnegie Commission on Higher Education indicated that 64 per cent identified themselves as Left or Liberal. The only piece of evidence suggesting economists are Right is the 1984 Carnegie Survey, which indicated that only 27.7 per cent of economists surveyed identified themselves as Left or Liberal. But the survey is small, 112, compared to the 1969 survey of 1250. And the reduction in Left or Liberal identification compared to 1969 is so massive that one is inclined to doubt the representativeness of the 1984 sample (see Hamilton and Hargens 1993, p. 624).
35. The R^2 of regressing economists responses on Democrat and Republican responses is 0.05.
36. Thomas Carlyle once wrote, 'If John Mill were to get up to heaven, he would hardly be content till he had made out how it all was. For my part, I don't trouble myself about the machinery of the place' (Whitaker 1975, p. 1033). This discontent of Mill in the face of incomprehension illustrates an attachment to reason. Shills judges, with regret, that Mill's concern to "make out the machinery" is absent from sociology students (1980).
37. Nassau Senior in 1852: 'I am for *bien-être*' (quoted in Levy 1970, n. 171).
38. Nassau Senior in 1852: 'I wish for comfort and security . . . If it were possible to secure a succession of perfectly wise and perfectly benevolent despots, I would surrender my liberty' (quoted in Levy 1970, n. 171). McCulloch expressed more moderately a similar sentiment (Grampp 1965, p. 107).

39. One may contend that a spurious value gap is not only useful to anti-economists when they suffer a deficiency in positive contentions. It is also useful when they suffer value deficiency. Thus the ridiculous spectacle of slaver anti-economists shamming humanitarianism (for example, George Fitzhugh) is an outcome of the audacious egotism of the slaver struggling, with difficulty, against the more public-spirited principles of economists.

8. The Religion of Love and the Science of Wealth

1. Machlup (1972) sketches a history of the controversy over the assumption of self-interest in economics.
2. Edmund Burke provided another (if only implicit) instance of a reproof by the Right of political economists on account of their supposedly over-extended sympathy for the poor. Burke sharply disapproved of the expression 'the labouring poor' that Smith had helped bring into use through its deployment in the *Wealth of Nations* (Chapter 8, Book 1). 'Nothing can be so base and so wicked as the political canting language, "The Labouring Poor"', said Burke. 'This puling jargon is not as innocent as it is foolish . . . Hitherto the name of the Poor (in the sense in which it is used to incite compassion) has not been used for those who can but for those who cannot labour – for the sick and infirm; for orphan infancy' (quoted in Coleridge 1972, p. 207).
3. It is significant that the one usage of egotism recorded before 1789 was in Rousseau's *Emile*.
4. An intricate discussion of the history in several languages of 'egotism' is provided by Price (1988, pp. 237–41). See also Bygrave (1986, pp. 1–9). Price shows that *amour-propre* (self-love) was in common usage by 1740 in France, but that it had only a diffuse denotation; variously denoting pride, vanity, self-esteem, self-interest.
5. Stendhal describes himself as knowledgeable of Smith and Say. Stirner had prepared what became the standard German version of Adam Smith's *Wealth of Nations*.
6. Malthus repeats this praise of self-love in the concluding paragraph of the second edition of the *Principle of Population* with nothing essential changed.
7. In classical economics it is frugality and industry that generally find praise, not self-love.
8. 'The object of the devoted attachment of the ancients, was their country – the united body of their fellow citizens. Each man learnt to feel how infinitely grander and more important than his own interest was this interest of the whole; each man felt that . . . the sacrifice of the self to what is greater than the self, is the one grand principle of all virtue' (Sismondi 1834, 2, p. 269).
9. 'We are disgusted with that clamorous grief, which, without any delicacy, calls upon our compassion with sighs and tears and importunate lamentations. But we reverence that reserved, that silent and majestic sorrow' (Smith [1759] 1979, p. 24).
10. 'During the 1830s and the 1840s, virtually everyone who considered himself a socialist claimed to be inspired by Christianity' (Berenson 1989, p. 543).
11. Ingram rightly writes: 'When Schmoller says, "The State is the grandest ethical institution for the education of the human race," he transfers to it the functions of the Church' (Ingram [1888] 1910, p. 245).
12. In the same vein Lilly and Devis complain (1904, p. xviii) that political economy does not recognise 'the State as an ethical organism'.

13. Comte: 'the inevitable decay of religious doctrine has left unsupported the generous part of the human heart, and everything is reduced to the most abject individuality' (quoted in Halévy 1967a, p. 46). And the Saint-Simonians declared: 'We know, gentleman, that to the superior men of our time . . . religious beliefs are nothing but absurd superstitions. But we also know that at the same time when this change in outlook was taking place in modern societies, egotism became dominant' (Enfantin [1828] 1972, p. 209).

14. 'Supposing the captain . . . were by any chance obliged to place his own son in the position of a common sailor: as he would treat his son, he is bound to treat everyone of the men under him' (Ruskin [1862] 1967, p. 27).

15. Another sympathiser of the GIIS declared: 'Almost always those national economists . . . urge that the inadequacy of the traditional theory . . . rest upon the narrowness with which it confines itself to the selfish endeavours of men in industry, so that it becomes a science of greed, while in reality men, even in their economic actions, are . . . stimulated by moral motives' (Philippovich 1912, p. 173). In the spirit of this criticism, Adolph Wagner in his *Grundlagen der Volkwirtschaft* (Foundations of Economics) of 1879 advanced as his fifth economic motive 'the remorse of conscience'.

16. David Syme in *Outlines of an Industrial Science* (1876) pursues a similar theme by way of contrasting 'Hemeistic' and 'Allostic' forces.

17. Anti-economists on the Right tended to approve of Malthus. Both Villeneuve-Bargemont and Bonald did so. Comte makes both positive and negative comments about Malthus. Wagner was a Malthusian. Roscher calls Malthus 'great'.

18. Mention may also be made of *De la Misère des Classes Laborieuses en Angleterre et en France* of Eugène Buret (1810–42). Malthus was 'cruel, almost barbarous' (Buret 1840, p. 32), and amounted to a reductio adabsurdam of political economy.

19. Leroux asks 'what commands political economy regarding children whose number appears superfluous to the need society has of them . . . ? It commands to *kill* them' (Leroux 1849, p. 141).

20. 'The theory of Malthus is the theory of political murder' (Proudhon 1886, p. 6).

21. The authors of the introduction to the *Book of Murder!* assert this member of 'the spurious school of Political Economy', proposes the 'MURDER OF MORE THAN ONE-HALF THE CHILDREN TO BE BORN INTO THE WORLD!'

22. The publishers of the *Book of Murder!* sought to make Francis Place culpable for the book's advocacy of infanticide. In his *Illustrations and Proofs of the Principle of Population* of 1822 Place stated he had no objection to infanticide if it would '*materially* and *permanently* benefit the working people in their pecuniary circumstances, without making them in other respects more vicious' (Place [1822] 1930, p. 143). Yet he also judged infanticide in the present 'condition' to be productive of 'intense suffering', and 'inefficient' in preventing overpopulation. Further, in judging the attempt to portray Place as a logical consequence of a cruel Mathusianism, it should be recognized that Place *opposed* the abolition of the Poor Laws. Malthus, said Place, was disadvantaged by an 'extreme ignorance of human nature', that led him to a denial of the right of the poor to means of subsistence that 'is, notwithstanding its absurdity, purely mischievous; its obvious tendency is to encourage and increase the hard-heartedness of the rich towards the poor' (Place [1822] 1930, p. 138).

23. In his *Thoughts Occasioned by the Perusal of Dr Parr's Spital Sermon* of 1801 Godwin wrote that he had no 'superstitious reverence' for the new born child. 'I had rather such a child should perish in the first hour of its existence, than

that a man should spend seventy years of life in a state of misery and vice' (quoted in Place [1822] 1930, p. 142).

24. Burr's biographer (Lomask 1982) records that Burr was solicitous of the welfare of his (several) children born out of wedlock. This tenderness does not seem consonant with visions of deadly gas.

25. One representative misrepresentation of classical economics is supplied by Lux (1990). He claims that Smith wishes to argue that 'self-interest is more effective in promoting the social good than benevolence' (Lux 1990, p. 82). To buttress this thesis he quotes Smith's well-known observation, 'It is not from the benevolence of the butcher, the brewer, or the baker, that we expect our dinner, but from regard of their own self-interest. We address ourselves, not to their human-ity but to their self-love, and never talk to them of our own necessities but of their advantages.' Contrary to Lux, this passage does not assert that the social good is more effectively promoted by self-interest than by benevolence; it says that self-interest is more effectively promoted by appeals to others' self-interest than by appeals to others' benevolence.

26. That economists assume rationality rather than self-interest was laboured as long ago as 1910 in Wicksteed's *Common Sense of Political Economy*.

27. If economics seeks to insinuate in its students an apology for self-interest, it has been singularly unsuccessful in doing so. A 1995 survey of 2248 students of economics, business administration and management tertiary institutions in 14 countries found a majority tended to agree with the proposition 'the market system is driven by greed and brings with it many inequities' (Goic 1996).

28. Frank's survey of 573 US academics found in fact that economists gave on average slightly *more* money to charity, and slightly *more* time to volunteer activities, than other disciplines. Interpretation of these differences should allow for the fact that economists have generally higher incomes than non-economists.

29. 'United Way Boards have come to favour "safe, uncontroversial agencies – crowd pleasers instead of boat rockers". Today the Boy Scouts, the Girl Scouts, the YMCA get about 31 percent of United Way funds. The implication is that United Way is quite purposely serving only blue-chip causes, that is those which will generate the smallest amount of controversy and which service individuals not economically distant from the donor' (Keating 1981, p. 118).

30. To explain the derivation: 77 per cent of sociologists have an income of $40,000 or over. But only 48 per cent pay the fee pertaining to $40,000 or over. Thus only 62.3 per cent (= 48/77) of those with incomes over $40,000 pay the right fee, and 37.7 per cent do not. The methodology assumes that the probability of a sociologist being a member of their professional society is invariant to their income.

31. After marriage Thornton gave one-third of his income to charity. See Hilton (1988, p. 101) and Owen (1964, pp. 93, 94). Their assessments seem to conflict.

32. As late as 1848 one contributor to that favourite journal of Tory anti-economists, *Fraser's Magazine*, argued in favour of flogging beggars. 'Let the Government be urged to protect honest industry against dishonest idleness by flogging every man or boy convicted of begging and every male parent whose child of tender years is found in the streets so employed' (Guy 1848, p. 402).

33. Mill: 'The certainty of subsistence should be held out by law to the destitute'.

34. 8th and 9th Will. III, 14th Eliz cap. 5 (1572), 7th Hen. IV cap. 17 (1405), 34th Ed. II (1360).

35. The Chancellor of the Exchequer John Charles Spencer (Viscount Althorp) (1782–1845) was a free trader and sympathiser with political economy.
36. Mill was opposed to the 10-Hours Bill not 'in principle', but on the ground it excluded women from some form of work.
37. 'At least until the 1760s there was almost total white acceptance of the use of black men and women as slaves' (Rice 1975, p. 155).
38. Perhaps the only economist in favour of preserving the legality of slavery was De Quincey.
39. Brougham in 1845 spoke against 'humanity mongers' who would restrict the hours of work of children in calico works (Fetter 1980).
40. A man of great feeling, Southey approved of the enforced incarceration of paupers (Eastwood 1989, p. 327). Carlyle believed that the New Poor Law was an improvement on the old (Carlyle [1849] 1899b, p. 129).
41. Aikin complained of charity that 'a positive *demand* for misery was created by the incessant eagerness manifested to relieve it' (Aikin 1864, p. 234).
42. Yet Ricardo suggested that the chief complaint of the poor 'is a want of sympathy' from the rich.
43. Archbishop Whately, a political economist, gave £8000 to famine relief. We might compare this sum to the £30,000 that the anti-economist Bishop Phillpotts spent on lawsuits during his lifetime (Soloway 1969, p. 89).
44. British officers involved in the reprisals reported: 'Nelson, at Port Antonio, is hanging like fun by court martial ... The soldiers enjoy it – the inhabitants here dread it. If they run on their approach, they are shot for running away' (quoted in Ford 1947–48, p. 222). The most authoritative account of the Governor Eyre case is Semmel (1962).

9.   Crusaders and Consumers

1. 'Not gloom, but merriment; not contempt for one's body and one's senses, but delight in one's physical being; not the exultation of pain, but the hymn to pleasure – this was the emotional basis of the scientific movement of the seventeenth century' (Feuer 1963, p. 7).
2. A 'Treatise on Public Happiness', was, for example, written by François Jean de Chastellux (1734–88), an inveterate traveller, reformer, and friend of the friends of humanity (including David Hume and Thomas Jefferson).
3. There was a debate in the eighteenth century over 'luxury'. Rousseau was representative of the hostility to luxury.
4. Quoted in Grampp 1973, p. 368.
5. Sombart, too, halts to pays homage at the shrine of work. Almost all societies elevate manual labour over cogitation, says Sombart. Except the Jews.
6. Raymond Williams memorably expresses a hostility to consumption born of its mindless passivity: 'It is an extraordinary word, "consumer". It is a way of seeing people as though they are stomachs or furnaces ... a very specialised variety of human being with no brain, no eyes, no senses, but who can gulp' (Williams 1995, p. 47).
7. A reverence for nature is congenial to a disregard of human comfort. We find both in Werner Sombart, who united them in a wish to reattach humanity and nature. 'Man lost his connection with nature' he lamented. 'The child of the city no longer knows the secret charms which nature offers in a thousand ways to the shepherd boy: the child no longer knows the song of the birds and has never

examined a bird's nest; he knows not the significance of the clouds, drifting across the sky; he no longer hears the voice of the storm' (Sombart 1937, p. 31).

8. 'Wales, until the late eighteenth century, had been ... ignored or denigrated. But ... before the end of the eighteenth century ... Merionethshire, formerly the rudest and roughest county of all Wales, had replaced the civilised county of Kent as a standard of ideal beauty' (Pepper 1984, p. 80).

9. See Vogel (1991) for consideration of the attraction to nature of Romantic critics of economics.

10. 'What Wordsworth described was nothing less than a religious experience, akin to that of the Old Testament prophets as they conversed with their wrathful God' (Cronon 1996, p. 11).

11. See Smith (1967, p. 1) and McLeod (1974, p. 231). The standard landmarks of atheism would be Ernest Renan's *Vie de Jésus* of 1863, and Darwin's *The Origins of Species* of 1859. The word 'agnosticism' was coined by T.H. Huxley in 1874.

12. 'Everywhere, to-day, it [political economy] is being denounced by thinking men as a false science – as a delusion and a snare – as an ignis fatis [delusive light], leading men away from the paths of happiness and true well-being, and guiding them towards the quagmires of unhealthy competition, poverty and discontent ... Surely a science like this – so narrow in its scope, so powerless for good, so utterly divorced from all considerations of morality, of justice, even of broad and enlightened expediency – should be treated as a blind and impotent guide, which, if any longer followed, will lead us on to social and political ruin' (Wallace 1895, pp. 126–8).

13. That environmentalism is the substitution of a newly sacred nature for an older sacred God is a theme that has been pressed by Bramwell (1989).

14. 'Throughout Europe, the late nineteenth century saw a spate of legislation and new institutions to safeguard historical monuments and natural areas' (Lowe and Goyder 1983, p. 17).

15. It was during this environmentalist wave of the late nineteenth century that Alfred Wallace made what is surely one of the first tilts against the tenets of political economy on environmental grounds. He maintained that free trade caused environmental degradation, and recommended as a consequence the restriction of free trade (1900, 2, p. 177).

16. The environmental historian Worster accuses Smith of taking a purely instrumental attitude to nature: 'Adam Smith ... saw nature as no more than a storehouse of raw materials for man's ingenuity' (1994, p. 53). No textual corroboration of this censure is supplied. Smith, incidentally, was an amateur natural historian.

17. If economics has not recognised an intrinsic value of nature, environmentalists have not sufficiently recognised the intrinsic value of human satisfaction; that is, human satisfaction has a value regardless of how much it serves (or harms) nature. Certainly, it has not been difficult for anti-environmentalist critics to discover inhumane professions by environmentalists; such as hailing AIDS as nature's antibody to the human plague (see Lewis, 1992, p. 30). 'On any homocentric scale of values the mortality [sic] of murder is clear-cut. It is not to be countenanced. But if humankind is not possessed of any moral "specialness" within nature, it is not immediately obvious that the taking of human life by human [sic] is more morally repugnant than the taking of other forms of life' (Hay 1988, p. 57).

18. In the same illiberal vein Sagoff protests a 'liberalism [that] defines every policy question as one of maximizing utility or enforcing rights. If liberalism makes these assumptions – which, perhaps, it need not – then it is plainly incompatible with environmentalism' (Sagoff 1988, p. 162). For another identification of consumer sovereignty as the reason 'why environmentalists hate mainstream economists' see Norton (1991).

19. Self also correlates the rise of political populism with the invasion of politics by 'public choice'. Public choice theory challenged the old presumption in Anglo-Saxon countries that the state was a valuable resource for implementing ideals more elevated than the base, self-regarding values of the market.

20. Ruskin also affirms the existence of intrinsic value with regard to ancient monuments. There is 'no question of expediency or feeling whether we shall preserve the buildings of past times or not', says Ruskin. *'We have no right whatever to touch them'* (quoted in Lowe and Goyder 1983, p. 21).

21. Les Murray's *Poems against Economics* (1972) is despite its title an artistic rage against the economic.

22. See McVeagh (1981) for the favourable portrayal of the capitalist in English literature during the period 1650–1750.

23. The first candid appeal for 'art for art's sake' is attributed to Théophile Gautier in 1836. Benjamin Constant uses the phrase in a diary entry in 1804 (Bell-Villada 1996, p. 36). Bell-Villada, contrary to our contention, argues that the notion of 'art for art's sake' is rooted in an Enlightenment author: Immanual Kant.

24. Primitivism as an aesthetic criterion is another reinforcement (or reflection) of this perception that civilisation is fatally polluting of art.

25. Southey's conviction of the aesthetic cost of industrialisation coheres easily with his doubts about 'luxury', that is, consumerism (see Eastwood 1989, p. 324).

26. However voracious or cosmopolitan its tastes, modern art has never tolerated 'relativism'. Any subjectivism humbles art. It is worth noting that Wordsworth reproved Smith for his tendencies to subjectivism in literary criticism.

27. D.H. Lawrence: 'If I had my way, I would build a lethal chamber as big as Crystal Palace . . . then I'd go out in the back streets and the main streets and bring them all in, all the sick, the halt and the maimed' (quoted in Carey 1992, p. 12).

28. Anti-economists have taken advantage of the common connotations of 'preferences' to make false distinctions between the motors of market conduct, and the motors of political conduct. 'Private and public preferences belong to different logical categories. Public "preferences" involve not desires or wants but opinions or views. They state what a person believes is best or right for the community or group as a whole' (Self 1975, p. 94). In truth, the 'private preferences' of economic theory may reflect 'what a person believes is best or right for the community or group as a whole'.

10.   Rival Gospels of Wealth

1. In agriculture, said Smith, nature labours with man. The analogy between parenthood, on one hand, and the complementarity of nature and labour, on the other, is due to Petty. Marx noted this, and sometimes himself wrote that labour works 'with' nature (Marx [1887] 1954, p. 565).

2. Physiocracy encouraged a gratitude to Nature (Worster 1994). Pierre Poivre, a physiocratic writer, has been identified as a landmark figure in the early environmental consciousness of France (Grove 1994, pp. 191–201).

3. Williams ([1982] 1995, p. 45): 'You keep hearing these phrases "conquest of nature", "mastery of nature", not only in the dominant bourgeois thought but also all through socialist and Marxist writing in the second half of the nineteenth century.' One form of 'bourgeois thought' where it is not heard is economics. Classical economists declined to entertain the conquest of nature: that posture has been maintained by their successors.

4. Environmentalists also see a class war between humanity and nature. But whereas Bogdanov took humanity's side, environmentalists took nature's side.

5. Technocracy denied any intellectual debt to Soddy.

6. Henderson is author of *Creating Alternative Futures: the End of Economics* (1978), *The Politics of the Solar Age. Alternatives to Economics* (1981), *Reconceptualization, the View beyond Economics* (1981), *Paradigms in Progress: Life beyond Economics* (1993). Her publicity indicates that she has been awarded 'an honorary doctorate from Worcester Polytechnic Institute for work in alternative economics and technology'. She writes 'This has been a 25-year-long crusade for me, and I've earned a lot of enemies in the economics profession. No one likes to be told that they will be obsolete.'

7. A more measured expression of the environmentalist elevation of energy physics is provided by Herman B. Daly in 'The Economic Growth Debate: What Some Economists Have Learned but Many Have Not' (1987).

8. Joseph Stalin.

9. The anti-economist William Cunningham used the 'Gospel of Work' as a title for his own attempt at deification of work. God, says Cunningham, is the 'Supreme Worker' (Cunningham 1902, p. 14).

10. James Stuart, for example, believed that labourers had a target income. See Baird (1997) for a closer discussion of eighteenth-century views on the responsiveness of the supply of labour to wages.

11. Carlyle misrepresents political economy. It was the planting interest, not political economy, that sought subsidised immigration. It was the advocates of the interests of their black neighbours who flourished political economy in opposition to such schemes (Goodwin 1968, p. 362).

12. Neither Marx nor Engels faulted economics on account of its opposition to slavery. Marx supported Lincoln in the American Civil War, despite the prospective disappearance of the United States if the North won.

13. Coleridge opposed slavery in youth, but was an apologist for it in his maturity. He longed for a 'powerful and wise government' to regulate the transatlantic transportation of slaves, and believed emancipation risked a 'monstrous calamity to the empire'. List proposed slavery be replaced by 'mild serfdom' rather than freedom. 'Can a barbarous race ever accomplish the change from natural freedom to civilisation without passing through the hard school of servitude?' (List 1909, p. 295).

11. The 'Unconquerable Private Interests'

1. Smith ([1776] 1937, p. 438).

2. While every vested interest will have a doctrine it dotes upon, not every doctrine will have a vested interest that dotes upon it. One such doctrine is economic liberalism.

3. But are there not rewards in having a diversified or, indeed, representative portfolio? Yes. But imperfections in capital markets allow heterogeneous portfolios to be optimal.

4. The anthropologist Peter Sutton: 'From 1968, equal wages for Aboriginal stock workers proceeded to be enforced, resulting in extremely widespread and typically undesired departures from small communities on pastoral holdings . . . into the gates of hell' (Sutton 2001, p. 130). 'None who knows the Kimberly could forget the despair of the refugee camps ringing the region's towns – home for years to thousands of Aboriginal pastoral workers and their families kicked off the cattle stations after the introduction of equal wages' (Peter Yu of the Kimberly Land Council, *Australian*, 15–16 September 2001).

5. Keynesian economics may also be prone to interested anti-economics. In the *General Theory* (1936, p. 373) Keynes approves of death duties, and wealth taxes, on the grounds that they increase the propensity to consume.

6. Plainly, in public finance wealth maximisation has not been the supreme criterion. 'Equal sacrifice' has appealed to economists at least since J.S. Mill. And, even more radically, many economists are committed to progressive income taxation with the purpose of financing the welfare state.

7. Ricardo wrote that 'the interest of the landlord is always opposed to the interest of every other class in the community. His situation is never so prosperous, as when food is scarce and dear' (Ricardo [1815] 1951, p. 21). Mill and Cairnes too believed land rent to have little legitimacy as an income. To Mill, landlords 'grow rich, as it were in their sleep, without working, risking or economizing. What claim have they, on the general principle of social justice, to this accession of riches?' (quoted in Lipkes 1999, p. 19).

8. The Church in Spain's jealousy of its social position encouraged it to oppose political economy episodically during the eighteenth century, and even place the *Wealth of Nations* on its 'Index'. Some prelates 'with a reputation of sanctity' hounded the economic societies (see Sarrailh 1954, p. 255). By contrast the Jansenist tendency in Spain, on the margins of society and with no social position to defend, welcomed political economy.

9. 'Resistance to the adoption of the precepts of Political Economy was very extensive within the Church [of England]' yet 'By the end of the 1830s indeed, the most influential of the Church leaders were all soaked in the attitude of Political Economy' (Norman 1976, pp. 42, 136).

10. Opposition of elements of the Church of England to the Poor Law also contained an element of purely interested opposition. Thus one of Oastler's 'objections to the new poor law was that it would prove fatal to the interest of the church' (Hewins 1882, p. 739).

12. 'The Infallible Dicta of the Holy Mother Church of Political Popery'

1. Robinson (1829, p. 511; 1827, p. 411).

2. Marx complained of a conspiracy of silence on the part of economic orthodoxy against his ideas. ('Official science tried, by a conspiracy of silence, to kill the works of Marx', Lenin [1916] 1996a, p. 15.) Any such conspiracy of silence was exceptionally unsuccessful.

3. The most spectacular and brutal arrogation of authority in economic questions was by a form of anti-economics; the 'Marxist Leninist political economy' of Stalinist regimes. In the 15 years following 1937 Stalin supervised with considerable attention the creation of an official text for political economy. In 1951 he advised

the authors that he appointed for this purpose: 'I care about the authority of the textbook. The textbook must have unquestioned authority' (Openkin 1991).

4. Destroying the authority of economics will assist in destroying the existence of economics, as the discipline can only reproduce itself if its practitioner bears some authority in the eyes of potential students. What students will undertake to struggle with texts, or attend to lectures, that bear no authority?

5. Kingsley on authority:

> I expect nothing from . . . who arrogantly talk of economics as a science so completely perfected, so universal and all important that common humanity and morality and reason must be pooh-poohed down, if they seem to interfere with its infallible conclusions. (Quoted in Flubacher 1950, p. 198)

6. Contrary to Robinson's contention, the use of Smith in parliamentary debates was respectful, but far from reverential (see Willis 1979).

7. Anti-economists have taken satisfaction in claiming renegade status. Linguet proclaimed that he had a youthful attachment to physiocrats when 'very young'. List owned that for 'many years I was not only a very faithful disciple of Smith and Say; but a very zealous teacher of the infallible doctrine' (List 1909, p. 173). Alison claimed that in his youth 'I took with . . . ardour to the study of political economy' (quoted in Roberts 1977, p. 160). Carlyle, too, claimed he had formerly sought to 'sail through the Immensities' on political economy (Carlyle [1850] 1898, p. 45).

8. See in the same vein Dillon:

> If the subjects of wages, population, and rent are susceptible to scientific treatment at all, the truth with regard to them ought by this time to be determined . . . as to negative the possibility of rational controversy. Yet what is the fact? . . . we have found that so far is it from being the fact that 'the period of controversy is passing away, and that of unanimity rapidly approaching', that, in truth, the 'period of unanimity' never at any time seemed farther off. (Dillon 1882, p. 58)

9. Surveys undertaken in 1980–81 in Western Europe, in New Zealand and Britain in 1990, and in Australia in 1992 also indicate support for these propositions in all countries, with one exception.

Economists Agreeing or Agreeing with Reservations (percentages)

	Tariffs	Cash payments	Minimum wage	Fiscal policy	Rents	Effluent taxes
Britain	74	60	69	82	77	59
Germany	94	78	70	87	94	66
France	72	78	39	95	54	56
Belgium	79	62	53	81	80	68
Switzerland	90	77	67	88	80	57
New Zealand	86	–	72	–	–	60
Australia	93	75	87	81	96	87

Sources: Britain, Ricketts and Shoesmith (1990); Western Europe, Frey et al. (1983); New Zealand, Coleman (1992); Australia, Anderson and Blandy (1992).

10. This argument for the excess force of the average opinion over any single opinion is as old as Condorcet's 1785 *Essai sur l'Application de l'Analyse à la Probabilité des Décisions Rendues à la Pluralité des Voix* (Baker 1975, p. 229). The argument has reappeared in demonstrations of the superiority of the average of forecasters' forecasts over a single forecaster's forecast (Graham 1996). Two remarks on the argument are warranted.

   1. The argument does assume the 'independence' of individual forecasts. This assumption is doubtless untrue. But the general point remains: as long as predictions are not perfectly correlate the average opinion will carry more authority than any individual opinion (see Graham 1996).
   2. The argument does assume that the probability of the event having been predicted (when it does occur) exceeds 0.5, and the probability of the event not having been predicted (when it does not occur) is less than 0.5. If the probability of the event having been predicted (when it does occur) is *less than* 0.5, and the probability of the event not having been predicted (when it does not occur) *exceeds* 0.5 then we have 'negative authority'. That is, a majority predicting an earthquake entitles us to conclude there will be no earthquake.

11. Frederic Harrison in 1883: 'if we seek for any measure of the decrepitude of the older school of economists, if we seek for a crucial test of its self-sufficient sophistry, we cannot do better than note how completely its predictions have been proved false by the event . . . ' (quoted in Adelman 1971, p. 186).

12. The forecast of inflation by an expectations augmented Phillips curve (*EAPC*) easily dominates the forecast of inflation by the US public (*SURVEY*) (Baghestani 1992).

   $$\text{Inflation} = \begin{array}{ccc} -0.292 & +0.151 \text{ SURVEY} & +0.869 \text{ EAPC} \\ (0.803) & (0.175) & (0.112) \end{array}$$

   $R^2 = 0.93$. Sample period: January 1978–December 1985.

13. Vauban and Boisguilbert resorted to public opinion after their failure to persuade political authority. But this still indicates a trust in public opinion.

14. 'As late as 1764, a Déclaration du Roi prohibited "the printing, selling or peddling" of any writings concerning the finance administration' (Faccarello 1998, p. 182).

15. The physiocrats combined a paranoid confidence in their strange doctrines with a universalist epistemology founded in 'evidence', that, taken at face value, repudiated any notion of 'estates in knowledge'. In practice Quesnay was 'the Master' who commanded with authority his disciples. But did they attempt to inculcate their doctrines by invoking authority?

16. Morellet's *Réfutation* of Galiani was banned in 1770.

17. Baudeau was later compensated for his discomfort by a grant from Necker of a *pension public* of 4000 livres.

18. 'Bentham and James Mill had taught him [Mill] that each individual was the best judge of his proper interests, authority should be distrusted, and education held the key to progress owing to its ability to improve people's judgements'

(Pickering 1993, p. 519). It is worth noting the earnest repugnance of Ricardo and Mill to any political guarantee of certain religious doctrine, and any prohibition on others.

19. Coleridge: 'To be a Musician, an Orator, a Painter, a Poet, an Architect, or even to be a good mechanist presupposes *Genius*; to be an excellent Artizan or Mechanic, requires more than an average degree of *Talent*; but to be a legislator requires nothing but *common Sense*' (Coleridge 1969b, p. 213).

20. In this advocacy of a clerisy Coleridge rebuked Smith for his 'pernicious Opinion' that endowed intellectuals and artists are less productive than those who earn their income from the market (Levy 1986).

21. Darwinism was one plain cause of the expiration of the aspiration to build an antipopular authority. It not only constituted a palpable crisis for traditional, non-rational, religious authority, but also damaged scientific authority, as scientific authority had been confidently used to dispose of the leading evolutionist before Darwin, Robert Chambers. In 1844 Robert Chambers's *Vestiges of the Natural History of Creation* advanced the thesis of evolution, achieving huge popular success (12 editions in 40 years) and the bitter, near unanimous contempt of scientific professionals. An amateur and outsider, Chambers despaired of a fair hearing from scientific authority, sought to find justice in the court of public opinion, and largely succeeded. Thus the Darwinian episode was as much a vindication of public opinion against scientific authority, as a victory of science over religion (Yeo 1984).

22. One way of making political economy more genial was to efface its commanding tone. Political economy was not an authority, said Mill, but merely a 'guide'. This was much more mannerly. Mill rebuked Robert Lowe for invoking political economy 'as if science was a thing not to guide our judgement, but to stand in its place' (quoted in Forget 1992, p. 55).

23. Mill was so successfully genial that he became an authority in the eyes of the public. It was this authority that Jevons resented. Jevons complained of 'the too great influence of authoritative writers in Political Economy. I protest against deference for any man, whether John Stuart Mill, Adam Smith or Aristotle, being allowed to check inquiry.' Jevons adds 'Our science has become far too much a stagnant one, in which opinions rather than experience and reason are appealed to' (quoted in Coats 1964, p. 95).

24. Economists 'tended to shift with the currents of the times. When the idea of liberalism was rising, a majority of economists extolled the virtue of competition, free enterprise and free trade. In the age of social reform, many became interventionists and even what the Germans called *Kathedersozialisten*, "socialists of the chair". The New Deal produced a crop of liberal economists (in Roosevelt's sense of the term). Democratic socialism caused economists to turn to planning in markets' (Niehans 1990, p. 517).

25. Neoclassical economics is not the ally of economic liberals that it is often taken to be: see the frustration that neoclassical theorising is easily capable of engendering in economic liberals. Buchanan: 'The economists of the 1980s are ... ideological eunuchs. They feel no moral obligation to convey and transmit to their students any understanding of the social process through which a society of free persons can be organised without overt conflict while at the same time using resources without [sic] tolerable efficiency' (Buchanan 1988, p. 127). See also the fury Hutt visits upon Joan Robinson for use of her thoroughly neoclassical 1930s micro theory for the purposes of deflating confidence in liberal measures (Hutt 1936, p. 210).

13. 'Economists, Glory to You and the Jews!': a Postscript on Anti-Semitism and Anti-Economics

1. Toussenel (Toussenel 1847, p. 177).
2. The anti-economist Möser was the author of an anti-Semitic tract that has been described as 'a semi-scurrilous attack on Judaism by a thoughtless official Christianity' (Knudson 1986).
3. On one occasion Cobbett discovered that the Gatcombe estate of David Ricardo had been acquired from a Mr Sheppard. This moved Cobbett to exclaim of the ancient gentry: 'Thus they go! Thus they are squeezed out of existence. The little ones are gone; and the big ones have nothing left for it, but to resort to the bands of holy matrimony with the turn of the market watchers and their breed' (Cobbett [1830] 1967, p. 375). Ricardo is identified by Cobbett as a 'sickening' turn of the market watcher. See Osborne (1984) for an account of Cobbett's anti-Semitism.
4. Anti-Semitic themes were briefly pursued again by Hobson in 1918 (Allett 1987, p. 111).
5. Cunningham (1896, p. 91) believed that the Jews of thirteenth-century England had been 'favourably considered in all other relations of life'.
6. 'Jewish rabble' (*Judengesindel*) is another of Marx's expressions (Silberner 1953, p. 7). Engels's anti-Semitism is discussed in Silberner (1949). Lassale was a 'greasy Yid' and Jews were synonomous with speculators. Engels's anti-Semitism subsided with the burgeoning of *völkisch* anti-Semitism after 1870.
7. Ruskin was, and was not, anti-Semitic. He opposed the bill of 1858 that proposed to extend basic civil and political rights to British Jews (Ruskin 1905, 12, p. 593), and believed that 'the Jews forfeited their prophetic power by taking up the profession of usury over the whole earth' (Ruskin, 1905, 33, p. 95). Yet he also commended the trading ethics of medieval Jewish merchants as an example to his contemporaries. Dickens's own compound of anti-Semitism and (late in life) philo-Semitism is discussed in Stone (1958–59).
8. Comte believed it was shameful to proscribe forever 'the entire Jewish nation to avenge one single victim' – a victim who submitted to death with the certitude of regaining life three days later. (I am grateful to Mary Pickering for enlightenment on this point.)
9. Ricardo's Jewishness attracted anti-Semitic remarks from anti-economists. Thus one anti-economist claimed that Ricardo ('a gentleman of Jewish origin') had misled Parliament in encouraging the return to gold in 1819, and had benefited from the return. The same adds that the banking crisis of 1825–26 was the work of the Jews (Grampp 1976).
10. See Reder (2000) for a study of anti-Semitism in Keynes and Hayek.

14. The Not-so-Puzzling Failure of Anti-Economics

1. It is not only the affirmations of economics that are misrepresented; so are the silences of economics. Thus economics advocates neither industrialisation or agrarianism, yet it is censured by both agrarians and industrialisers. In the same vein its tendency to a median position leaves it open to misrepresentation. That 'economic man' gains neither pleasure nor pain from others' utility, leaves economics open to presentation by moralists as holding an ungenerous (cynical, low) view of nature, and by realists as holding a generous (naive, guileless) view.

2. 'The subjects of every state ought to contribute towards the support of government...in proportion to the revenue they respectively enjoy' (Smith [1776] 1937, p. 777).
3. Hayek is the author of *The Counter-Revolution of Science: Studies on the Abuse of Reason* (1955) and *The Sensory Order: an Inquiry into the Foundations of Theoretical Psychology* (1963).
4. The full title of Keynes's pamphlet is, *How to Pay for the War. A Radical Plan for the Chancellor of the Exchequer*. The critic we have referred to finds the title 'appalling in its title and blatant in its intention'. (The title is not really Keynes's, it was borrowed from *How to Pay for the War: Being Ideas Offered to the Chancellor of the Exchequer by the Fabian Research Department*, edited by Sydney Webb (1916)). The reader will find no reference to war-making in Keynes's document. They will find a proposal for 'universal family allowances in cash, the accumulation of working class wealth under working class control, and a capital levy (or tax)' (Keynes 1940, p. iii).
5. Diderot, after initial enthusiasm, was a determined enemy of physiocracy; d'Alembert never did anything 'Oeconomist'; Jean-François de la Harpe was a literary critic cum revolutionist who 'detested' physiocracy. 'I didn't understand anything of political economy, but Necker who was acquainted with it, found the work of the Économistes detestable: so it must be' (quoted in Lebeau 1903, p. 118).
6. See Levy (2001, pp. 66–77) for an examination of the whitewashing of Carlyle.
7. Another illustration of the indulgence of anti-economists is how the anti-Semitism of several is lightly dismissed. One of Soddy's admirers dismisses Soddy's anti-Semitic gabble thus: 'Sometimes he had embellished his writings on the capitalist and monetary banking system with unnecessary comments on Jewish bankers...[but] I do not believe that these comments show other than run-of-the-mill Eurocentrism and anti-semitism' (Martinez-Allier 1987, p. 142). This is an inadequate response. An author who commends to his readers the *Protocols of the Learned Elders of Zion* is not a 'run-of-the-mill' Eurocentrist and anti-Semite.
8. For an examination, in an Australian context, of the prolific falsehood of anti-economics, see Coleman and Hagger (2001).
9. Senior's whole analysis is critically vitiated by his implicit self-contradiction regarding the rate of depreciation on fixed capital. He states he is assuming it to be 5 per cent. Yet his own numerical assumptions are grossly inconsistent. Proof: if we let Y = output, r equal the rate of profit, d equal the rate of depreciation, F equal fixed capital and V equal variable capital, then in equilibrium,

$$Y = [r + d]F + [1 + r]V.$$

And if we assume $F = 80,000$ (as Senior does), $V = 20,000$ (as Senior does), and $r = 10$ per cent (as Senior does), then $Y = 34,000$. Yet Senior takes Y to be 115,000, implicitly taking d to equal 1.0, not 0.05. If Senior had properly assumed Y equals 34,000 then the equality above implies that an 8.7 per cent reduction in Y (resulting from the working day being reduced from 11.5 hours to 10.5 hours) would merely reduce the profit rate to 7.0435 per cent. Further, if Senior had properly allowed the wage bill (V) to fall according to the ratio of 10.5/11.5, (since hourly wage rates were not increased to compensate for the reduction in hours worked) then the profit rate would be merely reduced to 8.9 per cent. The profitability is not 'destroyed'.

10. Coleridge: 'I think this country is now suffering grievously under an excessive accumulation of Capital, which having no field for its profitable operation, is in a state of fierce civil war with itself' (1969d, p. 372).

11. Is environmental degradation another issue where anti-economists rightly felt there was a problem, even if they could not articulate it? Ruskin's horror of industrial filth as reflected in the *Storm-Cloud* lectures has been instanced. But to distil the true meaning of such productions of this disturbed mind is not easy. He could express a horror of nature: 'Of all the things that oppress me, this sense of the evil working of *Nature herself* – my disgust at her barbarity – clumsiness-darkness-bitter mockery of herself – is the most devastating' (Watson 1972, p. 69).

12. The anti-economist is entitled to evaluate economics negatively on the basis of a comparison of economics with no economics at all; a complete state of economic innocence belonging to, say, the ninth century. This is the thesis of some anti-economists, including Patrick Pearse, 'Ye men and peoples burn your books of rent theories and land values and go back to your sagas' (Boylan and Foley 1991, p. 126).

13. In 1933 the general public was convicted of the same judgement of ignorance by the producer of a radio programme that is sufficiently curious to note. In that year the BBC broadcast a critical 'cross-examination' of an economist, Noel Frederick Hall, by members of the general public, using questions drawn from letters sent in by members of the public that had been solicited by the BBC. 'The ... intellectual enterprise shown by correspondents is surprisingly low. A few obvious exceptions apart, hardly a single writer appears to have tried to read a book on Economics (or to have succeeded in reading one to any purpose)' (King-Hall 1933, p. 215).

14. John Francis Bray quotes from Smith and Ricardo and many others (Henderson 1985, p. 73). 'Cayley shows himself to be familiar with the work of Smith, Ricardo, and Malthus all of whom he cites' (Dutton and King 1985, p. 206).

15. In 1824, Carlyle had also translated for the *Encyclopedia Britannica* Sismondi's essentially Smithian paper 'Political Economy' (Schneider 1995).

16. Ruskin's admirer and fellow anti-economist Frederic Harrison was of the opinion that Ruskin did not understand economics. 'The testimony of his friends Frederic Harrison and William Smart is that he did not understand traditional political economy' (Fain 1956, p. 48).

17. Major O'Keefe, the Honorary Secretary to the Royal and National Grand African Colonisation and Timbuctoo Civilisation Society decides to touch Miss Mabel Brook for a donation to his fraudulent Society. He announces that a 'most distinguished person has already placed at the disposal of the society a sum of £1000 to found a professorship of political economy in the great capital of Africa. The Rev Dr Mason, that celebrated writer and divine, has been pleased to place at our disposal all the unsold copies of his lectures of that science (and I assure you they amount to a large number of volumes), for the purpose of circulating them among the negroes' (Sewell [1845] 1976, 1, p. 370).

18. 'All the Romantics are manic-depressives' (Brunschwig 1974, p. 201).

19. 'Brain fever' = meningitis. Or an overdose?

20. Jenny Marx also attributed Marx's ailments 'to mental unrest and agitation' (Nelson 1999a).

21. Henry Drummond was an enthusiast of visionary religion who heard voices and on one occasion wrote to the Archbishop of York to advise him of the imminent end of the world.

22. By way of a final retort, reference might be made to the numerous cases of the unexplained but undeniable contiguity between creativity and madness (Andreasen 1987). But anti-economics is not so much a matter of creativity as of criticism. And the fertility of mental disturbance in criticism is doubtful.

23. That anti-economics has no logical content has been proposed before (Macaulay [1830] 1865, p. 25).

24. It is written of the anti-economist William Cunningham that 'Many who knew nothing of his economics long cherished his proclamation from the pulpit of Great St Mary's, Cambridge, that the joys of Heaven were incomplete if they did not feature the joy of conflict' (Maloney 1976, p. 441).

25. See Lewis (1875) for an exposition of the theme that an intellectual tradition that commands authority integrates and homogenises.

26. The one final possibility is the readoption of logical values and reintegration in the dominant mainstream.

27. The development in post-Meiji Japan of Marxism in a particular national form completely disconnected from the rest of the world can be contrasted with the abandonment in that period of indigenous Japanese mathematics ('wasan'), and the integration of Japanese mathematical learning with the rest of the world.

28. This integration contrasts strongly with disintegral forces present in other social sciences. Psychology: 'There is no commonly accepted body of psychological theory ... Rather than exchanging views with one another, they [psychologists] often find it easier and more natural to talk to academic neighbours outside of psychology' (Hudson 1985, p. 665). Anthropology: 'It would appear that "Mr Taylor's science" is in total disarray ... whether anything viable will emerge from the current chaos and ideological muddle is hard to see. What is more likely – and this is evident from the near collapse and "reorganisation" of the professional association – is that a series of relatively autonomous specialisms will diverge from one another and gravitate towards their nearest relatives in other fields' (Fox 1985, p. 32).

29. An intellectual tradition driven by rational criticism may lose that impulse and either fossilise or disintegrate. The Say tradition in France experienced various different outcomes. It froze (French liberals); it disintegrated (adapted by Saint-Simon and then bizarrely deformed by Saint-Simonism). It also developed and integrated (Walras).

30. The 'review article' is one vehicle for scholarship. But what is the prestige of a review article?

31. Does not a scientist need to be a good critic? A scientist needs to be a good critic respecting his own product, but the commensuration of different products is a special talent which successful scientists may not have.

Bibliography

Adams, John (1971), 'The Institutional Economics of Mahadev Govind Ranade', *Journal of Economic Issues*, 5(2).

Adelman, Paul (1971), 'Frederic Harrison and the "Positivist" Attack on Orthodox Political Economy', *History of Political Economy*, 3(1).

Adler, Franklin Hugh (1995), *Italian Industrialists from Liberalism to Fascism*, Cambridge: Cambridge University Press.

Ages, Arnold (1974), 'Bonald and the Jews', *Revue de l'Université d'Ottawa*, 44(1).

Aikin, Lucy (1864), *Memoirs, Miscellanies and Letters of the Late Lucy Aikin*, Philip Hemery le Breton, ed., London: Longman, Green and Co.

Aikin, William E. (1977), *Technocracy and the American Dream: the Technocrat Movement, 1900–1941*, Berkeley: University of California Press.

Albrecht, Catherine (1999), 'Continuities and Discontinuities in Business and Economic Education in Czechoslovakia, 1945–53', mimeo, University of Baltimore.

Albrecht, Catherine (2000), 'Professionalism in the Economic Institute of the Czechoslovak Academy of Sciences, 1953–1963', *Věda v Českolovebsku Letech 1953–1963*.

Alison, Archibald (1840), *The Principles of Population, and their Connection with Human Happiness*, 2 vols, Edinburgh: W. Blackwood and Sons.

Alison, Archibald (1845), 'Sismondi', *Blackwood's Magazine*, 67(355).

Alison, Archibald (1850), 'Thirty Years of Liberal Legislation', *Essays. Political, Historical and Miscellaneous*, vol. 1, Edinburgh: William Blackwood and Sons.

Allett, John (1987), 'New Liberalism, Old Prejudices: J.A. Hobson and the "Jewish Question"', *Jewish Social Studies*, 49(2).

Alston, Richard M., J.R. Kearl and Michael B. Vaughan (1992), 'Is There a Consensus among Economists in the 1990s?', *American Economic Review*, 82(2).

Amariglio, Jack (1987), 'Marxism against Economic Science: Althusser's Legacy', *Research in Political Economy*, 10.

Ambirajan, S. (1998), 'Dadabhai Naoroji: the First Economist of Modern India', *Research in the History of Economic Thought and Methodology*, 16.

The American Enterprise (1991), 'Politics of the Professoriate', *The American Enterprise*, 2(4).

Anderson, Malcolm and Richard Blandy (1992), 'What Australian Economics Professors Think', *Australian Economic Review*, 100.

Anderson, Martin (1992), *Impostors in the Temple*, New York: Simon and Schuster.

Andreasen, Nancy C. (1987), 'Creativity and Mental Illness: Prevalence Rates in Writers and their First-Degree Relatives', *American Journal of Psychiatry*, 144(10).

Anthony, Peter (1983), *John Ruskin's Labour: a Study of Ruskin's Social Theory*, Cambridge: Cambridge University Press.

Argyll, George Douglas Campbell (1893), *The Unseen Foundations of Society: an Examination of the Fallacies and Failures of Economic Science due to Neglected Elements*, London: John Murray.

Aris, Reinhold (1936), *History of Political Thought in Germany from 1789 to 1815*, London: George Allen and Unwin.

Arnold, Matthew (1871), *Friendship's Garland*, London: Smith, Elder and Co.

Ascher, Abraham (1963), 'Professors as Propagandists: the Politics of the Katheder Sozialisten', *Journal of Central European Affairs*, 23(3).

Ashley, W.J. (1926), 'Hildebrand', in *Palgrave's Dictionary of Political Economy*, vol. 1, Henry Higgs, ed., London: Macmillan.

Ashley, W.J. (1962), 'A Survey of the Past and Present Position of Political Economy', in *Essays in Economic Method*, R.L. Smyth, ed., London: Gerald Duckworth.

Ashton, T.S. (1931), 'The Origin of the "The Manchester School"', *The Manchester School*, 1.

Ashton, T.S. (1946), 'The Relation of Economic Theory to Economic History', *Economica*, 13(2).

Attali J. and M. Guillaume (1974), *l'Anti-économique*, Paris: Presses Universitaires de France.

Augello, Massimo M. and Marco E.L. Guidi (1996), 'The Emergence of the Economic Periodical Literature in Italy (1750–1900)', *History of Economic Ideas*, 4(3).

Ayres, Clarence Edwin (1935), 'The Gospel of Technology', in *American Philosophy Today and Tomorrow*, Horace M. Kallen and Sidney Hook, eds, New York: Lee Furman.

Bagehot, W. [1876] (1915), *The Works and Life of Walter Bagehot*, R. Barrington, ed., London: Longmans Green and Co.

Baghestani, Hamid (1992), 'Survey Evidence on the Muthian Rationality of the Inflation Forecasts of U.S. Consumers', *Oxford Bulletin of Economics and Statistics*, 54(2).

Baird, Bruce C. (1997), 'Necessity and the "Perverse" Supply of Labor in Pre-Classical British Political Economy', *History of Political Economy*, 29(3).

Baker, Keith Michael (1975), *Condorcet, from Natural Philosophy to Social Mathematics*, Chicago: University of Chicago Press.

Balogh, Thomas (1963), *Unequal Partners*, Oxford: Blackwell.

Balogh, Thomas (1982), *The Irrelevance of Conventional Economics*, London: Weidenfeld and Nicolson.

Banfield, Thomas Charles (1843), *Six Letters to the Right Hon. Sir Robert Peel, bart., being an Attempt to Expose the Dangerous Tendency of the Theory of Rent Advocated by Mr Ricardo, and by Writers of his School*, London: R. and J.E. Taylor.

Barkin, Kenneth D. (1970), *The Controversy over German Industrialization, 1890–1902*, Chicago: University of Chicago Press.

Barnett, Vincent (1994a), 'The Economic Thought of L.N. Yurovskii', *Coexistence*, 31.

Barnett, Vincent (1994b), 'As Good as Gold? A Note on the Chernovets', *Europe-Asia Studies*, 46(4).

Barnett, Vincent (1995), 'A Long Wave Goodbye: Kondrat'ev and the Conjuncture Institute, 1920–28', *Europe-Asia Studies*, 47(3).

Barnett, Vincent (1996), 'Trading Cycles for Change: S.A. Pervushin as an Economist of the Business Cycle', *Europe-Asia Studies*, 48(6).

Barnett, Vincent (1998), *Kondratiev and the Dynamics of Economic Development: Long Cycles and Industrial Growth in Historical Context*, Basingstoke: Macmillan Press – now Palgrave Macmillan.

Barrington, Donal (1954), 'Burke as an Economist', *Economica*, 21(3).

Barruel, Augustin [1797] (1800), *Mémoires pour Servir a l'Histoire du Jacobinsme*, Hamburg: P.F. Fauche.

Bastable, C.F. (1884), *An Examination of Some Current Objections to the Study of Political Economy*, Dublin: Hoggis, Figgis and Co.

Bate, Jonathan (1991), *Romantic Ecology: Wordsworth and the Environmental Tradition*, London: Routledge.

Beik, Paul H. (1956), 'The French Revolution Seen from the Right', *Transactions of the American Philosophical Society*, 56(1).

Beissinger, Mark R. (1988), *Scientific Management, Socialist Discipline and Soviet Power*, Cambridge, Mass.: Harvard University Press.

Bell-Villada, Gene H. (1986), 'The Idea of Art for Art's Sake: Intellectual Origins, Social Conditions and Poetic Doctrine', *Science & Society*, 50(4).

Bell-Villada, Gene H. (1996), *Art for Art's Sake and Literary Life*, Lincoln: University of Nebraska Press.

Beloff, Max (1968), 'A Plague of Economists?', *Encounter*, 30(3).

Belykh, A.A. (1990), 'A.A. Bogdanov's Theory of Equilibrium and the Economic Discussions of the 1920s', *Soviet Studies*, 42(3).

Berenson, Edward (1989), 'A New Religion of the Left: Christianity and Social Radicalism in France, 1815–1848', in *The Transformation of Political Culture, 1789–1848. The French Revolution and the Creation of Modern Political Culture*, vol. 3, Francois Furet and Mona Ozouf, eds, Oxford: Pergamon Press.

Berle, A.A. (1938), 'The Lost Art of Economics', *Virginia Quarterly Review*, Summer, 14(3).

Bernstein, Eduard [1899] (1993), *The Preconditions of Socialism*, ed. and translated by Henry Tudor, Cambridge: Cambridge University Press.

Bernstein, Samuel (1971), *Auguste Blanqui and the Art of Insurrection*, London: Lawrence & Wishart.

Berry, Christopher J. (1994), *The Idea of Luxury: a Conceptual and Historical Investigation*, Cambridge: Cambridge University Press.

Bestor, Arthur E. (1948), 'The Evolution of the Socialist Vocabulary', *Journal of the History of Ideas*, 9(3).

Betts, Raymond F. (1987), 'Du Pont de Nemours in Napoleonic France, 1802–1815', *French Historical Studies*, 5(2).

Betz, Horst K. (1993–94), 'From Schmoller to Sombart', *History of Economic Ideas*, 1(3)–2(1).

Beveridge, William (1937), 'The Place of Social Sciences in Human Knowledge', *Politica*, 2.

Biagini, Eugenio F. (1987), 'British Trade Unions and Popular Political Economy, 1860–1880', *Historical Journal*, 30(4).

Biddle, Jeff and Warren J. Samuels (1997), 'The Historicism of John R. Common's *Legal Foundations of Capitalism*', in *Methodology of the Social Sciences, Ethics, and Economics in the Newer Historical School: From Max Weber and Rickert to Sombart and Rothacker*, Peter Koslowski, ed., Heidelberg: Springer.

Black, R.D. Collison (1960), *Economic Thought and the Irish Question, 1817–1870*, Cambridge: Cambridge University Press.

Blandy, Richard (1992), 'Multiple Schizophrenia, Economic Rationalism and its Critics. Review of Pusey, Michael. *Economic Rationalism in Canberra: a Nation Building State Changes its Mind*', *Australian Quarterly*, 64.

Blanqui, Auguste (1885), *Critique Sociale*, Paris: Félix Alcan.

Blaug, Mark (1958), 'The Classical Economists and the Factory Act – a Re-Examination', *Quarterly Journal of Economics*, 72.

Blaug, Mark (1998), 'Disturbing Currents in Modern Economics', *Challenge*, 41(3).

Blendon, Robert J. (1997), 'Bridging the Gap between the Public's and Economists' Views of the Economy', *Journal of Economic Perspectives*, 11(3).

Bogdanov, Alexander [1908] (1984), *Red Star: the First Bolshevik Utopia*, Loren R. Graham and Richard Stites, eds, translated by Charles Rougle, Bloomington: Indiana University Press.

Böhm-Bawerk, E. [1896] (1949), *Karl Marx and the Close of His System*, New York: Kelley.

Boland, Lawrence A. (1992), *The Principles of Economics: Some Lies My Teachers Told Me* London: Routledge.

Bonald, Louis-Gabriel-Ambroise de [1806] (1864a), 'Sur les Juifs', *Oeuvres Complète de M. de Bonald*, vol. 2, Paris: J.-P. Migne.

Bonald, Louis-Gabriel-Ambroise de [1810] (1864b), 'Sur l'Économie Politique', *Oeuvres Complète de M. de Bonald*, vol. 2, Paris: J.-P. Migne.

Bonald, Louis-Gabriel-Ambroise de [1810] (1864c), 'De la Richesse des Nations', *Oeuvres Complète de M. de Bonald*, vol. 2, Paris: J.-P. Migne.

Boss, Ronald (1976), 'Linguet: the Reformer as Anti-Philosophe', *Studies on Voltaire and the Eighteenth Century*, 61.

Bourdieu, Pierre (1998), *Acts of Resistance: Against the Tyranny of the Market*, translated by Richard Nice, New York: New Press.

Bourdieu, Pierre (2000), *Les Structures Sociales de l'Économie*, Paris: Seuil.

Bowen, Ralph H. (1971), *German Theories of the Corporative State*, New York: Russel and Russel.

Boyd, William (1964), *The History of Western Education*, London: Adam and Charles Black.

Boylan, Thomas A. and Timothy P. Foley (1984), 'John Elliot Cairnes, John Stuart Mill and Ireland: Some Problems for Political Economy', in *Economists and the Irish Economy from the Eighteenth Century to the Present Day*, Antoin E. Murphy, ed., Dublin: Irish Academic Press.

Boylan, Thomas A. and Timothy P. Foley (1991), *Political Economy and Colonial Ireland: the Propagation and Ideological Function of Economic Discourse in the Nineteenth Century*, London: Routledge.

Bramsted, Ernest Kohn (1967), *Aristocracy and the Middle-Classes in Germany: Social Types in German Literature*, Chicago: University of Chicago Press.

Bramwell, Anna (1989), *Ecology in the Twentieth Century: a History*, New Haven: Yale University Press.

Breckman, Warren G. (1991), 'Disciplining Consumption: the Debate about Luxury in Wilhemine Germany, 1890–1914', *Journal of Social History*, 24(3).

Breton, Yves (1986), 'Les Économistes Libéreaux Français et l'Emploi des Mathématiques en Économie Politique 1800–1914', *Economies et Societies*, 20(3).

Brunschwig, Henri (1974), *Enlightenment and Romanticism in Eighteenth-Century Prussia*, translated by Frank Jellinek, Chicago: University of Chicago Press.

Buchanan, James M. (1985), 'Political Economy and Social Philosophy', in *Economics and Philosophy*, Peter Koslowski, ed., Tübingen: Mohr (Siebeck).

Buchanan, James (1988), 'Political Economy 1957–1982', in *Ideas, their Origins, and their Consequences: Lectures to Commemorate the Life and Work of G. Warren Nutter*, Washington: American Enterprise Institute for Public Policy Research.

Bücher, Karl (1912), *Industrial Evolution*, New York: Henry Holt.

Buckley, William F. (1951), *God and Man at Yale: the Superstitions of 'Academic Freedom'*, Chicago: Regnery.

Bukanin, Jack (1976), *Pierre Leroux and the Birth of Democratic Socialism 1797–1848*, New York: Revisionist Press.

Bukhonova, I.N. and E.V. Chilikova (1997), '"Ia Okazalsia Vybroshennym Iz Chelovecheskogo Obshchestva": A.V. Chainov v Kazhakstanskoi Ssylke' ['I Was Thrown out of Human Society': A.V. Chayanov in his Kazakhstan exile], *Otechestvennye Arkhivy*, 2.

Bullock, Allan (1998), *Hitler and Stalin: Parallel Lives*, London: HarperCollins.

Buret, Eugène (1840), *De la Misère des Classes Laborieuses en Angleterre et en France*, Paris: Paulin.

Burke [1790] (1968), *Reflections on the Revolution in France*, Conor Cruise O'Brien, ed., Harmondsworth: Penguin.

Butler, Marilyn (1981), *Romantics, Rebels and Reactionaries: English Literature and its Background 1760–1830*, Oxford: Oxford University Press.

Bygrave, Stephen (1986), *Coleridge and the Self: Romantic Egotism*, Basingstoke: Macmillan.

Byles, John Barnard (1904), *Sophisms of Free-Trade and Popular Political Economy Examined*, London: John Lane.

Byron, George Gordon (1982), *Don Juan*, T.G. Steffan, E. Steffan and W.W. Pratt, eds, Harmondsworth: Penguin.

Cairnes, John E. [1873] (1965), 'Political Economy and Laissez-Faire', in *Essays in Political Economy*, New York: Augustus M. Kelley.

Cannan, Edward (1894), 'Ricardo in Parliament', *Economic Journal*, 4(2–3).

Carey, Henry C. [1859] (1963), *Principles of Social Science*, vol. 3, New York: Augustus M. Kelley.

Carey, John (1992), *The Intellectuals and the Masses: Pride and Prejudice among the Literary Intelligentsia, 1800–1939*, London: Faber & Faber.

Carey, M. (1822), 'Addresses of the Philadelphia Society for the Promotion of National Industry', in *Essays on Political Economy*, Philadelphia.

Carey, M. [1829] (1970), *Autobiographical Sketches*, New York: Arno.

Carlson, Allan (1990), *The Swedish Experiment in Family Politics: the Myrdals and the Interwar Population Crisis*, London: Transaction Publishers.

Carlson, Julie (1991), 'Command Performances: Burke and Coleridge's Dramatic Reflections on the Revolution in France', *Nineteenth Century Contexts*, 15(2).

Carlyle, Alexander (1861), *Autobiography of Dr Alexander Carlyle*, Edinburgh: William Blackwood and Sons.

Carlyle, Thomas [1843] (1897), *The Collected Works of Thomas Carlyle: Past and Present*, vol. 10, London: Chapman and Hall.

Carlyle, Thomas [1849] (1899a), 'The Nigger Question', in *The Collected Works of Thomas Carlyle: Critical and Miscellaneous Essays* (vol. 4), vol. 29, London: Chapman and Hall.

Carlyle, Thomas [1849] (1899b), 'Chartism', in *The Collected Works of Thomas Carlyle: Critical and Miscellaneous Essays* (vol. 4), vol. 29, London: Chapman and Hall.

Carlyle, Thomas [1850] (1898), *The Collected Works of Thomas Carlyle: Latter-day Pamphlets*, vol. 20, London: Chapman and Hall.

Carlyle, Thomas (1980), *Carlyle, Books & Margins: Being a Catalogue of the Carlyle Holdings in the Norman and Charlotte Strouse Carlyle Collection and the University Library with a Transcription of Carlyle's Marginalia in John Stuart Mill's Principles of Political Economy and an Interpretative Essay Thereon*, Santa Cruz: University of California Press.

Carroll, John (1992), 'Economic Rationalism and its Consequences', in R. Manne and J. Carroll, eds, *Shutdown*, Melbourne: Text.

Cartmill, Matt (1993), *A View to a Death in the Morning: Hunting and Nature through History*, Cambridge, Mass.: Harvard University Press.

Carver, Terrell (1975), 'Editor's Preface', in *Karl Marx: Texts on Methods*, translated and edited by Terrell Carver, Oxford: Basil Blackwell.

Cassidy, John (1996), 'The Decline of Economics', *New Yorker*, 72(37).

Castles, Ian (1984), 'Economics and Anti-economics', 54th Congress of the Australia and New Zealand Association for the Advancement of Science.

Castles, Ian (1997), 'Directors Note', *Newsletter. Academy of the Social Sciences in Australia*, 3/1997.

Cate, George Allan (1988), *John Ruskin, a Reference Guide: a Selective Guide to Significant and Representative Works about Him*, Boston, Mass.: G.K. Hall.

Chandra, Bipan (1965), 'Indian Nationalists and the Drain', *Indian Economic and Social History Review*, 2(2).

Charlton, D.G. (1963), *Secular Religions in France 1815–1870*, London: Oxford University Press.

Charpentier, John (1935), *Napoléon et les Hommes de Lettres de son Temps*, Paris: Mecure de France.

Chase, Stuart (1933), *Technocracy: an Interpretation*, New York: John Day.

Checkland, S.G. (1951), 'The Advent of Academic Economics in England', *Manchester School*, 19(1).

Chevalier, Michel (1849), *L'Économie Politique et le Socialisme*, Paris: Guillaumin.

Choi, Young Back (1996), 'The Americanization of Economics in Korea', *History of Political Economy*, 28(0), Supplement.

Cinderella: a Manual of Political Economy for Free Men (1890), Sydney: Joseph Cook.

Clark, Evalyn A. (1940), 'Adolf Wagner: from National Economist to National Socialist', *Political Science Quarterly*, 55(3).

Clark, J.C.D. (1985), *English Society 1688–1832: Ideology, Social Structure and Political Practice during the Ancien Régime*, Cambridge: Cambridge University Press.

Clark, Kenneth (1969), *Civilisation: a Personal View*, London: British Broadcasting Corporation.

Coats, A.W. (1964), 'The Role of Authority in the Development of British Economics', *Journal of Law and Economics*, 7.

Coats, A.W. (1968), 'Political Economy and the Tariff Campaign of 1903', *Journal of Law and Economics*, 11(1).

Coats A.W. and S.E. Coats (1970), 'The Social Composition of the Royal Economic Society and the Beginnings of the British Economics "Profession", 1890–1915', *British Journal of Sociology*, 21(1).

Cobbett, William [1830] (1967), *Rural Rides*, George Woodcock, ed., Harmondsworth: Penguin.

Cobbett, William (1835), *Selections from Cobbett's Political Works*, vol.1, John M. Cobbett and James P. Cobbett, eds, London: Ann Cobbett.

Cocks, Geoffrey (1997), *Pyschotherapy in the Third Reich: the Göring Institute*, second edition, London: Transaction Publishers.

Cohen, D.K. (1969), 'The Vicomte de Bonald's Critique of Industrialism', *Journal of Modern History*, 41(4).

Cohen, J.M. (1993), *The New Penguin Dictionary of Quotations*, Harmondsworth: Penguin.

Cohn, Gustav (1874), 'Political Economy in Germany', *Fortnightly Review*, 54.

Colander, David C. (1991), *Why Aren't Economists as Important as Garbagemen? Essays on the State of Economics*, Armonk, NY: M.E. Sharpe.

Coleman, William (1992), 'Concord and Discord amongst New Zealand Economists: the Results of an Opinion Survey', *New Zealand Economic Papers*, 26(1).

Coleman, William (1995), *Rationalism and Anti-Rationalism in the Origins of Economics: the Philosophic Roots of Eighteenth-Century Economic Thought*, Cheltenham: Edward Elgar.

Coleman, William (1996), 'How Theory Came to English Classical Economics', *Scottish Journal of Political Economy*, 43(2).

Coleman, William (2001a), 'The Strange Laissez-Faire of Alfred Russel Wallace', in *Darwinism and Evolutionary Economics*, John Laurent and John Nightingale, eds, Cheltenham: Edward Elgar.

Coleman, William (2001b), 'Running Economics Down: Perceptions and Reality in the Presentation of Economists in the Media', School of Economics Discussion Paper 2001-12, University of Tasmania.

Coleman, William and Alf Hagger (2001), *Exasperating Calculators: the Rage over Economic Rationalism and the Campaign against Australian Economists*, Sydney: Macleay Press.

Coleridge, Samuel Taylor (1956), *The Collected Letters of Samuel Taylor Coleridge*, Earl L. Griggs, ed., 6 vols, Oxford: Oxford University Press.

Coleridge, Samuel Taylor (1969a), *The Collected Works of Samuel Taylor Coleridge. Lay Sermons*, R.J. White, ed., London: Routledge and Kegan Paul.

Coleridge, Samuel Taylor (1969b), 'The Friend' in *The Collected Works of Samuel Taylor Coleridge*, Barbara E. Rooke, ed., London: Routledge and Kegan Paul.

Coleridge, Samuel Taylor (1969c), 'Table Talk', vol. 1 in *The Collected Works of Samuel Taylor Coleridge*, Carl Woodring, ed., London and Princeton: Routledge and Princeton University Press.

Coleridge, Samuel Taylor (1969d), 'Table Talk', vol. 2 in *The Collected Works of Samuel Taylor Coleridge*, Carl Woodring, ed., London and Princeton: Routledge and Princeton University Press.

Coleridge, Samuel Taylor (1972), 'Lay Sermons', in *The Collected Works of Samuel Taylor Coleridge*, R.J. White, ed., 6 vols, London: Routledge and Kegan Paul.

Common, Michael (1995), 'Economists Don't Read *Science*', *Ecological Economics*, 15.

Commons, John R. (1907), *Race and Immigrants in America*, New York: Macmillan.

Commons, John R. (1924), *The Legal Foundations of Capitalism*, New York: Macmillan.

Comte, Auguste [1855] (1974), *The Positive Philosophy of Auguste Comte*, New York: AMS Press.

Comte, Auguste (1875), *System of Positive Polity*, 4 vols, London: Longman, Green and Co.

Constant, Benjamin (1988), *Political Writings*, Biancamaria Fontana, ed., Cambridge: Cambridge University Press.

Coombs, H.C. (1995), 'Corporate Takeover of Society's Values', *Australian*, 3 March, p. 13.

Cossa, Luigi (1880), *Guide to the Study of Political Economy*, London: Macmillan.

Courtois, Stéphane (1999), *The Black Book of Communism: Crimes, Terror, Repression*, translated by Jonathan Murphy, Cambridge, Mass.: Harvard University Press.

Coux, Charles de (1830), 'Économie Politique', *L'Avenir*, 29 December 1830.

Coux, Charles de (1832), *Essais d'Économie Politique*, Louvain: Vanlinthout and Vandenzande.

Coux, Charles de (1833), *Cours d'Économie Politique*, Louvain: Valinthout and Vandenzande.

Cox, E. (1995), *A Truly Civil Society*, Sydney: ABC Books.

Craster, Theophilus (1840), *A View of Manufactures, Money, and Corn Laws, Adverse to Every Theory of the Economists: with Observations Upon the National Worth of Machinery*, London: J. Hatchard and Son.

Cronon, William (1996), 'The Trouble with Wilderness; or, Getting Back to the Wrong Nature', *Environmental History*, 1(1).

Cunningham, Audrey (1950), *William Cunningham. Teacher and Priest*, London: SPCK.

Cunningham, William (1878), 'Political Economy as a Moral Science', *Mind*, 3.

Cunningham, William (1890), 'On the Comtist Criticism of Economic Science', Report of the 59th meeting of the British Association for the Advancement of Science, Newcastle 1889.

Cunningham, William (1892a), 'The Relativity of Economic Doctrine', *Economic Journal*, 2(1).

Cunningham, William (1892b), 'A Plea for Pure Theory', *Economic Review*, 2(1).
Cunningham, William (1892c), 'The Perversion of Economic History', *Economic Journal*, 2.
Cunningham, William (1894), 'Economists as Mischief-Makers', *Economic Review*, 4(1).
Cunningham, William (1896), 'The Expulsion of the Jews from England in 1290', *Economic Journal*, 6(1).
Cunningham, William (1902), *The Gospel of Work*, Cambridge: Cambridge University Press.
Cunningham, William (1911), *The Case against Free Trade*, London: John Murray.
Cunningham, William (1914), *Christianity and Economic Science*, London: John Murray.
Cypher, James M. (1993), 'The Ideology of Economic Science in the Selling of NAFTA: the Political Economy of Elite Decision Making', *Review of Radical Political Economics*, 25(4).
Daley, Kenneth (1997), 'From the Theoretical to the Practical: Ruskin, British Aestheticism, and the Relation of Art to Use', *Prose Studies*, 20(2).
Daly, Herman E. (1980), 'The Economic Thought of Frederick Soddy', *History of Political Economy*, 12(4).
Daly, Herman E. (1987), 'The Economic Growth Debate: What Some Economists Have Learned but Many Have Not', *Journal of Environmental Economics and Management*, 14(4).
Daly, Herman E. and John B. Cobb (1989), *For the Common Good: Redirecting the Economy toward Community, the Environment, and a Sustainable Future*, Boston: Beacon Press.
Daly, Mary E. (1994), 'The Economic Ideals of Irish Nationalism: Frugal Comfort or Lavish Austerity?', *Éire-Ireland*, 29(4).
Davies, R.W. (1989), *The Soviet Economy in Turmoil, 1929–1930*, Cambridge, Mass.: Harvard University Press.
Dawson, William Harbutt (1890), *Bismarck and State Socialism: an Exposition of the Social and Economic Legislation of Germany since 1870*, London: S. Sonnenschein & Co.
De Quincey, Thomas (1897), *De Quincey's Collected Writings*, vol. 9, London: Black.
De Tocqueville, Alexis [1835] (1945), *Democracy in America*, New York: A.A. Knopf.
Debray, Régis (1981), *Teachers, Writers, Celebrities: the Intellectuals of Modern France*, translated by David Macey, London: New Left Books.
Defarges, Philippe Moreau (1994), 'The French Viewpoint on the Future of the G-7', *International Spectator*, 29(2).
Delbanco, Andrew (1995), *The Death of Satan: How Americans Have Lost the Sense of Evil*, New York: Farrar, Straus, and Giroux.
Demming, W.E. (1993), *The New Economics for Industry Government and Education*, Cambridge, Mass.: MIT Press.
Denis, Henri (1951), *La Crise de la Pensée Économique*, Paris: Presses Universitaires de France.
Desaulniers, Mary (1995), *Carlyle and the Economics of Terror: a Study of Revisionary Gothicism in The French Revolution*, Montreal: McGill-Queen's University Press.
Desrousilles, G.D. (1976), 'Sismondi ou le Liberalisme Héroïque', in *Histoire, Socialisme et Critique de l'Économie Politique*, Paris: Institut de Sciences Mathématiques et Economiques Appliquées.
Diatkine, Daniel (1993), 'A French Reading of the *Wealth of Nations*', in *Adam Smith: International Perspectives*, Hiroshi Mizuta and Chuhei Sugiyama, eds, New York: St Martin's Press.
Dickens, Charles (1854), 'On Strike', *Household Words*, 203.

Dickens, Charles [1854] (1990), *Hard Times*, George Ford and Sylvère Monod, eds, New York: W.W. Norton.

Dillon, William (1882), *The Dismal Science. A Criticism of Modern English Political Economy*, Dublin: M.H. Gill and Son.

Dillon, William (1888), *Life of John Mitchel*, London: Kegan, Paul, Trench and Co.

Dinwiddy, John R. (1989), 'English Radicals and the French Revolution, 1800–1850', in *The Transformation of Political Culture 1789–1848*, François Furet and Mona Ozouf, eds, Oxford: Pergamon Press.

Dopfer, Kurt (1993), 'On the Significance of Gustav Schmoller's Contribution to Modern Economics', *History of Economic Ideas*, 1(2).

Dore, Mohammed, Sukhamoy Chakravarty and Richard Godwin (eds) (1988), *John von Neumann and Modern Economics*, Oxford: Clarendon.

Dovring, Folke (1996), *Leninism: Political Economy as Pseudoscience*, Westport, Conn.: Praeger.

Dow, Geoff (1992), 'The Economic Consequences of Economists', *Australian Journal of Political Science*, 27.

Drewnowski, Jan (1979), 'The Central Planning Office on Trial: an Account of the Beginnings of Stalinism in Poland', *Soviet Studies*, 31(1).

Dreyer, Jacob S. (1974), 'The Evolution of Marxist Attitudes toward Marginalist Techniques', *History of Political Economy*, 6(1).

Driver, Cecil (1946), *Tory Radical. The Life of Richard Oastler*, New York: Oxford University Press.

Drucker, Peter F. (1940), *The End of Economic Man*, London: Basic Books.

Durkheim, Emile (1967), *Socialism*, edited and with an introduction by Alvin W. Gouldner, translated by Charlotte Sattler, New York: Collier Books.

Dutton, H.I. and John King (1985), 'An Economic Exile: Edward Stillingfleet Cayley, 1802–1862', *History of Political Economy*, 17(2).

Eagleton, Terry (1999), *Scholars and Rebels in Nineteenth-Century Ireland*, Oxford: Blackwell.

Eastwood, David (1989), 'Robert Southey and the Intellectual Origins of Romantic Conservatism', *English Historical Review*, 104(411).

Eastwood, David (2000), 'History, Politics and Reputation: E.P. Thompson Reconsidered', *History*, 85(280).

Edwards, David W. (1977), 'Count Joseph Marie de Maistre and Russian Educational Policy, 1803–1828', *Slavic Review*, 36.

Edwards, Edward (1823), 'Ecclesiastical Revenues', *Quarterly Review*, 29(53).

Edwards, Ruth Dudley (1993), *The Pursuit of Reason*: The Economist, *1843–1993*, London: Hamish Hamilton.

Ekelund, Robert B. (1966), 'A British Rejection of Economic Orthodoxy', *Southwestern Social Science Quarterly*, 47(2).

Ekelund, Robert B. and Emilie S. Olsen (1973), 'Comte, Mill and Cairns: the Positivist-Empiricist Interlude in Late Classical Economics', *Journal of Economic Issues*, 7(3).

Eliade, Mircea (1959), *The Sacred and the Profane: the Nature of Religion*, New York: Harper and Row

Ellis, Gene (1981), 'The Backward-Bending Supply Curve of Labor in Africa: Models, Evidence and Interpretation – and Why It Makes a Difference', *Journal of Developing Areas*, 15(2).

Ely, Richard T. (1891), *An Introduction to Political Economy*, London: Swann Sonnenschein.

Enfantin, Barthélemy-Prosper [1828] (1972), 'The Doctrine of Saint-Simon' in *The Doctrine of Saint-Simon: an Exposition; First Year, 1828–1829*, translated by Georg

G. Iggers, New York: Schocken Books. (Published anonymously and written by Enfantin.)

Enfantin, Barthélemy Prosper (1832), *Économie Politique et Politique*, second edition, Paris.

Engels, F. [1844] (1973), 'Outlines of a Critique of Political Economy', in Karl Marx, *Economic and Philosophic Manuscripts of 1844*, Dirk J. Struik, ed., London: Lawrence & Wishart.

Engels, Friedrich [1845] (1948), *The Condition of the Working Class in England*, translated and edited by W.O. Henderson and W.H. Chaloner, Stanford: Stanford University Press.

Engels, Friedrich [1894] (1947), *Herr Eugen Dühring's Revolution in Science (Anti-Dühring)*, E. Wattenberg, ed., Moscow: Foreign Languages Publishing House.

Epstein, Klaus (1966), *The Genesis of German Conservatism*, Princeton: Princeton University Press

Epsztein, Leon (1966), *L'Économie et la Morale aux Débuts du Capitaliste Industrie en France et en Grande-Bretagne*, Paris: Armand Colin.

Evans, Eric J. (1976), *The Contentious Tithe: the Tithe Problem and English Agriculture, 1750–1850*, London: Routledge and Kegan Paul.

Eucken, Walter (1938), 'Die Uberwindung des Historismus' ('The Downfall of Historicism') *Schmollers Jahrbuch*, 62(2).

Eucken, Walter (1940), 'Wissenschaft [Science] im Stile Schmollers', *Weltwirtschaftliches Archiv*, 52.

Eucken, Walter (1948), 'Heinrich von Stackelberg', *Economic Journal*, 58(1).

Eysenck, H.J. (1990), *Rebel with a Cause*, London: W.H. Allen.

Faccarello, Gilbert (1998), 'Galiani, Necker and Turgot', in *Studies in the History of French Political Economy: from Bodin to Walras*, Gilbert Faccarello, ed., London: Routledge.

Fain, John Tyree (1956), *Ruskin and the Economists*, Nashville: Vanderbilt University Press.

Fetter, F.A. (1925), 'Economists and the Public', *American Economic Review*, 15(1).

Fetter, Frank Whiston (1958), 'The Economic Articles in the *Quarterly Review* and their Authors, 1809–1852', *Journal of Political Economy*, 66(1).

Fetter, Frank Whiston (1960), 'The Economic Articles in the *Blackwood's Edinburgh Magazine* and their Authors, 1817–1853', *Scottish Journal of Political Economy*, 66.

Fetter, Frank Whiston (1965), 'Economic Controversy in the British Reviews, 1802–1850', *Economica*, 32 (108).

Fetter, Frank Whiston (1980), *The Economist in Parliament: 1780–1868*, Durham, North Carolina: Duke University Press.

Feuer, Lewis S. (1963), *The Scientific Intellectual*, New York: Basic Books.

Fiering, Norman S. (1976), 'Irresistible Compassion: an Aspect of Eighteenth-Century Sympathy and Humanitarianism', *Journal of the History of Ideas*, 37(2).

Fitzhugh, George [1854] (1960), 'Sociology for the South or; the Failure of Free Society', in *Ante-Bellum*, Harvey Wish, ed., New York: Capricorn Books.

Flubacher, Joseph F. (1950), *The Concept of Ethics in the History of Economics*, New York: Vantage Press

Fontana, Biancamaria (1985), *Rethinking the Politics of Commercial Society: the Edinburgh Review 1802–1832*, Cambridge: Cambridge University Press.

Ford, George H. (1947/48), 'The Governor Eyre Case in England', *University of Toronto Quarterly*, 17.

Forget, E.L. (1992), 'J.S. Mill and the Tory School: the Rhetorical Value of Recantation', *History of Political Economy*, 24(1).

Fourier, Charles (1828), *Political Economy Made Easy. A Sketch*, London: Sherwood.

Fox, Robin (1985), 'Anthropology', in *The Social Science Encylopedia*, first edition, London: Routledge and Kegan Paul.

Foxwell, H.S. (1887), 'The Economic Movement in England', *Quarterly Journal of Economics*, 2(1).

Foxwell, H.S. [1899] (1962), 'Introduction', in Anton Menger, *The Right to the Whole Produce of Labour*, New York: Augustus M. Kelley.

Frank, André Gunder (1976), *Economic Genocide in Chile: Monetarist Theory versus Humanity: Two Open Letters to Arnold Harberger and Milton Friedman*, Nottingham: Spokesman Books.

Frank, Robert H., Thomas Gilovich and Dennis T. Regen (1993), 'Does Studying Economics Inhibit Cooperation?', *Journal of Economic Perspectives*, 7(2).

Frankel, Herbert S. (1992), *An Economist's Testimony: the Autobiography of S. Herbert Frankel*, Oxford: Oxford Centre for Postgraduate Hebrew Studies.

Frey, Bruno S. (1983), 'Consensus, Dissension and Ideology among Economists in Various European Countries and in the United States', *European Economic Review*, 23(1).

Friedman, Milton (1953), 'The Methodology of Positive Economics', *Essays in Positive Economics*, Chicago: University of Chicago Press.

Friedman, M. (1967), 'Value Judgements in Economics', in *Human Values and Economic Policy: a Symposium*, Sidney Hook, ed., New York: New York University Press.

Friedman, M. (1986), 'Economists and Economic Policy', *Economic Inquiry*, 24(1).

Fuller, Dan A., Rihad M. Alston and Michael B. Vaughn (1995), 'The Split between Political Parties on Economic Issues: a Survey of Republicans, Democrats and Economists', *Eastern Economic Journal*, 21(2).

Gaffney, Mason and Fred Harrison (1994), *The Corruption of Economics*, London: Shepheard-Walwyn.

Galiani, Ferdinando (1881), *L'Abbé F. Galiani Correspondance*, Luciu Perey and Gaston Maugras, eds, Paris: Calmann-Lévy.

Galiani, Ferdinando (1968), *Dialogues entre M. Marquis de Roquemaure, et Ms. le Chevalier Zanobi*, Philip Koch, ed., Frankfurt am Main: Klostermann.

Galt, John [1821] (1936), *Annals of the Parish*, D.S. Meldrum and William Roughead, eds, Edinburgh: John Grant.

Geddes, Patrick [1884] (1973), *John Ruskin. Economist*, Folcroft, Pa.: Folcroft Library.

Gellner, Ernest (1979), *Spectacles & Predicaments: Essays in Social Theory*, Cambridge: Cambridge University Press.

Gilder, George F. (1982), *Wealth and Poverty*, London: Buchan & Enright.

Gilmour, Robin (1967), 'The Gradgrind School: Political Economy in the Classroom', *Victorian Studies*, 11(2).

Gimpel, Jean (1969), *The Cult of Art: Against Art and Artists*, London: Weidenfeld & Nicolson.

Gittens, Ross (2001), 'Economical with Generosity', *Sydney Morning Herald*, 16 April 2001.

Glasberg, Victor M. (1974), 'Intent and Consequences: the "Jewish Question" in the French Socialist Movement of the Late Nineteenth Century', *Jewish Social Studies*, 36(1).

Godechot, Jacques (1971), *The Counter-Revolution. Doctrine and Action. 1789–1804*, New York: Howard Fertig.

Goic, Srecko (1996), 'Attitudes to the Market System (Market Economy) among Students of Economics (An International Comparison)', *Management*, 1(1).

Goldberg, Michael (1972), 'From Bentham to Carlyle: Dickens' Political Development', *Journal of the History of Ideas*, 33(1).

Golytsin, Dmitrii Alekseevich (1796), *De l'Esprit des Économistes ou les Économistes Justifiés d'avoir Posé leurs Principes es Bases de la Révolution Française*, Brunswick.

Goodwin, Craufurd D.W. (1968), 'Economic Ideas in the Development of Jamaica', *South Atlantic Quarterly*, 67(2).

Gordon, B.J. (1965), 'Say's Law, Effective Demand, and the Contemporary British Periodicals, 1820–1850', *Economica*, 32(128).

Gordon, Scott (1991), *The History and Philosophy of Social Science*, London: Routledge.

Gossett, Thomas F. (1963), *Race: the History of an Idea in America*, Dallas: Southern Methodist University Press.

Graham, John R. (1996), 'Is a Group of Economists Better than One? Than None?', *Journal of Business*, 69(2).

Graham, Loren R. (1993), *The Ghost of the Executed Engineer: Technology and the Fall of the Soviet Union*, Cambridge, Mass.: Harvard University Press.

Grampp, William D. (1960), *The Manchester School of Economics*, Stanford: Stanford University Press.

Grampp, William D. (1965), *Economic Liberalism: the Classical View*, New York: Random House.

Grampp, William D. (1973), 'Classical Economics and its Moral Critics', *History of Political Economy*, 5(2).

Grampp, William D. (1976), 'Scots, Jews and Subversives among the Dismal Scientists', *Journal of Economic History*, 36(3).

Gray, John (1995), *Enlightenment's Wake: Politics and Culture at the Close of the Modern Age*, London: Routledge.

Gray, John (1998), *False Dawn: the Delusions of Global Capitalism*, London: Granta Books.

Green, F. and Petter Nore (eds) (1977), *Economics, an Anti-Text*, London: Macmillan.

Green, Martin (1964), *Science and the Shabby Curate of Poetry: Essays about the Two Cultures*, London: Longman.

Green, S.J.D. (1995), 'The Tawney–Strauss Connection: on Historicism and Values in the History of Ideas', *Journal of Modern History*, 67.

Groenewegen, Peter (2000), 'The Political Economy of John Ruskin (1819–1900): a Centenary Assessment', unpublished paper, 2000 Conference of the History of Economic Thought Society of Australia.

Groenewegen, Peter (2001), 'Thomas Carlyle, "The Dismal Science" and the Contemporary Political Economy of Slavery', *History of Economics Review*, 34.

Gross, John (1991), *The Rise and Fall of the Man of Letters: Aspects of English Literary Life since 1800*, Harmondsworth: Penguin Books.

Gross P.R. and N. Levitt (1994), *Higher Superstition. The Academic Left and its Quarrels with Science*, Baltimore: Johns Hopkins University Press.

Grove, Richard (1994), *Green Imperialism. Colonial Expansionism, Tropical Island Edens, and the Origins of Environmentalism 1601–1860*, Cambridge: Cambridge University Press.

Guillaume, Marc (ed.) (1986), *L'État des Sciences Sociales en France*, Paris: La Découverte.

Gunton, George (1891), *Principles of Social Economics Inductively Considered and Practically Applied with Criticisms on Current Theories*, New York: G.P. Putnam's Sons.

Guy, W. (1848), 'The Plague of Beggars', *Fraser's Magazine*, 37.

Halévy, Élie [1928] (1949a), *The Growth of Philosophic Radicalism*, translated by Mary Morris, London: Faber & Faber.

Halévy, Élie (1949b), *The Liberal Awakening, 1815–1830*, translated by E.I. Watkin, London: Ernest Benn.

Halévy, Élie (1967), *The Era of Tyrannies: Essays on Socialism and War*, translated by R.K. Webb, London: Allen Lane.

Hall, Charles A.S. (1990), 'Sanctioning Resource Depletion: Economic Development and Neo-Classical Economics', *Ecologist*, 20(3).

Halle, Louis J. (1965), 'Marx's Religious Drama', *Encounter*, 25(4).

Halliday, James L. (1950), *Mr Carlyle, my Patient. A Psychosomatic Biography*, New York: Grune and Stratton.

Hamilton, C. (1994), *The Mystic Economist*, Canberra: Willow Park Press.

Hamilton, Richard F. and Lowell L. Hargens (1993), 'The Politics of the [US] Professors: Self-Identifications, 1969–1984', *Social Forces*, 1(3).

Harman, P.M. (1982), *Energy, Force, and Matter: the Conceptual Development of Nineteenth-Century Physics*, Cambridge: Cambridge University Press.

Harris, Abram L. (1942), 'Sombart and German (National) Socialism', *Journal of Political Economy*, 50(6).

Harrison, Alex (1994), 'Aspects of Nineteenth-Century Thought and National Socialism with Reference to the Economic and Social Ideas of Albert Speer and Otto Ohlendorf', thesis, University of Warwick.

Harrison, Frederic (1865), 'The Limits of Political Economy', *The Fortnightly Review*, 1.

Harrison, Frederic (1911), *Autobiographic Memoirs*, London: Macmillan.

Hasek, Carl William (1925), *The Introduction of Adam Smith's Doctrines into Germany*, New York: Columbia University Press.

Hay, P.R. (1988), 'The Contemporary Environment Movement as Neo-Romanticism: a Re-Appraisal from Tasmania', *Environmental Review*, 12(4).

Hayek, F.A. (1939), 'Introduction', in *An Enquiry into the Nature and Effects of the Paper Credit of Great Britain*, London: George, Allen and Unwin.

Hayek, F.A. (1952), *The Counter-Revolution of Science: Studies on the Abuse of Reason*, Glencoe, Ill.: Free Press.

Hayek, Friedrich A. von (1976), *Law, Legislation and Liberty: a New Statement of the Liberal Principles of Justice and Political Economy*, vol. 2, *The Mirage of Social Justice*, London: Routledge and Kegan Paul.

Hazlitt, William [1825] (1902), *The Plain Speaker: Opinions on Books, Men and Things*, William Carew Hazlitt, ed., London: George Bell and Sons.

Hebard, Grace Raymond (1958), 'Henry Charles Carey', *Dictionary of American Biography*, Allen Johnson and Dumas Malone, eds, New York: Charles Scribner's Sons.

Heilbronner, Robert L. (1970), 'On the Limited "Relevance" of Economics', *The Public Interest*, 21.

Henderson, Hazel (1978), *Creating Alternative Futures: the End of Economics*, New York: Berkley Publishing.

Henderson, Hazel (1981), *The Politics of the Solar Age. Alternatives to Economics*, New York: Anchor Press.

Henderson, James P. (1985), 'An English Communist, Mr Bray [and] his Remarkable Work', *History of Political Economy*, 17(1).

Henderson, W.O. (1982), 'Friedrich List and the Protectionists', *Journal of Institutional and Theoretical Economics*, 138(2).

Henderson, W.O. (1983), *Friedrich List: Economist and Visionary 1789–1846*, London: Cass.

Herbst, Ludolf (1982), *Der Totale Krieg und die Ordnung der Wirtschaft: die Kriegswirtschaft im Spannungsfeld von Politik, Ideologie und Propaganda 1939–1945*, Stuttgart: Deutsche Verlags-Anstalt.

Herold, J. Christopher (1955), *The Mind of Napoleon: a Selection from his Written and Spoken Words*, New York: Columbia University Press.

Heske, Henning (1986), 'German Geographical Research in the Nazi Period: a Content Analysis of the Major Geography Journals, 1925–1945', *Political Geography Quarterly*, 5(3).

Hewins, William Albert Samuel (1921), 'Oastler', in *Dictionary of National Biography*, Sir Leslie Stephen and Sir Sidney Lee, eds, London: L. Milford.

Heyne, Paul (1978), 'Economics and Ethics: the Problem of Dialogue', in *Belief and Ethics*, W. Widick Schroeder and Gibson Winter, eds, Chicago: Center for the Scientific Study of Religion.

Hicks, Granville (1937), 'The Literary Opposition to Utilitarianism', *Science and Society*, 1(4).

Higley, J., D. Deacon and D. Smart (1979), *Elites in Australia*, London: Routledge and Kegan Paul.

Hildebrand, Bruno (1848), *Der Nationalökonomie der Gegenwart und Zukunft*, Frankfurt.

Hilferding, Rudolf (1949), 'Böhm-Bawerk's Criticism of Marx', in Eugen Böhm-Bawerk, *Karl Marx and the Close of his System*, New York: Augustus M. Kelley.

Hill, Christopher (1964), *Society and Puritanism in Pre-Revolutionary England*, London: Secker & Warburg.

Hilton, Boyd (1988), *The Age of Atonement: the Influence of Evangelicalism on Social and Economic Thought, 1795–1865*, Oxford: Clarendon Press.

Hilton, Tim (1985), *John Ruskin: the Early Years, 1819–1859*, New Haven: Yale University Press.

Hobson, J.A. (1902), *Imperialism: a Study*, London: James Nisbet.

Hodgson, Geoffrey M. (2001), *How Economics Forgot History*, London: Routledge.

Hodgson, Judith F. (1974), 'Satan Humanized: Eighteenth-Century Illustrations of Paradise Lost', *Eighteenth Century Life*, 1(2).

Hofman, Amos (1993), 'Opinion, Illusion, and the Illusion of Opinion: Barruel's Theory of Conspiracy', *Eighteenth-Century Studies*, 27(1).

Hollis, Martin and Edward J. Nell (1975), *Rational Economic Man: a Philosophical Critique of Neo-Classical Economics*, London: Cambridge University Press.

Holloway, John (1953), *The Victorian Sage: Studies in Argument*, London: Macmillan.

Houghton, Walter E. (1952), 'Victorian Anti-intellectualism', *Journal of the History of Ideas*, 13(3).

Howard, M.C. and John King (1989), *A History of Marxian Economics*, vol. 1, London: Macmillan

Hudson, Liam (1985) 'Psychology', in *The Social Science Encyclopedia*, first edition, London: Routledge and Kegan Paul.

Hume, David [1777] (1975), *Enquiries Concerning Human Understanding and Concerning the Principles of Morals*, L.A. Selby-Bigge and P.H. Nidditch, eds, Oxford: Clarendon.

Hume, David (1985), *Essays, Moral, Political and Literary*, Eugene F. Miller, ed., Indianapolis: Liberty Classics.

Hunt, R.N. Carew (1963), *The Theory and Practice of Communism. An Introduction*, London: Geoffrey Bles.

Huskisson, W. (William) (1976), *Essays on Political Economy: in which are Illustrated the Principal Causes of the Present National Distress with Appropriate Remedies*, Canberra: Department of Economic History, Australian National University.

Hutchison, T.W. (1938), *The Significance and Basic Postulates of Economics*, London: Macmillan.

Hutchison, T.W. (1964), *'Positive' Economics and Policy Objectives*, London: George Allen and Unwin.

Hutchison, Terence W. (1988), 'Gustav Schmoller and the Problems of Today', *Journal of Institutional and Theoretical Economics*, 144(3).

Hutt, W.H. (1936), *Economists and the Public: a Study of Competition and Opinion*, London: Jonathan Cape.

Ikeo, Aiko (1996), 'The Internationalization of Economics in Japan', *History of Political Economy*, 28(0), Supplement.

Inglis, Brian (1971), *Poverty and the Industrial Revolution*, London: Hodder and Stoughton.

Ingram, John Kells [1888] (1910), *A History of Political Economy*, London: Adam and Charles Black.

Irwin, Douglas A. (1996), *Against the Tide: an Intellectual History of Free Trade*, Princeton, NJ: Princeton University Press.

Iurovski, Vladimir Evgen'evich (1995), 'Arkhitektor Denezhnoi Reformy 1922–1924 Godov' (The Architect of the Monetary Reform of 1922–24), *Voprosy Istorii*, 2.

Jasny, Naum (1972), *Soviet Economists of the Twenties: Names to be Remembered*, Cambridge: Cambridge University Press.

Jefferson, J.M. (1972), 'Industrialisation and Poverty: in Fact and Fiction', in *The Long Debate on Poverty*, London: The Institute of Economic Affairs.

Johnson, Chalmers and E.B. Keehn (1994), 'A Disaster in the Making. Rational Choice and Asian Studies', *National Interest*, 36.

Johnson, Harry (1968), 'Are the Economists to Blame?', *Encounter*, 30(5).

Johnson, Harry G. (1975), *On Economics and Society*, Chicago: University of Chicago Press.

Jolly, Pierre (1956), *Du Pont de Nemours: Soldat de la Liberté*, Paris: Presses Universitaires de France.

Jones, Richard [1831] (1956), *An Essay on the Distribution of Wealth and the Sources of Taxation*, New York: Kelley and Millman.

Judt, Tony (1986), *Marxism and the French Left: Studies in Labour and Politics in France, 1830–1981*, Oxford: Clarendon Press.

Kadish, Alon (1982), *The Oxford Economists in the Late Nineteenth Century*, Oxford: Clarendon Press.

Kadish, Alon (1986), *Apostle Arnold: the Life and Death of Arnold Toynbee 1852–1883*, Durham: Duke University Press.

Kanth, Ranjani Kannepalli (1997), *Against Economics. Rethinking Political Economy*, Brookfield, USA: Ashgate.

Kaplan, Fred (1983), *Thomas Carlyle. A Biography*, Cambridge: Cambridge University Press.

Kaplan, Steven L. (1976), *Bread, Politics and Political Economy in the Reign of Louis XV*, vol. 1, The Hague: Martinus Nijhoff.

Kates, Steven (1998), *Say's Law and the Keynesian Revolution: How Macroeconomic Theory Lost its Way*, Cheltenham: Edward Elgar.

Katsenelinboigen, Aron (1980), *Soviet Economic Thought and Political Power in the USSR*, New York: Pergamon Press.

Katsenelinboigen, Aron (1981), 'Jews in Soviet Economic Science', *Soviet Jewish Affairs*, 11(1).

Kaufman, B. (1994), *The Evolution and Origins of the Field of Industrial Relations*, New York: ILR press.

Keating, Barry (1981), 'United Way Contributions: Anomalous Philanthropy', *Quarterly Review of Economics and Business*, 21(1).

Keen, S. (2001), *Debunking Economics: the Naked Emperor of the Social Sciences*, Sydney: Pluto Press.

Kellock, James (1942), 'Ranade and After: a Study of the Development of Economic Thought in India', *Indian Journal of Economics*, 22.

Kelman, Steven (1981a), 'Economists and the Environmental Muddle', *The Public Interest*, 64.

Kelman, Steven (1981b), *What Price Incentives? Economists and the Environment*, Boston, Mass.: Auburn House.

Keohane, Nannerl O. (1978), 'The Masterpiece of Policy in our Century: Rousseau on the Morality of the Enlightenment', *Political Theory*, 6(4).

Keppler, Jan Horst (1994), 'Luigi Amoroso (1886–1965), Mathematical Economist, Italian Corporatist', *History of Political Economy*, 26(4).

Ketkar, V. Shridhar (1914), *An Essay on Indian Economics*, Calcutta: Thacker, Spink and Co.

Keynes, J.M. [1936] (1973), *The General Theory of Employment Interest and Money*, London: Macmillan.

Keynes, J.M. (1940), *How to Pay for the War. A Radical Plan for the Chancellor of the Exchequer*, London: Macmillan.

Khrushchev, N. (1971), *Khrushchev Remembers*, Edward Crankshaw, ed., London: Andre Deutsch.

King-Hall, Stephen and N.F. Hall (1933), *The Economist in the Witness Box*, London: Ivor Nicholson and Watson.

Kisaki, Kiyoji (1979), 'Controversy on the *Noblesse Commerçante* between Abbé Coyer and Chevalier D'Arcq', *Kyoto University Economic Review*, 49(1–2).

Kitchin, Donald K. (1933), 'Will Economics Follow the Robbins Road?', *Scrutiny*, 2(2).

Klein, Judy L. (1999), 'The Rise of "Non-October" Econometrics: Kondratiev and Slutsky at the Moscow Conjuncture Institute', *History of Political Economy*, 31(1).

Klinck, David (1994), 'The French Counterrevolution and the Rise of Sociology: the Question of Modernity of Louis de Bonald's Science of Society', *Consortium on Revolutionary Europe 1750–1850*.

Knudsen, Jonathan B. (1986), *Justus Möser and the German Enlightenment*, Cambridge: Cambridge University Press.

Koch, Mark (1989), 'Utilitarian and Reactionary Arguments for Almsgiving in Wordsworth's, "The Old Cumberland Beggar"', *Eighteenth-Century Life*, 3(3).

Kolm, S. (1978), 'Science Économique et Position Politique', *Revue Économique*, 29(4).

Kondratiev, Nikolai D. (1998), *The Works of Nikolai D Kondratiev*, 4 vols, Natali Makasheva, Warren J. Samuels and Vincent Barnett, eds, London: Pickering and Chatto.

Konow, James (1994), 'The Political Economy of Heinrich von Stackelberg', *Economic Inquiry*, 32.

Koot, Gerard M. (1975), 'T.E. Cliffe Leslie, Irish Social Reform, and the Origins of the English Historical School of Economics', *History of Political Economy*, 7(3).

Koot, Gerald M. (1977), 'H.S. Foxwell and the English Historical Economists', *Journal of Economic Issues*, 11(3).

Koot, Gerald M. (1987), *English Historical Economics 1870–1926*, Cambridge: Cambridge University Press.

Kopstein, Jeffrey (1997), *The Politics of Economic Decline in East Germany, 1945–1989*, Chapel Hill and London: University of North Carolina Press.

Krause, Günter (1998), 'Economics in Eastern Germany, 1945–1990', in *Economic Thought in Communist and Post-Communist Europe*, Hans-Jurgen Wagener, ed., London: Routledge.

Kristol, Irving (1980), 'Rationalism in Economics', in *The Crisis in Economic Theory*, Daniel Bell and Irving Kristol, eds, New York: Basic Books.

Krueger, Anne O. (1991), 'Report of the Commission on Graduate Education in Economics', *Journal of Economic Literature*, 29(3).

Krugman, Paul R. (1994), *Peddling Prosperity: Economic Sense and Nonsense in the Age of Diminished Expectations*, New York: W.W. Norton.

Kuczynski, Jürgen (1937), *New Fashions in Wage Theory: Keynes – Robinson – Hicks – Rueff*, London: Lawrence and Wishart.

Kuczynski, Jürgen (1939), *The Condition of the Workers in Great Britain, Germany and the Soviet Union*, London: Victor Gollancz.

Kuczynski, Jürgen (1952), *Die Politökonomische Apologetik des Monopolkapitals in der Periode der Allgemeine Krise des Kapitalismus*, Berlin: Dietz Verlag.

Kuczynski, Jürgen (1956), 'Bezwgledne Zubozenie a Sprawa Wyzywienia w Niemczech' [Absolute Impoverishment and the Problem of Food Consumption in Germany], *Kwartalnik Historyczny*, 63(4–5).

La Nauze, J.A. (1949), *Political Economy in Australia: Historical Studies*, Melbourne: Melbourne University Press.

Laband, David N. and Richard O. Beil (1999), 'Are Economists More Selfish Than Other, "Social", Scientists?', *Public Choice*, 100(1–2).

Lacy, George (1888), *Liberty and Law: Being an Attempt at the Refutation of the Individualism of Mr. Herbert Spencer and the Political Economists; an Exposition of Natural Rights, and of the Principles of Justice, and of Socialism; and a Demonstration of the Worthlessness of the Supposed Dogmas of Orthodox Political Economy. Addressed to the Youth of Great Britain and the Colonies*, London: S. Sonnenschein, Lowery & Co.

Ladd, Everett Carll and Seymour Martin Lipset (1975), *The Divided Academy: Professors and Politics*, New York: McGraw-Hill.

Lambi, Ivo Nikolai (1963), *Free Trade and Protection in Germany 1868–1879*, Weisbaden: Fritz Steiner Verlag.

Leamer, Edward E. (1983), 'Let's Take the Con Out of Econometrics', *American Economic Review*, 73(1).

Leavis, F.R. (1963), *Two Cultures? The Significance of C.P. Snow*, London: Pantheon.

Lebeau, Auguste (1903), *Condillac, Économiste*, Paris: Guillaumin.

Lebrun, Richard A. (1988), *Joseph de Maistre: an Intellectual Militant*, Kingston: McGill-Queen's University Press.

Leijonhufvud, Axel (1968), *On Keynesian Economics and the Economics of Keynes: a Study in Monetary Theory*, New York: Oxford University Press.

Leijonhufvud, Axel (1998), 'Three Items for the Macroeconomic Agenda', *Kyklos*, 51(2).

Lekachman, Robert (1976), *Economists at Bay. Why the Experts Will Never Solve Your Problems*, New York: McGraw-Hill.

Lenin, V.I. [1916] (1996a), *Imperialism: the Highest Stage of Capitalism: a Popular Outline*, London: Junius.

Lenin, V.I. (1996b), *The Unknown Lenin: from the Secret Archive*, Richard Pipes, ed., New Haven: Yale University Press.

Leontief, Wasilly (1982), 'Academic Economics', *Science*, 217(4554).

Lepenies, Wolf (1988), *Between Literature and Science: the Rise of Sociology*, Cambridge: Cambridge University Press.

Lerner, Abba (1938), 'New Fashions in Wage Theory. Keynes–Robinson–Hicks–Reuff', *Economic Journal*, 48(1).

Leroux, Jules (1841), 'Adam Smith', in *Encyclopédie Nouvelle*, Pierre Leroux and Jean Reynaud, eds, Paris: Charles Gosselin.

Leroux, Pierre (1849), *Malthus et les Économistes, ou y aura-t-il Toujours des Pauvres?*, Boussac.

Leroux, Pierre (1850), *Oeuvres de Pierre Leroux*, Paris: Société Typographique.

Leslie, T.E.C. (1888), *Essays in Political Economy*, London: Longmans, Green and Co.

Levere, Trevor H. (1981), *Poetry Realized in Nature: Samuel Taylor Coleridge and Early Nineteenth-Century Science*, Cambridge: Cambridge University Press.

Levy, David (1986), 'S.T. Coleridge Replies to Adam Smith's "Pernicious Opinion": a Study in Hermetic Social Engineering', *Interpretation*, 14.

Levy, David (2001), *How the Dismal Science Got its Name. Classical Economics and the Ur-Text of Racial Politics*, Ann Arbor: University of Michigan Press.

Levy, David and Sandra J. Peart (2001), 'The Secret History of the Dismal Science: Economics, Religion and Race in the Nineteenth Century', http://www.econlib.org/library/Columns/LevyPeartdismal.html.

Levy, Samuel Leon (1970), *Nassau W. Senior, 1790–1864: Critical Essayist, Classical Economist and Adviser of Governments*, Newton Abbot: David and Charles.

Lévy-Bruhl, Henri (1933), 'La Noblesse de France et le Commerce a la Fin de l'Ancien Régime', *Revue d'Histoire Moderne*, 8.

Lewis, George Cornewall (1875), *An Essay on the Influence of Authority in Matters of Opinion*, London: Longmans, Green.

Lewis, Martin W. (1992), *Green Delusions: an Environmental Critique of Radical Environmentalism*, Durham, NC: Duke University Press.

Lichtheim, George (1968), 'Socialism and the Jews', *Dissent*, July–August.

Liesse, André (1901), 'Un Professeur d'Économie Politique Sous La Restauration', *Journal des Economistes*, 56.

Lih, Lars T., Oleg V. Naumov and Oleg Khlevniuk (1995), 'Introduction', in *Stalin's Letters to Molotov, 1925–1936*, Lars T. Lih, Oleg V. Naumov and Oleg V. Khlevniuk eds, New Haven: Yale University Press.

Lilly, William Samuel (1907), *First Principles in Politics*, second edition, London: John Murray.

Lilly, William Samuel and Charles Stanton Devas (1904), 'Introduction', in *Sophisms of Free-Trade and Popular Political Economy Examined*, London: Lane.

Lindenfeld, David F. (1993), 'The Myth of the Older Historical School of Economics', *Central European History*, 26(4).

Lindenfeld, David F. (1997), *The Practical Imagination: the German Sciences of State in the Nineteenth Century*, Chicago: University of Chicago Press.

Linder, Marc (1977), *The Anti-Samuelson*, in collaboration with Julius Sensat, New York: Urizen Books.

Linguet, Simon Nicolas Henri (1767), *Théorie des Loix Civiles, ou Principes Fondamentaux de la Société*, London.

Linguet, Simon Nicolas Henri (1771), *Réponse aux Docteurs Modernes, ou, Apologie Pour l'Auteur de la Théories des Loix, et des Lettres sur cette Théorie. Avec la Réfutation du Système des Philosophes Économistes*, London

Linguet, Simon Nicolas Henri (1774), *Du Pain et du Bled*, London.

Linguet, Simon Nicolas Henri (1775), *Théorie du Libelle*, Amsterdam.

Linguet, Simon Nicolas Henri (1780), *Annales Politiques, Civiles et Litteraires*, 1.

Lipkes, Jeff (1999), *Politics, Religion and Classical Political Economy in Britain: John Stuart Mill and his Followers*, Basingstoke: Macmillan Press – now Palgrave Macmillan.

List, Friedrich [1827] (1909), 'American Political Economy', in *Life of Friedrich List and Selections from his Writings*, Margaret E Hirst, London: Smith, Elder and Co.

List, Friedrich [1841] (1909), 'National System of Political Economy', in Margaret E. Hirst, *Life of Friedrich List and Selections from his Writings*, London: Smith, Elder and Co.

Livingston, James C. (1973), 'Matthew Arnold and his Critics on the Truth of Christianity. A Reappraisal for the Centenary of Literature and Dogma', *Journal of the American Academy of Religion*, 41(3).

Locke, John [1691] (1823), *The Works*, London: Thomas Tess.

Lomask, Milton (1982), *Aaron Burr: the Conspiracy and Years of Exile 1805–1836*, New York: Farrar Straus Giroux.

Lonigan, Edna (1944), 'The Professors *versus* the People: Comment', *American Economic Review*, 34(2).

Louca, Francisco (1999), 'Nikolai Kondratiev and the Early Consensus and Dissensions about History and Statistics', *History of Political Economy*, 31(1).

Lovejoy, A.O. (1948), *Essays in the History of Ideas*, Baltimore: Johns Hopkins University Press.

Lowe, Philip and Jane Goyder (1983), *Environmental Groups in Politics*, London: Allen & Unwin.

Lui, F.T. (1975), 'Cagan's Hypothesis and the First Nationwide Inflation of Paper Money in World History', *Journal of Political Economy*, 83.

Lutfalla, M. (1976), 'Sismondi Aristophile', in *Histoire, Socialisme et Critique de l'Economie Politique*, Paris: Institut des Sciences Mathematiques et Économiques Appliquées.

Lux, Kenneth (1990), *Adam Smith's Mistake: how a Moral Philosopher Invented Economics and Ended Morality*, Boston: Shambhala.

Macaulay, T.B. [1830] (1865), 'Southey's Colloquies', *Lord Macaulay. Critical and Historical Essays*, London: Collins.

Macaulay, T.B. (1890), 'Bentham's Defence of Mill', in *Selected Essays and Miscellaneous Writings*, London: Routledge.

Macciò, Daniela Donnini and Roberto Romani (1996), 'All Equally Rich. Economic Knowledge in Italy, 1796–1799', *Research in the History of Economic Thought and Methodology*, 14.

Macfarlane, Allen (1987), *The Culture of Capitalism*, Oxford: Basil Blackwell.

Machlup, Fritz (1972), 'The Universal Bogey: Economic Man', in Maurice Peston and Bernard Corry, eds, *Essays in Honour of Lord Robbins*, London: Weidenfeld and Nicolson.

MacIntyre, Alasdair (1981), *After Virtue: a Study in Moral Theory*, London: Duckworth.

Mallet, Bernard (1902), *Mallet du Pan and the French Revolution*, London: Longmans, Green and Co.

Mallet, Charles Edward (1927), *A History of the University of Oxford*, vol. 3, London: Methuen.

Mallet du Pan, Jacques (1793), *Considérations sur la Nature de la Révolution de France*, London.

Maloney, John (1976), 'Marshall, Cunningham, and the Emerging Economics Profession', *Economic History Review*, 29(3).

Maloney, John (1985), *Marshall, Orthodoxy and the Professionalisation of Economics*, Cambridge: Cambridge University Press.

Maloney, John (1987), 'English Historical School', in *The New Palgrave: a Dictionary of Economics*, John Eatwell, Murray Milgate and Peter Newman, eds, vol. 3, London: Macmillan.

Malthus, T.R. [1803] (1986), *An Essay on the Principle of Population*, second edition, E.A. Wrigley and David Souden, eds, London: W. Pickering.

Malthus, T.R. [1798] (1993), *An Essay on the Principle of Population*, first edition, Geoffrey Gilbert, ed., Oxford: Oxford University Press.

Mandeville, Bernard [1732] (1924), *The Fable of the Bees: or Private Vices, Public Benefits*, F.B. Kaye, ed., Oxford: Clarendon.

Manne, Robert (1982), *The New Conservatism in Australia*, Melbourne: Oxford University Press.

Manne, Robert (1993), 'Economic Rationalism', in *Economic Rationalism: Dead End or Way Forward?*, S. King and P.J. Lloyd, eds, Sydney: Allen & Unwin.

Manoïlesco, Mihaïl (1931), *The Theory of Protection and International Trade*, London: P.S. King and Son.

Manoïlesco, Mihaïl (1934), *Le Siècle du Corporatisme*, Paris: Félix Alcan.

Marchal, André (1953), *La Pénsee Économique en France Depuis 1945*, Paris: Presses Universitaires de France.

Marchal, André (1951), 'La Crise Contemporaine de la Science Économique', *Banque*, January.

Marcus (1839), '*The Book* of *Murder!* Vade-mecum for the Commissioners and Guardians of the New Poor Law Throughout Great Britain and Ireland, Being an Exact Reprint of the Infamous Essay on the Possibility of Limiting Populousness*, London.

Martin, David A. (1985), 'R.H. Tawney's Normative Economic History of Capitalism', *Review of Social Economy*, 43(1).

Martinez-Allier, Juan (1987), *Ecological Economics: Energy, Environment, and Society*, Oxford: Basil Blackwell.

Marwell, Gerald and Ruth E. Ames (1981) 'Economists Free Ride, Does Anyone Else?: Experiments on the Provision of Public Goods, IV', *Journal of Public Economics*, 15(3).

Marx, Karl [1844] (1963), review of 'Bruno Bauer's, "Die Fähigkheit der Heutigen Juden und Christen, Freiz Zu Werden"', in *Karl Marx: Early Writings*, translated and edited by T.B. Bottomore, London: CA Watts

Marx, Karl [1847] (1963), *The Poverty of Philosophy*, New York: International Publishers.

Marx, Karl [1875] (1969), 'Critique of the Gotha Program', *Karl Marx and Friedrich Engels: Basic Writings on Politics and Philosophy*, Lewis S. Feuer, ed., London: Collins.

Marx, Karl [1887] (1954), *Capital. A Critique of Political Economy*, Moscow: Progress Publishers.

Marx, Karl and Friedrich Engels (1983), *Letters on 'Capital'*, translated by Andrew Drummond, London: New Park.

Maser, Werner (1974), *Hitler's Letters and Notes*, translated from the German by Arnold Pomerans, New York: Harper & Row.

Masuda, Etsusuke and Peter Newman (1981), 'Gray and Giffen Goods', *Economic Journal*, 91(364).

Mathews, R. (1991), 'Free Market Policies have been Disastrous', *Canberra Times*, 14 November.

Mauduit, Roger (1929), *Auguste Comte et la Science Économique*, Paris: Felix Alcan.

Mayer, Thomas (1980), 'Economics as a Hard Science: Realistic Goal or Wishful Thinking?', *Economic Inquiry*, 18(2).

Mayer, W. (1988), 'Schmoller's Research Programme, his Psychology, and the Autonomy of the Social Sciences', *Journal of Institutional and Theoretical Economics*, 144(3).

McCloskey, Donald N. (1983), 'The Rhetoric of Economics', *Journal of Economic Literature*, 21.

McCulloch, J.R. (1831), 'An Essay on the Distribution and Wealth, and the Sources of Taxation', *Edinburgh Review*, 54(107).

McCulloch, J.R. (1843), *A Dictionary Practical, Theoretical and Historical of Commerce and Commercial Navigation*, vol. 2, London: Longman, Brown, Green and Longmans.

McLeod, Hugh (1974), *Class and Religion in the Late Victorian City*, Connecticut: Archon Books.

McVeagh, John (1981), *Tradefull Merchants: the Portrayal of the Capitalist in Literature*, London: Routledge and Kegan Paul.

Mendes-Flohr, Paul R. (1976), 'Werner Sombart's: *The Jews and Modern Capitalism*. An Analysis of its Ideological Premises', *Year Book Leo Baeck Institute*, London: Secker & Warburg.

Mendès-France, Pierre and Gabriel Ardant (1955), *Economics and Action*, London: William Heinemann.

Middendorf, J.H. (1961), 'Samuel Johnson and Adam Smith', *Philological Quarterly*, 40(2).

Mill, James [1836] (1966), *Selected Economic Writings*, Chicago: Oliver and Boyd.

Mill, John Stuart [1848] (1965a), *Principles of Political Economy (Books I and II)*, vol. 2, *The Collected Works of John Stuart Mill*, London: Routledge and Kegan Paul.

Mill, John Stuart [1848] (1965b), *Principles of Political Economy (Books II–V)*, vol. 3, *The Collected Works of John Stuart Mill*, London: Routledge and Kegan Paul.

Mill, John Stuart [1873] (1924), *Autobiography*, New York: Columbia University Press.

Mill, John Stuart (1963), *The Earlier Letters, 1812–1848*, vol. 12, *Collected Works of John Stuart Mill*, London: Routledge and Kegan Paul.

Mill, John Stuart (n.d.) *Collected Works*, vol. 12, Toronto: University of Toronto Press.

Mills, C. Wright (1963), *The Marxists*, Harmondsworth: Penguin.

Mises, Ludwig von (1962), *The Ultimate Foundation of Economic Science: an Essay on Method*, Princeton, NJ: Van Nostrand.

Mishan, E.J. (1969), *Growth: the Price We Pay*, London: Staples Press.

Mishan, E.J. (1981), *Introduction to Political Economy*, London: Hutchinson.

Mitchell, Broadus (1958), 'Mathew Carey', in *Dictionary of American Biography*, Allen Johnson and Dumas Malone, eds, New York: Charles Scribner's Sons.

Mitchell, Harvey (1965), 'Hobson Revisited', *Journal of the History of Ideas*, 26(3).

Moffat, Robert Scott (1878), *The Economy of Consumption: an Omitted Chapter in Political Economy*, London: C. Kegan Paul & Co.

Molsberger, Josef (1985), 'Eucken, Walter' *New Palgrave Dictionary of Economics*, vol. 1, John Eatwell, Murray Milgate and Peter Newman, eds, London: Macmillan.

Mommsen, Hans (1991), 'The Political Legacy of the German Resistance: a Historiographical Critique', in *Contending with Hitler: Varieties of German Resistance in the Third Reich*, David Clay Large, ed., Cambridge: Cambridge University Press.

Morley, Neville (1998), 'Political Economy and Classical Antiquity', *Journal of the History of Ideas*, 59(1).

Morris-Suzuki, Tessa (1989), *A History of Japanese Economic Thought*, London: Routledge.

Morrow, Glenn R. (1969), *The Ethical and Economic Theories of Adam Smith*, New York: Augustus M. Kelley.

Morrow, Glenn R. (1939), 'Plato and Greek Slavery', *Mind*, 48.

Morrow, John (1990), *Coleridge's Political Thought: Property, Morality and the Limits of Traditional Discourse*, Basingstoke: Macmillan, Press – now Palgrave Macmillan.

Mozley, Thomas (1843), 'Agricultural Labour and Wages', *British Critic*, 33.

Murray, Les A. (1972), *Poems against Economics*, Sydney: Angus and Robertson.

Myrdal, Gunnar (1957), *Rich Lands and Poor: the Road to World Prosperity*, New York: Harper & Row.

Myrdal, Gunnar [1929] (1953), *The Political Element in the Development of Economic Theory*, translated from the German by Paul Streeten, London: Routledge & Kegan Paul.

Myrdal, Gunnar (1977), 'The Nobel Prize in Economics', *Challenge*, 20(1).

Nelson, Anitra (1999a), 'Marx and Medicine. Part I: Before the Publication of Das Kapital', *Journal of Medical Biography*, 7.

Nelson, Anitra (1999b), 'Marx and Medicine. Part II: After the Publication of Das Kapital', *Journal of Medical Biography*, 7.

Nicholls, A.J. (1994), *Freedom with Responsibility: the Social Market Economy in Germany, 1918–1963*, Oxford: Clarendon Press.

Nicholson, J.S. (1903), 'The Uses and Abuses of Authority in Economics', *Economic Journal*, 13.

Niehans, Jurg (1990), *A History of Economic Theory: Classic Contributions, 1720–1980*, Baltimore: Johns Hopkins University Press.

Nielson, Kia (1983), 'Engels on Morality and Moral Theorising', *Studies in Soviet Thought*, 26(3).

Nitti, Francesco S. [1895] (1911), *Catholic Socialism*, London: George Allen and Unwin.

Norman, E.R. (1976), *Church and Society in England, 1770–1970: a Historical Study*, Oxford: Clarendon Press.

Norton, Bryan G. (1991), 'Thoreau's Insect Analogies: Or Why Environmentalists Hate Mainstream Economists', *Environmental Ethics*, 13(1).

O'Brien D.P. (1975), *The Classical Economists*, Oxford: Clarendon Press.

O'Brien D.P. (1977), 'Torrens, McCulloch and Disraeli', *Scottish Journal of Political Economy*, 24(1).

O'Malley, Joseph (1976), 'Marx's "Economics" and Hegel's Philosophy of Right: an Essay on Marx's Hegelianism', *Political Studies*, 24(1).

Oakley, Allen (1994), *Classical Economic Man: Human Agency and Methodology in the Political Economy of Adam Smith and J.S. Mill*, Aldershot: Edward Elgar.

Oncken, A. (1926), 'Roscher', in *Palgrave's Dictionary of Political Economy*, vol. 3, Henry Higgs, ed., London: Macmillan.

Openkin, L.A. (1991), 'I.V. Stalin: Poslednii Prognoz Budeschchego' [Joseph Stalin: Last Prognosis for the Future], *Voprosy Istorii KPSS*, 7.

Ormerod, P. (1994), *The Death of Economics*, London: Penguin Australia.

Osborne, John W. (1984), 'William Cobbett's Anti-Semitism', *The Historian*, 47(1).

Owen, David (1964), *English Philanthropy, 1660–1960*, Cambridge, Mass.: Harvard University Press

Ozanam, Frederic (1865), 'Le Protestantisme et la Liberté', *Oeuvres Complètes de A.F. Ozanam*, Paris: J. Lecoffre.

Palter, Robert (1995), 'Hume and Prejudice', *Hume Studies*, 21(1).

Palyi (Melchior) [1928] (1966), 'The Introduction of Adam Smith on the Continent', in *Adam Smith, 1776–1926: Lectures to Commemorate the Sesquicentennial of the Publication of 'The Wealth of Nations'*, New York: Augustus M. Kelley.

Parker, Richard (1993), 'Can Economists Save Economics?', *American Prospect*, 13.

Paskoff, Benjamin (1983), *Linguet: Eighteenth-Century Intellectual Heretic of France*, Smithtown, N.Y.: Exposition Press.

Peacock, T.L. [1831] (1924), *The Misfortunes of Elphin and Crotchet Castle*, London: Constable.

Pearson, Heath (1999), 'Was There Really a German Historical School?', *History of Political Economy*, 31(3).

Pepper, David (1984), *The Roots of Modern Environmentalism*, London: Croom Helm.

Perrot, Jean-Claude (1984), 'Nouveautés: l'Économie Politique et ses Livres', *Histoire de l'Édition Francaise*, vol. 2, *Le Livre Triomphant: 1600–1830*, Paris: Promodis.

Persky, Joseph (1998), 'Wage Slavery', *History of Political Economy*, 30(4).

Péteri, György (1991), 'Academic Elite into Scientific Cadres: a Statistical Contribution to the History of the Hungarian Academy of Sciences, 1945–49', *Soviet Studies*, 43(2).

Péteri, György (1996), 'Controlling the Field of Academic Economics in Hungary, 1953–1976', *Minerva*, 34.

Péteri, György (1997), 'New Course Economics: the Field of Economic Research in Hungary after Stalin, 1953–6', *Contemporary European History*, 6(3).

Petrella, Frank (1963–64), 'Edmund Burke: a Liberal Practitioner of Political Economy', *Modern Age*, 8.

Petridis, Ray (1994), 'The Disappearance of Australian Economics: a Review Essay', *Research in the History of Economic Thought and Methodology*, 12.

Petropolous, Jonathan (2000), *The Faustian Bargain: the Art World in Nazi Germany*, Harmondsworth: Penguin.

Philippovich, Eugen von (1891), 'The Verein für Sozialpolitik', *Quarterly Journal of Economics*, 5.

Philippovich, Eugen von (1912), 'The Infusion of Socio-Political Ideas into the Literature of German Economics', *American Journal of Sociology*, 18(3).

Phillips, George Lewis (1949), *England's Climbing-Boys: a History of the Long Struggle to Abolish Child Labor in Chimneys*, Boston: Baker Library, Harvard Graduate School of Business Administration.

Pickering, John (1847), *The Working Man's Political Economy*, Cincinnati: Thomas Varney.

Pickering, Mary (1993), *Auguste Comte: an Intellectual Biography*, vol. 1, Cambridge: Cambridge University Press.

Place, Francis [1822] (1930), *Illustrations and Proofs of the Principle of Population*, by Francis Place, London: Allen & Unwin.

Pocock, J.G.A. (1985), *Virtue, Commerce, and History: Essays on Political Thought and History, Chiefly in the Eighteenth Century*, Cambridge: Cambridge University Press.

Polanyi, Karl [1944] (1957), *The Great Transformation*, Boston: Beacon Press.

Polanyi, Michael (1962), *Personal Knowledge: Towards a Post-Critical Philosophy*, second corrected edition, Chicago: University of Chicago Press.

Pons, Jordi (1999), 'Evaluating the OECD's Forecasts for Economic Growth', *Applied Economics*, 31(7).

Porwit, Krzysztof (1998), 'Looking Back at Economic Science in Poland, 1956–96', in *Economic Thought in Communist and Post-Communist Europe*, Hans-Jürgen Wagener, ed., London: Routledge.

Posnett, Macaulay Hutcheson (1882), *The Historical Method in Ethics, Jurisprudence and Political Economy*, London: Longmans Green and Co.

Postan, M. (1968), 'A Plague of Economists', *Encounter*, January.

Price, Russel (1988), 'Self-love, "Egoism" and *Ambizione* in Machiavelli's Thought', *History of Political Thought*, 9(2).

Priddat, Birger P. (1995), 'Intention and Failure of W. Roscher's Historical Method of National Economics', in *The Theory of Ethical Economy in the Historical School*, Peter Koslowski, ed., Berlin: Springer-Verlag.

Proudhon, P.J. (1846), *Systeme des Contradictions Économiques, ou Philosophie de la Misère*, Paris: Guillaumin.

Proudhon, P.J. (1886), *The Malthusians*, London: International Publishing Company.

Pusey, M. (1991), *Economic Rationalism in Canberra*, Cambridge: Cambridge University Press.

Quennell, Peter (1949), *John Ruskin. The Portrait of a Prophet*, New York: Viking Press.

Radcliffe, Evan (1993), 'Revolutionary Writing, Moral Philosophy and Universal Benevolence in the Eighteenth Century', *Journal of the History of Ideas*, 54(2).

Rae, John [1895] (1965), *Life of Adam Smith*, New York: A.M. Kelley.

Ramstad, Yngve and James L. Starkey (1995), 'The Racial Theories of John R. Commons', *Research in the History of Economic Thought and Methodology*, 13.

Ranade, M.G. [1892] (1899), 'Indian Political Economy', in *Essays on Indian Economics*, Bombay: Thacker and Co.

Rashid, Salim (1978), 'David Robinson and the Tory Macroeconomics of Blackwood's Edinburgh Magazine', *History of Political Economy*, 10(2).

Rashid, Salim (1979), 'Richard Jones and Baconian Historicism at Cambridge', *Journal of Economic Issues*, 8(1).

Rashid, Salim (1982), 'Josiah Tucker, Anglican Anti-Semitism, and the Jew Bill of 1753', *Historical Magazine of the Protestant Episcopal Church*, 51(2).

Rashid, Salim (1986), 'Economists and the Age of Chivalry: Notes on a Passage in Burke's Reflections', *Eighteenth-Century Studies*, 20(1).

Rashid, Salim (1994), 'John von Neumann, Scientific Method and Empirical Economics', *Journal of Economic Methodology*, 1(2).

Ravenstone, Piercy (1821), *A Few Doubts as to the Correctness of Some Opinions Generally Entertained on the Subjects of Population and Political Economy*, London: John Andrews.

Reder, Melvin W. (2000), 'The Anti-Semitism of Some Eminent Economists', *History of Political Economy*, 32(4).

Reiss, Hans Siegbert (1955), *The Political Thought of the German Romantics, 1793–1815*, Oxford: Blackwell.

Reybaud, Louis (1864), 'Les Chairs d'Économie Politique en France', *Revue des Deux Mondes*, 54.

Ricardo, David [1815] (1951), 'An Essay on the Influence of the Low Price of Corn on the Profits of Stock', in *The Works and Correspondence of David Ricardo*, Piero Sraffa, ed., vol. 4, Cambridge: Cambridge University Press.

Ricardo, David [1817] (1951), *On the Principles of Political Economy and Taxation*, Piero Sraffa, ed., Cambridge: Cambridge University Press.

Ricardo, David (1952a), *The Works and Correspondence of David Ricardo*, Piero Sraffa, ed., vol. 6: *Letters, 1810–1815*, Cambridge: Cambridge University Press.

Ricardo, David (1952b), *The Works and Correspondence of David Ricardo*, Piero Sraffa, ed., vol. 9: *Letters July 1821–1823*, Cambridge: Cambridge University Press.

Rice, C. Duncan (1975), *The Rise and Fall of Black Slavery*, London: Macmillan.

Ricketts, Martin and Edward Shoesmith (1990), *British Economic Opinion: a Survey of One Thousand Economists*, London: The Institute of Economic Affairs.

Rieter, Heinz and Matthias Schmolz (1993), 'The Ideas of German Ordoliberalism 1938–45: Pointing the Way to a New Economic Order', *European Journal of the History of Economic Thought*, 1(1).

Riha, Tomas J.F. (1985), 'Spann's Universalism – The Foundations of the Neoromantic Theory of the Corporative State', *Australian Journal of Politics and History*, 31(2).

Ringer, Fritz K. (1969), *The Decline of the German Mandarins. The German Academic Community, 1890–1933*, Cambridge, Mass.: Harvard University Press.

Roberts, David (1977), 'The Social Conscience of the Tory Periodicals', *Victorian Periodicals Newsletter*, 10(3).

Roberts, David (1979), *Paternalism in Early Victorian England*, London: Croom Helm.

Robinson, David (1827), 'The Faction', *Blackwood's Edinburgh Magazine*, 22 (131).

Robinson, David (1829), 'Political Economy', Nos. 1 and 2, *Blackwood's Edinburgh Magazine*, 26.

Robison, J. (1798), *Proofs of a Conspiracy against all the Religions and Governments of Europe, Carried on in the Secret Meetings of Freemasons, Illuminati and Reading Societies*, Edinburgh.

Roche, George Charles (1971), *Frédéric Bastiat: a Man Alone*, New Rochelle, NY: Arlington House.

Rogers, J.E.T. (1888), *The Economic Interpretation of History*, London: T. Fisher Unwin.

Roon, Ger van (1971), *German Resistance to Hitler: Count von Moltke and the Kreisau Circle*, translated by Peter Ludlow, London: Van Nostrand Reinhold Co.

Röpke, Wilhelm (1935), 'Fascist Economics', *Economica*, 2.

Röpke, Wilhelm (1947), *The Solution of the German Problem*, translated by E.W. Dickes, New York: G.P. Puttnam's Sons.

Röpke, Wilhelm (1960), 'National Socialism and Intellectuals', in *The Intellectuals: a Controversial Portrait*, George B. de Huszar, ed., New York: Free Press.

Roscher, Wilhelm (1878), *Principles of Political Economy*, translated by John H. Lalor, Chicago: Callaghan and Co.

Rose, R.B. (1998), *Tribunes and Amazons: Men and Women of Revolutionary France 1789–1791*, Sydney: Macleay Press.

Rosefielde, Steven (1996), 'Stalinism in Post-Communist Perspective: New Evidence on Killings, Forced Labour and Economic Growth in the 1930s', *Europe-Asia Studies*, 48(6).

Rothbard, Murray Newton (1995), *Economic Thought before Adam Smith: an Austrian Perspective on the History of Economic Thought*, Aldershot: Edward Elgar.

Rousseau, Jean-Jacques [1755] (1997a), 'Discourse on Political Economy', in *The Social Contract and Other Later Political Writings*, Victor Gourevitch, ed., Cambridge: Cambridge University Press.

Rousseau, Jean-Jacques (1997b), *The Social Contract and Other Later Political Writings*, Victor Gourevitch, ed., Cambridge: Cambridge University Press.

Ruskin, John [1862] (1967), *Unto This Last: Four Essays on the First Principles of Political Economy*, Lloyd J. Hubenka, ed., Lincoln: University of Nebraska Press.

Ruskin, John [1872] (1891), *Munera Pulveris. Six Essays on the Elements of Political Economy*, London: George Allen.

Ruskin, John (1905), *The Works of John Ruskin*, E.T. Cook and Alexander Wedderburn, eds, London: George Allen.

Ryan, Cheyney C. (1981), 'The Fiends of Commerce: Romantic and Marxist Criticisms of Classical Political Economy', *History of Political Economy*, 13 (1).

Sadler, Michael Thomas [1830] (1971), *The Law of Population: a Treatise in Six Books, in Disproof of the Superfecundity of Human Beings and Developing the Real Principle of Their Increase*, Shannon: Irish University Press.

Sagoff, Mark (1988), *The Economy of the Earth: Philosophy, Law, and the Environment*, Cambridge: Cambridge University Press.

Sandelin, Bo and Ranki Sinimaaria (1997), 'Internationalization or Americanization of Swedish Economics?', *European Journal of the History of Economic Thought*, 4(2).

Sargent, William Lucas (1887), *Inductive Political Economy*, London: Simpkin Marshall.

Sarrailh, Jean (1954), *L'Espagne Eclairée de la Seconde Moitié du XVIIIe Siècle*, Paris: Imprimerie Nationale.

Sauer-Thompson, Gary and Joseph Wayne Smith (1996), *Beyond Economics: Postmodernity, Globalization and National Sustainability*, Aldershot: Avebury.
Saul, John Ralston (1996), *The Unconscious Civilization*, New York: Free Press.
Say, Jean-Baptiste (1840), *Cours Complet d'Économie Politique Pratique*, Paris: Guillaumin.
Say, Jean-Baptiste (1865), *A Treatise on Political Economy*, Philadelphia: J.B. Lippincott.
Say, Jean-Baptiste (1997), *An Economist in Troubled Times*, selected and translated by R.R. Palmer, Princeton: Princeton University Press.
Scanlan, James P. (1999), 'The Case against Rational Egoism in Dostoevsky's Notes from Underground', *Journal of the History of Ideas*, 60(3).
Schafer, Simon (1991), 'The History and Geography of the Intellectual World: Whewell's Politics of Language', in *William Whewell: a Composite Portrait*, Menachem Fisch and Simon Schaffer, eds, Oxford: Clarendon.
Schefold, B. (1987), 'Schmoller, Gustav von', in *The New Palgrave: a Dictionary of Economics*, John Eatwell, Murray Milgate and Peter Newman, eds, vol. 4, London: Macmillan.
Schmitter, Philippe C. (1979), 'Still the Century of Corporatism', in *Trends Towards Corporatist Intermediation*, Philippe C. Schmitter and Gerhard Lehmbruch, eds, Beverly Hills: Sage.
Schmölders, Günter (1948), 'Jens Jessen', *Economic Journal*, 48(1).
Schmoller, Gustav von (1894), 'The Idea of Justice in Political Economy', *Annals of the American Academy*.
Schmoller, Gustav von (1906), *Principes d'Économie Politique*, 8 vols, Paris: V. Giard and E. Brière.
Schmoller, Gustav von [1907] (1991), 'Adam Smith by Gustav von Schmoller', *Review of Social Economy*, 49(2).
Schnapp, Alain and Eric Vigne (1982), 'Quand les Nazis se Faiseaient Archéologues: un Entretien avec Alain Schnapp', *Histoire*, 43.
Schneider, Michael (1995), 'Two Early Critics of Economic Rationalism: Sismondi and Carlyle', mimeo, La Trobe University.
Schönwälder, Karen (1996), '"Taking Their Place in the Front-line"?: German Historians during Nazism and War', *Tel Aviver Jahrbuch für Deutsche Geschichte*, 25.
Schumacher, E.F. (1973), *Small is Beautiful: Economics as if People Mattered*, New York: Harper & Row.
Schumpeter, Joseph A. (1954), *History of Economic Analysis*, New York: Oxford University Press.
Scott, H. (1933), 'Technology Smashes the Price System', *Harpers Magazine*, 166.
Scott, William Robert (1937), *Adam Smith, as Student and Professor*, Glasgow: Jackson.
Scrope, George Poulett (1831), 'The Political Economists', *Quarterly Review*, 44.
Scrope, George Poulett (1835), *Political Economy Versus the Hand-Loom Weavers. Two Letters of George Poulett Scrope, Esq., M.P. to the Hand-Loom Worsted Weavers of the West Riding of York*, Pamphlet, Bradford.
Scrope, George Poulett (1873), *Political Economy for Plain People*, London: Longmans Green and Co.
Sekine, Thomas T. (1975), 'Uno-Riron: a Japanese Contribution to Marxian Political Economy', *Journal of Economic Literature*, 13(3).
Self, P. (1975), *Econocrats and the Policy Process: the Politics and Philosophy of Cost-Benefit Analysis*, London: Macmillan.
Semmel, Bernard (1962), *The Governor Eyre Controversy*, London: MacGibbon & Kee.
Senior, Nassau [1860] (1962), 'Statistical Science', in *Essays in Economic Method*, R.L. Smyth, ed., London: Gerald Duckworth.

Sent, Esther-Mirjam (1998), *The Evolving Rationality of Rational Expectations: an Assessment of Thomas Sargent's Achievements*, Cambridge: Cambridge University Press.

Sewell, William [1845] (1976), *Hawkstone*, New York: Garland Publishing.

Shelley, Percy Bysshe (1965), *The Complete Works of Percy Bysshe Shelley*, Roger Ingpen, ed., New York: Gordian Press.

Shelton, George (1981), *Dean Tucker and Eighteenth-Century Economic and Political Thought*, London: Macmillan.

Sherman, Clifton Lucien (1929), 'Aaron Burr', *Dictionary of American Biography*, vol. 3, Allen Johnson, ed., London: Humphrey Milford.

Shills, Edward (1980), *The Calling of Sociology and other Essays on the Pursuit of Learning*, Chicago: University of Chicago Press.

Shovlin, John (2000), 'Towards a Reinterpretation of Revolutionary Antinobilism: the Political Economy of Honour in the Old Regime', *Journal of Modern History*, 72(1).

Shubik, Martin (1970), 'A Curmudgeon's Guide to Microeconomics', *Journal of Economic Literature*, 8(2).

Sibalis, Michael David (1988), 'Corporatism after the Corporations: the Debate on Restoring the Guilds under Napoleon I and the Restoration', *French Historical Studies*, 15(4).

Sidgwick, H. (1901), *The Principles of Political Economy*, London: Macmillan.

Silberner, Edmund (1949), 'Friedrich Engels and the Jews', *Jewish Social Studies*, 11.

Silberner, Edmund (1952), 'British Socialism and the Jews', *Historia Judaica*, 14.

Silberner, Edmund (1953), 'The Anti-Semitic Tradition in Modern Socialism', Pamphlet, Hebrew University.

Simon, M. Walter (1955), *The Failure of the Prussian Reform Movement, 1807–1819*, Ithaca, NY: Cornell University Press.

Sismondi, J.-C.-L. Simonde de (1834), *A History of the Fall of the Roman Empire*, 2 vols, London: Longman, Rees, Orme, Brown, Green & Longman.

Sismondi, J.-C.-L. Simonde de [1827] (1991), *New Principles of Political Economy: of Wealth in its Relation to Population*, translated and annotated by Richard Hyse, New Brunswick, NJ: Transaction Publishers.

Skousen, M. (1991), *Economics on Trial*, Homewood, Illinois: Business One Irwin.

Sluga, Hans (1989), 'Metadiscourse: German Philosophy and National Socialism', *Social Research*, 56(4).

Small, Robin (1987), 'Origins of the Marxian Programme for Education', *History of Education Review*, 16(2).

Smith, Adam [1759] (1979), *A Theory of Moral Sentiments*, Indianapolis: Liberty Classics.

Smith, Adam [1776] (1937), *An Inquiry into the Nature and Causes of The Wealth of Nations*, New York: The Modern Library.

Smith, Adam (1977), *The Correspondence of Adam Smith*, Ernest Campbell Mossner and Ian Simpson, eds, Oxford: Clarendon.

Smith, Joseph Wayne, Graham Lyons and Gary Sauer-Thompson (1999), *The Bankruptcy of Economics: Ecology, Economics and the Sustainability of the Earth*, Basingstoke: Macmillan Press – now Palgrave Macmillan.

Smith, Warren Sylvester (1967), *The London Heretics, 1870–1914*, London: Constable.

Smith, Woodruff D. (1991), *Politics and the Sciences of Culture in Germany, 1840–1920*, Oxford: Oxford University Press.

Smolinski, Leon (1967), 'Planning without Theory 1917–1967', *Survey: a Journal of Soviet and East European Studies*, 64.

Smolinski, Leon (1971), 'The Origins of Soviet Mathematical Economics', *Jahrbuch der Wirtschaft Osteuropas*, 2, Munich: Günter Olzog Verlag.

Smolinski, Leon (1973), 'Karl Marx and Mathematical Economics', *Journal of Political Economy*, 81(5).

Smyth, Paul and Bettina Cass (1998), *Contesting the Australian Way: States, Markets and Civil Society*, Oakleigh: Cambridge University Press.

Sockwell, W.D. (1994), *Popularizing Classical Economics: Henry Brougham and William Ellis*, New York: St Martin's Press – now Palgrave Macmillan.

Soddy, Frederic (1922), *Cartesian Economics. The Bearing of Physical Science upon State Stewardship*, London: Hendersons.

Soddy, Frederick (1926), *Wealth, Virtual Wealth and Debt: the Solution of the Economic Paradox*, London: Allen & Unwin.

Soloway, R.A. (1969), *Prelates and People. Ecclesiastical Social Thought in England, 1783–1852*, London: Routledge & Kegan Paul.

Sombart, W. (1930), *Die Drei Nationalokonomien: Geschichte und System der Lehre von der Wirtschaft*, Munchen: Verlag von Duncker & Humblot.

Sombart, W. [1934] (1937), *A New Social Philosophy [Deutscher Sozialismus]*, Princeton: Princeton University Press.

Sombart, W. (1939), *Weltanschauung, Science and Economy*, New York: Veritas.

Sombart, Werner [1911] (1951), *The Jews and Modern Capitalism*, translated by M. Epstein, Glencoe, Illinois: Free Press.

Soros, George (1994), 'The Theory of Reflexivity', MIT Department of Economics World Economy Laboratory Conference, Washington, DC, http:/www.soros.org/textfiles/speeches.

Southey, Robert [1832] (1971), 'State of the Poor', *Essays, Moral and Political*, Shannon: Irish University Press.

Southey, Robert (1803), 'An Essay on the Principles of Population', *Annual Review*, 2.

Southey, Robert (1831), 'Moral and Political State of British Empire', *Quarterly Review*, 44.

Sovani, N.V. (1973), 'Indian Economics and Indian Economists', *Indian Economic Journal*, 21.

Spann, Othmar [1912] (1930), *Types of Economic Theory*, translated by Eden and Cedar Paul, London: George Allen & Unwin.

Speer, Albert (1981), *The Slave State: Heinrich Himmler's Masterplan for SS Supremacy*, translated by Joachim Neugroschel, London: Weidenfeld and Nicolson.

Stafford, William (1987), *Socialism, Radicalism and Nostalgia. Social Criticism in Britain, 1775–1830*, Cambridge: Cambridge University Press.

Stalin, J. [1952] (1972), *Economic Problems of Socialism in the U.S.S.R.*, Peking: Foreign Languages Press.

Stalin, J. (1995), *Stalin's Letters to Molotov, 1925–1936*, Lars T. Lih, Oleg V. Naumov and Oleg V. Khlevniuk, eds, New Haven: Yale University Press.

Starck, Johann August (1804), *Der Triumph der Philosophie in Achtzehnten Jahrhunderte*, Germantown [Augsburg].

Staum, Martin S. (1987), 'The Institute Economists: from Physiocracy to Entrepreneurial Capitalism', *History of Political Economy*, 19(4).

Staum, Martin S. (1998), 'French Lecturers in Political Economy, 1815–1848: Varieties of Liberalism', *History of Political Economy*, 30(1).

Steiner, P. (1990), 'Comment Stabiliser l'Ordre Social Moderne? J.-B. Say, l'Économie Politique et la Révolution', *Economies et Societies*, 24(7–10).

Steiner, P. (1997), 'Politique et Économie Politique Chez J.-B. Say', *Revue Française d'Histoire des Idees Politiques*, 1(5).

Stephen, L. [1900] (1950), *The English Utilitarians*, New York: P. Smith.

Stephens, W. Walker (1895), 'Life of Turgot', in *The Life and Writings of Turgot*, W. Walker Stephens, ed., London: Longmans, Green and Co.

Stigler, George J. (1982), *The Economist as Preacher*, Oxford: Blackwell.

Stocking, George W. (1968), *Race, Culture and Evolution: Essays in the History of Anthropology*, Chicago: University of Chicago Press.

Stone, Harry (1958–59), 'Dickens and the Jews', *Victorian Studies*, 2(3).

Streeten, Paul (1970), 'Thomas Balogh', in *Unfashionable Economics: Essays in Honour of Lord Balogh*, Paul Streeten, ed., London: Weidenfeld and Nicolson.

Summers, Lawrence H. (1991), 'The Scientific Illusion in Empirical Macroeconomics', *Scandinavian Journal of Economics*, 93(2).

Sutela, Pekka (1991), *Economic Thought and Economic Reform in the Soviet Union*, Cambridge: Cambridge University Press.

Sutton, Peter (2001), 'The Politics of Suffering: Indigenous Policy in Australia since the 1970s', *Anthropological Forum*, 11(2).

Syme, David (1871), 'On the Method of Political Economy', *Westminster Review*, 52(1).

Syme, David (1876), *Outlines of an Industrial Science*, London: H.S. King.

Szporluk, Roman (1988), *Communism and Nationalism: Karl Marx Versus Friedrich List*, New York: Oxford University Press.

Taine, Hippolyte [1868] (1903), 'Saint Odile et Iphigénie en Tauride', *Derniers Essais de Critique et d'Histoire*, Paris: Hachette.

Taine, Hippolyte [1876] (1962), *The Ancient Regime*, translated by John Durand, New York: Peter Smith.

Taine, Hippolyte [1893] (1903), 'Fondation de l'École Libre des Sciences Politiques', *Derniers Essais de Critique et d'Histoire*, Paris: Hachette.

Tawney, R.H. (1972), *R.H. Tawney's Commonplace Book*, J.M. Winter and D.M. Joslin, eds, Cambridge: Cambridge University Press.

Terrill, Ross (1973), *R.H. Tawney and his Times: Socialism as Fellowship*, New York: Harvard University Press.

Thomas, Louis (1941), *Alphonse Toussenel. Socialiste National Antisemite (1803–1885)*, Paris: Mecure de France.

Thomas, Paul (1976), 'Marx and Science', *Political Studies*, 24(1).

Thompson, E.P. (1971), 'The Moral Economy of the English Crowd in the Eighteenth Century', *Past and Present*, 50.

Thompson, N.W. (1984a), 'The Attitude to Political Economy of Writers in the Working Class Press, 1816–1834', *Research in the History of Economic Thought and Methodology*, 2.

Thompson, N.W. (1984b), *The People's Science: the Popular Political Economy of Exploitation and Crisis, 1816–34*, Cambridge: Cambridge University Press.

Thompson, Robert Ellis (1875), *Social Science and National Economy*, Philadelphia: Porter and Coates.

Thurow, Lester C. (1983), *Dangerous Currents: the State of Economics*, Oxford: Oxford University Press.

Todd, Francis Murray (1957), *Politics and the Poet: a Study of Wordsworth*, London: Methuen.

Toussenel, Alphonse (1847), *Les Juifs, Rois de l'Époque*, Paris: Gabriel de Gonet.

Toynbee, A. (1913), *Lectures on the Industrial Revolution*, London: Longmans.

Treml, Vladimir G. and Dimitri M. Gallik (1973), 'Teaching the History of Economic Thought in the USSR', *History of Political Economy*, 5(1).

Tribe, Keith (1988), 'Friedrich List and the Critique of "Cosmopolitical Economy"', *Manchester School*, 56(1).

Trollope, Frances [1840] (1968), *The Life and Adventures of Michael Armstrong, the Factory Boy*, London: Cass.

Tu, Pierre N.V. (1969), 'The Classical Economists and Education', *Kyklos*, 22(4).

Tucker, Robert C. (1972), *Philosophy and Myth in Karl Marx*, second edition, Cambridge: Cambridge University Press.

Tudor, Henry (1999), 'Introduction', in Eduard Bernstein, *The Preconditions of Socialism*, Cambridge: Cambridge University Press.

Turner, C.B. (1969), *An Analysis of Soviet Views of John Maynard Keynes*, Durham, NC: Duke University Press.

Valdes, Juan Gabriel (1995), *Pinochet's Economists: the Chicago School of Economics in Chile*, Cambridge: Cambridge University Press.

Van-Lemesle, Lucette le (1980), 'La Promotion de l'Économie Politique en France au XIXe siècle jusqu' à son Introduction dans les Facultés, 1815–1881', *Revue d'Histoire Moderne et Contemporaine*, 27(2).

Veblen, Thorstein [1915] (1939), *Imperial Germany and the Industrial Revolution*, London: Secker and Warburg.

Villeneuve-Bargemont, Alban de (1839), *Histoire de l'Économie Politique*, Brussels.

Villey, Daniel (1946), 'Economique et Morale', in *Pour une Économie Libérée*, Paris: SPID.

Viner, Jacob (1963), 'The Economist in History', *American Economic Review*, 53(2).

Viner, Jacob (1965), 'Guide to John Rae's *Life of Adam Smith*', in *Life of Adam Smith* by John Rae, New York: A.M. Kelley.

Vogel, Ursula (1991), 'Markets and Communities – a Romantic Critique', in *The Market and the State: Studies in Interdependence*, Michael Moran and Maurice Wright, eds, New York: St Martins Press – now Palgrave Macmillan.

Vronskaya, Jeanne and Vladimir Chuguev (1989), *A Biographical Dictionary of the Soviet Union, 1917–1988*, London: Saur.

Vyverberg, Henry (1970), 'Limits of Nonconformity in the Enlightenment: the Case of Simon-Nicholas-Henri Linguet', *French Historical Studies*, 6(4).

Walker, Mark (1989), 'National Socialism and German Physics', *Journal of Contemporary History*, 24.

Walker, Mark (1996), 'National Science under Socialism', *Dimensions*, 10(2).

Wallace, Alfred (1895), 'The Social Economy of the Future', in *The New Party*, Andrew Reid, ed., Melbourne: E.W. Cole.

Wallace, Alfred (1900), *Studies Scientific and Social*, 2 vols, London: Macmillan.

Walras, Leon (1860), *L'Économie Politique et la Justice*, Paris: Guillaumin.

Waring, Marilyn J. (1988), *Counting for Nothing: What Men Value and What Women are Worth*, New Zealand: Allen and Unwin.

Watson, Francis (1972), 'The Devil and Mr Ruskin', *Encounter*, 38(6).

Watson, George (1973), *The English Ideology: Studies in the Language of Victorian Politics*, London: Allen Lane.

Watts, Cedric (1990), *Literature and Money. Financial Myth and Literary Truth*, New York: Harvester Wheatsheaf.

Weatherall, David (1976), *David Ricardo: a Biography*, The Hague: Martinus Nijhoff.

Webb, Beatrice (1968), 'The Jews of London', in *Charles Booth's London*, Albert Fried and Richard M. Elman, eds, New York: Random House.

Webb, R.K. (1992), 'A Crisis of Authority: Early Nineteenth-Century British Thought', *Albion*, 24(1).

Webb, Sidney (ed.) (1916), *How to Pay for the War: Being Ideas Offered to the Chancellor of the Exchequer by the Fabian Research Department*, London: Allen & Unwin.

Welch, Cheryl B. (1984), *Liberty and Utility. The French Idéologues and the Transformation of Liberalism*, New York: Columbia University Press.

Weisskopf, Walter A. (1971), *Alienation and Economics*, New York: E.P. Dutton.

West, Edwin G. (1983), 'Marx's Hypothesis on the Length of the Working Day', *Journal of Political Economy*, 91.

Whatmore, Richard (1998), 'The Political Economy of Jean Baptiste Say: Republicanism', *History of Political Thought*, 19(3).

Wheatcroft, Stephen (1996), 'The Scale and Nature of German and Soviet Repression and Mass Killings, 1930–45', *Europe-Asia Studies*, 48(8).

Whitaker, J.K. (1975), 'John Stuart Mill's Methodology', *Journal of Political Economy*, 83(5).

Wiener, Joel (1980), 'Richard Carlile and *The Republican*', *Victorian Periodicals Review*, 13(3).

Wiener, Martin (1979), 'Some Leaders of Opinion and Economic Growth in Britain, 1918–74', *Journal of Contemporary History*, 14(2).

Wiles, Peter J.D. (1979–80), 'Ideology, Methodology, and Neoclassical Economics', *Journal of Post Keynesian Economics*, 2(2).

Wilhelm, John Howard (1993), 'The Soviet Economic Failure: Brutzkus Revisited', *Europe-Asia Studies*, 45(2).

Williams, Perry (1991), 'Passing on the Torch: Whewell's Philosophy and the Principles of English University Education', in *William Whewell: a Composite Portrait*, Menachem Fisch and Simon Schaffer, eds, Oxford: Clarendon.

Williams, Raymond (1967), *Culture and Society*, London: Chatto and Windus.

Williams, Raymond [1982] (1995), 'Socialism and Ecology', *Capitalism, Nature, Socialism*, 6(1).

Willis, Kirk (1979), 'The Role in Parliament of the Economic Ideas of Adam Smith, 1776–1800', *History of Political Economy*, 11(4).

Winch, Donald (1970), 'Introduction', in *Principles of Political Economy*, by John Stuart Mill, Harmondsworth: Penguin.

Winch, Donald Norman (1978), *Adam Smith's Politics: an Essay in Historiographic Revision*, Cambridge: Cambridge University Press.

Winch, Donald (1996), *Riches and Poverty: an Intellectual History of Political Economy in Britain, 1750–1834*, Cambridge: Cambridge University Press.

Woehrlin, William F. (1971), *Chernyshevskii. The Man and the Journalist*, Cambridge, Mass.: Harvard University Press

Wolowski, L. (1878), 'Preliminary Essay', in *Principles of Political Economy*, by William Roscher, Chicago: Callaghan and Company.

Wordsworth, William (1922), *The Ecclesiastical Sonnets of William Wordsworth*, A.F. Potts, ed., New Haven: Yale University Press.

Wordsworth, William (1841), 'The Sonnets of William Wordsworth', *Quarterly Review*, 69.

Wordsworth, William (1947), *The Poetical Works of William Wordsworth*, E. de Selincourt and Helen Darbishire, eds, Oxford: Clarendon Press.

Wordsworth, William (1974a), 'A Letter to the Bishop of Landaff', *The Prose Works of William Wordsworth*, vol. 1, W.J.B. Owen and J.W. Smyser, eds, Oxford: Clarendon Press.

Wordsworth, William (1974b), 'Two Addresses to the Freeholders of Westmorland', *The Prose Works of William Wordsworth*, vol. 3, W.J.B. Owen and J.W. Smyser, eds, Oxford: Clarendon Press.

Worster, Donald (1994), *Nature's Economy. A History of Ecological Ideas*, second edition, Cambridge: Cambridge University Press.

Worswick, G.D.N. (1972), 'Is Progress in Economic Science Possible', in *Uses of Economics*, G.D.N. Worswick, ed., Oxford: Basil Blackwell.

Wootton, B. (1938), *Lament for Economics*, London: Allen and Unwin.

Yeo, Richard (1984), 'Science and Intellectual Authority in mid-Nineteenth-Century Britain: Robert Chambers and Vestiges of the Natural History of Creation', *Victorian Studies*, 28(1).

Yurovskii, L.N. (1925), *Currency Problems and Policies of the Soviet Union*, London: Leonard Parsons.

Index